*Praise for*

**The Inheritance**
**by David E. Sanger**

"A brilliant *tour d'horizon* of world trouble spots, world crises and world-class challenges. . . . This volume has the title of a policy book but the air of a non-fiction page-turner, in the spirit and example of David Halberstam. . . . Put the remote and the BlackBerry away, Mr. President, and start reading."

—David Shribman, *Toronto Globe & Mail*

"Prescient, relevant—and great reading for people who want to have insomnia."

—Jon Stewart, *The Daily Show*

"Superb."

—Nicholas D. Kristof, *New York Times*

"Highly instructive."

—Edward Luce, *Financial Times*

"Well reasoned and compelling . . . Sanger's book merits close reading, inside the White House and out."

—Doug Childers, *Richmond Times-Dispatch*

"An in-depth look . . . at where America stands in the world, why in-depth reporting by the Fourth Estate keeps government honest, and how the Obama Administration faces global challenges not of its own making."

—Mike Smith, *The Huffington Post*

"A sobering, often chilling account."

—Brian MacArthur, *The Telegraph*

For Jenny Furlong—
With thanks,

# THE INHERITANCE

❖

## The World
## Obama Confronts
## and the Challenges
## to American Power

# DAVID E. SANGER

Harmony Books
New York

For Sherill
and
Andrew and Ned

Copyright © 2009 by David E. Sanger

All rights reserved.

Published in the United States by Three Rivers Press,
an imprint of the Crown Publishing Group,
a division of Random House, Inc., New York.
www.crownpublishing.com

Three Rivers Press and the Tugboat design are registered
trademarks of Random House, Inc.

Originally published in hardcover in the United States
by Harmony Books, an imprint of the Crown Publishing Group,
a division of Random House, Inc., New York, in 2009.

Library of Congress Cataloging-in-Publication Data is available.

ISBN 978-0-307-40793-1

Printed in the United States of America

*Design by Nancy Beth Field*

1 3 5 7 9 10 8 6 4 2

First Paperback Edition

# Contents

# Preface

Let us learn our lessons. Never, never, never believe any war will
be smooth and easy, or that anyone who embarks on that strange
voyage can measure the tides and hurricanes he will encounter.
The Statesman who yields to war fever must realise that once the
signal is given, he is no longer the master of policy but the slave
of unforeseeable and uncontrollable events. Antiquated War
Offices, weak, incompetent or arrogant Commanders,
untrustworthy allies, hostile neutrals, malignant Fortune, ugly
surprises, awful miscalculations—all take their seats at the
Council Board on the morrow of a declaration of war.

—Winston Churchill, *My Early Life,* 1930

THIS IS A BOOK ABOUT the world that Barack Obama inherited
on that bitterly cold Inauguration Day on the steps of the Capitol in
January, 2009, and the complex, often agonizing choices he now
faces. It looks backward at the seismic events that led America to
lose so much standing and leverage in the world. But it also looks
forward to reimagine ways in which we can rebuild our influence
and power and learn to live in a world in which the United States
acknowledges its limitations while continuing to advance its ideals.

From the steps of the Capitol on that Inauguration Day, you
could almost hear much of the nation—and the world—exhale in relief. But in the ensuing months, you could also hear millions inhale
with apprehension as they recognized that it was one thing to call
for change, and another to bring it about. The global euphoria that
greeted Barack Obama's ascension has begun to fade. Americans,

and the world, have come to realize that while installing a new occupant of the Oval Office can dramatically change the tone and image of the United States, it does not make the knot of Afghanistan easier to untangle, the mullahs of Iran more pliant, the political problems of global warming or energy use, or the rise of new global competitors less urgent. In the first few months of the new administration, all seemed possible. Now, as Obama himself often says to his advisers, the biggest challenge is coping with impatience.

No American president since Franklin Delano Roosevelt, the commentators reminded us too many times during those inaugural ceremonies, had inherited a range of problems so seemingly intractable and complex, or a country less certain of its future. Two wars, an economic crisis that seemed at risk of tipping the country into a second Great Depression, and a range of new threats that had festered while the country's attention and resources were focused on Iraq seemed to prove Churchill's famous caution.

In the years before Barack Obama's election, America knew that it had taken its eye off the ball. Iraq had proven to be the great distraction—the war so all-consuming for the top leadership of the country that more potent threats went unaddressed, many huge opportunities unexploited.

In an American presidential election like none before, Obama had promised to refocus America's attention—to withdraw from Iraq so that America could focus anew on a war in Afghanistan that he argued was at the center of America's security concerns; to stop Iran's steady march toward acquiring the capability to build a nuclear weapon; and to deal with North Korea and other failing states with nuclear ambitions. He vowed to redefine our relationships with China and hit the Reset button with Russia. Obama promised to reverse America's detention and interrogation policies, which had tragically diminished the country's standing in the eyes of the world. He vowed to reverse an economic crisis that threatened not only jobs but also America's power and influence. Most important, Obama promised to end an era of huge opportunity costs—and to regain the credibility to confront more imminent threats to our security than Saddam Hussein's Iraq ever posed.

Yet campaigning is one thing; governing is entirely another. It is a lesson that Obama's friend and political adviser, former Representative Lee Hamilton, noted at the end of 2009 that Obama has learned "with a vengeance." In racing to quell an economic disaster, manage two wars, and enact a broad social agenda, the new president stretched the system to the breaking point—much as FDR did in 1933. "The central question that emerges after these months," Hamilton said, "is can he make it all work?"

In his first year, Obama shifted the way the world viewed us and the way we conduct ourselves around the globe. Rather than making American demands about how other nations must change, he talked of the "rights and responsibilities" of all nations. That was one way of saying that no nation—including the United States—can expect to operate by its own rules, a rejection of the American exceptionalism of the Bush years. Such talk instilled a sense of hope that America was changing course, that it was finding itself again. This sense was reinforced by Obama's decision to reach out to the Muslim world in a way that no American president ever has before—even though few Islamic nations reached back.

In Europe there was jubilation that America had turned over a new leaf. So much jubilation, in fact, that the Nobel Committee awarded the young president a peace prize for his aspirations and for changing the tone of America's dealings with the world, rather than for any concrete accomplishments. As Obama himself said that morning, he would accept the award "as a call to action, a call for all nations to confront the challenges of the twenty-first century."

But it was telling how in America the reaction was quite different. Here the Nobel was something of a political liability—awarded at the outset of a contest rather than at its finish line. There was an irony in the fact that the new peace laureate was receiving his medal just as he was deciding whether to accelerate America's involvement in an increasingly unpopular war in Afghanistan—one he had called a "war of necessity"—and to take far more forceful action to prevent Iran and nations like it from obtaining the world's worst weapons.

*The Inheritance* is an exploration of the tests Obama faces as he heads into the heart of his presidency, with the sober recognition that the glow surrounding his election has begun to wear off. America is still grasping the complexities of the tasks it has handed him.

The grand ambition of the Bush presidency after 9/11 was to create "a rip in time," to reorder the Middle East and the wider world. Bush's theory was that the combined effect of America's military power and our newly declared intolerance for accepting risks to our security or our interests around the world—particularly nuclear threats—would convince other nations to surrender their weapons of mass destruction. The preemption doctrine would put nations on warning. Our successes in Afghanistan and then Iraq, Bush argued, would sow the seeds for democratic revolutions. Repressed people would find the confidence to rise up against self-interested mullahs and oil-soaked dictators. Some of these events would happen right away. Others, like democracy's rise, would become what Condoleezza Rice called "a generational project."

But just as Bush dismissed the Powell Doctrine calling for overwhelming force, he repeatedly ignored Churchill's warning about the need to prepare for "unforeseeable and uncontrollable events." Seven years of covering the Bush administration day by day, traveling with him around the world and around the country, and circling back to talk with the leaders who had dealt with him, left me less surprised by the administration's combination of arrogance and ideological fervor than by the president's inexplicable resistance, until the final quarter of his time in office, to changing course as events and outcomes turned against him. Adjustments to strategy and negotiations with enemies were seen as signs of weakness. For Bush to acknowledge that the country was paying a heavy, unforeseen price for his decision to invade Iraq, to turn away from Afghanistan, to coddle a Pakistani dictator in the hope he would fulfill his promises, and to scorn big diplomatic initiatives would be to acknowledge that he and his aides had not fully thought through the consequences of their policies. We were not only slow to adjust to the war we were fighting. We were too slow and too unimaginative to confront the far more potent threats, many of them nuclear, that were emerging while we were otherwise engaged. The "decider" became the ditherer, and the nation was set adrift.

America's challengers were quicker to adapt. They understood the futility of directly taking on the American military. They probed instead for our other vulnerabilities and found plenty. Terrorists in Iraq and Afghanistan designed roadside bombs that hit the soft underside of our armored personnel carriers. The Iranians designed a nuclear strategy based on the wager that the Iraq experience so damaged our credibility and so overstretched our military that we would be unable to rally the world to stop Tehran from acquiring the knowledge and material to build a bomb—especially if Iranian leaders stopped just short of actually fabricating one. Al Qaeda saw its chance to regroup; the Taliban saw its chance to retake old territory; and other militants saw their chance to destabilize a nuclear Pakistan. The North Koreans—those starving, savvy hermits—set off two nuclear blasts. The Chinese realized that a distracted America could not react effectively to their rapid rise as the dominant power in Asia, the world's fastest-growing consumer of energy, and the banker of last resort for America's soaring deficits.

Bush's second term was a significant improvement. Even while denying that he was changing course, he experimented. His defense secretary, Robert Gates, whom Obama retained, publicly questioned why America has more members of military marching bands than foreign service officers and why we spend vastly more to prepare to fight wars than to prevent them. But the holes dug during the beginning of Bush's first term proved too deep to crawl out of by January 20, 2009. Bush could not find it in himself to make the dramatic, Nixon-to-China reversals of strategy that the moment in history required.

At the moment when we most needed to act like a truly enlightened superpower, we let fear trump judgment, we depleted our political capital and moral authority, and we sullied our reputation as the world's safest, best-regulated place to invest. The scorecard at the end of eight years was unforgiving: Barack Obama inherited a country in far more peril—strategically and economically—than Bush did when he took office.

While Obama's opportunity remains great, he has discovered that his options are limited. The symbolism of electing a biracial president with the middle name "Hussein" proved a powerful antidote to the stereotyped image of America as an intolerant, hegemonic power. Yet symbolism goes only so far in restoring our leverage and redeploying our portfolio of influence around the world. Eight years after 9/11, we are still struggling to understand how to balance building schools by day and blowing up terrorist safe-havens by night—sometimes in the same village—and how to talk to our enemies without also empowering them.

As described in a new epilogue for this paperback edition, rebuilding American credibility and authority became the greatest challenge of Obama's first year. Even as he works to reestablish our economic influence, he needs to restore the leverage that comes from backing up diplomacy with the explicit or implicit threat of military action. He has made clear that withdrawing from the world—the path America has periodically taken, with disastrous results—is no longer an option. Nor is it realistic to expect that the United States will retain the huge lead over rising powers that it enjoyed for the first sixty years after World War II. Yet the world still seems to crave leadership from Washington, and one of the unanswered questions of the Obama era is whether his style—inquisitive, measured, deliberate—appears decisive enough to blaze the path.

To shape the world we now confront will require more than restoring the moral power of our example, more than talking to our enemies, more than freeing up our military, more than once again making America the most alluring place to invest, to study, and to pursue dreams. It will require a mixture of ingenuity, sacrifice, and risk-taking that Americans have summoned at more trying moments in our history and that we can find in ourselves again.

*David E. Sanger*
*Washington, D.C.*
*December, 2009*

# INTRODUCTION

# THE BRIEFING

THE MOTORCADE pulled up to the side of the gleaming new FBI building on Chicago's west side at midmorning on the first Tuesday in September, just as the 2008 presidential campaign was shifting into its final, most brutal phase. There was a brief pause as Secret Service agents made one last check of the surroundings and radioed back to their headquarters that the man they had codenamed "Renegade" had arrived. Barack Obama emerged silently, a few foreign policy advisers in tow, and quickly took a waiting elevator to the tenth floor. The candidate strode past the long corridor lined with identically framed portraits of the special agents-in-charge who have run the FBI's operations there since the era when bank robbers such as John Dillinger were still considered Public Enemy Number 1. Obama and his team were headed for the FBI's secure conference room—a "bubble" that deflects any electronic intercepts—for one of the quietest rituals of the quadrennial presidential campaign season: a ninety-minute, classified briefing about the world that the winner of the 2008 presidential election would confront.

Waiting for him in the windowless room was a man who, unlike Obama, had been able to walk into the FBI building almost completely unnoticed. At sixty-five, J. Michael McConnell, the director of national intelligence, was pale, a bit stooped because of a bad back, and wearing wire-rim glasses that made him look like a well-heeled consultant—the job he had held until President Bush convinced him to return to government at the lowest point of Bush's presidency, as Iraq was dissolving into chaos in the fall of 2006.

The two men who shook hands in the bubble could not have come from more different worlds. When Obama was a six-year-old living in Jakarta, McConnell was patrolling the Mekong Delta on a small Navy boat, seeking out the Vietcong. In 1991, the same year Obama graduated from Harvard Law School, McConnell was already a veteran of the Cold War, directing the National Security Agency, the biggest and most technologically complex of the intelligence agencies. By the time Obama was heading into government service in the Illinois state legislature, McConnell had already retired from the covert world and had started a second career earning millions from corporations desperate to protect their computer systems.

Bush had enticed McConnell back to take over a demoralized, disorganized "intelligence community" that was anything but communal. It employed 100,000 people spread over sixteen agencies and had become more famous for its internal rivalries than for the quality of its analysis. McConnell's first job was to bind those agencies together. But early in 2008, McConnell and his top aides had identified the first twelve months after the presidential election as a period of critical vulnerability. It would mark the first transfer of power since the 9/11 attacks, and McConnell and other top intelligence officials believed America's rivals and enemies would seek to exploit the inevitable disruptions of a government transition—even a smooth one—to test a new president.[1] In 2009 there would be little time to get up to speed. The plan for dealing with al Qaeda had been sitting on Condoleezza Rice's desk at the White House on the morning of September 11, waiting for discussion. The administration's slowness to understand the threat was sharply criticized by the 9/11 Commission; after that searing experience, a similar mistake by a new administration would be unforgivable. But McConnell had a second motive: After the intelligence disasters leading up to the Iraq War, the new president would come to office deeply suspicious of anything that landed on his desk in a red "classified" jacket. McConnell needed to demonstrate that the agencies he oversaw had learned and evolved.

The spy chief commissioned a stack of digestible reports for Obama and his rival, Senator John McCain, as a sort of field guide to American vulnerabilities at the end of the Bush era. "We came up with thirteen topics," McConnell said. "If you made a list, you'd probably get eleven or twelve of the thirteen."[2]

Among the reports was a grim assessment that al Qaeda—the terror group whose middle ranks Bush used to claim were being decimated—had not only reconstituted but had more allies and associates than ever along the forbidding border between Pakistan and Afghanistan.[3] There was a description of how the Taliban were making huge inroads into Afghanistan and how other militants saw an opportunity over the next two years to attempt the first violent overthrow of a nuclear-armed state: Pakistan. The country was ripe for the picking: Its weak, corrupt government faced national bankruptcy, an insurgency raged on the doorstep of the capital, and the Pakistani government had no comprehensive strategy to confront either threat. Nor did it seem to want one. McConnell himself had come to the conclusion months before that Pakistan's aid to the Taliban was no act of rogue intelligence agents but instead was government policy. Nonetheless, Washington kept paying billions in "reimbursements" for counterterrorism operations to the Pakistani military.*

Another report summarized the huge strides Iran had made in its nuclear program while America was focused elsewhere: By Inauguration Day, Iran was estimated to have amassed enough partially enriched uranium to manufacture a single bomb—if the Iranians could find a covert way to finish the enrichment process. The report's timeline made it clear that in his first term, the new president will have to

---

* The encounters with Pakistani officials that led McConnell to this conclusion are described in chapter 8, "Crossing the Line."

decide whether to live with a nuclear Iran or attempt—by diplomacy, stealth, or force—to disarm it.

There was a study of the economic and military implications of China's rise, and another detailed Russia's angry mix of nationalism and its perpetual sense of victimization—a dangerous brew on display just weeks before, during Russia's invasion of parts of Georgia. Yet another report focused on a recent analysis of North Korea's nuclear arsenal, which had expanded dramatically on Bush's watch. There was even a report on the national security implications of global climate change—not the usual fare for the intelligence community.

For ninety minutes Obama listened, sometimes tipping back his chair at the long, beechwood-toned conference table. His aides were largely quiet as they looked around the room that was decorated in government-issue flags at one end and screens for secure video links at the other.

Obama wanted to know more—much more—about Iran's race for the bomb, the subject of a confusing, internally contradictory "National Intelligence Estimate" that he had read in its full, classified version in late 2007. How much time would the next president have to conduct talks with Iran—negotiations Obama promised during the campaign—before the Iranians got the bomb?

Obama also had questions about Afghanistan, to which he had committed to send more troops while accelerating the American exit from Iraq. He had already publicly argued that the Afghanistan-Pakistan border was the real "central front" in the war on terrorism and rejected Bush's insistence that the true battle was in Iraq. Everything in the reports McConnell provided backed up Obama's assertion. As Michael V. Hayden, the director of the CIA, put it a few months later, "Today, virtually every major terrorist threat my agency is aware of has threads back to the tribal areas."[4]

Over the course of their discussion the two men wandered onto McConnell's favorite subject: America's huge, unaddressed exposure to cyber threats that could paralyze the country's banks, its power stations, and its financial markets. "They spent a fair bit of time on that," one of the participants said. "More than you might expect." (It was a subject that struck close to home: Both the Obama and Mc-Cain campaigns' computer systems were hacked during the race, the kinds of attacks the federal government and American businesses face each day. The intrusions appeared to have come from abroad.)[5]

It was a daunting set of conflicts as broad and complex as those that Britain faced a century ago or that Franklin Roosevelt faced in 1933. It was a lot to digest. Obama and McConnell vaguely agreed to try to meet again before the election for another "deep dive"—McConnell's phrase for a plunge into specific subjects, something he did frequently with Bush.

The follow-up session did not happen before Election Day. Two weeks after the briefing came the second September shock of the Bush era: the collapse of Lehman Brothers, followed by the terrifying plunge of America's financial markets—and then the world's. The last eight weeks of the campaign were dominated by questions of how to right the economy: bailout plans were announced, discarded, reformulated, and announced again by Bush and his treasury secretary, Henry Paulson. There were emergency meetings at the White House that in one case put both Obama and McCain at the same table in the Roosevelt Room, with Bush in the middle; and a $700 billion authorization by Congress, reluctantly supported by both Obama and Mc-Cain, to save some of America's biggest institutions and try to stabilize a crumbling market. It was rocky territory for McCain, who had regularly praised deregulation and declared on the day of the Lehman collapse that "the fundamentals of the economy are strong," a sentence that seemed so out of touch with reality that it cost him immeasurably.

Then, at a little past eleven p.m. Eastern time on Tuesday, November 4, exactly nine weeks after that meeting at the FBI, McConnell's world of problems became Obama's future. In a night that shimmered with history, Americans decisively—but not overwhelmingly—repudiated George W. Bush and his approach to the world. They embraced a candidate with less experience than Jack Kennedy had in

1960 and elected the first black president since George Washington, a slave-holder, took the oath of office.

His victory secure, Obama appeared at a huge rally in Chicago's Grant Park. He had canceled the campaign's plans for fireworks and strode to the oversized wooden podium with a relaxed air of command, but little sign of jubilation.

"If there is anyone out there who still doubts that America is a place where all things are possible, who still wonders if the dream of our founders is still alive in our time, who still questions the power of our democracy, tonight is your answer," Obama said as he peered out over a crowd of more than 100,000, a pastiche of a new America: white and black and Hispanic and Asian. It was a crowd whose many dreams had been poured into the man just elected the forty-fourth president of the United States.

But Obama knew that while parts of the world would welcome him as the anti-Bush, it would not be long before he would be tested. Something in McConnell's thirteen briefing papers—or something that the intelligence apparatus did not anticipate—would soon erupt. Then would come the moment to show that he, like another young senator propelled into the presidency on soaring oratory and a nation's hope for a fresh start, had a spine of steel. In a speech that Obama crafted to sound less like a victory celebration and more like an inaugural address, he added some Kennedy-esque lines that suggested that while an Obama administration would be about diplomacy and dialogue—with enemies as well as friends—it would not be about weakness.

"To those who would tear the world down: We will defeat you," he told the throng. "To those who seek peace and security: We will support you."

It was an inspiring declaration, aimed at an audience far beyond America's shores. But Obama's neat separation of the world into builders and destroyers had echoes of the man leaving the White House, the president who had famously declared early in his first term to all the nations of the world that "you're either with us or against us in the fight against terror."* Bush quickly discovered that the nations of the world refused to choose sides quite that clearly and that some of the nations he needed most, starting with Pakistan, would be with him on Tuesdays and Thursdays, but against him on Mondays and Fridays. Many things might change with the arrival of a new president. This fact of geopolitics would not.

Thirty-six hours after Obama's victory, McConnell slipped back into Chicago and the two men met in the same FBI conference room. This time the director came with the day's "PDB," the President's Daily Brief, the summary of intelligence that occupies the first hour of the president's day. This briefing, Obama's first as president-elect, was unlike the one before. At Bush's orders, the candidates' previous briefings had been restricted to the problems America faced around the world. This time, McConnell came armed with the PDB's descriptions of covert actions, classified "special action programs," and other steps that the nation's intelligence agencies, sometimes in concert with the Pentagon, were taking at a moment when most Americans were understandably focused on the crumbling of the American economy. It would be weeks—maybe months—before Obama would be able to get a full sense of the secret efforts that Bush had launched, the legal authorities that justified them, and the political land mines he was about to inherit.

"Bush wrote a lot of checks," one senior intelligence official told me in the early summer of 2008, "that the next president is going to have to cash."

UNTIL 1952, incoming American presidents rarely had a clue of what they were getting into.

With the Korean War raging, Harry Truman declared that none

---

* Bush uttered the famous phrase several times, but most clearly at a joint news conference in the Rose Garden with Jacques Chirac, then the president of France, on November 6, 2001.

of his successors should enter office as ignorant as he had been about the world he was about to face. It was twelve days after Franklin Roosevelt's death in April 1945, that Truman was fully briefed on a project he had heard only vague rumors about: the huge undertaking in the deserts of New Mexico to build a nuclear weapon. Within weeks, he would have to decide whether to drop the first atomic bomb on Japan, the momentous decision that cost hundreds of thousands of Japanese lives and likely saved untold numbers of Americans slated to invade Honshu, my father, Kenneth Sanger, among them.

At Truman's instigation, a quadrennial tradition began: The newly created CIA briefed both the Republican nominee, Dwight D. Eisenhower, and the Democratic nominee, Adlai Stevenson. (In one of those odd accidents of historical geography, Stevenson received briefings at the Illinois governor's mansion in Springfield, two blocks from where Obama began his political rise a half century later.) Unlike Obama and McCain in 2008, Eisenhower and Stevenson did not get the same briefing. The agency trusted only Eisenhower, the hero of World War II, with the fruits of its communications intercepts.[6]

By the time John F. Kennedy ran for president in 1960, the briefings centered on the most contentious issue of the campaign: the bitter argument over the alleged "missile gap" between the Soviets and the United States. Kennedy charged that Eisenhower and Nixon had allowed the United States to become dangerously vulnerable. There was also the question of who would be tougher in the defense of Taiwan against Communist China: Nixon alleged Kennedy didn't have the steel to face down Mao's forces. Then there was Cuba. Kennedy's campaign accused the sitting administration of doing too little to help Cuban exiles oust Castro. Nixon later wrote he "assumed" that Kennedy's CIA briefings included news of the covert program already under way to send exiles onto the island to lead an overthrow of Castro. That program, of course, launched the biggest disaster of Kennedy's first year, the abortive Bay of Pigs invasion. The fiasco unfolded less than three months after Kennedy took office, before the young, inexperienced president had learned the strengths and weaknesses of his advisers and before he understood that even the most confident-sounding intelligence officers and military officials blow smoke—and underestimate what can go wrong. It was a bitter lesson for Kennedy in 1961 and an even more bitter one for Bush in 2003.[7]

Obama was born four months after the debacle on the coast of Cuba. But forty-eight years later, as he prepared to take office, several of his top national security aides were asking the same question Kennedy's young aides had asked then: What *weren't* they hearing? "The Bay of Pigs is the right analog here," one of Obama's national security advisers told me the week of the presidential election. "We can *guess* what we are walking into. But until you turn over the rocks, you really don't know what's there."

It turned out there were a lot of rocks.

In the last year of his presidency, Bush secretly opened several new fronts in what he called the war on terrorism—the defiantly ill-defined, ever-evolving conflict that became the raison d'être of his presidency.

In January 2008, and then more dramatically in July, Bush rewrote the rules of war against the militants who had built a seemingly impervious sanctuary inside the tribal areas of Pakistan, where they could strike in two directions: against the Western coalition in Afghanistan and against Pakistan itself. Publicly, Bush insisted that he was respecting Pakistan's sovereignty, that its inept government was a "partner" in rooting out terrorists. In reality, he had faced up to the fact that the Pakistani government was aiding both sides of the conflict, and he ordered regular strikes inside the Pakistani border—both by Predator drones and, when necessary, by his favorite branch of the military, the Special Forces. It was an act of desperation, driven in part by the fact that more than seven years after the defining, awful morning of his presidency, Osama bin Laden and his chief lieutenant, Ayman al-Zawahiri, had reconstituted al Qaeda. "The idea that he would go home to the ranch in

Crawford with these two guys still walking around ate at the president," one of Bush's aides told me. "He didn't say it, but you could see it in the new strategy." During the campaign, Obama voiced support for going into Pakistan to hunt al Qaeda. But what Bush had ordered was something far more extensive: a search for extremists of many stripes—a very different kind of undeclared war, and one that, as Bush left office, was already prompting a ferocious backlash among Pakistanis.

Obama would soon learn of another major covert operation, also born of desperation. This time the target was Iran.

Sanctions had taken their toll on the Iranian economy but had not changed the regime's behavior. Secretary of Defense Robert Gates had made clear that a military strike, while possible, would have awful repercussions. Whatever his inner thoughts, Bush professed to agree. "I think it's absolutely absurd," Bush insisted to a group of White House reporters in early 2007, "that people suspect I am trying to find a pretext to attack Iran." He was talking as if his first term, and the preemption doctrine, had never happened.

Early in 2008, Bush authorized something just short of an attack: a series of new covert actions, some that the United States would conduct alone, others designed in consultation with the Israelis and the Europeans. Most were centered on a last-ditch effort to undermine the industrial infrastructure around Natanz, the site of Iran's largest known nuclear enrichment plant. Such attempts had been made before, even during the Clinton administration, but now the clock was ticking faster. Few believed the effort would amount to much. "We may be past the point of stopping the Iranians," one senior intelligence official acknowledged to me months after Bush signed the orders. But the hope was that the covert actions would at least slow down Iran's effort to produce enough nuclear fuel for several weapons.

Obama had vowed never to allow Iran to get a nuclear weapon. During the post-election transition, however, several of his top advisers acknowledged that the harder question, never discussed on the campaign trail, would be how close to that goal Obama would allow the Iranians to get. Should he take the risk of letting the CIA's covert efforts move forward before he understood their scope and what could go wrong—the mistake that Kennedy made? "I wouldn't want to bet my country on any of these," one skeptic of the covert programs told me, being careful not to reveal more than what was already circulating about the highly classified projects. Similar efforts had been tried before, he said, and while they worked briefly, the Iranians had soon discovered them. "I hope," he confided, "someone's ready to tell the next president there's not much chance any of this crap is going to work."

The Israelis had apparently arrived at the same conclusion. In Bush's last months in office, they feared that Obama, if elected, would enter endless, ultimately fruitless negotiations with the Iranians. So they came to the White House in 2008 asking for help with a plan of their own—a military option to try to neutralize Iran's known nuclear facilities. The secret approach triggered a panic in the Bush White House that the Middle East would again be in flames as Bush left office, with the United States quickly sucked into the attacks and counterattacks that would almost certainly follow. The Israelis were deliberately vague about their intentions, and Bush deflected the request. His aides were hoping that with Israel's leadership engaged in a power struggle to succeed Prime Minister Ehud Olmert, the question of military action against Iran would be put on hold for a while. But the Israeli threat—and the crisis it could provoke—was bound to be among the most pressing of the issues on Obama's desk when he walked into the Oval Office.*

◆

---

* The secret Israeli approach to the Bush White House is discussed at greater length in chapter 4, "The Israel Option."

EXACTLY A WEEK after the huge stock-market plunge in September 2008, Robert Gates, the former CIA chief who had been appointed to the Pentagon to undo the damage done by Donald Rumsfeld, offered America the words it had been waiting five years to hear. Understandably, given the din of collapsing banks, few heard it.

"I have cautioned that, no matter what you think about the origins of the war in Iraq, we must get the endgame there right," he told a Senate committee. "I believe we have now entered that endgame."

When Gates took the job in 2006, he told colleagues that he had one overarching goal: to guide Bush to that "endgame" as quickly as possible. From his post as president of Texas A&M, he had been mystified by Bush's constant talk of "victory" and appalled by Bush's brief sojourn into describing America's struggle as one against "Islamofascism," a misguided effort to cast the war in World War II terms, a step that even Bush's own aides believed inflated the enemy's perception of itself. As a member of the Iraq Study Group—the bipartisan panel that made the case for an accelerated move toward the exits by early 2008—Gates had visited Iraq and was sobered by the strategic disarray.[8]

But Gates's "endgame" comment wasn't intended to be taken simply as a progress report on Iraq. Instead, seizing on the success of the "surge," he was testifying about the need to turn more attention toward Afghanistan and Pakistan. It was there, he said, "the greatest threat to the homeland lies." This was the unclassified, watered-down version of what McConnell was telling the candidates—and it appeared to give the imprimatur of a Republican former chief of the CIA to one of Obama's campaign themes.

Just a year earlier, such a comment would have been heresy in the Bush administration. But Gates was bulletproof. He hadn't sought this job. And while he was a skilled bureaucratic player who made sure he didn't openly contradict Bush, he was blistering in his descriptions of how the United States had gotten into this mess. "We are at war in Afghanistan today," he told an audience at West Point in April 2008, "in no small measure because we mistakenly turned our backs on Afghanistan after the Soviet troops left in the late 1980s." (At that time George H. W. Bush was in office, and Gates himself was at the CIA.) He pulled no punches about the NATO allies in Afghanistan, asking the question of what to do when "some of your allies don't want to fight." By his own account, he had learned during his years in the intelligence world to frame the question in this way: "If we do this, what will they do? Then what? And then what?" He would never say so, but he was trying to force an administration and a president who had spent the first term imagining how a quick victory in Iraq would beget a resurgence of American power to adjust themselves to a world in which some investments go bad.

"We are overinvested in Iraq; it's fixing us in place," one of Gates's closest high-ranking allies told me in the Pentagon one day in the summer of 2007. The war was about to become America's longest military commitment, save for the American Revolution, and he compared his and Gates's problem to one of managing a portfolio with some money-losing stocks—the familiar trap of sunken costs. "It's like you invested in a bad mutual fund. You know, then you get your emotions tied up in the investment. You had an objective in mind—maybe sending the kids to college. But you become so enamored of the fund that over time you lost track of the objective. And suddenly you find that you are getting negative returns, but you just can't get yourself out."

Gates's hope was to get down to ten combat brigades in Iraq by the time Bush left office—which was about half the fighting force at the time we spoke. (He didn't make it, but came close; as Bush was preparing to leave office, the force was down to fourteen combat brigades.)

Once America got on the path out of Iraq, Gates said to me in his office a few months before his Senate testimony, a new president could begin to prepare the American public for the fact that we would need a far, far longer commitment to Afghanistan. That was clearly a message Obama's faithful did not want to hear.

Yet Afghanistan was not Iraq. Overwhelming military force wouldn't work, Gates argued, because it would be impossible to maintain "a much larger Western footprint in a country that has never been hospitable to foreigners, regardless of why they are there." But the American people, the Congress, and the European allies had not yet learned this lesson, he worried. They were not yet prepared for the kind of world in which we were forced to pour many kinds of talent and resources—not just troops—into the failing states that now rank among our gravest national security threats.

For the next president, Gates said, the deeper lesson of Afghanistan, Pakistan, and problems like them is that America's challenge is much more far-reaching. "The structures of national security are outdated," he told me. "They are sixty years old; they were products of lessons learned from World War II and what we needed to fight the Cold War, and they were great for that. They worked. But we live in a different and much more complex world."

Obama was about to discover how much more complex. In the weeks after his election, it became increasingly obvious that the architecture of the world's financial institutions, also created in the 1940s, was as outdated as the national security infrastructure. It had been designed for a world in which economic crises could be contained in individual countries or regions; the assumption was that the United States and other large economies would be healthy enough to pull the world through. But this crisis was different from the one that struck Mexico in 1994 or Asia in 1997. The crash that began with falling property prices in Florida and California and everywhere in between was radiating out around the world. At home, Obama was confronted by the prospect of the collapse of General Motors and other automakers. Abroad, fragile nations, unable to attract loans or capital, were being pushed to the brink. At a meeting of his foreign policy advisers, Obama was told that Pakistan was in about the same shape as GM: It would run out of cash in months. What looked like a domestic economic crisis was, simultaneously, a global crisis.

Obama's advisers agreed his first priority had to be the deepening recession at home. An America wracked by credit freezes, foreclosures, bankruptcies, deflation, and unemployment would have little leverage in the world. But the reports coming in to Obama once he began to regularly receive the President's Daily Brief made it clear that America's rivals around the world were not waiting for his economic initiatives. Seizing on the moment of transition, the Russians were threatening to base missiles near Poland, in hopes of forcing Obama to back away from Bush's missile defense plan for Eastern Europe. The North Koreans were reneging on the deal they had struck with Bush on nuclear inspections. The Taliban and their associates were fracturing Afghanistan, tribe by tribe, village by village, compound by compound. An attack on Mumbai, the commercial capital of India once known as Bombay, threatened a resurgence of the six-decade-long conflict with Pakistan and once again put the volatile subcontinent on a hair trigger. And in Iran, perhaps the problem Obama had the least time to solve, the mullahs were getting closer to the day when they could claim they had everything they needed for a nuclear arsenal.

# PART I

## IRAN

# THE MULLAHS' MANHATTAN PROJECT

# CHAPTER I

# DECODING PROJECT 111

Fate changes no man, unless he changes fate.

— Epigraph on the opening page of a status report prepared by
engineers of Project 111, the Iranian military's effort to design
a nuclear warhead

BY THE TIME President Bush's national security team gathered in the Situation Room the Thursday before Thanksgiving 2007, the rumor had already raced through the upper reaches of the administration: America's much-maligned spy agencies had hit the jackpot.

With a mix of luck and technological genius, they had finally penetrated the inner sanctum of Iran's nuclear weapons program. For weeks the dialogues, laboratory drawings, and bitter complaints of Iran's weapons engineers had secretly circulated through the headquarters of the CIA and the National Intelligence Council, the small organization charged with putting together classified, consensus "estimates" about the long-term security challenges facing the nation. Now the highlights were crammed into a draft of a 140-page National Intelligence Estimate (NIE) that was stacked in front of every chair in the Situation Room's new, high-tech conference center, where Vice President Cheney, National Security Adviser Stephen Hadley, Secretary of State Condoleezza Rice, and others prepared to pick through it. Though it would never be explicitly discussed that morning, the memories of another NIE—the disastrously wrong-headed one on Iraq in the fall of 2002—was the subtext of their deliberations. No future NIE on weapons of mass destruction could escape from under that cloud.

But this report was different in every respect. It detailed the names of each of the Iranian engineers and program managers, along with excerpts from their deliberations about the nuclear program and speculation about the political travails inside Iran's fractious circle of top leaders. What those exchanges revealed turned out to be so mind-blowing that it threatened to upend Washington's strategy toward Tehran for months, maybe years, to come. The estimate concluded, in short, that while Iran was racing ahead to produce fuel that would give it the capability to build a bomb, it had suspended all of its work on the actual design of a weapon in late 2003. No one knew whether the weapons programs—what the Iranians referred to as "Project 110" to develop a nuclear trigger around a sphere of uranium, and "Project 111" to manufacture a warhead—had been resumed since then. The discovery cut the legs out from under Bush's argument that Iran harbored an active nuclear-weapons program that needed to be stopped immediately.

To those who delved into the report, starting with Robert Gates, the former director of the CIA who was now defense secretary, the intelligence estimate was one of the most imprecisely worded, poorly assembled intelligence documents in memory. Later, Gates would declare that in his whole career in intelligence he had never seen "an NIE that had such an impact on U.S. diplomacy." He did not mean it as a compliment.

"The irony is it made our effort to strengthen the political and the financial sanctions more difficult because people figured, well, the military option is now off the table," Gates told me a few months after the estimate was released.

To many of Gates's colleagues on the national security team, it seemed clear that Bush and Cheney were paying the price for twisting the intelligence on Iraq. Either out of a new sense of caution or out of fear that Bush was laying the predicate for war, the authors of the intelligence report had hemmed the president in, leaving Bush little justification for military action unless, as Gates put it, "the Iranians do something stupid."

The summary opened with a set of "key judgments," the first section of every National Intelligence Estimate, and sometimes the only pages that top officials read. To this day, those judgments are the only part of the intelligence estimate that has been made public—a decision prompted largely by the realization that once the classified version went to Capitol Hill, the main conclusion would leak instantly. The key judgments were written in a shorthand that emphasized the remarkable new discovery that some powerful Iranian had ordered a halt to the weapons design work. But it failed to say what sophisticated readers instantly understood: Designing the weapon is the easiest step in putting together a nuclear bomb. It could be done relatively quickly later on in the development process, presuming the Iranians had not already purchased a workable design from the Russian nuclear scientists who kept jetting into Tehran after the fall of the Soviet Union, or from the Pakistanis. The hard part of bomb-building is obtaining the fuel—the part of the project that was still speeding along in public view. The omission of that distinction in the NIE summary had to do with its intended audience. "We never wrote this to be read by the general public," one of the authors of the report told me. "So it is missing a lot of the context."

But once the key judgments became public, the reaction astounded everyone from President Bush to Michael McConnell, the director of national intelligence, and Michael Hayden, the CIA director. No one was more astounded than the authors of the report inside the National Intelligence Council, who had written the document with the assurance that it would never be made public. Around the world, critics of America's many intelligence failures in Iraq trumpeted the Iran report's conclusion to make the case that even the Americans now had their doubts that Iran was pursuing a bomb. As a consequence, the Germans delayed plans to announce new sanctions; the Russians and the Chinese said they would not vote for stiffer action against Iran.

Readers of the full classified version of the NIE, however, walked away with a very different impression. In their copies, the report contained the first allegations of a complex, covert program by the Iranians to enrich uranium at sites other than the giant facility outside the ancient city of Natanz, where inspectors were counting every gram of nuclear material. The covert enrichment program, too, had been halted, the classified sections of the report concluded.

"I'm not saying we saw centrifuges spinning on the edge of the Caspian Sea," said one senior intelligence official who was deeply involved in reviewing the intelligence with Bush. "But there was a secret enrichment program too." That was important, he said, because "none of us believe that they will create weapons-grade fuel at Natanz. What they are producing at Natanz is a body of knowledge there that they can transfer elsewhere."

Whatever the truth—that Iran wants a bomb, that it wanted a bomb until it realized the cost, or that it simply wants the *capability* to build a bomb someday should the mullahs decide to take the last step—it is now clear that the effect of the intelligence report was far more detrimental than anyone realized at the time. The NIE's findings, or at least the awkwardly worded declassified version, sent a go-back-to-sleep message around the globe. In the intelligence community's overcaution about not repeating its mistakes in Iraq, analysts may have actually erred the other way, veering toward the kind of mistakes they made when they underestimated the Soviet effort to build a bomb sixty years ago or the pace of the Chinese, Indian, and Pakistani efforts that followed. It may turn out that one of the great post-Iraq paradoxes was that in crying wolf about Iraq, the American intelligence community found itself unable to raise the alarm about Iran.

Certainly the Iranians think so. The country's messianic president, Mahmoud Ahmadinejad, not only celebrated the intelligence findings, he sped up the deployment of new centrifuges, continuing to enrich uranium as fast as possible. The goal seemed clear: Create such a large infrastructure and inventory of nuclear fuel that the rest of the world will conclude it is simply too late in the game to get it back.

The result is that the next administration inherits an Iran newly emboldened to race ahead with its nuclear program and become ever more dominant in the region. By the middle of 2008, other nations that have historically feared Iran—a group of countries led by the Saudis—were nearly apoplectic. They were publicly talking about building up their own nuclear capabilities. And suddenly the world turned upside down: When the Israelis staged a clearly provocative military exercise that simulated a hundred-plane attack on Iran's nuclear facilities, the Saudis issued not one word of protest.

"You know," one of Bush's top aides said to me in the summer of 2008, after returning from a Middle East trip with his boss, "there are a lot of people in Iran who are afraid we are going to bomb them. And there are a lot of other people in the region who are afraid we aren't."

IT FELL TO Michael McConnell, the man who oversees the president's daily briefings, to tell Bush about the intelligence breakthrough in the summer of 2007, while the rest of Washington was fleeing for the cooling climate of the mountains and the beach. Just weeks before, a draft of the NIE that was circulating through the intelligence community had read a lot like the previous reports on Iran, though in a fit of Iraq-induced caution it said that the intelligence community now had only "moderate" confidence that Iran was determined to build a weapon, which was down from "high confidence" a few years before. The change had been made because in the interim there had been no new evidence of nuclear work—and no one wanted to repeat the mistake they made with Saddam's program, which analysts asserted must have been progressing because there was no reason it should have stopped.

But now, McConnell told Bush, a team of CIA analysts had come to Hayden with the fruits of an astounding technological breakthrough. After twenty years of watching via spy satellites or relying on international inspectors who were playing a running game of cat-and-mouse with the Iranians, the United States finally had found a way to glean the intentions of Iran's leaders and nuclear engineers.

How they did so ranked among the biggest secrets in Washington. Officials insist there were several sources; they would not have relied on a single source of intelligence for a finding of such magnitude. But clearly a good deal of the success came from the penetration of Iranian computer networks.

For four or five years American spy agencies, led by the code breakers at the National Security Agency in Fort Meade, Maryland, had worked on perfecting a series of technologies that enabled them to tunnel through computer networks—with astounding results. In Iraq, they had successfully bored into the computers of suspected al Qaeda terrorists, in one case even manipulating data to lure someone into a trap. Iran was a far harder target, with much more sophisticated computer security. The country's nuclear designers report to one of the most elite and secretive units of the Iranian Revolutionary Guard Corps.

The details of exactly how the United States got inside the Iranian network are highly classified.[1] But the cyber invasion gave Americans access to a treasure trove of reports that detailed, with remarkable specificity, Iran's covert efforts to design a weapon and eventually to make it small enough so that it could fit atop a Shahab-3, an Iranian missile capable of hitting Israel or parts of Europe. It was all there—designs, sketches, and most important in this case, a running dialogue among engineers detailing what was going well and what wasn't.

Hayden was intrigued, but suspicious enough that he immediately sent the whole package of evidence to what is known at CIA headquarters in Langley as the CIC, the Counterintelligence Center. It is a corner of the agency that is staffed by professional paranoids who examine every major new piece of evidence to determine whether it amounts to "strategic deception," information planted by someone looking to deceive the agency with false data. The analysts came back saying they thought the evidence was genuine, but just in case, they recommended reducing the agency's level of confidence in the trustworthiness of the new finding.

"We didn't do that," one senior intelligence official told me. "These are guys who wouldn't trust that their mother was telling the truth if she said, 'You were a beautiful baby.'"

Hayden told McConnell that he needed more time to assess the discovery, and that despite the pressure from Congress to report on what was happening in Iran, a thorough analysis of the credibility of the new information would take until Thanksgiving.

McConnell knew that he would have to handle Bush carefully—and he did. The "good news," claimed McConnell, was that the intelligence appeared to confirm what Bush had long alleged but could never before prove: Despite their years of denials, the Iranians had constructed a secret military program devoted to solving the mysteries of building a bomb. There could be no other explanation for why engineers were tinkering with warhead designs.

But there was a serious hitch, McConnell warned. The flood of computer data that was still being translated and picked apart left it completely unclear who gave the order to shut down the weapons program. There was no indication of whether the bomb design effort had subsequently been turned back on.

Later, Bush's national security adviser, Stephen J. Hadley, told me he thought that a combination of events in 2003 must have led the Iranians to fear that the heart of their weapons-design program was about to be exposed. If the program was discovered, it would rip the cover off the story Iran was telling about how it was merely pursuing its right to produce reactor fuel. Hadley argued that it was no coincidence that the order to suspend the work came eight months or so after the American invasion of Iraq and just two months after the seizure of nuclear centrifuges headed for Libya. The noose was clearly tightening around Iran's first big supplier of centrifuge technology, the Pakistani nuclear engineer A. Q. Khan. The Iranians knew he was likely to talk and reveal Iran's purchases—if he hadn't already.

Whatever the motivation, the intelligence now in the hands of senior administration officials in Washington revealed that Iranian engineers, like engineers everywhere, were fuming about the idiocy of their technologically clueless masters. (Those masters were never named in the material.) The engineers believed their bosses were making a huge mistake. After years of work and huge sums of money expended, Iranian scientists had finally been making progress toward a Persian bomb, one that would level the playing field with Israel, leap ahead of the Saudis, and help restore Iran to a day of glory and influence it had not enjoyed for centuries. It had taken decades to get this far: The program had run into technological roadblocks, political opposition in Tehran, and covert efforts by the United States and others who, among other things, sabotaged the power supplies for Iran's centrifuges so that the equipment would blow up if it were turned on. But all those setbacks were temporary.

McConnell's warning to Bush in the summer of 2007 could not have come at a more critical moment.[2] The capital had been buzzing for a year with speculation about whether Bush and Cheney would decide on one last, big confrontation before they left office—or whether the Israelis, concerned that Bush was too bogged down in Iraq to pay attention to a growing Iranian threat, would execute an attack on Iran themselves.

The left was convinced that Bush and Cheney would attack;

some on the right, belatedly realizing that Iran was a far more serious threat than Saddam's Iraq had ever been, were afraid Bush would be paralyzed after the Iraq debacle. Bush himself, some of his friends said, was worried about how history would judge him if he left office with a legacy of invading a country that had no weapons, ignoring North Korea as it built six to eight of them, and leaving his successor to handle an Iran that was on the verge of getting a nuclear option, if not a bomb. Soon the perception of imminent confrontation had taken on a life of its own.

Senator John McCain, in the heat of a presidential primary campaign, had already declared that "there's only one thing worse than the United States exercising a military option. That is a nuclear-armed Iran."[3] That led some to conclude that his threshold for attacking Iran was relatively low—and that his statement could tempt Bush to act before the end of his term. Seymour Hersh, the veteran investigative reporter, fueled speculation about an impending attack with a series of articles in *The New Yorker* describing the Pentagon's contingency plans to take out Iran's nuclear facilities.[4] What Hersh failed to mention is that there are Pentagon plans for scores of contingencies—probably somewhere in the back of a file cabinet, even plans to invade Canada. But in the hothouse atmosphere in Washington, contingencies and intentions were thoughtlessly blurred in the rumor mill—or deliberately blurred in hopes of worrying the Iranians.

With speculation about Bush's objectives swirling, the National Intelligence Estimate on Iran took on an unusual urgency. Not since the intelligence agencies rushed to turn out their disastrous estimate of Iraq's weapons capabilities—also produced in response to a congressional demand—had the prospect of war seemed to be riding on a single political document. The authors of the Iran report knew they needed to demonstrate that the intelligence agencies had learned two lessons from that disaster. The first was that you can start a war—or fail to stop one—by drawing hasty conclusions about what kind of weapons a country *may* be able to manufacture, given enough time, talent, and political will. But there was a second subtext to the Iran NIE. Many intelligence analysts wanted to show that they could stand up to political pressure and deliver a message the president and his team did not want to hear.[5]

"This community is consumed with not repeating the mistakes that were made in 2002," McConnell said to Lawrence Wright of *The New Yorker* shortly after the National Intelligence Estimate was published.[6] Another senior intelligence official who was deeply involved in putting together the NIE was more blunt over dinner one night. "If we screw up on Iran the way we screwed up on Iraq," this official told me as the administration was coming to grips with the new discovery in Iran, "we're finished."[7]

The Israelis were not convinced. They insisted that the CIA was blind to the evidence because it was overcompensating for mistakes made in Iraq. The Israelis complained that the International Atomic Energy Agency (IAEA)—the organization responsible for ensuring that civilian nuclear programs and facilities were not being used as part of a weapons program—was being duped. Iran, the Israelis alleged, was hiding secret nuclear facilities and programs from the international inspectors. But like the Americans, the Israelis had little recent evidence to support their claims.[8] Israeli politicians feared that Bush's stand against Iran was weakening and maintained they could not accept the possibility of an Iranian nuclear weapon. They were, after all, in range of Ahmadinejad's missiles and at the receiving end of his apocalyptic threats.

One of Washington's favorite parlor games at the end of the Bush presidency was trying to figure out how Bush and Cheney would react if the Israelis declared one day that they were going to bomb Iran's facilities on their own. By running a huge military exercise in the Mediterranean in early June 2008, in which F-15s and F-16s flew 900 miles to simulate a strike on Natanz, the Israelis were clearly signaling they were prepared to take action. But part of that was bravado. One senior Air Force officer who studied the problem in detail for the administration told me in the spring of 2008 that he doubted the Israelis had the capability to hit the twelve to fourteen sites that would need to be destroyed. "I'm not sure *we* could do it," he said. One thing was clear: If it ever came to mounting an attack, whoever struck the blow that crippled Iran's program, Washington would be blamed.

TO BUSH, the whole idea that Iran had suspended its covert weapons design work sounded suspicious. Sure, he told his aides, the Iranians may have stopped work on the most incriminating part of the program, designing the actual weapons. But they could quickly resume the weapons design work. His anger shone through when he was questioned about the intelligence after he landed on his first trip to Israel as president, early in 2008. "That's the CIA's view, it's not necessarily my view," he told his hosts.[9]

Even though the final analysis was incomplete, the implication of McConnell's warning was clear: If the Iranian order to suspend designing the weapon proved to be real—a huge "if," McConnell quickly acknowledged—everything Bush had been saying for years about the Iranians' actively working to produce a nuclear weapon was technically wrong. The intelligence community still believed that Tehran wanted nuclear weapons and was strategically advancing toward that goal, but technically they had stopped the actual design of a weapon—and probably not resumed it.

"Mike needed to warn the president not to go too far out on a limb before we figured this out," a senior intelligence official mentioned to me.[10]

Bush was brittle because he knew that the NIE report undercut the last bit of leverage he had with the Iranians: his ability to credibly threaten military action if they crossed some invisible line in their drive to make a bomb. It was a loss of leverage he could not afford. In 2003, in the glow of "Mission Accomplished," he had squandered his best moment to strike a deal with the Iranians. He had toppled their greatest enemies. He had installed a Shia-dominated government in Baghdad friendly to Tehran. He had put 150,000 American troops in easy reach of Iran's elite Quds Force, which supplied Iraqi militants with next-generation, armor-piercing IEDs, used to horrific effect in the worst moments of anti-American violence in Iraq. It was exactly the "empowerment" of Iran warned about in the intelligence reports sent to Bush in 2002. Whether Bush ever read those warnings is unclear.

Now the next American president faces not only a budget deficit at home and a troop deficit in Afghanistan, but a huge leverage deficit with Iran. Bush left his successor with two grim choices: Accept the reality that Iran will continue producing its own nuclear fuel and live with the clear risk that Tehran could ultimately use it for weapons, or try to force the country to disassemble nuclear production facilities that had blossomed during the Bush years. The first course could send Iran down the path blazed by North Korea, now a nuclear-weapons state. The second could easily lead to economic sanctions, oil embargos, and, perhaps, military confrontation.

EVEN AFTER McConnell's warning, Bush kept talking about Ahmadinejad, Iran's fiery but shaky president, in apocalyptic terms. "We've got a leader in Iran who has announced that he wants to destroy Israel," Bush said to reporters during a press conference two months before the NIE was published, but after he already knew much of its contents. He told reporters that at a just-completed summit meeting he had said to his counterparts: "If you're interested in avoiding World War III, it seems like you ought to be interested in preventing them from having the knowledge necessary to make a nuclear weapon."[11] What jumped out of his statement was his use of the word "knowledge." Even if Iran didn't *have* a weapon, he was arguing, no one can take the risk that they would soon learn how to make one.

And it was pretty clear that the Iranians *were* learning how. In two years' time, the country had gone from installing a few gas centrifuges at a test facility at Natanz to putting more than 3,800 centrifuges into operation—a threshold number. If the Iranians could somehow keep that many machines spinning largely uninterrupted for a year, they could produce enough fuel for a nuclear weapon. In early 2008 the machines were still crashing regularly. But international inspectors reported that the Iranian engineers appeared to be solving the problem.

The Iranians tried to explain away the centrifuges. As they liked to point out to anyone who would listen, the Japanese had them, as did many non-nuclear states in Europe, and no one was complaining about their nuclear programs. To the rest of the world, that was beside the point: Iran had hidden its activities for seventeen years, disqualifying them from ordinary treatment.

Of course, if the Iranians got caught running a secret military program to design a weapon, their benign explanation would evaporate. "It would be game-over," one of the authors of the National Intelligence Estimate told me. Instead, the Iranians developed a strategy that took advantage of what they termed their "right to a civilian nuclear program,"[12] which allowed them to develop the capability to make a nuclear weapon while living within the letter of the Nuclear Non-Proliferation Treaty.

The Iranians have thrived on nuclear ambiguity. They understood the reality of post–Cold War power: To attain influence in the Middle East and beyond, the mullahs did not need a ruinously expensive arsenal patterned after the Americans or the Russians. That would simply give the rest of the world a target.

What Iran needed was a convincing capability to build a weapon on short notice. And as McConnell pointed out to Bush, the United States may never know when the Iranians decide to make the leap from a civilian nuclear program to a weapon. As long as the mullahs keep that uncertainty alive, they win.

◆

MIKE MCCONNELL often reminded his colleagues of the caution that he received in the late 1980s and early '90s when he worked for Colin Powell. "Tell me what you know, then tell me what you *don't* know, and only then can you tell me what you think," McConnell recalled Powell saying. "Always keep those separated."[13] Powell's colleagues—and Powell himself, his critics argue—forgot that maxim in the run-up to Iraq. In the case of Iran, McConnell needed to make sure the intelligence agency relearned Powell's rules.

McConnell had arrived at the National Security Agency just before the Clinton years, as the Internet and e-mail were catching on and were about to revolutionize the world of high-tech eavesdropping. Breaking into computer systems was nothing new for the agency: For years, in country after country, American spies had learned how to insert Trojan programs that collected data without detection. They had learned how to insert devious programs into the VAX computers that the Soviets were buying up through front companies around the world—programs that led to slight miscalculations that were undetectable for all intents and purposes but just big enough to result in fatal errors in missile designs or weaponry.

The rise of the Web changed the nature of espionage: Suddenly engineers around the world were putting their computers on the Internet, offering the NSA a new keyhole. McConnell presided over the agency just as it was making a technological leap to the next big challenge in detection and interception.

But after four years McConnell gave up the job, heading off, as he later put it bluntly, to "become rich." He became one of corporate America's leading consultants on cyber threats, a lot more profitable pursuit than working in the government. He thought he was done with intelligence work until Bush pulled him back into service in late 2006, putting him in the newest and most difficult job in the spy world, director of national intelligence. There he was to preside over sixteen intelligence agencies that constantly battle for influence and assets.

It was only after he had settled into that job that McConnell fully understood the magnitude of the quiet revolution that had happened in his absence. When he had left the NSA, the main way to determine the status of a nuclear program was by looking through the periscope of spy satellites. From low Earth orbit, the satellite images could identify where the North Koreans were getting ready to conduct a nuclear test or what was being delivered to the Iranian nuclear facility at Natanz. Now, all of a sudden, McConnell and his colleagues were peering through what my colleague Bill Broad called "the world's biggest microscope."

The microscope was the ability to reach inside computer networks—a gift the world of the Internet had given to the world of spycraft. Inside the operations rooms of the NSA and counterterrorism centers, twentysomethings with cans of Diet Coke spent their days conducting cyber missions into foreign computer systems. Once they were able to crack the computer systems of rogue states, they could see through into the networks—and copy the plans, the intentions, and the frustrations of engineers who had to make it all happen. Unlike with art thieves, they did not need the original paintings: A perfect digital copy was just as valuable.

"It's pretty astounding," said one former intelligence official who has reviewed similar penetrations of foreign computer systems. "You have to assume that anybody in Iran, or anywhere else, who is computer savvy, knows that we can read e-mail," he said. "But they assume that most of their communications are needles in the haystack—lost in the huge volume of traffic." Oftentimes, that is a mistaken conclusion.[14]

In Iran's case, the effort required far more than simply capturing e-mails. The reports and conversations cited in the classified version of the NIE bore no date or time stamps. It was unclear who exactly was doing the writing and when the key conversations took place. Lurking in the background was the risk that the data being harvested was disinformation, designed to convince Washington that the weapons program had been halted.

So until the analysis was complete, Hayden and McConnell were not about to send raw, unanalyzed intelligence into the Oval Office. Hayden was determined that there would be no "slam-dunk" moments akin to the mistake George Tenet, the former director of the CIA, famously made as he presented Bush with evidence on Iraq's WMD programs. Nor, he vowed, would the intelligence community blind itself to inconsistencies, as many did when they ignored evidence that "Curveball"—the wonderfully named source for much of the intelligence about Iraq's weapons of mass destruction—was a known fabricator.

WHEN THE NIE was ready, Hayden fulfilled his promise to deliver it before Thanksgiving. It happened at one of those meetings that doesn't show up on any public schedule, in which the top members of the national security team gather in the Situation Room for a briefing—without the president. These meetings enable more open debate, including a discussion of what to present to the president. As they trickled into the room, whose low windows look out on West Executive Avenue, the president's advisors were in familiar but still somewhat unaccustomed surroundings: The Situation Room had been reopened just months earlier, after the first full renovation since the time of John F. Kennedy.

During the Cuban Missile Crisis, Kennedy had realized that there was no single place where top officers of the United States government could gather to review up-to-date intelligence and argue over strategy without being seen entering and exiting the Cabinet Room or the Roosevelt Room by the Oval Office. The Situation Room first came into operation toward the end of Kennedy's presidency. But for decades the facility was a disappointment to anyone who stepped inside: It was cramped and filled with paper and the buzzing of fax machines. There was a kitchen with no sink. The place looked much like it did when Lyndon Johnson used to head downstairs into the maze of rooms to micromanage the Vietnam War. Communications with other arms of government were haphazard at best, even a few years ago. There were moments in the early days of the Iraq War when Bush tried to talk to his generals in Baghdad, and the screens went blank, events that one of the president's aides said, with some care, had been known to "prompt a presidential outburst."[15] On the morning of 9/11, the place was not only chaotic, it was dangerously underequipped: There were only two rooms where it was even possible to have a video conference, and the ambient noise was so bad that often participants could not hear what was going on. Even before 9/11 the Bush White House had begun planning to turn the Situation Room into something resembling a modern facility. After 9/11, said Joe Hagin, the deputy White House chief of staff who oversaw the project, "what at first seemed desirable suddenly seemed urgent."

It took more than a year of renovations to create a Situation Room that finally began to live up to Hollywood's depictions. The main conference room where the national security team gathered that morning had six flat-screen televisions that could pipe in generals from the field, as well as the British prime minister from 10 Downing Street. Bush was so enamored with the technology that he had it installed at Camp David, in a trailer just outside the ranch in Crawford, and on *Air Force One*.

ON THIS MORNING, every participant had been given the draft entitled "Iran: Nuclear Intentions and Capabilities." The opening pages explained that like all NIEs this was supposed to reflect the consensus of all sixteen intelligence agencies. But it is rarely that easy.

Every year, roughly a dozen or so NIEs are published, sometimes prompted by a presidential question or demanded by Congress. They range in subject matter from the status of al Qaeda and other terror groups to the possible consequences of global economic meltdowns. Until the Iraq War, few outside the circulation list even knew when an NIE was being prepared.

This one had been wordsmithed by Hayden and a murder board of other experts, and every phrase was chosen carefully. It put the new news first.

"We judge with high confidence," the first line read, "that in fall 2003, Tehran halted its nuclear weapons program; we also assess with moderate-to-high confidence that Tehran at a minimum is keeping open the option to develop nuclear weapons."

It went on to portray the Iranians as rational actors who "are guided by a cost-benefit approach rather than a rush to a weapon irrespective of the political, economic and military costs." It argued that the weapons work had stopped "in response to international pressure"—presumably the invasion of Iraq and the arrival of inspectors. It was impossible to know, the report's summary concluded, whether Iran "currently intends to develop nuclear weapons."

If this latest report was right, it would mark a huge change not only in the assessment of Iran but in how Washington watched its enemies. Inside the Situation Room, Cheney, Rice, Gates, and Hadley, among others, wasted no time trying to poke holes in the sourcing and the logic. They peppered Vann Van Diepen, the national intelligence officer for weapons of mass destruction who oversaw the writing of the report, with questions about how the network was infiltrated and whether the Iranians could have deliberately allowed a "back door" to their system to remain open, precisely for the purpose of feeding disinformation to Washington. Van Diepen detailed the steps that the "red team"—the counterintelligence analysts who had examined the interceptions from Iran to determine if they were deliberate deceptions—had taken to test the proposition that the entire discovery was actually intended for American eyes. Their conclusion, he reported that morning, was that none of what they had in hand was "feed," the agency's shorthand for information planted to take the Americans off course. "This wasn't a document that the Iranians ever intended for us to see," one of the intelligence officials who prepared the report concluded.

Most of the president's aides were deeply skeptical. "It wasn't just Cheney who wondered if we were missing something," one of the officials who took part in the briefing told me later.

What if the Iranians had a second, competing team working on the weapons design and the intelligence agencies missed it? And what if Iran's intentions suddenly changed and the mullahs decided to resume the weapons program? Would we know? Could we be assured that the same technology that got the intelligence agencies into the Iranian networks would continue to yield results, especially once the Iranians figured out what was going on?

Those were possibilities, of course, that Van Diepen could not rule out, and the report was filled with carefully worded hedges. Those who read it closely saw that its authors cautioned that they "do not have sufficient intelligence to judge confidently" whether the Iranians were willing to continue their suspension of work, or whether they have plans "to restart the program" after solving other technical problems down the road. On balance, the authors concluded that sooner or later, the Iranians probably planned to build a bomb.

"In our judgment, only an Iranian political decision to abandon a nuclear weapons objective would plausibly keep Iran from eventually producing nuclear weapons—and such a decision is inherently reversible," the estimate concluded.

However, that caution was buried far down on the list of "key judgments." What gave many in the room heartburn was the fact that the document, for the first time, seemed to redefine a nuclear-weapons project. Everyone in the room had read reports on covert nuclear programs for years. They knew that putting together a crude but devastating nuclear bomb of the kind America dropped on Hiroshima is not all that challenging, especially given that so many elements of the design are readily available online. Learning how to enrich uranium—what Hadley, the national security adviser, told reporters later was "the long pole in the tent"—is far more difficult.

Yet a footnote on the bottom of page one of the NIE made it clear that the report considered the enrichment secondary: "For the purposes of this Estimate, by 'nuclear weapons program' we mean Iran's nuclear weapon design and weaponization work and covert uranium conversion-related and uranium enrichment related work; we do not mean Iran's declared civil work related to uranium conversion and enrichment."[16]

In other words, the report redefined the process. It largely ignored the public production of nuclear fuel that the international inspectors were watching. It focused only on the big discovery—that the Iranians had halted their work on the final step, the physical construction of the weapon.

Two months later, Thomas Fingar, the chairman of the National Intelligence Council, explained the reasoning for the decision this way:

"We were writing something that we fully expected to remain a classified document," he said, clearly still smarting from the criticism that greeted the effort. "We were writing for officials who were fully familiar with the issue. We were making assumptions about our audience. And it was important to get right to the new element and not make people hunt around or go down forty pages to get to what was new."[17]

Fingar had plenty of reason to believe that the document would stay classified. Since taking over as the director of national intelligence, McConnell had been determined to end the practice—born of the Iraq debacle—of making NIEs public. He insisted that unless some secrecy was restored, his analysts would begin pulling their punches, writing with an eye on how their assessments would read on front pages. Just weeks before the Situation Room meeting, McConnell had signed off on an order that said summaries of NIEs would no longer be released; he soon afterward told a conference of intelligence analysts in Washington that he did not expect the conclusions on Iran to ever see the light of day.[18]

But as soon as Hadley, Rice, and Gates flipped through this NIE, they knew its conclusions were so explosive that it would never stay secret. The document rewrote the main story line of the Iranian nuclear program.

When Bush was briefed, according to people who were in the room, he told McConnell that the conclusion was so dramatic it would have to be made public—despite the director's orders a few weeks before that all intelligence estimates should remain secret. Clearly, the Iraq intelligence failure was weighing on Bush. He told McConnell, "I can't be in a position of saying something publicly that's not true, backed up by your intelligence." Had Bush uttered that same line to his intelligence chiefs in 2003, before the Iraq invasion, he might have rescued his place in history.

HADLEY KNEW THAT the inevitable headlines—"Iran Halts Nuclear Weapons Work, CIA Concludes"—would derail the sanctions on Iran. He was right. To the rest of the world, it looked as if Bush's rationale for driving the United Nations to impose sanctions on Iran had disappeared overnight. The irony was that the sanctions were rooted in Iran's refusal to suspend the enrichment of uranium—the main action that the Iranians were continuing, even speeding up. But as Bush himself later admitted, the NIE undercut the American assertion that the only reason Iran wanted to enrich was to supply a secret bomb program.

Now that argument was gone. Yet everyone at the White House knew that they could not order the intelligence agencies to rewrite the report for public consumption, with a greater emphasis on the dangers of allowing the Iranians to continue enriching uranium. That would have looked suspiciously like Bush was manipulating intelligence reports. But to leave the NIE in its current, less-than-subtle form would completely undermine the rationale for sanctions.

The problem was resolved with a muddy compromise that made everything worse. The NIE's "key judgments" were released essentially as written, save for a few omissions to protect sources and methods, chiefly the penetration of the computer networks and the direct references to Projects 110 and 111. Stephen Hadley appeared in the White House pressroom to put his own spin on the findings, stressing that the estimate concluded that Iran had, indeed, sought a weapon—and might again someday restart the weaponization program.

But he could not paper over the fact that the Iranians had played the game brilliantly. By suspending the military part of the program—and getting caught suspending it—they had eviscerated five years of efforts by the United States and its allies to build momentum for confronting Tehran. All of a sudden, the Americans seemed to be endorsing the view of the IAEA which had said that while Iran's efforts were deeply suspicious, there was no evidence of an ongoing weapons program.

Mahmoud Ahmadinejad, meanwhile, claimed a "great victory" for Iran. He was entitled to celebrate. The new intelligence estimate relieved the international pressure on Iran—the same pressure that the document itself claimed had successfully forced the country to suspend its weapons ambitions.

The Iranians responded by beginning to install their next generation of centrifuges—the so-called IR-2—a vastly improved model based on the advanced designs that A. Q. Khan had sold them more than a decade before. By early 2008, the first machines were up and running. If they could amass the parts to build these more-stable machines, the Iranians could enrich uranium faster than ever. The justification for developing the IR-2 centrifuge, as with the older models, was that Iran had to be ready to feed its own nuclear power plants—even though the only facility anywhere close to going into operation, at Bushehr, would use Russian fuel that had already been delivered.

Iran's Middle Eastern neighbors—from the Saudis to the Israelis—complained to the Bush administration that the accelerated Iranian uranium enrichment program was Washington's fault. The NIE had emboldened Iran, they said. They could not understand why Bush would let that happen. After all, wasn't this the president who had declared just a few years ago that he would never "tolerate" an Iran that could build nuclear weapons?[19]

This was true, but he was also a president who had denied, for years, that the invasion of Iraq would empower Iran. Now, even as the U.S. strategy for Iran was falling apart, a few members of the administration began to admit the obvious. Zalmay Khalilzad, the former American ambassador to Iraq and later to the United Nations, for example, told students at Columbia University one Friday afternoon in the winter of 2008 that Iran had emerged as perhaps the biggest winner of the Iraq War.

"It's helped Iran's relative position in the region, because Iraq was a rival of Iran," Khalilzad explained. "The balance there has disintegrated or weakened." As the American inability to control the chaos in Iraq grew more evident, so did the ability of Iran's mullahs to frustrate America's interests across the region—from supporting Hezbollah in Lebanon to arming Hamas in the Palestinian territories.

By the end of the Bush administration, the Iranians could imagine the future: a Persian sphere of influence that extended to the western banks of the Euphrates River. For a country that had terribly mismanaged its economy, that had been frozen out of the international community for a quarter-century, it could be the beginning of a revival. Not a new Persian empire, but a Persian influence far beyond its own borders.

That is where a nuclear capability—not even a weapon itself, but the mere ability to make one—could greatly bolster Iran's position. The Iranians had no hope of challenging the American nuclear umbrella, the ultimate defensive shield that Washington extended over its closest European and Asian allies. But Pakistan, India, and North Korea had taught the Iranians a lesson in modern power politics: Washington does not mess with countries that have nuclear arsenals, even small ones. Saddam Hussein never learned that lesson, and one day his American jailers delivered him to a noose. Kim Jong-Il, however, learned it well, and after he set off a nuclear test, the Americans dropped by to negotiate.

Iran's Arab neighbors looked at the NIE and came to a quick conclusion: The Iranians are getting the bomb. The only question is how long it will take, and whether, for the purposes of plausible deniability, the mullahs stop just short of turning the last screws. The Arab reaction was predictable. Suddenly, most of Iran's oil-rich neighbors became keenly interested in "peaceful" civilian nuclear projects. They are too smart to rekindle the arms race. Instead, they are in a *capabilities* race—figuring out how to assemble all the elements without assembling the bomb. As a senior Egyptian official told me, "Once the Iranians take the next step, everyone else is going to have to go the same route. No one would have a choice."[20]

# CHAPTER 2

# REGIME-CHANGE FANTASIES

NINE MONTHS AFTER the Iranian revolution in 1979, a thirty-six-year-old man from Wichita, Kansas, found himself sitting in a hotel in Algeria facing a motley collection of some of the world's most famous revolutionaries.

The young man was Robert Gates, a fast-rising career intelligence officer temporarily on loan to the White House from the CIA. Three decades later, after running the agency, serving four presidents, and giving up his favorite job as president of Texas A&M, he would return to Washington to try to rescue the Bush administration from some of its worst mistakes. Iran's nuclear program and spreading influence in the Middle East would rank among his most pressing problems, after figuring out a way to extract the United States from Iraq. Thanks in large part to his venture in Algiers, he would bring with him many thoughts about the right way—and the wrong way—to confront the Iranians.

But to look at him that day in Algeria, you might have thought he was another one of the clean-cut Midwesterners who, moving from one oil-rich dictatorship to another, sold drilling equipment or Rolls-Royces to newly minted billionaires. His hair was cropped close, his broad face had a winning smile, and he had a plain way of speaking that hid a biting sense of humor and one of the sharpest analytical minds in Washington. He didn't look like what he was— an expert in the workings of the Soviet Union and one of the nation's most skilled cold warriors.

But for this trip he was largely a note-taker for his boss, Zbigniew Brzezinski, President Carter's national security adviser. Officially, they had come to the Mediterranean coastal city for an anniversary celebration of the Algerian revolution, not usually an event that attracts high-level American attention. Needless to say, they had another agenda.

The collection of revolutionaries who showed up in Algiers that week ranged from egomaniacs to accomplished guerrilla fighters to novices feeling their way through the underground world of militant networks. It was, Gates recalled later, "an intelligence officer's dream come true. All the principal thugs in the world were present."

Yasser Arafat was there, his signature pistols in his belt. So was Hafiz al-Assad, the Syrian strongman. At the banquet, where Gates tried to circulate anonymously, he saw Gen. Vo Nguyen Giap, the Vietnamese strategist who was responsible, as much as any man except perhaps Ho Chi Minh, for plotting the victory that led to the United States' forced departure from South Vietnam, a moment of humiliation that would shape the world Gates later had to navigate.

The people Brzezinski and Gates were focused on, however, were less well known around the world: a delegation sent by Iran's clerics, representing the government formed by the Islamic revolutionaries who were still basking in the glory of their huge and improbable success, the ouster of the American-backed Shah of Iran.

By any measure, theirs was a stunning achievement. They had taken over one of the largest oil-producing countries in the world, unseating one of Washington's greatest allies. Just eight months before, Iran's most famous Shiite cleric-in-exile, the cunning, enigmatic Ayatollah Khomeini, had returned to Tehran. Almost immediately the country plunged into what Gates later called a "reign of terror."

Much as is the case today, no one in Washington could quite figure out who was really in charge in Iran. The intelligence agencies had gotten it wrong. Less than a month after Khomeini arrived in Tehran, they told Brzezinski and Gates they doubted the cleric had enough political power to survive. (Khomeini did just fine; he named himself "supreme leader" and stayed in power until he died a decade later.)

As they maneuvered around Algiers, Brzezinski and Gates were unsure how this revolutionary government would deal with the United States. As much as the clerical leaders reviled America, Khomeini regarded the Soviets as a great threat to Iran as well. Brzezinski was there to reassure the Iranians that the United States was willing to recognize their new government and was prepared to talk about resuming the sale of military equipment.

Together, Brzezinski and Gates showed up at the hotel suite to meet the Iranian delegation. Waiting for them was Iran's newly installed prime minister, Mehdi Bazargan, a French-trained engineer already in his early seventies, who had been imprisoned by the Shah several times. He was clearly already uncomfortable with the radical clerics who were micromanaging Iran's every move. But he was Washington's best hope, the moderate realist that Americans are always seeking in the Iranian leadership. He was accompanied by the Iranian foreign minister, Ibrahim Yazdi, an aide to Khomeini during his exile in Paris, and Defense Minister Mustafa Ali Chamran.

Gates knew there was no way this was going to be an easy encounter. The United States had installed Mohammad Reza Shah in a CIA-backed coup, and for more than two decades he was viewed as an American puppet. Washington had sold him his weapons, cooperated in neutralizing his enemies, supported his feared intelligence service, SAVAK, and overlooked his repressive policies—and his imprisonment of dissidents like Bazargan—in the name of supporting an anticommunist ally. In a mistake that would be repeated time and time again—from Latin America to Pakistan—the United States backed an autocrat even as it was becoming clear that his star was fading and his ability to hold on to power was eroding.

By the time a popular revolt forced the Shah to flee Iran in January 1979, the Carter administration was locked in a fierce internal debate about what to do about him. The man who once was the darling of the CIA and a series of American presidents was suddenly royalty without a country. Brzezinski was pushing to offer him refuge in the United States; Secretary of State Cyrus Vance was warning that such an offer would inflame the Iranians. Just days before Brzezinski and Gates landed in Algiers, President Carter invited the Shah to the States, chiefly on humanitarian grounds; by then the ousted monarch was desperately ill with lymphoma and needed sophisticated medical care.

As Gates recalled later, the State Department had checked with the new Iranian government, "explained the circumstances, and received assurances that Americans in Iran would be protected" if the Iranian public reacted badly. On October 23, the Shah arrived on American soil. A few days later came Brzezinski's first meeting with the new government, meant to explore whether the United States could live and cooperate, if uneasily, with Khomeini's Shiite theocracy.

As they entered the hotel room, Gates recalled later, "their greeting and the tone of the entire meeting were surprisingly friendly under the circumstances."[1] Brzezinski, ever the realist, suggested to the aging Bazargan that Iran and America shared a common interest in opposing the Soviet Union. Global realities and mutual national interests, he suggested, should trump past differences.

But as Gates described the session to me twenty-nine years later, in his office at the Pentagon, one image stuck in his mind—one that guided how he would deal with the Iranians years later.

"Bazargan, Chamran, and Yazdi," Gates said with a smile, "all said, 'Give us the Shah. Give us the Shah.' Back and forth, back and forth, 'Give us the Shah!'"

"This was our first dialogue with the Iranians," he said, shaking his head, 'Give us the Shah!'"[2]

The demands went on endlessly. Finally, Gates recalled, Brzezinski stood and said with some drama in his voice, "To return the Shah to you would be incompatible with our national honor."

To Gates's surprise, the reaction inside the room to Brzezinski's declaration was subdued, but it did not take long for the meeting to break up. Later Gates remembered thinking that despite the differences, the parting seemed friendly.[3]

Whatever feelings of goodwill existed when they left the room did not last.

"Three days later," Gates said to me, "the embassy was seized and two weeks later all three of those guys were out of power." Khomeini backed the hostage-takers; Bazargan and his government resigned in protest, declaring that the taking of the hostages was not in Iran's interest. It was the beginning of a crisis that would dominate the rest of Carter's presidency, ultimately contributing to his undoing in the 1980 elections. Relations between Iran and the United States were poisoned for more than a quarter of a century.

"So passeth the first dialogue between the United States and Iran," Gates said as he tipped back his chair at the round conference table in the middle of the secretary of defense's office at the Pentagon. "Every president since has tried to open a dialogue with the Iranians and none of them have turned out well. And a couple nearly got presidents in jail."[4]

IN ALGIERS, Brzezinski and Gates were trying to recover from bad bets that Washington had placed on Iran—and that still haunt us. The first was that the Shah would somehow find a way to cling to power. The second gambled that the United States could safely give the Shah the tools he needed to create his own civilian nuclear program. Of course, to help Iran produce nuclear energy, the program would include the basic tools needed to make bomb fuel. Washington had forgotten the ironclad mathematical realities of nuclear politics: While the half-life of the average dictator's tenure is about fifteen years, the half-life of uranium-235 is about 700 million years. Rulers may come and go, but the nuclear material they amass will outlast generations of Middle Eastern leaders, from the beneficent to the brutal.

America began fulfilling the Shah's nuclear ambitions in the 1950s, under Eisenhower's tragically misnamed "Atoms for Peace" program. At the heart of the program was what seemed, for decades, to be a simple bargain: If a country agreed it would never seek nuclear weapons, the United States (and ultimately the IAEA) would help it develop its nuclear power industry. Only decades later—long after the Shah was gone—would the huge loopholes in that bargain become evident, as Iranian scientists, Syrian engineers, and North Korean "radio-chemists" developed skills that could be used for making energy or for making weapons. But at the time, supporting nuclear development in Iran seemed like a no-brainer.

By the mid-1960s, the Iranians were running a small research reactor in the center of Tehran—that was similar in size to the reactor the North Koreans built a few years later. In the 1970s, when the Shah still seemed a reliable if repressive friend in the Middle East, a fervent anticommunist and an insurance policy against the threat of Arab oil embargos, Washington agreed to take the next step. It signed a deal to sell the Shah upwards of eight nuclear reactors. (When the deal was coming together in 1976, Dick Cheney—who later became the chief proponent of using any means necessary to keep the Iranians from learning how to make nuclear fuel—was the White House chief of staff.)

The Shah made clear, though, that he wanted more than just reactors. Like a very different generation of Iranian leaders who would come to power decades later, he yearned to master the secrets of the nuclear fuel cycle so that he would never have to depend on a foreign power for the supply of uranium. At the time, the risk seemed theoretical and remote. Few seemed worried that once the equipment and training were in place, Iran could divert that fuel for nuclear weapons. After all, the Shah was a friend. When you troll through the public discussion of the deal at the time, few if any American officials were asking the obvious question that the Bush administration made a staple of its talking points decades later: Why would a country with huge oil reserves want to spend billions on nuclear power?

The Shah made little progress in realizing his dream before he fled the country in 1979. During the Iranian Revolution the program ground to a halt. Remarkably, Ayatollah Khomeini ignored it. Khomeini was far more interested in the purity of the country's Shia faith than in the purity of its uranium, and he viewed the project as "a suspicious Western innovation."[5] Early work at Bushehr, the site of Iran's first two nuclear plants, stopped dead, a setback that ultimately cost the Iranians decades.

Until Khomeini's death in 1989, the Iranian nuclear program was an on-again, off-again effort, pressed largely by the country's technocrats. Yet in 1985, during the depths of the Iran–Iraq War, the country began experimenting with gas-centrifuge technology and bought small facilities for converting raw uranium into a gas, the first step toward enriching the material. The motive was clear: nuclear parity with Saddam Hussein.

Saddam understood what the Iranians had in mind. Just as the Israelis had bombed Saddam's reactor at Osirak in 1981, Saddam bombed Iran's reactor site at Bushehr. He was not about to allow the mullahs to obtain nuclear fuel ahead of him. Toward the end of the Iran–Iraq War, Saddam used chemical weapons on the Iranians, an act of barbarism that convinced Tehran that it needed a far greater deterrent than conventional weapons could offer. The Iranians began stockpiling chemical weapons of their own and told the country's Atomic Energy Organization that it was time to think about a nuclear option.

With Bushehr in ruins, their best hope was to learn how to produce uranium. The process was complicated, but it could be hidden. Many of the purchases, they knew, could be conveniently disguised as equipment for the oil industry. But mastering the centrifuge technology, the key to the uranium route to a bomb, seemed beyond Iran's capabilities at the time.

Their timing, however, was spectacular. Pakistan was years ahead of them and desperately needed money. The mullahs reached out to establish a formal relationship with the generals running Pakistan, one that resulted in a paper agreement in 1986 to cooperate on civilian nuclear energy.

Unfortunately for the Iranians, the accord resulted in little on-the-ground progress. Pakistan's prime minister, Zia al-Haq, was a devout Sunni Muslim and deeply suspicious of the Shia leadership in Tehran, particularly Ayatollah Khomeini.[6] He told his aides to "play around" with the Iranians "but not to yield anything substantial at any cost."[7]

It did not take the Iranians long to figure out that they were being strung along. But they had a Plan B: a separate deal with Abdul Qadeer Khan, the metallurgist behind the Pakistani bomb. The Iranians set up a meeting with Gotthard Lerch, a German who had been an early supplier to Khan, and Mohammed Farooq, an Indian who lived in Dubai and thrived in the city's regulation-free culture. If the authorities in Dubai, one of the seven principalities in the United Arab Emirates, were on to what was happening, they averted their eyes. After all, a lot of contraband moved through Dubai; that fact earned the city its reputation as the Singapore of the Persian Gulf.

In retrospect, the meeting with the Iranians was the true beginning of what became the Khan network. Iran's shopping list, as pieced together years later by international inspectors, contained all the elements that Khan would later ship to Libya and North Korea: drawings of centrifuges, a few prototypes of the same machines for the Iranians to reverse-engineer, and the layout for a full uranium enrichment plant.[8] These were the building blocks that Iran would later use to construct its huge enrichment plant in the desert near the city of Natanz, supplied by small centrifuge-manufacturing workshops spread around the country. The process took years; it was not until the summer of 1994 that the Iranians arranged to buy a more sophisticated centrifuge, called the P-2, from Khan and his Malaysian cohort, Buhari Sayed abu Tahir, who ran Khan's operations in Dubai. Later that year, two officials of Iran's Revolutionary Guards showed up at the Dubai office with suitcases stuffed with $3 million in cash—a partial payment—and left with detailed plans for the P-2 and with parts that fit an older model.[9] The Iranians were angry about the inferior equipment, but Khan's help jump-started their construction effort. Astoundingly, American intelligence agencies missed the operation for years; they still had no clue that Khan had turned from a buyer into a seller.

A formal nuclear cooperation agreement between Iran and Pakistan gave Khan the political cover to travel to Tehran. He toured the wreckage of Bushehr, which helped create the impression that he had come to aid the Iranians' civilian nuclear efforts. In reality this was the first of several trips on which he could both act as a consultant and push his wares, pointing to the products that made possible the Pakistani bomb project. Along the way, Khan began to spin out his self-justification for the deals: He was helping another Muslim state break the American and Israeli stranglehold on nuclear technology. That played well in Tehran and around the Islamic world. In fact, his operation was mostly about money, and eventually money— and the Iranian realization they had been sold some old and unreliable technology—broke up the relationship.

It was around this time that the Iranians received—presumably from Khan himself, but perhaps from one of his deputies—a fifteen-page series of drawings and instructions that explained how to cast uranium metal into two hemispheres. For anyone familiar with nuclear weapons technology, the document rings alarm bells. Casting uranium into hemispheres is essential in building a nuclear weapon, but it has no utility in a civilian nuclear project. Years later, in 2005, Iran showed the document to international inspectors but forbade them to take a copy of it back to Vienna. (The Pakistanis have since confirmed that it matched one in their files.) The Iranians insist that they never sought the diagrams and never paid for them. They came, the Iranians argue, along with the prototypes and designs for the P-1, the first-generation centrifuge, sort of the way a car dealer might throw in a CD player. Later those drawings would become part of the circumstantial case that Iran was trying to design a weapon. But the key part of the transaction was Pakistan's P-1 centrifuges—the model for most of the centrifuges the Iranians installed at Natanz through the summer of 2008.*

By the late 1980s, there were new leaders in Pakistan and Iran, but intelligence agencies in Washington and Europe still did not understand the depth of the connections between Islamabad and Tehran. There were plenty of hints. As tensions rose with Pakistan over American demands that it close down its own nuclear program, there were periodic threats from the Pakistanis that they would respond to the pressure by selling their growing nuclear know-how. The American embassy in Islamabad reported that the Pakistani Army chief of staff, Gen. Mirza Aslam Beg, had gone beyond open support of the Iranians. He had threatened American officials that he would sell nuclear technology to Tehran if the United States ever made good on its threat to cut off arms sales to Pakistan.[10] Beg also pressed Benazir Bhutto, then prime minister, to strike a $4-billion deal with Iran to exchange nuclear technology for some mix of money and oil.

Bhutto said later she shot down the idea, and she professed ignorance of Khan's activities. "I find it very hard to comprehend that A. Q. Khan would have dared to do this," she said in a conversation in London two years before she was assassinated in Pakistan, "be-

---

* The P-1 is an old and inefficient design. The Iranians quickly set to work on the next generation, making their own modifications and calling it the IR-2 to designate it as Iranian-made. By early summer 2008, they were installing IR-2s at Natanz and told inspectors that they expected to focus on manufacturing the more modern version, which can enrich significantly more uranium in the same amount of time as the original.

cause if I found out about this I would have sacked him, and he knew that I was that type of prime minister who would sack somebody if they breached the law."[11] Perhaps, but Khan also knew that Bhutto was weak, and lacked support in the army. He manipulated her and her successors for years to come.

As the Iranians gradually came to realize that the Pakistanis were selling outdated technology at sky-high prices, they began to cast a far wider net for alternative suppliers. They turned to the Chinese for new equipment to conduct laser enrichment of uranium at the Tehran Nuclear Research Center, the facility that had been set up with American help years before. President George H. W. Bush, far more concerned about Iraq than about Iran, said little to Beijing, even though, as the first American representative there, he knew most of the leadership personally. The Clinton administration was not much more vocal. The CIA was watching Iran's nuclear developments, and it was watching A. Q. Khan, suspecting that he was secretly importing nuclear components for the Pakistani nuclear weapons program. But America's spy agencies missed the crucial turn of events in the Khan empire: that he had flipped the switch, and begun to sell Pakistan's wares. It was a devastating failure to connect the dots.

"We saw Iran's activities, and we knew Khan was buying up supplies for Pakistan," Gary Samore, who headed nonproliferation efforts for the Clinton White House, recalled in 2004, as the Khan network was unraveling. "But I don't think there was ever a moment where we saw Khan helping the Iranians."

The Iranians said years later that they had no choice but to operate in great secrecy because the Americans were doing everything they could to choke the country off. On that point there is no dispute. Under American pressure, Germany turned down an Iranian request to complete the Bushehr project. The United States intervened with Argentina when it appeared that the country might help the Iranians learn how to produce fuel. Nonetheless, the Iranians claimed their share of victories. By greasing the wheels of commerce with petrodollars, they obtained high-strength materials and equipment they could plausibly claim were intended for oil production. In time, the Iranian supplier network stretched from Beijing to Berlin, from St. Petersburg to Istanbul.

It was not until 1997 that the Clinton administration was able to get the Chinese to cut off their assistance to Iran, including shipments of raw uranium. (The Chinese drove a typically hard bargain, consenting to stop the shipments only in return for an American agreement to export nuclear power reactors to China.)

Meanwhile, the Iranians brilliantly exploited Russia's simmering anger at being left behind as bankrupt, geopolitical roadkill after the Cold War. Nuclear technology ranked as one of Russia's few growth industries, and Moscow courted the Iranians. Soon they became partners in an effort to get the rusting reactors at Bushehr running. More surreptitiously, a deal was struck for missiles, that enabled the Iranians to move beyond their old North Korean Nodong missiles to something with far greater range that eventually became the Shahab-3. Broke and angry at the West, the Russian establishment responded in the late 1990s by delivering most of what the Iranians ordered.

"It seemed like every couple of months I was over in Russia, meeting Yeltsin's latest ministers—they changed every few months—and describing to them once again the programs that we had uncovered," John McLaughlin, the former deputy director of the CIA, told me later.[12]

McLaughlin got little for his exertions except frequent-flier miles. The Iranians paid well, and in dollars. Over the next few years the Russians sped or slowed their deliveries to Iran depending on the political mood of the moment. When things were tense, they would claim that payment problems were holding up shipments. When the Iranians gained the upper hand, such as when the 2007 National Intelligence Estimate was published, the Russians unblocked delivery. With Bush's reluctant consent, the Russians delivered the nuclear fuel the Iranians so desperately needed. Bush did extract a concession from Vladimir Putin, however, that Russia would take back the spent fuel that resulted from its deliveries to ensure that Iran could not reprocess the spent fuel rods into plutonium for weapons, as the North Koreans had done so successfully.

Bush told me in 2007 that he believed containing Iran's nuclear ambitions was one of the few areas in which he and Putin could cooperate. "There aren't going to be many, so we should focus on this one," he said, though none of us could have envisioned just how bad the relationship with Moscow would get as Bush prepared to leave office. The Russians, he argued, are as vulnerable to a nuclear Iran as the rest of Europe. But, he fumed, "We're up against economic interests, and it's very hard to get people to put those aside."[13]

IN THE HOURS after the World Trade Center fell, Americans were in such shock that few paid attention to the reaction in Tehran. What they would have seen were candlelight vigils held for the victims, a reaction that was spontaneous, unanticipated, and symbolic of opportunities that would be missed as the United States sped into a series of ill-fated ventures in the Middle East.

The vigils took place across Iran. Before a soccer game in Tehran, there was a minute of silence. At Friday prayers, the ritual chant of "Death to America" was skipped—not exactly what one might call a warm gesture of friendship, but a welcome departure from the norm.[14]

After more than two decades of hostile relations between Washington and Tehran, this fleeting moment offered at least the hope of some common ground. Instead, the opportunity was lost in the administration's zeal to divide the world into two camps—Bush's version of geography in which countries had to declare that they were with us or against us. Eventually the president learned that the world doesn't operate that way. By that time it was too late to take advantage of the chance to change the relationship with Tehran.

At the Pentagon and the State Department, where preparations began immediately after 9/11 to go to war in Afghanistan, some senior officials quickly recognized that Iran could be a natural ally of convenience in that fight. For years the Iranians had heavily supported the Northern Alliance, the band of Afghan rebels whose central role in taking down the Taliban—with American support—has been underappreciated in the popular narrative of the war. Iran's motive in that struggle was far from altruistic. The Taliban did everything they could to repress Afghanistan's Shia minority. Just three years before 9/11, Iran and Afghanistan came to the brink of conflict over the murder of Iranian diplomats—and many Afghan Shia—in Mazar-e Sharif.[15]

Not since 1979, when diplomatic relations between Washington and Tehran were terminated amid the hostage crisis, had the two countries found themselves on the same side of a common fight. The newly espoused Bush Doctrine called on governments around the world to declare whether they were "with us or against us." Many wavered. Remarkably, for this one brief moment, the Iranian military chose to declare that they were with us, even though they could not talk to us, at least directly.

In discussions that took place through intermediaries, Tehran offered to allow U.S. pilots to land in Iran if they ran into emergencies while flying sorties over Afghanistan. After the Taliban's fall, the Iranians showed up at the conference in Bonn that created a framework for the new Afghan government and proved to be marginally helpful. They held a series of secret meetings with Zalmay Khalilzad and Ryan Crocker—a duo that teamed the administration's only Afghan-born neocon with one of its most respected career diplomats. These meetings marked the first time in recent memory that Iran and the United States broached the subject of dealing with terrorism. If not a breakthrough, at least it was a historic opportunity.

It is hard to say who was more suspicious about the utility of talking to the enemy—the mullahs or Dick Cheney. The mullahs

tended to move at a slow diplomatic pace and saw an American conspiracy behind many events in which Americans had no role. Cheney
and his staff, along with many neoconservatives, wanted to move at
warp speed in bringing the Iranian regime to its knees. Negotiations
would serve simply to prolong the regime's survival. In Tehran, the
Iranian government was, as always, deeply divided about how to deal
with the "Great Satan."

"The intelligence out of Iran suggested a huge fight," one administration official said to me, "that sounded a lot like our fight."

Astoundingly, Bush never tested the possibilities. This was his
moment to do what wartime leaders are supposed to do: Divide your
enemies. FDR seized his moment to form an alliance of convenience
with Stalin against Germany. The United States sided with the Mujahideen to expel the Soviets from Afghanistan. The list goes on.
This was Bush's chance to exploit the longtime divisions between
the Persian Shia who saw themselves as the legitimate ruling power
in the Middle East and the Arab Sunni extremists who had planned
and executed the attack on the United States. But for a White House
that was already well on its way to rallying the country against what
the president, several years later, called "Islamofascism," those dis-
tinctions seemed more obfuscating than compelling.

Bush's instinct during his first term was to lump all of America's "enemies" in one camp, from the 9/11 plotters (but not the
country they came from, Saudi Arabia), to Taliban remnants, Shia
militias, and everyone else who wished America ill. He ignored the
natural fault lines that might have enabled him to do what Roosevelt had done.[16] Why? It is a question I asked in interview after interview, year after year, usually to get pabulum about engaging the
American public in a broad "war against terrorism." It was only late
in the administration that senior officials began to acknowledge
that the "GWOT," as the Pentagon called the Global War on Terror,
was the wrong phrase—it encouraged generals and politicians to
fight a tactic without addressing its causes.

Within three months the administration dug a deeper hole,

when it let rhetoric drive American foreign policy, instead of the other way around. In writing his State of the Union address in January 2002, Bush's speechwriters, Michael Gerson and David Frum, were searching for a phrase that would capture this new era that pitted America against a world of shady actors with nuclear ambitions. They settled on "axis of evil" to describe Iran, Iraq, and North Korea. Many senior foreign policy officials in the administration told me in interviews that they never even saw the language before Bush gave the speech.*

The president, his fist clenched as he stood at the podium the night of January 29, 2002, delivered the lines with gusto. The three Axis members, he said, were "arming to threaten the peace of our world," amassing weapons of mass destruction and harboring terrorists.

"We will be deliberate, yet time is not on our side," he said, foreshadowing what became, months later, the key element of the preemption policy in his national security strategy. "I will not wait on events, while dangers gather. I will not stand by, as peril draws closer and closer. The United States of America will not permit the world's most dangerous regimes to threaten us with the world's most destructive weapons."

"States like these and their terrorist allies," he concluded, "constitute an axis of evil."[17]

The "axis" phrase evoked the imagery of the "Axis powers" of Germany, Italy, and Japan during World War II, suggesting a similar kind of alliance among Iran, Iraq, and North Korea.

Bush particularly singled out Iran, saying that it "aggressively pursues these weapons and exports terror, while an unelected few repress the Iranian people's hope for freedom."[18] His phraseology, I wrote in the *Times* the next morning, "seemed to be outlining a ra-

---

* The speech was closely held, and early drafts did not contain the "axis of evil" phrase, or its exact context. Colin Powell, among others, has said that he did not see a final draft.

tionale for future action, if he deems it necessary, not only against terrorists but against any hostile states developing weapons of mass destruction."[19]

Colin Powell hated the rhetoric. As his biographer Karen De-Young wrote later, "It reminded him of Ronald Reagan's 'evil empire,' a phrase much beloved by neoconservatives but one he considered unnecessarily provocative and relatively meaningless in the context of the pragmatism he knew had marked U.S.–Soviet relations in the final years of Reagan's presidency."[20]

In fact, a war was under way between Powell's forces and the White House over how to think about Iran. The day after the speech, a White House official told me that "there are people in the State Department who want to think Iran is changing because everyone's drinking Coca-Cola, but the evidence isn't there."[21]

Publicly, though, the White House quickly backed away from the notion that the three Axis nations were colluding. The day after the speech, the White House spokesman, Ari Fleischer, was sent out to declare that the "axis" line was "more rhetorical than historical." In fact, earlier drafts of the speech had gone even further by describing links among the three nations, until someone pointed out that, for example, North Korea had more exchanges of missile technology with Pakistan—America's newest ally in the war on terrorism—than with Iran.

"So we pared back to the essential warning," one official told me, "if you develop these weapons, and if you mess with terrorists, sooner or later we will make you regret it."[22]

Even years later, it is difficult to explain fully what led Bush off this rhetorical cliff. Some of his aides told me at the time that although he was impressed with Iran's offers of support after 9/11, his mind was changed a few weeks later by the Israeli seizure of a ship, the *Karine A*, that was delivering smuggled arms from an Iranian port to Palestinian forces. That convinced Bush "that the Iranians weren't serious," one of the aides said. (Others in the White House could barely recall the seizure in the blitz of events that followed.)

In the supercharged mix of emotions and ideological fervor inside the White House after the attacks, there was a conviction that any language vilifying the hardline Iranian leadership would empower the country's young people—the same young people who were lighting those candles after 9/11.

Instead, the words gave the Iranian leadership a reason to crush the moderates. One Iranian reformer told my colleague Michael Slackman, "When Bush named Iran as the Axis of Evil, the hardliners became happy. . . . They can then mobilize the part of the country that supports them."[23]

Days later, at the Davos World Economic Forum, which had been moved to Manhattan as a sign of post-9/11 solidarity, Powell was taken aside by one world leader after another, all of whom said they had cringed at the president's words. Bill Clinton, who had held forth until two in the morning at an after-dinner session, warned that it was unwise to treat the "Axis" as a single entity.

"We have to take these countries each in turn," he cautioned. "They may all be trouble, but they are different." Iran had two governments, he said—one with progressive elements, one with hardliners—and he thought North Korea was ready to make a deal when he left office.[24] Bush brushed off the criticisms as the hand-wringing of those who were not thinking globally about the threats facing America, and who did not have to stay awake at night devising strategies to deter a second attack. Time altered his view. In his far more pragmatic second term, Bush never uttered the "axis of evil" phrase. By the end of his time in office, he was doing exactly what Powell had urged: sending out probes to find out if the Iranians were serious. By that time, though, it was too late.

DAYS AFTER THE "Axis of Evil" speech was delivered, Colin Powell sent word to the Iranians that they could relax a little: It was Saddam Hussein who was in Bush's sights, not the mullahs. "With respect to Iran and with respect to North Korea, there is no plan to start a war with these nations," he said. Iraq was a different story, he said, and regime change "would be in the best interests of the region, the best interests of the Iraqi people. And we are looking at a variety of options that would bring that about."

Among Powell's small cluster of advisers, many hoped the Iranians would get the message: Forget what Bush says, just watch what he does. To Tehran, the advantages of having the Americans remove Saddam Hussein, Iran's mortal enemy, were immediately clear. But the mullahs were trapped in their own anti-American rhetoric, just as Bush was trapped by his "Axis of Evil" speech.

Then, in August 2002, an Iranian resistance group publicized the existence of a covert uranium enrichment site in Natanz. "We had watched it for years," one senior intelligence official told me. "But until it was publicly revealed, we had a hard time getting people interested." The American press didn't pick up the story until December 2002, just a few months after similar uranium-enrichment efforts in North Korea had been disclosed. The revelation of the existence of Natanz led the IAEA to realize they had been duped by the Iranians, who had failed to declare the existence of the facilities. Naturally, Iranian officials claimed that the site was part of a peaceful nuclear program, though if it was, why not declare it to the international inspectors, who were already looking at other parts of Iran's nuclear energy program? As Colin Powell said, once caught, the Iranians protested with vigor but never really explained the underlying economics of their program. "We've always found it curious," he said, "as to why Iran would need nuclear power when they are so blessed with other means of generating electricity."[25]

SOON A NEW IRANIAN ambassador was dispatched to the United Nations: Javad Zarif, whose perfect English, hip attire, and diplomatic pragmatism had caught the attention of American officials during the Afghan talks in Bonn (like Condoleezza Rice, he was a graduate of the University of Denver). Zarif made it clear from the start that he sided with those in Iran who sought a "grand bargain" with Washington—a faction in Tehran whose ideas, unfortunately, have always exceeded their influence. A series of meetings in early 2003 between Zarif, Khalilzad, and Crocker gave the Iranians their first understanding of American intentions in Iraq—and how they might benefit.

The Iranians were not the only ones thinking about the consequences of an American invasion of Baghdad. The CIA, the same agency that was getting everything wrong about Saddam's weapons, had it right about the benefits to Iran if Bush ordered troops into Iraq. In October 2002, it issued a report, "Iran Wary of a U.S. Attack on Iraq," that laid out the options for Bush.

"The more that Iranian leaders—reformists and hardliners alike—perceived that Washington's aims in Iraq did not challenge Tehran's interests or threaten Iran directly, the better the chance they would cooperate in the postwar period—or at least not actively undermine U.S. goals," the intelligence report read. It argued for "guaranteeing Iran a role in the negotiations on the fate of post-Saddam Iraq—as it had at the Bonn conference for Afghanistan." Those negotiations, it continued, "might give Tehran a stake in its success."[26]

The CIA report also warned that "some elements in the Iranian government could decide to try to counter aggressively the U.S. presence in Iraq or challenge U.S. goals following the fall of Saddam" by sowing dissent among Shia and Kurds. The message was clear: The best chance of avoiding trouble was to talk to the Iranians early and often.

But Bush was not in a mood to talk to the Iranians about Iraq—not until 2007, when American forces were in such trouble, partly because of Iran's covert assistance to the insurgents, that the Iranians had far more influence in the southern part of Iraq than the United States did. The moment to talk, as it turned out, arrived during the same week that the United States seemed at the pinnacle of its power in the Middle East. The week that Bush, a former Air National Guard pilot, donned a flight suit and—with an expert pilot at his elbow—landed a small jet on the deck of the USS *Abraham Lincoln*.

It was May 1, 2003, and that evening Bush delivered what became the most widely mocked speech of his presidency—the "Mission Accomplished" address to the nation. Those words never appeared in his text; they were on the banner behind him. But on that crisp California night off the coast of San Diego, I didn't run into a single member of the administration who objected to the giant banner hanging behind the president, emblazoned with the two words Bush would spend the rest of his presidency trying to disown. "Because of you," Bush declared, "our nation is more secure. Because of you, the tyrant has fallen, and Iraq is free."

Even the truest believers in the Bush White House identify that week as the beginning of a dangerous era of triumphalism. There are few other convincing explanations for the administration's decision to ignore, that same week, what might have been the best opportunity in years to start remaking the U.S. relationship with Iran—and with it, America's role in the Middle East.

The opportunity was contained in a long missive, apparently from the Iranian government, that showed up on a fax machine at the State Department. It quickly became known as "the offer," a proposal to build what amounted to an opportunistic alliance of convenience.

The fax came with a cover letter from the Swiss ambassador to Iran, Tim Guldimann, who was responsible for representing American government interests in Tehran in the absence of a formal diplomatic relationship between the United States and Iran. The offer itself had been edited by Iranian diplomats—chiefly Zarif—and had supposedly been seen by both Iran's Supreme Leader, Ayatollah Khamenei, and the weakened sometime reformist who was serving as president, Mohammad Khatami.[27]

Whether those two leaders—whose own relationship was badly strained—truly stood behind the offer is impossible to know. But the words were beyond dispute. The document began by ticking off a list of "Iranian aims," including the perennial "Halt in U.S. hostile behavior," with the "Axis of Evil" speech noted as an example. The offer proceeded to call for "full access to peaceful nuclear technology, biotechnology and chemical technology," and the "pursuit of anti-Iranian terrorists." Under "U.S. aims," the first item listed was "full transparency for security that there are not Iranian endeavors to develop or possess WMD," and "decisive action against any terrorists (above all al Qaida)." Iranian help in establishing democratic institutions in Iraq was also listed, though Iran seemed like an unusual choice as an exporter of democratic institutions. Then it called for talks, working groups, and road maps.[28] It was vague, but so was Bush's other "road map," for a grand bargain between the Israelis and the Palestinians.

Like the Israeli-Palestinian peace process, though, this offer seemed to envision a fundamental shift in the relationship. If it was for real—a big if—it had the potential to be a game-changer. The problem for the administration—even for those in the State Department who had been pushing for just such an approach—was that no one was clear about the offer's origins, authorship, or sincerity. Some suspected that it was nothing more than a Swiss attempt to get talks started under the guise of an Iranian offer. Others thought it could be an unauthorized probe sent out by the moderates in Iran surrounding President Khatami. ("How many times," Rice asked one of her subordinates in exasperation, "have we pursued the elusive Iranian moderates," only to discover they had no power?)[29] A few hardliners in the administration saw the offer as the confirmation of their wisdom in invading Iraq. The mullahs, they figured, had tuned in to CNN in time to see the video of Saddam's statue being pulled down and feared that unless they did something, downtown Tehran could be the next stop on the preemption parade.

"There were a lot of questions," said Richard Haass, who was running Iran policy for the State Department at the time. "But I thought it was worth testing it, to find out whether it was real. That was the only way we were going to find out."[30] Haass described to Powell the advantages of opening talks with the Iranians, and even dangling some incentives, including dropping American objections to Iran's entry into the World Trade Organization, a longtime Iranian goal. "I didn't see what we had to lose," Haass said later. "I did not share the assessment of many in the administration that the Iranian regime was on the brink."[31]

The hawks—not only Cheney, but many in his office—convinced themselves that the mullahs were just one step from the cliff's edge, and that quick American success in Iraq could push them into the abyss. To them, the Iranian offer sniffed of weakness and fear. For that reason, they immediately and vigorously rejected it. John Bolton, the Cheney protégé who was undersecretary of state for arms control and proliferation at the time, described the offer as "a fantasy."

"Time is the only thing they can't purchase with their oil revenue, but they can get time if they can dupe Europeans or Americans into negotiations," he said later.[32] The speed with which the Iraqi Republican Guard was vanquished by American forces stoked the hawks' confidence that the United States should not negotiate. They argued that the United States would have even more clout once the Middle East was transformed by a wave of liberal democratic reforms. In retrospect, that was the true fantasy. When the war in Iraq began going badly, America's leverage was lost. When oil tripled in price, Iran was suddenly in the driver's seat again. The rest of the Bush years were spent trying to regain some leverage over Iran—without success.

Nonetheless, talks were already under way. Zarif was meeting secretly with Americans, including Khalilzad, about the possibilities of exchanging intelligence about al Qaeda and Mujahideen-e Khalq, or MEK, a rebel group that has waged a violent struggle against the clerical regime in Iran since 1981. The MEK is Iran's largest opposition group, and for years it operated out of Iraq with Saddam Hussein's support. When America invaded Iraq, Iran demanded that

American forces treat the MEK as enemy combatants. Instead, U.S. soldiers disarmed members of the MEK but did not arrest them.

As the offer was being faxed to the State Department, the Iranians proposed a swap: MEK for al Qaeda. If the Americans would turn over the MEK members, the Iranians would hand over to Washington the al Qaeda leaders who had escaped into Iran and were now under house arrest. In short, the Iranians were proposing setting up a kind of terrorist bazaar. It was unseemly, but given that at the time the United States was snatching terror suspects out of towns and cities throughout the world and dropping them into a netherworld of secret detention camps, stranger things were happening.

Khalilzad was not ready to bargain on terrorist exchanges. However, he did warn the Iranians about a suspected terrorist plot in the Persian Gulf area and pressed the Iranians to interrogate the al Qaeda members in their midst and provide the information needed to preempt the attack. The Iranians never took the warning very seriously.

Then, on May 12, 2003, just eleven days after the "Mission Accomplished" speech, four bombs went off in Western housing compounds in Riyadh, Saudi Arabia, just ahead of a visit to the country by Powell. Nine Americans were killed and hundreds of people were injured. The Bush administration was convinced that the al Qaeda members in Iran had been in close contact with the perpetrators of the plot. Enraged at the intransigence—or at least the indifference—of the Iranians, the administration promptly cut off any negotiations. Zarif arrived in Geneva twelve days later for another meeting with Khalilzad, but Khalilzad never showed up. Any discussion about a "grand bargain" was dead. The relationship quickly reverted to its normal state of open hostility.

WITH NO NEGOTIATIONS under way, the Bush administration found itself facing a familiar dead end. Like the North Korean government, the Iranian regime had stubbornly refused to collapse. If there was an American strategy for guiding the next move, it was a mystery to Washington's allies. Bush seemed to be passing the buck to the Europeans (including the French, who had fervently opposed the Iraq War), hoping they would deal with Iran while the United States cleaned up in Iraq.

For a while it looked as if the Europeans might make progress. In September 2003, the IAEA board of governors, in a rare moment of unity, demanded that the Iranians fully disclose their nuclear program and resolve outstanding legal issues. The resolution set a deadline of October 31, touching off a flurry of vigorous and belligerent Iranian rebuttals.[33] Days after the resolution was announced, the head cleric of Iran's Guardian Council questioned publicly why Iran should stay in the Nuclear Non-Proliferation Treaty.[34]

By late October, it was clear that the Iranians would require some convincing if they were to come clean. With the United States notably absent, the foreign ministers of France, Germany, and the UK flew to Tehran desperately seeking to avoid the looming showdown between the IAEA and Iran. What emerged was a hopeful-sounding agreement in which Iran agreed to cooperate with the IAEA and voluntarily suspend its uranium enrichment. In return the EU offer hinted at the possibility of future nuclear technology assistance and affirmed Iran's right to civilian nuclear energy.[35] The United States stayed silent; it refused to endorse the European effort.

Two months later it looked as if the inspections might get someplace, when Iran signed an agreement with the IAEA that permitted, at least on paper, inspections of any facilities that international inspectors demanded to see. By November 2004, Iran and the Europeans signed an accord, called the Paris Agreement, in which the Iranians agreed to suspend all their uranium-enrichment activities while negotiations continued. Again the Americans stayed silent.

But within weeks of Bush's second inaugural—where he called for America to make the spread of freedom around the world its number-one goal—Rice quickly discovered that Bush's stony silence was untenable. On her first trip to Europe as secretary of state, "everyone beat the hell out of her" about Iran, one of her traveling companions said. It was clear that the Europeans, still angry that Bush had rolled over their objections to invading Iraq, believed he was headed to another disastrous confrontation.

It was the first test of whatever explicit or implicit understanding Rice had cut with Bush at Camp David when he first broached the idea of removing Powell and putting her in his place. Rice's failings as national security adviser were obvious to everyone. She never had the clout to oppose Cheney and Rumsfeld openly, and she seemed to view her job as staffing Bush and measuring his mood, rather than shaping the debate. The results had been disastrous. Now she seemed willing to conduct end runs around Cheney and Rumsfeld in a way she never managed during her time as national security adviser.

"Something changed in Condi," said one of her top aides who followed her to the State Department. "I think she knew that her time at the White House was a failure because, for whatever reason, she was constantly measuring the wind direction rather than guiding the policy. At the White House she felt like staff. Now she felt like she had the power to make changes."

But the changes were incremental. She embraced the European negotiating effort. She dropped the American objections to Iran's application to enter the World Trade Organization. Yet she was unwilling to make the one change that might have made a difference: allowing American diplomats to join the talks with the Iranians.

"This is our way of making clear that we will join the Europeans in giving Iran positive reasons to give up its program," one administration official said to me.[36]

When Bush traveled to Europe for a summit meeting, he made a deal with his European counterparts: He would support their negotiations, but in return Britain, France, and Germany had to agree to join an escalating series of sanctions at the Security Council if Iran balked. The Europeans feared they had been to this movie before—just eighteen months earlier, when Bush used Security Council resolutions demanding that Iraq disarm as "authorization" for the American invasion. Some European leaders feared being sucked into a deal that, eventually, would give Bush an excuse for military action. But with Bush increasingly pinned down in Iraq, the risk seemed low.

To the Iranians, of course, negotiations were a way to buy time. The Iranian regime was consumed with bitter infighting, but the leadership understood two things. Bush had his hands full in Iraq—a problem the Iranian Quds Force knew how to make worse—and the United States could not afford to get involved in yet another Middle East war.

IN THE SUMMER OF 2004, almost exactly twenty-five years after the meeting in Algeria and the hostage crisis that immediately followed, Gates and Brzezinski found themselves thrown together again with the same mission: to find a way to deal with Iran.

This time there were no awkward banquets in Algiers. Bazargan, the prime minister they had dealt with, had died nearly a decade before, banished from power since his resignation in the opening days of the hostage crisis. Chamran, the former aide to Ayatollah Khomeini and defense minister, had been killed during the Iran-Iraq War by an Iraqi mortar. Only Yazdi survived, as a dissident seeking a more open and democratic Iran. He had gotten nowhere.

In Washington, Brzezinski and Gates were trying to save the Bush administration from itself. They directed a joint study at the Council on Foreign Relations to explore how to move forward with Iran. There was a lot of catching up to do. There had been virtually no direct, official talks between the two countries for a quarter century, save the clumsy deals struck during the Reagan administration that became the Iran-Contra scandal.

The idea was to steer the government out of a dead end—gently, without overt criticism. Gates, relishing his time away from the politics of Washington, was president of Texas A&M. Brzezinski was comfortably ensconced as a counselor at the Center for Strategic and International Studies in Washington.

Reports such as theirs are published in Washington every week. They usually circulate among a few hundred influential policymakers and occasionally get a few paragraphs deep in the International section of the *Times*. But given Gates's and Brzezinski's stature, this one had the potential to be different.

They started by bursting the hardliners' balloon. The fall of the current regime in Iran, they said, was not going to happen anytime soon. America's clear-cut interests in Iran's behavior necessitated direct engagement—working through the Europeans wouldn't suffice. As a member of the panel told me, "There are some things in life that don't work when you have other people do them for you. Among them are sex, drinking, and negotiating with Iran."

But Gates and Brzezinski argued that an all-encompassing grand bargain would not work, at least not yet. They pushed for "selective engagement," a mix of economic inducements and threatened penalties that could bring serious progress on key issues, starting with the nuclear program and Iran's support for Hamas, Hezbollah, and other terror groups.

The central recommendation was that the United States not waste time. The leverage that America had gained by invading Iraq and Afghanistan was a dwindling asset, they argued. Moreover, it was their sense that the internal rifts in Iran could be exploited.

"Most revolutions—the Bolshevik Revolution, the Chinese Revolution—most revolutions tend to get more moderate as time goes along, and leaders sort of deal with the real world in a more realistic way," Gates said when we talked about the report he issued. When Mao saw that happening to his revolution, Gates noted, he launched the Cultural Revolution to bring back the fervor—but that just delayed the inevitable. "It looked to me like the same thing was happening in Iran with Khatami and Rafsanjani and all these guys."

Gates's and Brzezinski's recommendations were immediately put in the back of a file drawer by the Bush White House. The administration was hoping that as the Iranians headed into elections in 2005, the combination of negotiations and escalating sanctions would lead Iran's younger generation to decide that the nuclear program was not worth the pain.

They did not anticipate Iran's version of the Cultural Revolution: the rise of the mayor of Tehran, Mahmoud Ahmadinejad, a man whose rhetoric outstripped his competence.

Ahmadinejad's election took everyone by surprise—Bush, Rice, Hadley, and the intelligence agencies. He was a populist with little base in national politics and a predilection for talking in apocalyptic terms about Israel disappearing from the earth. He often rambled, and had never been considered a serious player, but rather more of a fringe element. "Nobody really thought he was going to win, but it is not as if exit polling is something that we understand well, especially in Iran," Rice told me later.[37]

Ahmadinejad turned out to be a skillful politician who knew in his gut that what Iranians cared about most was the restoration of their country to the position of the greatest power in the Middle East. The Bomb—or at least the debate over giving in to the West's demands—was the way to exploit that emotion. Iranians did not like sanctions, and they did not like isolation. But as long as the situation could be cast as another effort by the Americans to deny the Iranians their rightful place in the world, Ahmadinejad would enjoy support. The more he baited Bush, and the more Bush went for the bait, the better off he would be. It wasn't much of a strategy, but it was better than anything the Bush administration had yet devised.

# CHAPTER 3

# AHMADINEJAD'S MONOLOGUE

MAHMOUD AHMADINEJAD was late to his meeting with the old guard of the American foreign policy establishment. That was part of the act.

The Iranian president, dressed in his usual baggy jacket and open-collared shirt, had begun the day at the podium of the United Nations, denouncing President Bush. However, his carefully planned effort to seize the spotlight—and to sidestep an American effort to contain his visit as well as his country—was overshadowed by his partner in America-bashing, President Hugo Chávez of Venezuela. It was Chávez, not Ahmadinejad, who dominated the airwaves by declaring, from the same podium where Bush had just spoken a few hours earlier, that he smelled the lingering whiffs of sulfur.

But if Chávez had the quotable line, it was Ahmadinejad who had assembled the better road show. Although his visa didn't extend as far west in Manhattan as the theater district, it didn't matter. He was ready to perform at length, with his signature habit of answering every question with a question, and of starting down the road of a reasonable answer, only to veer off into a conspiracy theory. He had packed the day with television interviews and meetings with academics and pundits, trying to demonstrate that he was willing to take on all comers. If Washington would not talk to Iran, Ahmadinejad would talk to everyone. Or, rather, he would talk *at* everyone. He had his diatribes down pat, from questioning Israel's legitimacy while attacking America for not caring about the Palestinians, to asking what gave a country with several thousand nuclear weapons the right to insist that Iran possess not a single one.

His last stop that day in the fall of 2006 was a dinnertime meeting at the InterContinental Hotel in New York, with thirty or forty invited members of the Council on Foreign Relations. When Richard Haass, the council's president and the man who had advocated testing the Iranian offer of a "grand bargain," called Condoleezza Rice to tell her he was holding the dinner, she was distinctly unhappy.

"It's fair to say that Dr. Rice thought this was a bad idea," one senior State Department official told me that day. "A really, really bad idea."

As did leaders of several Jewish groups, whom Haass had invited. They promptly asked if the Council would have invited Hitler to address them in the 1930s. "Some of us considered quitting to make it clear how offensive this is," said Abraham Foxman, the national director of the Anti-Defamation League, who was one of the Jewish leaders whose attendance Haass sought.

But after a flurry of phone calls, including one with Elie Wiesel, the Nobel Peace Prize winner, writer, and Holocaust survivor, they decided against a mass resignation. The session was downgraded to a "meeting" rather than a dinner. (This was accomplished by putting light hors d'oeuvres on a side table, which Ahmadinejad never touched.)

Among the invitees were two of Rice's mentors: Brent Scowcroft, who had hired Rice, then a young scholar at Stanford, for a midlevel position at the White House in the 1980s and had openly split with her on Iraq; and Robert Blackwill, whom she had reported to in those days. As national security adviser, she had brought the gruff Blackwill back to Washington to coordinate Iraq policy. There were multimillionaire members of the establishment, including Peter Peterson of the Blackstone Group, the insurance magnate Maurice Greenberg, and nuclear experts such as Ashton B. Carter of Harvard.

Initially it was supposed to be a closed-door, off-the-record meeting. But at the last minute four journalists were added, all members of the Council, after Haass realized that if the session remained off the record, he would end up relaying, and perhaps interpreting, Ahmadinejad's Holocaust-denying pitch to the world.* After all, Jewish groups were still in an uproar that the Iranian leader had been invited at all, and undoubtedly the conspiracy theorists who thought the Council kept a fleet of black helicopters on its roof would have a field day denouncing a secret dinner with a certified member of the Axis of Evil, one with whom America was arguably conducting a proxy war in Iraq.

Ahmadinejad came into the room flanked by a half-dozen obsequious aides and Ambassador Zarif, who had put together the 2003 offer—by now long forgotten. The guest of honor wore a big grin and an even bigger chip on his shoulder. He barely acknowledged his hosts, nodding briefly as he took his seat, shook no hands, and asked for no introductions. After all, he wasn't there to listen. He was there to perform. He launched into a familiar lecture on why Iran was just like every other nuclear power on earth, and conducted a Socratic monologue on the arrogance of American power.

It was evident how Ahmadinejad had managed to become such an object of fascination and revulsion in New York and Washington. His was the voice of an angry, aggrieved Iran that saw its chance, thanks to American blunders in Iraq, to restore itself to a position of dominance in the Middle East. His bellicose rhetoric had been a key component of his election in 2005, a campaign that had been carefully thought out by Ayatollah Khamenei, the most

---

* The four were the author, Fareed Zakaria of *Newsweek*, Robin Wright of the *Washington Post*, and Charlie Rose, the public affairs talk-show host. Recordings were prohibited. I am indebted to several participants who were willing to share their notes, which I was able to compare with my own.

powerful man in the country. Ahmadinejad actually wields little power; it is Khamenei who commands the army and the intelligence agencies, and the Revolutionary Guards, which is responsible for the nuclear program. Khamenei needed someone he could control, and the presumed winner of the election, Rafsanjani, had talked openly about chipping away at Khamenei's powers. It proved easy to portray Rafsanjani, a moderate, as a lapdog of the West.

By the time the Council dinner took place, however, the mullahs may have been experiencing some buyer's remorse. Ahmadinejad was an unguided missile. He was incapable of managing the domestic economy, which was his main job. Unemployment was rampant, inflation was out of control. Abroad, he seemed oblivious to how he was undercutting his own cause. He seemed far more interested in scoring rhetorical points than in winning his audience over to his point of view.

None of us knew where to start, but Ahmadinejad did, with his insistence that we need to "continue studying" whether the Holocaust ever happened. This provocation seemed less about his genuine doubts than about his desire to goad the audience.

Never raising his voice, and thanking each questioner with a tone that oozed polite hostility, he launched immediately into the issue that he knew would rile his New York audience: his view that the treatment of the Palestinians was at least as bad as anything that had happened to the Jews sixty years ago. His technique was to spew out a series of disconnected questions that sought to create equivalencies. "If Western countries support Israel not because of the Holocaust, why is there so much bias and prejudice toward Palestine?" he demanded. "We can't hide the truth. The truth is that in Palestine there are people who came from all around the world and established a state on a homeland where others lived. We think of other historical events freely. Why is there not bias and prejudice about other genocides? Is it because the Holocaust relates to some conflicts we see today?"

He went on in this manner for fifteen minutes, expressing

doubts that there was any evidence the Holocaust had happened, suggesting that photographs could easily have been fabricated and witness reports massaged to create a pretext for the founding of the Jewish state.

Within the limits of diplomatic etiquette, and when they could get a word in edgewise, his hosts made it clear to Ahmadinejad that they thought his characterizations of Israel and the Holocaust were repugnant. Martin S. Indyk, a former American ambassador to Israel, told Ahmadinejad that Iran "did everything possible to destroy" efforts to bring peace between Israel and the Palestinians. The Iranian responded, "If you believe Iran is the reason for the failure, you are making a second mistake." Why, he asked, should the Palestinians be asked to "pay for an event they had nothing to do with" in World War II, referring to the systematic killing of Jews—if those killings, of course, had happened at all?

"In World War II about sixty million people were killed," Ahmadinejad had said at one point, when he was pressed again on his refusal to accept that the Holocaust had happened. "Why is such prominence given to a small portion of those sixty million?" he asked.

Then Hank Greenberg, who had been on a slow boil throughout the evening, spoke up. He had been a young soldier at the end of the war, and participated in the liberation of the camps. "I went through Dachau in the war and saw with my own eyes," he said. Most people might stop and ask an eyewitness what, exactly, he saw. Not Ahmadinejad.

"How old are you?" he asked Greenberg.

"Eighty-one," Greenberg said.

"OK, you were there and I'm glad nothing happened to you."

"Things did happen to me," Greenberg shot back. "I'd like an answer regarding whether you think the Holocaust occurred."

"I think we should allow more impartial studies to be done on this," Ahmadinejad said, in what turned out to be a prelude to a farcical conference in Tehran on just this topic.

After forty minutes on the Holocaust, the conversation turned nuclear—and it sped further downhill, if that was possible. Brent Scowcroft, perhaps the closest friend of Bush 41 and his former national security adviser, went right to the heart of the issue that, months later, would become the focus of debate about the National Intelligence Estimate.

Iran has claimed that its nuclear efforts are for peaceful purposes, Scowcroft said, and "the U.S. thinks it is for weapons. I don't know which is true." But, he continued, "the basic problem is that once you have the capability to enrich uranium, making a bomb is simple." Enrichment, he argued, was foolish for the Iranians to pursue. The effect would simply lead the Egyptians, the Saudis, and the Turks "to do the same thing. It will make the world more dangerous for all, and especially for you." Why not simply suspend the work and see how the negotiations proceed?

Ahmadinejad traced the history of fifty years of unfulfilled deals with the United States, Germany, France, and others—skipping over the Iranian Revolution and the hostage-taking that followed—and concluded, "How can we rely on these partners?" His solution? The United States should shut down its own nuclear fuel production and "within five years, we will sell you our own fuel, with a fifty-percent discount!" He settled back into his seat with a broad smile that some might describe as a smirk.

Ahmadinejad went on to insist he was fully cooperating with the International Atomic Energy Agency, a claim that was derided in the room, given the brazenness with which Iran had ignored the agency's questions for years. He neatly steered the whole conversation toward Iran's rights under the Nuclear Non-Proliferation Treaty, ignoring an effort by Ashton B. Carter, a Harvard professor, to get him to answer whether the nuclear effort was worth the cost to Iranian society.

"I could ask the same question. Why do some insist that we should not enrich, if it is our right?" he asked. Then he turned to the question that President Bush never openly addressed, at least in public: How could Washington argue that it was critical to stop new countries from joining the nuclear club while it sped ahead with building "second- and third-generation bombs in the U.S.?"*

"The U.S. and Europe don't speak for the whole world," Ahmadinejad continued, noting that at a meeting of nonaligned nations in Cuba the previous weekend, "118 countries defended the right of Iran to enrich."

Haass finally steered him toward Iraq, by asking Ahmadinejad how he could call the U.S. "occupiers" who pursued "covert and overt efforts to heighten insecurity," when Iranian forces were doing just that, arming Shia militias around the country? Ahmadinejad gave another of his Cheshire-cat smiles and made a version of the case he had made about nuclear weapons: that America was hardly in a position to lecture anyone.

How could Washington accuse Iran of meddling in Iraq—a neighbor—when it was clearly meddling itself? "I think U.S. leaders are confused over Iraq and that is why they accuse others," Ahmadinejad said. "We have no forces in Iraq. The U.S. has over 160,000 troops and military bases."[1]

This encounter clearly was going nowhere, and after an hour and a half, Haass called a halt to the sparring. "We have barely scratched the surface," he said, adding that he hoped for a "future dialogue." Ahmadinejad, though, could not resist the temptation to end with a jab at his hosts.

---

* Ahmadinejad was presumably referring to research efforts in the United States to build new, more reliable weapons, including the "Reliable Replacement Warhead," and bunker-busting nuclear weapons. Most of these efforts had been held up in Congress by the end of the Bush administration. Advocates of the projects argued that as long as the United States acted as the nuclear umbrella for its allies, it was critical that the arsenal remain up to date, reliable, and safe. (Some argued that if it deployed the "Reliable Replacement Warhead," the United States could reduce the number of weapons in its arsenal.) All those arguments would have been effective had Bush linked them, publicly, to a plan to dramatically reduce the American stockpile. But Bush rarely spoke about that issue in public after the signing of the Moscow Treaty in 2002.

"In the beginning of the session you said you are independent, and I accepted that," he said. "But everything you said seems to come from the government perspective."

Haass decided he couldn't let that stand unanswered. "There may be some overlap between these individuals and the government," he said. "The message for you to take away is that views toward Iran are held broadly and deeply," and added, "it would be wrong for you to leave this meeting thinking that you heard unrepresentative views."

"Don't worry," Ahmadinejad said as he got up to leave. "We know you."

It was, to say the least, an unsatisfying dialogue. Everyone had to admit at the end of the experience that Ahmadinejad was about as skillful a debating partner as modern Iran had ever produced. It would be hard to imagine President Bush opening himself up to ninety minutes of argument with foreigners openly hostile to his policies. But Ahmadinejad's technique of answering every question with a question was a way, of course, of avoiding taking positions—and of covering up the roiling debate inside Iran about whether the country was undercutting its own interests by letting Ahmadinejad pursue such a confrontational course with the West.

"He is a master of counterpunch, deception, circumlocution," Scowcroft leaned over and whispered, as Ahmadinejad left the room. Blackwill, a former ambassador to India, emerged from the conversation wondering how the United States would ever be able to negotiate with this Iranian government.

"If this man represents the prevailing government opinion in Tehran, we are heading for a massive confrontation with Iran," he said. I had to agree. If the dinner was a glimpse of what it would be like to negotiate with Iran, if we ever got that far, this probably wouldn't end well.

◆

AHMADINEJAD'S ELECTION sounded the death knell of the effort by the Europeans to come to a negotiated solution. In August 2005, he essentially torched the talks, saying the Iranians were preparing to go back to producing centrifuges. In January 2006, they did exactly that—and inspectors who toured Natanz watched as a small research-and-development project turned into an industrial-sized effort to enrich uranium. Clearly the Iranian strategy was to emulate the Pakistanis and the North Koreans—to create an infrastructure so large that it would be harder and harder for the West to force the country to give it up.

For that reason, Ahmadinejad rejected a proposal that would have allowed Iran to buy enriched Russian nuclear material for use in a civilian nuclear energy program. The aim of the Russian program was to establish a way to provide the fuel for nuclear energy without allowing Iran to develop the domestic capacity to make its own fuel—which could be diverted to make nuclear weapons. Iran's prompt response reinforced the administration's belief that Ahmadinejad didn't want to resolve his showdown with the West—he wanted to make a bomb.

So the Bush administration quickly headed into new territory, pressing the Security Council for globally enforceable sanctions against Iran. Not surprisingly, many countries balked, starting with two of Iran's most important business partners, Russia and China. They argued that there was no hard evidence that Iran was building a bomb—adding, moreover, that the intelligence estimates warning of Iran's nuclear progress had come from the same agencies that had warned the world about Saddam Hussein's weapons programs.

IT WAS AN ARGUMENT that stung. So perhaps it was no surprise that the CIA began offering tentative glimpses into the latest Iranian enigma: what had been known inside the American intelligence world as the "Laptop of Death," the bitterly wry nickname some of the analysts gave the machine.

In mid-2004 the CIA had gotten its hands on a laptop computer that arrived courtesy of a senior Iranian technician. Recruited at a scientific conference outside of Iran, the technician appeared to be in his forties or early fifties. He made it clear that he despised the Iranian regime, and strongly hinted to his handlers that he had access to the evidence that Iran was trying to design a weapon.

Soon he was engaged in a huge gamble, one that likely cost him his life. The technician either possessed or was provided with a laptop computer, and he agreed to move onto its hard drive the designs and projects that his fellow Iranian engineers had on the drawing boards.

Over time, he copied thousands of pages of Iranian computer simulations, accounts of experiments written in Farsi, and detailed schematic diagrams. The information revealed a progression of development projects, from 2001 until sometime in late 2003, that ranged from designing detonators that could fire simultaneously (essential to making a nuclear core implode) to digging a 400-meter-deep shaft and hooking it to an ignition system that could be operated from miles away. There was also the computer image of a schematic drawing of what international inspectors benignly called a "reentry vehicle." The rest of the world would call it a warhead. (In 2008, in its first public description of the evidence, the IAEA said that the dimensions and the layout showed that the warhead design was "quite likely to be able to accommodate a nuclear device.") The evidence copied onto the laptop made it clear the warhead would be sent aloft by the Shahab-3 missile, Persian for "Shooting Star."[2]

Eventually the technician suspected that Iran's feared counterintelligence teams were on to him. As he grew increasingly nervous, he gave the laptop to his wife, who managed to get out of the country with their children. Within weeks, CIA analysts poring over the computer files were astounded to find incredibly detailed information about Iran's secret efforts to design a weapon, much more than America had ever known before. But the technician himself never made it out of Iran. "We never figured out whether he was impris-

oned or executed," one former intelligence official who was involved in the operation told me. "But you have to think that it did-
n't work out well for him."[3]

For the CIA, still under siege in 2004 for its failures in Iraq, the
laptop was simultaneously a gift from the heavens and an enormous new risk. Every week the agency's top officials were answering
questions about how they had extrapolated from spotty data to
conclude that Saddam had restarted his programs to build
weapons of mass destruction, and naïvely bought into the account
of an Iraqi defector, wonderfully code-named "Curveball," who fabricated tales of extensive Iraqi weapons programs. First the 9/11
Commission, then the lesser-known WMD commission, then investigations by the Senate intelligence committee and some criminal
inquiries, had left the agency reeling. They had been charged, accurately, with failing to connect the dots before 9/11, then seeing dots
that did not exist before the invasion of Iraq.

Compared to Iraq, Iran was an even bigger black hole for American intelligence. The same WMD commission that examined the intelligence failures on Iraq expressed shock, in a classified section of
its report, that so little was known about Iran.[4] Now the laptop offered a chance to show that the agency had not forgotten everything
it once knew about good spycraft. It potentially could provide exactly the kind of window into the Iranian weapons program that was
missing in the case of Iraq: a detailed look at what the engineers had
accomplished and, more important, what they had failed to achieve.

"The big mistake in Iraq was that we assumed they had the talent and the drive to make steady progress," one senior official who
returned to the intelligence world after the Iraq debacle told me.
"Of course, they were making no progress." The intelligence world's
top weapons experts knew that the only thing more career-
impairing than being wrong about Iraq's WMD would be to repeat
the mistake with Iran's program.

The first question was whether the technician was another
"Curveball," this time of the Persian variety. With that bitter experi-

ence in mind, experts at the CIA, the Energy Department, and the national laboratories started going through the laptop's diagrams and notes to figure out whether the technician had given them actual nuclear-related designs or something less fearsome, perhaps plans for a conventional warhead.

Relatively quickly, they determined that the documents in the Laptop of Death were not likely to be forgeries. "All the information was so sophisticated and so technical that it would be very difficult for someone to fabricate," one official who was briefed on the material said a few months later.

But as the White House and the world learned in Iraq, circumstantial evidence doesn't prove the existence of a weapons program. Nothing on the hard drive actually proved that Iran was really building a nuclear device, rather than just exploring what would be required. Nor did it answer the question of whether Iran's leadership had decided to speed ahead, put the program on hold, or scrap the whole thing. The Laptop of Death was tantalizing, but it was not definitive.

That reality became clear in the early summer of 2007. The new evidence that arrived during the preparation of the National Intelligence Estimate sent everyone scrambling back to the laptop. But the last documents found on the computer, it appeared, were written just before someone in the Iranian hierarchy pulled the plug on direct work on weapons designs. The laptop was a snapshot in time—it did not establish that the Iranians were working on a bomb design now.

There was no question, however, that the laptop revealed that a team of Iranian scientists had been deeply engaged in solving the hardest problems involved in weaponization. And the schematics they left on their hard drives looked, to amateurs and experts alike, a lot more useful for building a nuclear bomb than for building a nuclear power plant.

◆

WITH ITS CREDIBILITY in tatters after the humiliations of the intelligence failures in Iraq, the Bush administration faced a vexing problem: How could it tell the world about the new evidence? The White House was hardly about to send the president out to declare that he now possessed a "smoking" laptop. Nor could it repeat the pre-Iraq stunt of publishing a "white paper" highlighting the sanitized, declassified case against the Iranian regime—one that, in the case of Iraq, made no mention of the dissenting opinions. They had been through all that in late 2002 and 2003, and the result was that American intelligence findings would be tainted for years to come, whether or not they turned out to be right. Bush's first term was coming to an end, and the plan was to maintain a steely silence about the Iran evidence until the second-term team settled in.

But then Colin Powell said something that he shouldn't have.

Powell was on his way to Santiago, Chile, for one of his last big meetings as secretary of state. Before he left, he had gotten his usual intelligence briefing, up in the small study next to his office, where he was surrounded by memorabilia from his Army days and models of the cars he loves to tinker with. The briefers had told him the tale of the laptop, which he viewed with a bit of suspicion after his bitter experience making the case against Saddam Hussein at the United Nations. (As the most credible voice in the Cabinet, Powell had been tapped by the president to make the argument, much to Powell's lasting regret.)

Powell paced through the whole tale of the laptop story with the briefers, prodding them for details about how they had convinced themselves of the laptop's authenticity. If it wasn't a con job, he later remembered thinking, it was pretty persuasive. Within days he was headed out on one of his last official trips, still grappling with the question of whether there was anything he could initiate with Iran in his final days as secretary of state. When questions came up about Iran during a refueling stop, Powell told the reporters traveling with him that he had seen evidence that Iran was "actively working" on a program to enable its missiles to carry nuclear weapons. He said that "should be of concern to all parties." The reporters seized on his words, and pressed him. Realizing that he had probably revealed too much, he retreated. "I knew it was news," he said later, "but I didn't think it would be that big."

It was that big. Among those reporters who followed the Iran issue closely, the statement set off alarm bells—and a search to understand what, exactly, Powell had learned. Clearly there was some new evidence floating around Washington suggesting that Iran's motives were not as benign as the Iranians liked to claim.

The laptop was among the government's most highly classified discoveries, and inside Washington, intelligence experts were shocked that someone as normally cautious as Powell had spilled the news. "We were looking at each other with that kind of expression that says, 'He said *what*?'" recalled John McLaughlin, the deputy director of the CIA at the time.[5]

Desperate to stuff the genie back into the bottle, the Bush administration decided it would offer no help to reporters who began asking about the nature of the new evidence. But silence was not an option for long. Bush and Rice, who was preparing to become Powell's successor, knew that in the second term they would have no practical military options with Iran. As Rice said to Bush in another context—regarding Bush's desire to send troops to help stop the slaughter in Darfur—"I don't think you can invade another Muslim country during this administration, even for the best of reasons."[6]

That left economic sanctions as the only viable option to step up pressure on Tehran. And if they were going to persuade the members of the UN Security Council to back a ratcheting up of sanctions against a country that provided much of the world's oil, they needed airtight evidence that the Iranians were lying. The French, the British, and the Germans were already convinced. But the laptop, it was clear, represented the administration's best shot at convincing the rest of the world.

Soon the order went out for the State Department and the intelligence agencies to work up an unclassified but confidential briefing on the laptop—essentially a PowerPoint presentation that danced around the question of how the evidence had ended up in American and European hands. There were two skeptical audiences who needed to be convinced: the IAEA, which spent much of 2003 shooting down the administration's contention that Iraq was buying uranium in Africa, and the members of the Security Council, who were reluctant to ramp up sanctions.

The administration knew it had burned most of its bridges at the IAEA. Before the Iraq War, Cheney had mocked the agency as incompetent, describing Mohamed ElBaradei, the director general of the IAEA, and his inspectors as a bunch of naïve fools who wandered around countries aimlessly, missing evidence that was right in front of their faces. ElBaradei had just survived an American-led effort to block him from getting a second term, in what looked to the rest of the world like an effort at payback considering that he had been right about Iraq. Along the way, the IAEA had discovered its phones and e-mails were being monitored, presumably by American intelligence agencies. Visitors to the IAEA's imposing towers in Vienna did not have to hang around the cafeteria for long before they heard long, angry diatribes about Bush and Cheney, who had never acknowledged that the agency was a lot closer to right about Iraq than was the American intelligence community.

Into this poisoned atmosphere, a team of American diplomats and intelligence officers showed up in the spectacular top-floor conference room of the American mission to the IAEA on July 18, 2005. Below, the Danube River flowed through Vienna's grand cityscape. They had invited the agency's top inspectors to walk across the street from the UN's complex to see a presentation of the new evidence, and to judge for themselves whether the Iranians were hiding anything.

On the screen, and spread out on the table, were thousands of pages of Iranian computer simulations and accounts of experiments. None had ever been seen by the agency before, though the Iranians had maintained they were showing inspectors everything they had. The American presenter pointed to marginal notes indicating that the Iranians were not only mapping things out on paper, they were conducting experiments. "This wasn't just some theoretical exercise," he insisted.

A number of the IAEA experts were impressed by the scope and detail of the evidence, and thought it was the most credible proof they had seen. "They've worked problems that you don't do unless you're very serious," one nuclear-weapons expert who saw the evidence said of the Iranians. Many agreed. The most impressive part of the American presentation, they said, was the work the Iranians had done on creating a sphere of detonators to ignite conventional explosives that, in turn, compressed radioactive fuel to start a nuclear chain reaction. There were sketches showing how to position a heavy ball—presumably one of nuclear fuel—inside the warhead so that it would be stable during a fiery flight toward a target. There were notes about how to detonate a warhead at 2,000 feet, strongly suggesting a nuclear weapon because that altitude would be unsuitable for detonating a warhead containing a conventional explosive charge.

All the arrows pointed toward nuclear weapons. But a few in the room couldn't help thinking that they had been through all this before. Just because the Iranians had worked out the plans, they warned, that did not prove they were carrying them out. Nothing in the Nuclear Non-Proliferation Treaty prohibits a country from studying how a nuclear weapon works. It just prohibits them from building one.

"I can fabricate that data," one senior European diplomat who had seen the presentation told me and my colleague Bill Broad later. "It looks beautiful, but it is open to doubt."[7]

The information was classified, and the Americans refused to allow the IAEA to confront the Iranians with it. That prohibition lasted for three years, a huge mistake on the part of the administration because it enabled the Iranians to claim to the public that there was no reason for suspicion. But with a showdown vote at the Security Council looming, American officials quickly started taking their show on the road.

Robert Joseph, the longtime aide to Condoleezza Rice and an expert in nuclear strategy, showed it to the president of Ghana, and other administration officials took it to leaders of Argentina, Sri Lanka, Tunisia, and Nigeria—all of whom were temporarily sitting on the Security Council. One of the leaders turned to Joseph after the presentation and thanked him. "It's the first time I've seen anything like this," he said. "We don't have an intelligence service."

While Bush was willing to share the evidence with countries like Sri Lanka, he refused to talk about it with the two audiences who mattered most: the people of the United States and the people of Iran. If the nuclear standoff led to military confrontation, those were the two populations with the most to lose. Yet Bush never publicly cited the evidence to back up his claims about Iran's intentions. Once, and only once, he acknowledged that the damage to his credibility from selling the Iraq War meant he would have trouble convincing the American public about the evidence against Iran.

That moment arrived shortly after the *Times* published its first lengthy story on the laptop and its contents. It was Bush's last news conference of 2005, held in the East Room.

When I asked him about the laptop, he tried to deflect the issue, asking, "Is that classified?" When the room broke out in laughter, he added, "No, never mind." I pressed him on the question of why he was not making a public case against Iran, as he had two years before against Saddam Hussein.

"Where it is going to be most difficult to make the case is in the public arena," he acknowledged. "People will say, you know, if we're trying to make the case on Iran, you know, well, your intelligence failed in Iraq, therefore how can we trust the intelligence in Iran?"[8]

But he plunged right ahead into his argument that Iran was so dangerous that it could never be allowed to get its hands on nuclear fuel. "The next step," he said, "is to make sure that the world understands that the capacity to enrich uranium for a civilian program would lead to a weapons program. And so therefore we cannot allow the Iranians to have the capacity to enrich."

BY THE SPRING OF 2006, it was clear that Bush was losing that argument. His fragile coalition against Iran was falling apart.

In late March, Rice attended a disastrous meeting in Berlin with European foreign ministers, who described to her how Ahmadinejad's government was brilliantly exploiting fissures among the Europeans, the Russians, and the Chinese, and enjoying considerable success. The Iranians were playing off Moscow's greed and Beijing's thirst for oil, persuading diplomats to water down their sanctions and offering lucrative oil exploration contracts and investment opportunities in return. Iran understood the American-led strategy at the United Nations, a strategy of starting with small sanctions and steadily raising the threshold of economic pain, and it was looking to short-circuit the process.

At a dinner in Washington with the Russian foreign minister, Sergey Lavrov, Rice and Hadley learned how effectively Iran's effort to undermine the Bush strategy was working. Rice could barely stand Lavrov, whom she viewed as a parrot for a Kremlin that was increasingly obsessed with the goal of using Russia's oil wealth to restore the country to the ranks of a real superpower. But she could not dismiss the scenario he painted that night of how Iran would respond to growing pressure. He warned that Ahmadinejad and the mullahs would be tempted to follow the North Korean playbook, throwing out all the international inspectors and exiting the Nuclear Non-Proliferation Treaty, then negotiating from a position of strength as a country speeding toward acquisition of the bomb.

It seemed more than plausible. It seemed like the kind of stunt that would appeal to Ahmadinejad. But while he threatened that move, he did not make it. His first step was to bring talks with the Europeans to a halt, and to move ahead with enriching uranium. As soon as a tiny amount was produced, he appeared at a celebratory event that included the waving of flags, a release of doves, and declarations about the start of a great new nuclear era for Iran. Dancers passed a vial—supposedly of the real stuff, enriched uranium—around on the stage.

The ceremony was pure hype. At that point the Iranians had not made enough uranium to irradiate a microwave dinner. But the deeper message was clear: Iran was building centrifuges faster than Washington could win approval for new UN sanctions.

In the small dining room behind the Oval Office—accessible only by what White House wags called the "Monica hallway" because it was the site of Monica Lewinsky's tryst with Bill Clinton—Rice presented Bush with the kind of bad news only she could deliver. The Iran strategy, she said, was failing.

In private, Bush had already told her and Hadley that he worried that unless something changed he might soon be forced to choose between two potentially disastrous choices. "He said he doesn't want to be left in a situation where he has only one of two options, accepting a nuclear Iran or contemplating the military option," one senior official who dealt with Bush on the issue told me.

If the Iranians were allowed to begin large-scale enrichment on their own soil, Bush was certain it would eventually lead to a bomb. If Bush ordered a military strike against the nuclear sites, the blowback could be enormous—international condemnation, attacks on American forces in Iraq, and, most probably, a wave of nationalistic fervor in Iran that would benefit the hardline clerics.

"I need another choice," Bush told Rice.[9]

Rice's alternative was right out of the Colin Powell playbook: an offer of direct, face-to-face negotiations with Iran, exactly what the administration had passed up in 2003. But she knew that she would run headlong into opposition from Cheney and others. So she came up with a face-saving condition: Iran would have to agree to suspend its work on producing uranium in return for a suspension of all sanctions. That was the only way the Iranians would get the United States, including Rice herself, to join the Europeans at the bargaining table. Rice made it clear that she would open the negotiations personally.

Rice told Bush that the condition would ensure that Iran was not building centrifuges while the negotiations dragged on. It was a way to coax Bush into what amounted to a partial about-face. Of course, it was something that Bush could have attempted years before, when he still had the upper hand over the Iranians, after the successful early operations in Iraq and before Ahmadinejad was elected to power. But as one of Rice's top aides said to me later, the deal was something "he never would have allowed Colin to pursue."

Over the Easter weekend, Rice retreated to her apartment at the Watergate and drafted a two-page paper that turned the idea into a formal proposal. It was classic Rice: The United States faced a choice of three paths, she wrote, including a course of "coercive measures," both military and economic; an alternative course of negotiations laced with what Rice called "bold" incentives for Iran to give up all production of nuclear fuel; and, finally, a set of sanctions that the United States and some allies could impose if the United Nations refused to act against Iran. The proposal was accompanied by a three-color chart that Rice herself had drawn because of the great secrecy surrounding the idea. It included all sorts of timelines for action as the Iranians responded. (Hadley took a look at it and said later that it was "brilliant and completely indecipherable.")

I met with Rice and Hadley for an hour and a half in Rice's office when she made the offer public and both were all but certain the Iranians would jump at the deal. After all, it gave the Iranians what the administration assumed they wanted most—a face-to-face negotiation—and the only price they had to pay was reinstituting the "voluntary" suspension of their nuclear work. If Iran's nuclear negotiators didn't like how the negotiations were going, they could always restart the centrifuges.

In the end, however, the Iranians didn't bite. They never really responded to the offer. Ahmadinejad simply repeated his mantra: Enrichment was Iran's "natural" right, and he wasn't going to give it up. For Bush and the Europeans, the result was disastrous. In the next eighteen months, while Washington and Tehran exchanged invective, the Iranians went from running a single cascade of 164 centrifuges to running more than 3,800. By early 2008, they had begun installing the next generation of nuclear technology and were modifying A. Q. Khan's designs for a more advanced centrifuge that could pump out uranium faster than ever before.

WHILE THE WHITE HOUSE was trying to focus public attention on ratcheting up the pressure on Iran, the CIA and other intelligence agencies were well along on a campaign of their own—one designed to sabotage Iran's nuclear operations.

Today, few secrets are more closely held in Washington than the details of the CIA's operations in Iran, which in recent years have ranged from planting detection devices inside the country to try to scope out secret nuclear facilities, to fiddling with the crucial nuclear components Iran was trying to buy around the world, in hopes of throwing a wrench into their works. The CIA was not alone in conducting such covert actions: Britain, Germany, and other intelligence services helped, and the Israelis have had the strongest incentive of all.

Few of these covert actions had come to light—until investigators began unraveling the sordid tale of the Tinner family. Two generations of the Swiss engineers had a relationship with A. Q. Khan that dated back to the days when he was first attempting to obtain the equipment Pakistan needed for its bomb.

Khan had started his dealings three decades before with Friedrich Tinner, an inventor and mechanical engineer who specialized in vacuum technology—the mazes of pipes, pumps, and valves that evacuate air from machinery. Assuring a perfect vacuum is particularly vital in centrifuges, which can enrich uranium only if they are spinning at phenomenal speeds. The elder Tinner owned American patents for some of his valves, and he proved invaluable to Khan during Pakistan's race to catch up to India in nuclear technology.

When Khan went into business for himself, striking his deals with Iran and Libya to sell centrifuge components and plans, he reached out to Friedrich Tinner again. By that time, Tinner had been joined in the business by his sons, Urs and Marco. Friedrich lived un-ostentatiously in a modest house in Haag, near the Liechtenstein border. But looks were deceiving. This was a global enterprise. Eventually it was agreed that one of the sons would go to Malaysia to help set up a factory that ultimately would provide centrifuge parts to Libya and to Iran, among other clients. (Even today, investigators are unnerved by the fact that they have never accounted for all the centrifuges that Khan sold, most of them using technology furnished by the Tinners.)

The family, it turned out, was pressed for cash, and eventually their operation became known to the CIA. But rather than bust it down, the agency saw its chance to turn at least one member of the family—paying him at first to provide information, then to help sabotage some of the equipment.[10]

It was a huge, if largely unheralded, success for the CIA—an operation that "was very significant," said Gary Samore, who ran the nonproliferation office at the National Security Council under President Clinton when the infiltration into the Khan network began. "That's where we got the first indications that Iran had acquired centrifuges," he said.

Clinton left office before the spying relationship blossomed. But it soon became crucial to the Bush administration's efforts to penetrate two nations' nuclear programs: Libya's and Iran's.

Thanks in part to the Tinners, the CIA had the Khan manufacturing plant in Malaysia fully monitored, tapping into conversations and computer traffic involving Khan and his bevy of scientists and engineers. Then, in the winter of 2003, CIA officers rendezvoused with the Tinners at a hotel in Innsbruck, Austria, to discuss the terms on a new operation—one that would not only involve sharing information, but would also involve gaining access to the equipment bound for Iran.

The details of this have come out, to the embarrassment of American intelligence officials, largely through an investigation conducted by the Swiss and the IAEA—at least until the United States persuaded the Swiss to drop the case and destroy the materials they found in the Tinners' files. But some of that information revealed that on June 21, 2003, just two months after Baghdad fell, Marco Tinner signed a formal agreement with two CIA agents. For a million dollars, the agency bought the rights that the Tinners held for manufacturing vacuum gear. The money went to a front company Marco Tinner had established in Road Town, Tortola, the capital of the British Virgin Islands. Clearly someone involved in the transaction had a sense of humor: The contract was signed by two CIA agents who used cover names—W. James Kinsman and Sean D. Mahaffey—and they were supposed to work for a company called Big Black River Technologies Inc., apparently a play on "black" intelligence operations. The headquarters was supposed to be in an office building just three blocks from the White House, on I Street. (No one there has any memory of the company.)

Four months after the signing of the contract, American and European authorities seized centrifuge parts bound for Libya aboard the BBC *China*, a freighter. When they hauled the ship into an Italian port, they knew exactly which containers they wanted to look into. That was no accident. "The Tinners were a source," one former Bush administration official told me and my colleague Bill Broad.

That seizure helped convince the Libyans to give up their nuclear project, and it was turned over to the Americans, lock, stock, and centrifuge—including some parts sold by the Tinners. Bush heralded the seizure as a major intelligence coup, and to this day the Libyan operation stands out as one of the administration's biggest intelligence successes, though the Libyans remain bitter that they did not get the kind of benefits they believed were coming to them.

For the Tinners, the deal was the beginning of the end: The secret double lives of the family unraveled. In Malaysia, they were accused in a police report of being key members of Khan's network. The factory was cleaned out. In Switzerland, one of the sons was charged and jailed.

The Swiss soon discovered they were holding an American spy. For more than two years, President Bush was receiving regular updates on the dealings with the Tinners, and those briefings helped firm up his view that Iran was hell-bent on acquiring a bomb. It also gave the administration a moment to play havoc with the Iranians' program—and set them back, albeit briefly.

The sabotage first became obvious when inspectors from the IAEA traveled to Iran and Libya in 2003 and 2004 and discovered identical vacuum pumps in both countries. Not only were they identical, they had been damaged cleverly so they looked perfectly fine, but did not operate properly. Swiss investigators and the IAEA traced the route of the defective parts from Pfeiffer Vacuum in Germany to, of all places, the Los Alamos National Laboratory in New Mexico, the birthplace of the atomic bomb. There, according to a European official who studied the case, American nuclear experts had made sure the pumps "wouldn't work." It's unclear when the Iranians figured out what happened, or whether they ever traced them, as the Europeans did, to the same laboratories where the nuclear age began in the 1940s. Whatever the case, they buy their goods elsewhere these days.

A more serious disruption involved a power supply shipped to Iran from Turkey, where the Khan network did business with two makers of industrial control equipment. The Iranians put the machine to work at their nuclear complex at Natanz, where they needed precisely controlled electrical feeds to keep the centrifuges spinning. But it turned out that something had happened to the power supplies that caused them to turn out a highly unstable wave of electricity—just enough to make the interiors of the centrifuges spin out of control and explode. That happened to about fifty centrifuges before the Iranians caught on—a serious though temporary setback.

What happened next was described by Gholamreza Aghazadeh, who heads the Atomic Energy Organization of Iran. Talking to Iranian reporters, he recalled that the previous spring "they called me at two o'clock in the morning and said that all the fifty centrifuges have exploded because the UPS [uninterruptible power supply] in charge of controlling the electricity had not acted properly. Later we found out that the UPS that we had imported through Turkey had been manipulated; and after this incident we checked all the imported instruments before using them." His next call was from Ahmadinejad, he said.

"'Build these machines even if they explode ten times more,'" Aghazadeh recalled being told.[11]

To this day, American intelligence officials will not talk about their multimillion-dollar effort to sabotage the Iranian program. When I showed a top American counterproliferation official the transcript of Aghazadeh's account, he smiled broadly and said to me, "Accidents do happen. It's a shame, isn't it?"[12]

WHILE THE INTELLIGENCE world focused on covert action, the administration spent the better part of eighteen months on what turned out to be a bad bet: that escalating UN sanctions would make life so difficult for Iran that it would throw in the towel. The process started in July 2006, when the Security Council adopted a resolution demanding that Iran suspend its uranium enrichment. The idea was simply to get countries on record opposing the Iranian action so that later the administration could argue that the UN's credibility required that sanctions must be imposed.

Predictably, the Iranians ignored the Security Council. It took six months for the United States and its allies to pass the first resolution imposing penalties. It placed restrictions on some high-tech exports to Iran, and banned technological assistance that would aid the regime in acquiring nuclear material or delivery capabilities. Iranian businesses involved in the program were targeted, and countries were urged to restrict the travel of those engaged in military research programs.

In March 2007, after an even greater uphill climb, the United States succeeded in getting a third resolution passed. China and Russia balked at any sanctions that would have real teeth, but the resolution did include action against an expanded list of personnel and sanctions on Bank Sepah, an Iranian-owned financial institution, making it difficult for the bank to operate abroad. There was also a ban against buying Iranian arms.

All this might have had some effect, but the rising price of oil meant that Iran's revenue flow kept rising too. No one on the Security Council would risk sanctions against Iran's oil exports or limit the flow of refined petroleum into Iran—two steps that would have really gotten the country's attention. At Natanz, the installation of centrifuges sputtered along, then surged in 2008.

Eventually the Bush administration all but gave up on UN sanctions, figuring that it was better to take joint measures with Europe to limit Iran's access to capital. The French firm Total, a big investor in oil fields, said it would no longer put money into Iran. Many banks shied away from business. The sanctions began to hurt, but not enough to get the Iranians to halt their nuclear work.

ON A COLD DAY at the end of January 2008, I went to see Nick Burns, the administration's top Iran negotiator, just as he was packing up the trappings of a twenty-seven-year career in American diplomacy. Back in the autumn, before the National Intelligence Estimate was published, he had told Rice that he had decided to go ahead with a long-held plan to leave his post as America's most senior foreign service officer.

No one could blame him; Burns had three children, all of college or graduate-school age, and a government salary was clearly not going to be enough to cover tuitions. He was only fifty-one, and like many who leave the upper reaches of American diplomacy, he would be a hot commodity for any corporation seeking access to some of the world's most profitable markets. (Ultimately, Burns would choose to go to Harvard to teach foreign policy.) Without question, Burns had one of the most valuable Rolodexes on the planet. Around the world, every prime minister and foreign minister would take his call.

But some of his friends suspected something else was going on as well. The NIE had effectively ended American diplomacy with Iran, Burns's project since Condoleezza Rice handed him the world's most complex nuclear problem in early 2005. And many voiced the belief that Burns was looking for some ideological purification as well. In the Bush White House, Burns had often been treated with some suspicion. After all, he had served—and prospered—under the Clinton administration. He walked and talked like a pro-negotiation Democrat. His protection stemmed from his ties to Rice, an old friend since the two worked together in the days of Bush 41.

At a ceremony announcing his departure, a wistful-sounding Rice acknowledged that back then—before Iraq and Abu Ghraib, before Iran and other second-world challengers to American power— the world seemed to be going America's way. "It was a heady time, a time of the end of the Cold War, when Eastern Europe was being liberated, when Germany was being unified, and when the Soviet Union was well on its way to peaceful collapse," she said. "And they were great times for two people in their thirties who thought they had the world by the tail. It was a great time to be there and a great time to be friends working together on those issues."

Now they were both in their early fifties, and things seemed different. She thanked him for being along for what she gently termed "more trying times for our country."[13]

They were certainly more trying times for Burns, who clearly believed, as did many others in the State Department, that the Bush administration had missed some huge opportunities in the world, including with Iran. As we settled into the back office where we had had many previous conversations, the subject gradually turned from the question of where he would display all the Red Sox memorabilia in his office—not at home, his wife had decreed—to what he would have done differently in dealing with Iran.

"I would have dropped the conditions for our opening a direct discussion with Tehran," he said with an openness that surprised me. This, of course, was precisely the critique that many Democrats (along with a few Republicans) had long made about the Bush administration's approach to the world. Bush and Cheney had always regarded negotiations with another country as a reward granted to foreigners for good behavior. That approach explained why, in the first term, the administration talked to neither North Korea nor Iran.

Rice loosened that stricture in 2006, when she persuaded Bush to propose talks with the Iranians if they first suspended enriching uranium, however briefly. "With the benefit of hindsight, we should have just offered to negotiate with them" without caveats about suspending production, Burns told me. Burns admitted he was as responsible as anyone for the decision to demand conditions in the first place. "But the conditions became a political football" inside Iran for eighteen months, "and gave them an excuse not to negotiate." Those were the critical months during which Iran went from spinning a few hundred centrifuges to spinning a few thousand. What's more, the very act of holding fast against the American conditions became a rallying cry for Ahmadinejad and raised his stature as he portrayed himself as the man who stood up to the American behemoth. He was able to silence his critics inside Iran, Burns noted, by exploiting his image as the unwavering Persian David, holding off the imperialist Goliath.

Burns had been among the authors of the plan to hold talks with Iran once the country suspended its nuclear enrichment activity. But after the Iranians refused to respond, and kept building centrifuges, he started to urge Rice in 2007 and others in the administration to consider opening a direct channel to Iran, without conditions.

"Imagine the tremendous diplomatic advantage if we had simply said, 'We are willing to talk,'" Burns told me that day. "Offering to talk would have increased our leverage any way those talks worked out. If the Iranians accepted the offer to talk, we would have been able to probe their bottom line. If they declined, we would have strengthened our ability to argue for stronger sanctions with the Russians and the Chinese. We haven't had a real conversation with these people for twenty-eight years. We would have been able to figure out whether there was a coherent government on the other side that could have a real conversation with us." He suspected that the Iranians would not have been able to resolve their own factional splits, which would have left the United States in a stronger position from which to argue for tougher sanctions.

"This penchant that we have that we don't talk to our enemies simply does not make sense," Burns said, echoing a position many of the administration's critics made. "As Yitzhak Rabin said, 'You don't need to talk to make peace with your friends. You need to make peace with your enemies.'"

It was a battle Burns had fought until he left the department, but always behind the scenes because of his loyalty to Rice. It was never clear where Rice herself stood on the issue; inside the State Department, she seemed to acknowledge that the administration's policy was failing, but she said she could simply not persuade her White House colleagues to attempt a new approach.

"Condi's view of this shifted back and forth," one of her close colleagues said. "There were times she thought that if we hung tough, the Iranians would come around. There were times she despaired this would never work."

In the end, Cheney and Hadley won the day with the argument that agreeing to negotiate would be seen as a sign of weakness born of our troubles in Iraq. The Iranians, the argument went, would conclude that if we were willing to give in by coming to the negotiating table, we would be willing to give in on allowing Iran to continue producing uranium. All they would have to do was wait us out.

Hadley, usually the calm lawyer, was particularly vociferous on this point. Give in to the Iranians, he argued, and you might as well invite the Saudis and the Egyptians to start up their own nuclear weapons projects.

The result of this internal war within the administration was disastrous.

Like North Korea, Iran quickly recognized that time was on its side. In the months and years after the start of the Iraq War, the "Dear Leader" in North Korea built his nuclear arsenal; the Supreme Leader in Iran put together a nuclear "capability" that would be difficult if not impossible to persuade the country to dismantle. Iran did not get everything it needed to build a bomb. But it got almost everything—designs, centrifuges, plenty of foreign expertise. The Iranians were just smarter about it than the North Koreans. They realized that as soon as they built a weapon, they would cross a line that would inflame the Sunni Arab states and make the country a target of Israel and the West. Ambiguity is their friend. In the Second Nuclear Age, countries don't need to compile huge stockpiles of the sort that the Americans and Soviets amassed during the Cold War. All they need is a "virtual bomb," a credible capacity to build one in a few months and a credible willingness to do so.

Iran didn't invent this strategy; the Japanese have employed it effectively for more than a decade, although they deny doing so. But the Iranians figured out that, skillfully executed, it was the smartest path to becoming a nuclear weapons state.

# CHAPTER 4

# THE ISRAEL OPTION

ON A FRIGID Monday in Vienna in late February 2008, Olli Heinonen summoned ambassadors and experts from dozens of countries into the boardroom of the International Atomic Energy Agency, posting guards outside the doors.

For two months, Heinonen had watched as political leaders around the world had seized on the ambiguities of the Bush administration's National Intelligence Estimate on Iran for their own purposes. As the agency's chief inspector, Heinonen and his team had spent several years of their lives trying to extract answers from the Iranians, and he understood better than anyone what questions they had promised to answer and then avoided. He kept a list in his head of the obfuscations they had generated when presented with specific evidence that they were designing warheads, or that military units appeared involved in what the Iranians insisted was a completely civilian effort to produce nuclear power.

Every few weeks, Heinonen's inspectors were visiting Iran to track the construction of each new "stand" of centrifuges used to enrich uranium. It was clear that 2008 was a breakthrough year. The summer before, Heinonen had predicted that by the end of 2008, the Iranians would likely be running upward of 4,000 of the high-speed machines—enough to make a bomb's worth of uranium in a year's time if they chose to enrich to bomb-grade purity. His prediction proved just about right.

Now in his early sixties, Heinonen had been in the nuclear inspection business for a quarter of a century. It had all started as something of a lark. At thirty-five, he was eager for a new challenge, and could no longer stand Helsinki, where he was employed at Finland's Technical Research Centre. "The winter was endless," he told me one night, relaxing over a beer in the Stadtpark, one of the perfectly groomed parks in downtown Vienna. "Snow, horrible weather, I was ready to get out." But the job did offer him an opportunity to get around a bit, and during a free day while attending a nuclear conference in Austria, he signed up for a river cruise in Hungary. Along the way, Heinonen happened upon a flyer advertising openings for "safeguards inspectors" at the IAEA, the sleepy United Nations outpost in Vienna that was responsible for monitoring all of the world's nuclear facilities. He knew little about the agency, but most of the jobs it posted were for assignments in the Far East, a region of the world that he had always dreamed of traveling around. This seemed the perfect match of nuclear expertise and opportunity for wanderlust. He returned to Helsinki, where a messy mix of snow and rain the following Monday convinced him to apply for the job. Soon Heinonen and his wife and daughter were settling into the quiet Tokyo neighborhood of Shiroganedai, a district of tiny streets, ancient Japanese gardens, and a few surviving old wooden houses, where the "Yakimo man," a seller of sweet potatoes, still came through with his cart now and again, a reminder of a faraway time.

Heinonen loved it. His job was to inspect Japan's nuclear industry, one of the largest in the world. It was in Tokyo that he learned much about the process of making nuclear fuel. It was also a fast lesson in nuclear realities: Heinonen discovered how easy it would be for a determined country to use the same technology—even the same machinery—to go the extra few steps necessary to turn reactor fuel into bomb fuel. The Japanese never took that step—or insisted they had never taken it. But he left viewing the country and others that possessed similarly sensitive technologies as "virtual" nuclear-weapons states. There was plenty of anecdotal evidence that Japanese engineers had drawn out, with their usual precision, exactly what it would take to make a weapon if the country ever decided that it could no longer depend on the American nuclear umbrella. No one who had ever visited Japanese laboratories believed it would take very long, if Japan ever decided to do so, for the nation that invented the Walkman to design a warhead.

After three years Heinonen was posted back to the headquarters in Vienna. His adventure over, he was preparing to quit the IAEA and return to his old, less-exciting life in Helsinki. That is, until he settled his children into school, found an apartment, and then discovered that it would require him to give up a prized possession.

"It was a Saab," he said. "A thing of beauty." He had bought it in Vienna, and had planned to take it to Finland tax-free. But that required a waiting period of a year—and his former boss told him that if he wanted his old job at the Technical Research Centre, he had to show up within six months. When Heinonen said he needed more time, he got a stiff letter from the company's legal department telling him to show up on schedule or the offer would disappear. Angry, he never responded. He stayed in Vienna. As it turned out, his decision to stick with the Saab changed his life—and, years later, the course of the West's confrontation with Iran.

By October 1986, Heinonen was in Iraq for the first time, examining Saddam Hussein's civilian nuclear program—the program that the agency discovered, after the Gulf War in 1991, had come perilously close to building an atomic weapon. Later he was in North Korea, trolling through the grim nuclear facilities at Yongbyon. These were his first entanglements with two of the world's most complex covert nuclear weapons projects. The combination of Hussein's megalomania and North Korea's use of its nuclear program as a bargaining chip for state survival got him hooked. He rose slowly through the ranks, until he was selected by the IAEA's Egyptian-born director general, Mohamed ElBaradei, to run all of the agency's "safeguards" program—the gentle name used for the division that is responsible for ensuring that countries are not trying to build a bomb. It is a job that puts Heinonen in the interesting position of assessing the quality of the estimates that the world's intelligence agencies drop at his doorstep. And, with varying degrees of candor, everyone from the CIA to German intelligence to the Mossad all share what they have learned—because Heinonen has the legal right to ask questions and demand answers of every country that is a signatory of the Nuclear Non-Proliferation Treaty. But the IAEA's relationship with its member countries is always rife with tension.

ElBaradei spent most of his tenure at war with Washington. And Heinonen will never forget the Bush administration's willingness to skew intelligence to fit its political agenda. At that dinner in Stadtpark in 2007, the conversation turned to evidence the CIA had provided to the IAEA on Iraq in the last months before the war in 2003. He was still angry at the contempt that Dick Cheney heaped on the agency, which the vice president had portrayed as a group of incompetent fools who wouldn't recognize a nuclear program if it was dropped in the courtyard of their headquarters. Of course it was the IAEA that quickly determined that the most important single piece of evidence supporting Bush's allegation that Saddam Hussein was "seeking uranium in Africa" was an obvious forgery. As ElBaradei rarely tired of mentioning, the IAEA was right and Cheney was wrong.

ElBaradei and Heinonen got the last laugh when the Egyptian nuclear chief and his staff won the Nobel Peace Prize. But in 2007 Washington and Vienna were at war again, this time over Iran. ElBaradei, concerned that Bush might be setting the pretext for war with Iran, decided to take diplomacy into his own hands. He negotiated a separate agreement with Iran, a "work plan" for the Iranians to answer questions they had long ignored—with the implicit promise that if they complied, ElBaradei would give the country a clean bill of health. Bush and Rice were outraged: The IAEA chief was overstepping his bounds and undercutting the Security Council's sanctions against Iran, they said. Rice complained that ElBaradei and his agency were supposed to be inspectors, not negotiators; other administration officials charged, as two of my colleagues wrote, that ElBaradei was "drunk with the power of his Nobel."[1] Even some of ElBaradei's own staff worried he was naïve in cutting his deal with the Iranians—Tehran would string him out, they feared, and never answer all the questions.

But at the beginning of 2008, the tables had turned. Suddenly, Heinonen worried that the American-produced intelligence estimate was so muddled that the Bush administration was actually taking the pressure *off* the Iranians.

The timing of the American intelligence report could not have been worse. It came out just as the deadline was approaching for Iran's negotiators to answer all the outstanding questions the IAEA had put to it—about documents that seemed to involve crude bomb designs and about evidence of work on warheads. Few of the answers ever arrived in Vienna; the Iranians sensed that the pressure was off. Neither the Americans nor the Europeans could threaten harsher sanctions against a country that was judged to have suspended its weapons design, even if it was still violating UN resolutions. Ahmadinejad had claimed victory, saying that the NIE was a "declaration of surrender" by the United States.

Heinonen's inspectors felt the effects. When they visited Iran, their freedom was more limited than ever. Iran had backed away from its commitment to ratify an "additional protocol" that allowed the inspectors to demand to see just about anything in the country they wanted. They could no longer visit sites that Iran had not declared to be part of the nuclear program—which cut out a long list of suspected facilities. It was exactly those kinds of inspections that, five years before, had revealed the secret centrifuge-making facilities behind a false wall in a clock-making factory in downtown Tehran and raised questions about a host of military sites.

"We are going blind," Heinonen complained. And that was the point. The Iranians knew that as long as they could keep playing three-card monte with the inspectors, they could profit from the ambiguities about their program. The Russians and the Chinese were eager to preserve their lucrative oil and natural gas contracts with the Iranians; if the Americans thought active weapons work halted in 2003, what was the case for sanctions? The Europeans disbelieved the American report, but their plan to get their banks and other financial institutions to cut off more of Iran's access to the world's credit markets fell apart the moment the American intelligence estimate was published.

"I'm sure this is part of a brilliant American strategy," a senior French diplomat told R. Nicholas Burns, the State Department's former negotiator on Iran, his voice dripping with sarcasm, when they discussed the intelligence findings. "Would you mind letting us know what it is?"

The Arab states, who were as alarmed as the Israelis by the prospect of a nuclear Iran, could not believe Bush allowed the report to be published. As Rice later noted, the Arab countries "never heard of an independent intelligence community, because almost none of them have one." While Iran's Arab neighbors were saying little publicly, privately they were asking Bush administration officials when they were going to solve this problem for them. For one of the rare moments in the history of Arab–Israeli conflict, the Arabs and the Israelis were on the same side.

HEINONEN HAD CALLED the meeting in the boardroom because he felt he had no choice but to create new pressure on the Iranians. So, in a forum where he knew the evidence would quickly leak, he presented a detailed accounting of the most intriguing, incriminating evidence the Iranians refused to talk about. Now, with more than a hundred representatives of different governments sitting in hushed silence, he asked for the lights to be lowered. On the giant screen at one end of the room, images from his treasure trove of evidence appeared. For most of those present—except the Americans and some of the Europeans—these were Iranian documents and drawings they had never seen before. Nor had the Iranian delegation seen them; for months the Iranians had declared that all the evidence consisted of "fabrications," and they refused even to look at it, much less answer questions about it.

For two long hours, Heinonen talked his audience through documents and sketches that appeared to come from Iran's military laboratories—the same laboratories that had been the target of the American spy agency's intercepts of computer traffic.[²] In his oral report, Heinonen discussed the mysterious role of Mohsen Fakrizadeh, the Iranian military scientist sitting atop the entire nuclear project. Heinonen laid out the organization of Fakrizadeh's empire, and described how the Iranian academic taught a few classes, but reported directly to the Iranian ministry of defense.

There, on the screen, were memorandums from Fakrizadeh. Some were budget documents. But others were memos to the various Iranian nuclear projects that reported to him, chastising them for putting the names of real employees in their reports. Those were to be stricken from all future memos, Fakrizadeh insisted. He was clearly obsessed with secrecy. That did not prove anything, Heinonen said, but it was suspicious.

Then Heinonen delved into the operations of Fakrizadeh's organization. There was Project 5, he said, a sprawling effort to mine uranium and convert it to gas that can be turned into nuclear fuel. There was Project 110, he continued, responsible for what appeared to be an effort to design a warhead. He showed sketches that diagrammed a "spherical device" that could be detonated using a complex system of high explosives. It was a classic "nuclear trigger." Anticipating Iran's response—that there are industrial applications for conducting controlled explosions, including for drilling—Heinonen looked out over the crowd and told them that the specific design work he was showing them was "not consistent with any application other than the development of a nuclear weapon."

He saved Project 111 for last. Here, he said, was "some of the information that the agency had wanted to show Iran but that they had not been in a position to see." The members of the Iranian delegation, who had already been jeering at Heinonen, suddenly began looking at one another. Realizing that some detailed Iranian memorandums about Project 111 were about to be thrown onto the screen, they whipped out their cell phone cameras to take photographs and video; back in Tehran, people would want to see exactly what Heinonen possessed, and presumably try to figure out how it leaked.

The first slide was a "status report" on Project 111, written in Farsi. The opening page bore an epigraph, which Heinonen's staff had translated: "Fate changes no man, unless he changes fate." The remainder of the slides, also in Farsi, detailed work on how to design a warhead so that it could be placed in the nose cone of Iran's most sophisticated long-range missile, the Shahab-3. The cramped space inside the nose cone looked as if it was designed to accommodate a sphere like the one the diplomats had just seen, the one surrounded by detonators. But it was unclear exactly how the two projects related, and nowhere in the documents was there any reference to a *nuclear* warhead. That was the implication, but the Iranians could argue that this was just a conventional weapon—and thus none of the IAEA's business.

Heinonen told the group that he had a lot of questions for Mr. Fakrizadeh. But so far the Iranians had come up with a string of excuses about why he was not available to be interviewed—and never would be available.

The Iranians in the room had seen enough. Ali Asghar Soltanieh, the head of the Iranian delegation to the IAEA, stood up and told Heinonen he was headed down "a very dangerous road." Later, other Iranians yelled, "The work plan is over," a threat that they would abandon entirely the plan that ElBaradei had painstakingly negotiated with the Iranians to get answers to outstanding questions.

Heinonen looked unperturbed by Soltanieh's outburst. He had come to expect it; brinkmanship was all part of the Iranian strategy.

He continued to display other documents from the same vault of evidence, which he assured the audience of diplomats came from several countries and several sources—his way of saying he wasn't shilling for the CIA. One of the hardest documents for the Iranians to explain was a chronology showing the arc of a missile's flight. It indicated when the altitude meters would be switched on, when the detonators in the warhead would be fired, and it showed the warhead exploding at about 600 meters above the ground.

There was silence in the room.

Heinonen's message was clear: No one would detonate a conventional weapon at that height; it would be a wasted boom, doing no damage. But as any nuclear weapons designer would attest, that is roughly the height at which an atomic bomb, detonated over a city, can do the most damage. (The bomb dropped on Hiroshima was an airburst, at a similar altitude.)

Warming to his subject, the Finn ended with a video animation—another Iranian production, he said. It appeared to have been designed for dignitaries visiting Project 111. It showed a warhead from all angles, and preparations to test it. As the lights came up, Soltanieh insisted again that it was all a fraud.

Heinonen had stopped just short of accusing the Iranians of making a bomb. These documents were the basis of questions, he said, questions that the Iranians had promised to answer, but had long ignored. Their "file," he added, would not be closed until satisfactory answers were delivered. The diplomats filed out, raced back to their offices, and cabled home. Within hours, the news of the briefing leaked, just as Heinonen knew it would.

HEINONEN'S PRESENTATION surprised everyone in the room that day—including the Americans. Much of the evidence they knew about, of course; some of it had come from the laptop. But this was the first time they heard public discussion of the role of Mohsen Fakrizadeh. For more than two years the Iranian engineer's name had been plastered all over classified briefings to Bush, Cheney, Rice, Hadley, and Gates, among others. As Iranian scientists go, he was not hard to find—he lectured every week at the Imam Hossein University in downtown Tehran. He had also once headed the Physics Research Center, where he'd helped develop the country's first project to enrich uranium. The academic work, American intelligence officials believed, was real, but also a perfect cover for experiments that were far more interesting to the Iranian Revolutionary Guards, of which Fakrizadeh appeared to have been a member as a young man after the 1979 revolution.

To this day American officials have never talked publicly about his suspected role in the nuclear program, though his name was included among those of a number of military commanders and nuclear officials designated for travel bans and other sanctions in a 2007 United Nations resolution. In July 2008, his name was added to a list of Iranian officials whose assets in the United States were ordered frozen—though there was no evidence he had any here. Heinonen made no mention of it during his presentation, but it was Fakrizadeh's unit that had been the subject of the intense American intelligence scrutiny that showed weapons-development work had been ordered halted in 2003. (Curiously, some of the documents Heinonen showed ran through January 2004.)

There was no question that the American effort to understand Iran's intentions focused intently—though not exclusively—on Fakrizadeh and his staff and their links to the Iranian military. "These guys are target number one," one senior official told me.

While Fakrizadeh's name does not appear in the declassified "key judgments" of the National Intelligence Estimate on Iran, he is a central figure in the classified chapters. Those chapters are filled with accounts of his role in Projects 110 and 111 and document his close links with the Iranian military. But the report makes clear that Fakrizadeh is more like the Robert Oppenheimer of the mullahs' Manhattan Project—he is running the operation, not deciding when and whether to build a weapon.

In fact, like the Americans, Heinonen could not prove Fakrizadeh and his colleagues were making a bomb. He could prove only that at some point, engineers in Projects 110 and 111 had tackled the most difficult problems any bomb designer faces sooner or later: how to make a warhead small enough to fit atop a missile, and how to time its detonation. But the Iranians are hardly the only country to play out those issues on paper—or to stop short of constructing a weapon. As the Iranians liked to point out, the IAEA could put together a pretty good slide show about Israel, too.

WITH LESS THAN a year remaining in the Bush presidency, the fierce internal debate about what should—and could—be done to stop the Iranian program went into overdrive. By this point, Bush and his top advisers felt they had tried all the classic incentives and disincentives. They needed something new. The arguments were familiar. Some officials surrounding Cheney and other hawks were still talking about reviving the Pentagon's well-honed plans to bomb the facility. At the State Department, Nicholas Burns had left in frustration, never once permitted to engage the Iranians in a real, one-on-one, diplomatic conversation. Though he had spent three years in charge of American strategy toward Iran, he was part of that large generation of American diplomats who had never been permitted to set foot in the country, let alone meet with an Iranian in an official capacity where he could engage in the give-and-take of diplomacy. He had argued, time and time again, for the chance. Each time the same answer came back: It would legitimize the Iranian government to meet them. It would be a victory for the Holocaust-denying Ahmadinejad. It would undercut Israel. Burns believed the arguments were shortsighted. "If you fear that there could be a confrontation," he told me after he left the State Department, "it's our moral responsibility to do everything we can—*everything* we can—to head it off."

The moment to engage in that kind of direct diplomacy was in 2005 and 2006, when the Iranians had assembled only a small number of centrifuges at an "experimental" facility at Natanz. At the time, the Iranians had lots of ambitions, lots of plans, and lots of new facilities—but they had barely produced any uranium. The mullahs had little negotiating leverage: They could not yet threaten, as they can today, that they would pull out of the Nuclear Non-Proliferation Treaty and turn their reactor fuel into bomb fuel. But Bush felt bogged down in Iraq, and Rice feared that even an experimental stand of centrifuges was unacceptable. "The problem isn't the number that they have," she told me. "The problem is that they have them. The problem is that they're experimenting and learning."

The administration's reluctance ran deeper, though. Cheney and others had yet to give up on the dream of regime change in Iran. Some lived in the fantasy that the Iranians would bow to escalating economic pressure and do what the Libyans had done—surrender it all for the prospect of a good relationship with Washington.

But the cases were not analogous. As the price of oil rose, Washington's leverage diminished. The Iranians correctly calculated that there were limits to the Europeans' willingness to impose sanctions; they would never go along with actions that could prompt a severe backlash. As Dennis Ross, the longtime Middle East negotiator, put it, "the pace of Iran's nuclear development outstripped the pace of the sanctions."

Now time was short. For the past year or two the Bush administration had focused on the Iranians' biggest vulnerability, their failing economy. Iranian oil output was declining; they were operating at 300,000 barrels a day below the production quota that OPEC had set for Iran. They simply could not meet the target, and it was costing them tens of millions of dollars every day. Even Ahmadinejad's acolytes were upset about his mismanagement of the economy. Oil accounts for 85 percent of the government's revenue—and the Bush administration had successfully dissuaded many countries from allowing their firms to strike new oil and gas agreements with Iran, or to provide the financing for them. Using squeeze techniques honed in isolating North Korea, the treasury secretary,

Henry Paulson, exerted leverage on Iran by making it dangerous for banks and financial institutions to lend the country money. To ratchet the pressure a little higher, he warned of "the extraordinary risks that accompany those who do business with Iran," making it clear it could affect their own access to American markets. Meanwhile, Ahmadinejad was dealing with a restive populace, unhappy with inflation, shortages of commodities, and sporadic government services. For a populist, he wasn't delivering much.

Condoleezza Rice insisted that the sanctions strategy was working; the Iranians were hurting. She was right, they were hurting. But no matter how much the Americans and the Europeans tightened the noose, even cutting off access to bank credits, the Iranians simply would not slow down the nuclear program. To the contrary, they sped up. "There was a moment when we discussed cutting off their supplies of refined gasoline," one former administration official who was in on these discussions told me later. But the Pentagon responded that the Iranians had what strategists called "escalation dominance"—they could inflict more pain on American consumers than we could inflict on the Iranian government. "The fear was that oil might shoot up to eighty dollars a barrel—that doesn't sound like much now, but it did then," one official said to me. "And there were all kinds of models under which this led to military confrontation in the Straits," he said, referring to the Strait of Hormuz, where the Iranians were patrolling more vigilantly than ever. Tied up in Iraq, the Pentagon chiefs told Bush that the last thing they could handle was a conflict with a country twice as populous and far more powerful than the nation they were already trying to pacify.

Ahmadinejad responded to the economic pressure by appealing to Iranian nationalistic sentiment. Give the Americans our centrifuges, he said, and they will soon want the rest of the country. "If we would take one step back in our confrontation with the arrogant powers regarding our nuclear program," he argued, "we would have to keep taking more and more steps back till the very end."[3]

By the last year of the Bush presidency, even the hawks inside the White House had shut up about regime change in Iran. "I haven't heard that discussed for a long time," one of Bush's aides told me one day. But they had also given up on the strategy of seeking ever-escalating Security Council resolutions. Each resolution required an enormous diplomatic effort and yielded very minimal results. The Iranians had ignored them anyway, and just kept building their centrifuges. Bush needed another option.

"The administration is in real disarray," said David A. Kay, the nuclear specialist who led the fruitless search for weapons of mass destruction in Iraq after the invasion and who famously declared when he got home that "we were all wrong." A former senior official in the first term who was talking to the White House about Iran put it this way: "The hawks—Cheney and his boys—haven't fully given up the dream of just taking out the nuclear program. But they haven't figured out a way to do it, or a way to handle what happens next."

On most days, the debate about attacking Iran was well hidden—not only from the public, but from members of Congress, from European allies, often from the State Department's own negotiators. Periodically, stories appeared about rumors of a new plan for a military strike, but when you dug into them, you usually discovered that the Pentagon was updating old plans.

Those plans had been on the table for a long, long time—well back into Rumsfeld's tenure at the Department of Defense. As one senior administration official put the choice to me back in January 2006, when I first wrote about those options, "Could we do it? Sure. Could we manage the aftermath? I doubt it." That calculus has not changed.

The obvious targets for airstrikes were the big nuclear facilities that everyone knew about. The Air Force's main target would be Natanz, where 4,000 centrifuges were spinning away at 80 percent of their capacity, according to IAEA inspectors. If that pace continued, Iran could accumulate enough material for a single bomb by the time

Bush left office, though it would have to send its uranium through additional enrichment before it could be used for a weapon. American intelligence estimates indicate it will be 2010 to 2012 before Iran has enough material to make a few weapons, but that is educated guess-work.

Under the Air Force's carefully honed plan, there would also be strikes on the nuclear complex at Isfahan, where uranium ore mined from Project 5 was turned into gas, one of the steps in creating fuel for nuclear weapons. Presumably, other targets would include Bushehr, where the Russians were completing Iran's civilian nuclear reactors; if those reactors went into production, the Iranians would have a supply of spent fuel to produce plutonium, the route the North Koreans took to the bomb. And there was a new reactor under construction at Arak, which will eventually be capable of producing plutonium.

Military experts who have studied the options say an airstrike could be devastating. But it wouldn't be quick, like the Israeli attack a quarter of a century ago on Osirak, Saddam Hussein's reactor in the Iraqi desert. An air attack in this case would more closely resemble all-out war. "You are talking about something in the neighborhood of a thousand strike sorties," W. Patrick Lang, the former head of intelligence for the Middle East and South Asia at the Defense Intelligence Agency, told me. "And it would take all kinds of stuff—air, cruise missiles, multiple restrikes—to make sure you've got it all."[4] After each day's bombing, satellite photos would be taken to figure out if the destruction had gone deep enough underground. New attacks would have to be launched—and of course, after the first one, the Iranians would be ready. Doing an airstrike right, by some estimates, would take a week or two. The Iranians would almost certainly lash out in retaliation, either through the Quds Force—their most elite unit—or through terror groups like Hamas and Hezbollah. The targets could include American forces in Iraq, as well as Lebanon and Israel.

Would a preemptive strike be worth it? Even inside the Bush administration, I found few who thought so. Most of the internal estimates at the Pentagon and the Energy Department—where the nuclear expertise is located—suggested that an attack would set Iran's program back by two years or so. In other words, it might delay the day that Iran built a weapon to 2015, or even a year or two later. But the political cost would be huge. Even the young, educated, Westernized, visa-desperate generation would likely be radicalized.

That was certainly the view of Robert Gates, who, a generation after his first encounter with the Iranians in Algeria, found himself at the center of the new debate about whether to attack the country. At his confirmation hearing as secretary of defense, he laid out his view with words never before heard from a Bush administration official. "I think that we have seen, in Iraq, that once war is unleashed, it becomes unpredictable," Gates told the committee. "And I think that the consequences of a military conflict with Iran could be quite dramatic." If asked by Bush, he said, "I would counsel against military action except as a last resort and if we felt our vital interests were threatened."[5]

Once in office, Gates made the same argument, even more forcefully. Because of his status as a former CIA director, he integrated both intelligence reports and the military's conclusions to buttress his points. "This was done very differently in the second term," said one official who had seen Gates's behind-the-scenes work. "He knew he had an authority on these issues that few defense secretaries have ever had. He pressed the case hard."

Grudgingly, even some of the hawks in the Bush White House came to the conclusion that Gates was correct in his analysis of the issue. Attacking the nuclear facilities might be a satisfying last act, they acknowledged, but it would probably rally support around an unpopular theocracy and an economically incompetent president. "There are some people who think Ahmadinejad is actually trying to goad us into an attack," one cabinet official told me at the end of Bush's presidency, "because it's the best way for him to save his own skin." In the end, the official said, "I think that's the argument that registered with President Bush."

But there was also a more practical argument against a strike, one that President Obama will undoubtedly confront soon after he takes office. It is the problem that military and intelligence officials brought to Bush in 2008: After years of intelligence reviews, of spy-satellite photographs and reports from insiders, neither the Pentagon nor the intelligence agencies can identify with assurance what targets in Iran should be destroyed.

A whole chapter of the classified version of the NIE, according to several who have read it, is filled with descriptions of other suspected nuclear sites in Iran far from Natanz, far from the facilities visited by Olli Heinonen's inspectors. (There is a brief reference to those sites in the unclassified version, but nothing that suggests the detailed treatment of the subject in the classified version.)

The official who had cautioned me that "I'm not telling you that we saw centrifuges spinning on the Caspian" made the point that a covert program would be enormously appealing to the Iranians. They saw what the Israelis did at Osirak in 1981 and in Syria in 2007. Those attacks were Exhibits A and B, he said, of "the dangers of assembling a nuclear program all in one place." The Iranians made clear to IAEA inspectors that parts for centrifuges had been spread out in stockpiles and small factories around the country. They were insurance, it seemed, against losing the whole program at once. The message to the United States and Israel was clear: If you hit Natanz, we're ready to speed up elsewhere.

FACED WITH NO good options, Bush did what many presidents do in the absence of a workable military plan: He turned to the CIA.

In the spring of 2008, Bush notified the heads of the intelligence committees and leaders in Congress that he was issuing a "finding" authorizing covert action in Iran aimed at its nuclear program. Such findings are highly classified, and while those familiar with the documents would not discuss the details, they said that the wording was maddeningly vague. "My understanding is that it would allow the president to do a lot of things and come back later and say, 'That's covered in the finding,'" said one former official who had been consulted on the issue.

The bulk of the efforts appeared to focus on disrupting Natanz and other sites. This was, in reality, an effort to revive old programs that dated back to the Clinton era, when the CIA used Russian scientists in a series of efforts that ultimately failed to slow the Iranian program.[6] If the past is any indication, that means efforts to interfere with the power supply to nuclear facilities—something that can sometimes be accomplished by tampering with computer code, and getting power sources to blow up. Some of the programs focused on ways to destabilize the centrifuges, in hopes they would shut down or spin out of control and explode.

Several of the efforts were coordinated with European intelligence agencies, and several with the Israelis. There have been periodic reports, hard to confirm, of U.S. Special Forces teams being inserted briefly into Iran, but Bush's program does not appear to have focused on putting many people on the ground. Instead, the plan was largely to penetrate the supply chain that the Iranians were relying on for their nuclear programs. One person familiar with the planning called these efforts "science experiments," and another argued that it was a little late in the game for Bush to be refocusing on sabotage. "It was not until the last year that they began to get really imaginative about what one could do to screw up the system," one official told me. "None of these are game changers."

Naturally, Bush's top aides would not discuss what the president had or had not authorized. But I thought the reaction of one of those officials was revealing, during an interview early in the summer of 2008.

I asked whether prudence dictated allowing the Iranians to go ahead with a low level of uranium enrichment—not enough to produce a weapon, but enough to serve as a salve to Iranian pride. In return, the United States would insist on regular, rigorous inspections, including restored rights for the IAEA inspectors to travel to any suspect sites. If the inspectors were blocked, or thrown out of the country, Iran's actions would be ample evidence of "breakout"—its intention to build a bomb. Moreover, this approach would leave the next administration with a diplomatic process rather than an immediate confrontation.

The official, who rarely got riled, stood up and started pacing around the office. "All of you who think you want to leave Iran with a route to a nuclear weapon, please raise your hand," he said, talking to an imaginary audience of incoming officials. There ought to be a serious national debate, he said, about whether America could afford to drop the demand that Iran agree to halt all uranium production before the United States engages in real negotiations.

"If you say now you're going to drop that precondition and you're going to go talk to them, you are telling the Iranians and everybody else in the international community, 'They are going to end up with an enrichment program.' And that means they end up with a path to the bomb."

He started pacing faster and faster. "And you better tell the Egyptians and the Saudis and all the rest of them that right now so they can start their bomb programs, too. I mean, let's get real about this."

AT THE END of September 2008, American military officials quietly deployed a high-powered radar—called X-band—in Israel as part of an effort to put together a joint defense against any missile attacks by Iran.

The system was the same kind that had already been installed in northern Japan to warn of a missile attack from North Korea. This was no experiment, the United States said; the radar was there for good.

The radar installation was written about in the military trade press, but it didn't exactly make big news. In fact, the radar was a small part of a much bigger request that the Israelis sent to Washington in the spring of 2008—a request that made many in the administration believe that the prospect of an Israeli attack on Iran's nuclear facilities was significantly more likely. By this time, Bush had become so risk averse that he was intent on quashing any Israeli threat.

Except for the radar, the core of Israel's request was kept secret in both capitals. A series of delegations sent to Washington had asked for precision-guided bunker-busting bombs from the U.S. arsenal, according to American officials who described Israel's interchanges with the administration. The Israelis already possess some bunker-busters, American officials told me, but they knew that in addition to its traditional arsenal, the United States had a limited number of specially produced, conventional weapons that were specifically designed to pierce underground nuclear sites—like those in North Korea and Iran.

The Israelis had another request: They wanted overflight rights in Iraq so that Israeli fighters and bombers could hit Iran's facilities. The Israeli aircraft have only limited range, and without the overflight rights, an attack on Natanz or other facilities would border on the impossible. "The chief of the Air Force says they can do it even without overflight [of Iraq]," one senior American official told me. "We're not convinced." The defense radars were all about planning for the Iranian response: If Iran launched missiles toward Israel with conventional warheads atop them, the Israelis wanted to see them coming.

Bush stalled, saying neither yes nor no. The additional bunker-busters were never delivered, but as a consolation prize the Americans stepped up discussions with Israeli intelligence about covert operations that might achieve the same end—slowing down the Natanz project—without a highly visible attack that would almost certainly provoke a response, if not a war. The most problematic issue for the White House was the threat that Israel might try to overfly Iraq on its way to Natanz. The United States still controlled Iraqi airspace. On this issue, American officials say they gave a firm "no" to the Israelis. The reaction in Iraq, they feared, would be overwhelming. It would likely force Iraqi politicians of all stripes to condemn the United States—exactly the kind of split Bush was desperately hoping to avoid. It could drive Iraqi politicians into the arms of the Iranians. And it might be used by the Iranians as an excuse to make a major incursion into Iraq—setting up a confrontation with the United States.

Inside the White House, there was a deeper concern. What if the Israelis flew over Iraq anyway, without Washington's permission? Would the American military be ordered to shoot them down? Not likely. So, by the time the first bomb dropped, Washington would be accused of being complicit in the Israeli attack, whether the United States was part of it or not. "This one is a nightmare," one national security official told me.

TAKEN TOGETHER, Bush's decision to start up additional covert actions against Iran so late in his presidency and the Israeli effort to prepare an attack or try to convince Washington that one was coming, were signs that the Bush administration had run out of gas on Iran. Bush had spent years assembling sanctions, to little avail. He had put together some modest incentives to try to induce the Iranians to give up their nuclear program, but nothing that pointed toward a big, strategic change in the relationship—nothing that would lead young Iranians to pressure their ossified government to embrace a vastly new relationship with the United States.

The arrival of a new administration creates that opportunity. It may be too late; the Iranians may be so close to a bomb—a few screwdriver turns away—that there is no hope of stopping the country from becoming nuclear capable. But if there is hope, it lies in using what Dennis Ross, the Mideast negotiator, calls vastly bigger carrots and vastly bigger sticks.

Barack Obama adopted that approach—but deliberately stopped short of explaining it in detail—in the 2008 campaign. He tangled with his opponent, Senator John McCain, on the question of whether he would negotiate with the Iranians "without preconditions," and McCain used the exchange to try to portray Obama as naïve. But the real issue isn't whether to negotiate, it is whether the United States has leverage to change Iran's behavior. And now, there is reason to hope that we might.

Ahmadinejad is on the ropes; his popularity has plummeted, and at the end of 2008 he appeared on the verge of physical collapse. Some Iranians seized on his weakness to suggest he should not run for reelection. He was humiliated by his own parliament, which removed a member of his cabinet. Whatever happens, the new president should try to make Iranian elections about one issue: whether Iran wants to continue to be a revolutionary republic, defying the world at great economic cost to its own citizens, or whether it wants to become a normal nation.

The best way to influence the outcome is to spell out to the Iranians exactly what they have to gain: diplomatic recognition, a lifting of all sanctions, visas for Iranian students. The more public the offer, the tougher the pressure on the Iranian regime. The Iranian people have to hear the American message, and they should hear it directly from the new American president.

That would set the stage for a real negotiation, one in which the "bigger sticks" could also be described. At the opening session, the secretary of state would not only sit at the table; the Americans should be at the head of the table. That would send the signal that we respect the Iranian people, and we are prepared to deal with their government.

But the message would also have to be clear that America has leverage again. With the war in Iraq beginning to wind down and oil prices dipping, at least temporarily, the United States is finally in a position to threaten Iran with far greater economic pain. Obama talked in his campaign about taking the step that Bush rejected: cutting off the fuel that keeps Iranian daily life going. "If we can prevent them from importing the gasoline that they need," he said in one presidential debate, "and the refined petroleum products, that starts changing their cost-benefit analysis." The threat sounded strong on the campaign trail, but in reality it would mean preparing for a violent Iranian reaction. The new president will have to show that if his "grand bargain" fails, he is committed to far harsher sanctions than Bush ever threatened. And he would have to be willing to make it clear to our European allies that if the Iranians failed to negotiate a grand bargain, every European investment in the Iranian oil industry will have to stop, every loan will have to cease. The gasoline cutoff—the ultimate sanction—will have to be enforced by everyone, including NATO. Countries that balk will risk their relationship with Washington, and with the new president in whom they have invested so many hopes. It will be a huge test of whether, with Bush gone, America's influence is on the rebound.

At first the Iranians would likely reject a grand bargain and claim that the West was seeking its destruction. But the pressure might well build, particularly after Iran's own elections. Bigger sticks and bigger carrots might not work. But what we've tried for the past eight years has clearly failed. If we stay on the current path, Iran is getting the Bomb.

# PART II

## AFGHANISTAN

# How the Good War
# Went Bad

# CHAPTER 5

# THE MARSHALL PLAN
# THAT WASN'T

A scrimmage in a Border Station—
A canter down some dark defile—
Two thousand pounds of education
Drops to a ten-rupee *jezail*—
The Crammer's boast, the Squadron's pride,
Shot like a rabbit in a ride!

No proposition Euclid wrote,
No formulae the text-books know,
Will turn the bullet from your coat,
Or ward the tulwar's downward blow.
Strike hard who cares—shoot straight who can—
The odds are on the cheaper man.

— Rudyard Kipling, "Arithmetic on the Frontier" (1886),
    describing what happened when an overeducated, heavily outfitted
    British force confronted Afghan tribesmen armed only with the
    *jezail*, a homemade musket

GEN. DAN MCNEILL, the bullheaded American commander of all 52,000 NATO troops in Afghanistan, was never very skilled at suffering fools or managing hesitant allies. An old infantryman with four decades of military experience, McNeill was already in his sixties when he took on his last command—an age when most generals are retired, some settling into lucrative contracts with Fox and CNN second-guessing their former colleagues. McNeill was now one of a dwindling number of active generals, familiar with the art of counterinsurgency honed during the height of the Vietnam War. He knew what failure to contain an insurgency looked like.

But this job—managing troops from twenty-six fractious countries that couldn't figure out whether they were there to rebuild Afghanistan or save it from falling yet again to the Taliban—differed from anything he had confronted in his storied career. He had always commanded well-oiled military machines that knew their mission, from small combat squads in Vietnam to platoons and, eventually, the famed 82nd Airborne Division, the pride of Fort Bragg.

Along the way, he never expended much energy on the politics of managing a war. He disdained the process of massaging his masters in Washington. It showed. He was, his colleagues agreed, the polar opposite of his better-known counterpart in Iraq, Gen. David Petraeus, widely considered a political master, with a direct line to the Oval Office and an unerring sense of how the political mood was turning back home. McNeill had neither that kind of access nor that kind of radar.

McNeill's first exposure to Afghanistan came, unexpectedly, during a drinking session at the Russian Airborne Academy in 1998, when he was still leading the 82nd Airborne. His Russian counterparts put on a dinner for him, with the requisite rounds of vodka, not McNeill's favorite drink. But they insisted he join them for round after round—including the third toast, the one to fallen soldiers.

"They were quite drunk, and in tears, as they talked about Afghanistan," McNeill told me later, as his own tour in Afghanistan was ending. "Until then the only thing I knew about the country came from pictures in *National Geographic*. But their constant refrain was, 'This was our Vietnam, and we got our asses kicked.'"[1] One of his hosts, while doing shots, told him the story of being in a convoy of 140 Russian soldiers. They were ambushed by the Mujahideen: Only seventeen survived.

McNeill arrived in Afghanistan determined never to let that

happen to NATO. But he spent much of every day hand-holding commanders from Germany, Italy, and Turkey, or from one of twenty-three other nations, most of whom were under instructions from back home to avoid sending their troops into regions of the country where casualties were likely. In short, they could fight everywhere but where they were most needed.

"I'm a simple soldier," McNeill liked to say. "The problem with alliance warfare is that every country puts its national interest first and the alliance second. Every decision takes longer. Plans leak. It's an interesting way to try to win a war."

So it was no surprise that McNeill regularly got under the skin of the NATO allies, with his insistence that they fight like a unified force, with a common strategy. No sooner had he settled into his office in Kabul than he ordered up the production of a vivid chart illustrating the deficiencies of what President Bush had grandiloquently named the "Coalition of the Willing."

At a glance, the chart illustrated which tasks the troops from nations in the alliance were willing to perform to combat the Taliban, who, with the help of their al Qaeda allies, were seeping back into the country from their sanctuary in Pakistan—territory off limits to McNeill and his troops. More precisely, the chart illustrated what America's allies were *unwilling* to do—go out on patrol far from camp, or travel beyond their assigned sector, even if fellow NATO troops were in trouble in a firefight. Soldiers from many countries, including France, Germany, and Italy, would not even venture into the south, down near Kandahar, where the fight for the control of Afghanistan was taking place.

McNeill's chart hung in his office, where no visitor could miss it. That was the point. It was a graphic depiction of alliance dysfunction. Bright red blocks highlighted "caveats" that countries insisted on as a condition for contributing troops to Afghanistan. Yellow blocks denoted missions they were willing to consider only if they got approval first from their capitals. It was a process, everyone knew, that would take so long that the target would be long gone by the time word came back from Ottawa or Berlin or London. Each block, on the chart, amounted to an explanation of why NATO was so often on the defensive against an enemy that knew the territory by heart and that tailored its strategy to inflict enough casualties among reluctant NATO allies that Europe's parliaments would eventually order a withdrawal. In short, it wasn't exactly the kind of battle-map graphic that Churchill would have been proud to hang in his World War II bunker where he ran the war during the Blitz, or that Roosevelt would have put in the Map Room of the White House.

Instead, it was a reminder that NATO had come to Afghanistan chiefly to provide political cover, not covering fire. For the grand alliance that was designed to repel a Soviet invasion of Europe, this was the first "out of area" operation beyond Europe. After opposing NATO's involvement in the war for two years, the Bush administration ultimately invited the alliance in, realizing that it needed to share the burdens for the long haul. NATO's presence gave the operation an international patina intended to displace the feel of an American occupation.

From the start it was clear the NATO allies had arrived in Afghanistan with a different mission from that of the United States. Rather than focusing on counterterrorism operations and rooting out al Qaeda and the Taliban, the core of the American mission, the allies signed on as a peacekeeping force. Making matters worse, each nation operated under its own combat rules, often including strict prohibitions about wandering beyond their designated territory. The contrast was striking. For example, German forces were prohibited from conducting offensive operations or going on patrols at night, whereas British soldiers, doing a significant portion of the heavy fighting in the south, were permitted to use airstrikes against suspected Taliban formations, conduct preemptive strikes, and set up ambushes.[2] Quickly the Taliban turned the disunity to its advantage, acutely aware that some Europeans had no stomach for risk, not to mention casualties.

But when McNeill complained that this was no way to fight a war, much less win one, the White House and the Pentagon told him to keep his complaints private. An unspoken rule of the Bush administration barred public criticism of the allies, for fear that European parliaments would refuse to renew their troop commitments. Always the good soldier, McNeill was careful when he returned to Washington to give periodic updates on progress in Afghanistan, as he did at the end of 2007, to put a highly optimistic gloss on events. He talked about successes NATO was enjoying in winning hearts and minds with new roads and hospitals and, best of all, 6.2 million Afghan children going to school each morning.

These were undeniable accomplishments and exactly the kind of statistics Bush liked to hear. Reporters who followed the president quickly learned his favorite number: the tally of Afghan girls attending school after the Taliban had been routed in 2001. Afghanistan, Bush insisted throughout his 2004 reelection campaign, was a prime example of how "freedom is on the march," as America restored God-given liberties to some of the world's poorest people, just as it had restored them to Germans and Japanese who once lived under a tyrant's heel. It was a way of trying to fuse what Bush called "the transformational power of liberty," the creation of a more peaceful world through the advancement of freedom and democracy, with what he hoped would become the storyline of his presidency through the examples of Iraq and Afghanistan. Among the faithful, it never failed to elicit wild applause.[3]

But by the end of 2007, McNeill knew that freedom in Afghanistan was on the retreat. When NATO troops arrived, schools opened; when NATO troops left, they were often burned. There was no hiding the bigger picture in Afghanistan: It was not the triumph of democratic stability that Bush had advertised. Four enervating years in Iraq had soaked up Washington's attention and resources, and by early 2008 there was no question that the "good" war had gone bad.

The reasons were pretty clear. The Taliban had never been defeated, they had merely moved a hundred miles east and south. A July 2007 National Intelligence Estimate (NIE) concluded that al Qaeda had not only reestablished "a safe haven in the Pakistan Federally Administered Tribal Areas," but now had successfully "regenerated key elements of [their] Homeland attack capability" against the United States. For a president who had vowed that another 9/11 would never happen, it was a searing reminder of the price of distraction.

Whether or not al Qaeda was plotting against America, it was certainly scheming against Afghan president Hamid Karzai. In the spring of 2008, militants linked to al Qaeda mounted an attack on a ceremony intended to celebrate the ouster of the Soviets two decades before. They sprayed the area with bullets. Karzai survived the attack, along with the American ambassador; three other parade attendees were not so lucky. Within weeks, Karzai charged that Pakistan's intelligence service had been complicit in the attack—a charge American officials said they could not prove but that was likely accurate. In another brazen attack the following month, the Taliban drove into the outer limits of Kandahar, blew open the main gates of the huge prison outside the city, and celebrated as 1,200 of their compatriots ran to freedom. Shortly thereafter, other Taliban-related forces took control of several districts near Kandahar. Eventually NATO and Afghan forces retook the area, at least for a while. There was relatively little fighting, however, as the Taliban melted back into the countryside, waiting to fight another day.

The list of such events went on and on in 2008—bombings, coordinated and uncoordinated attacks, rising casualties. It created a sense of a country under siege, and the fear that at the end of Bush's term, Afghanistan was in danger of falling back into the chaos that existed when he took office.

And while Washington rightly celebrated the arrival of rudimentary democracy to the country, for most Afghans it was something old—corruption—that seemed more a part of everyday life than the arrival of new liberties. When McNeill drove by poppy fields, he said, "What [I] saw was AK-47s," because he knew the drug trade paid for the insurgency and for its guns. Repeated American and British attempts at eradication had failed; by early 2008, the CIA warned in a classified study that the drug trade had expanded to a $4-billion business, making Afghanistan the world's largest narco-state. (By comparison, revenue for the Afghan government budget for 2008 was $716 million, with much of that coming from international aid.)

One evening in Kabul during the long winter of 2008, McNeill decided to tell the president what victory in Afghanistan would require.

His mistake was that he decided to do so via secure video during a full National Security Council meeting, with no warning to either Bush or Secretary of Defense Robert Gates. When McNeill's image appeared on the screen in the White House Situation Room, he briskly laid his plan on the table: If Bush really wanted to win in Afghanistan, rather than just talk about winning, he needed to send more American troops—a lot more.

The American force needed to be increased by about 50 percent, he said. His plan was to put two full American combat brigades in the south, where NATO troops were operating, essentially proposing a replication of the American forces on the eastern side of the country. McNeill knew he needed more troops in this area, free from the "caveats" that were hampering NATO forces, to engage a resurgent and reconstituted Taliban and al Qaeda threat. He wanted a full division headquarters in the south as well, which would require massive amounts of resources.

"He just floored everyone," one participant in the discussion recalled later. "Everyone knew that in a few weeks Petraeus would be back in Washington and the president would sign on" to a gradual end to the "surge" in Iraq, one that would eventually free up troops, but not quickly enough to allow a rapid shift back to Afghanistan.

"We didn't have two combat brigades," the participant said. "We didn't have a spare division headquarters. And McNeill knew it." The only way to fulfill McNeill's request, everyone in the room knew, was to continue a policy of deploying troops for fifteen months and giving them only twelve months back at home—a huge strain on the force. (In fact, Bush soon reduced deployment times.)

Months later McNeill conceded to me, with a tight smile, that "there were a lot of unhappy people" in the Situation Room that day. He was told never to cite in public the number of additional troops he had asked for; if the numbers leaked, the White House feared, they would become a political football in the argument about whether the United States had tied itself down in Iraq. Of course, they would also provide evidence, as if more were needed, that the combined American, NATO, and newly trained Afghan force that seemed sufficient in 2004 and 2005 was no longer big enough to handle the challenge.

McNeill never got his additional troops. He retired in June 2008. Prodded by Secretary of Defense Robert Gates, Bush promised at a NATO meeting to send additional forces in 2009. But everyone in the room knew he would be president for only the first twenty days.

The irony, of course, was lost on no one. This was the president who had declared emphatically that he "listened to his generals" and gave them whatever they needed to win. In practice, Bush's promise seemed to extend only to Iraq. Time and again, Afghanistan—the country where the 9/11 plot was hatched—was overshadowed by the war in Iraq. Early successes had made it easier to ignore the deepening challenges as the conflict wore on. As resources shifted west, toward Baghdad, plans for a robust reconstruction program evaporated. The initial appearance of an easy victory was masked by the fact that the Taliban had never been defeated, but simply had moved across the border into the safety of the tribal areas in Pakistan.

No one wanted to face the hard reality that in Afghanistan, "winning" meant holding the fort for decades to come, lest the country fall back into the Taliban's reign of terror that had allowed al Qaeda to thrive.

"The truth is that you have to think about this problem in

thirty-year terms," Gen. Douglas Lute, the "czar" for Iraq and Afghanistan, told me one day in 2007, as he was preparing for the thankless task of trying to rescue the administration from several years of errors. "That's simply what it is going to take." One night in early summer 2008, I asked Lute whether he was sticking to that estimate. No, he said, he had rethought the numbers. "I've revised it to closer to fifty years."[4]

During the 2008 presidential campaign, no candidates wanted to utter anything quite that honest. But inside the Pentagon and the White House, everyone had long since internalized the strategy: Fight a hot war in Iraq and a holding war in Afghanistan, and pray the hot war wouldn't last much longer. The chairman of the Joint Chiefs of Staff, Mike Mullen, summed it up during testimony in late 2007.

"In Afghanistan we do what we can," he said. "In Iraq, we do what we must."[5]

UNFORTUNATELY, THE TALIBAN figured out America's priorities long before Admiral Mullen acknowledged them to Congress. The Taliban reached an obvious conclusion: Their greatest weapon was not the car bomb or the roadside IED, the improvised explosive devices that caused devastating injuries. Instead, it was American tentativeness, an unwillingness by Bush or other officials to commit troops, money, and resources for the years, if not decades, it would take to rebuild the country. Bush's hesitance was understandable: His briefing books were overflowing with tales of Afghan aversion to outside occupation, a legacy of British colonialism.

But the Taliban needed no briefing books, and they were masters of intimidation. Any suggestion that NATO—or even the United States—had one foot out the door enabled the Taliban to threaten that it would maim or kill any local "collaborators." In towns like Musa Qala, which the British had defended in 2006 at the cost of the lives of seven of their soldiers, the Taliban moved back in only four months after a "peace" deal with tribal elders led to the British withdrawal. The Taliban immediately executed several of the villagers for collaborating with the British. They jailed the tribal elders for agreeing to the truce. It was the kind of brutality that reinforced the message that while NATO might be around for a while, the Taliban were here for good. In late 2007, British, American, and Afghan forces retook the town. But the residents of Musa Qala had to wonder, what happens after they withdraw again?

Even if McNeill had received the additional troops he asked for—a total of 37,000 Americans on the ground—he freely admits he could not have overcome the Taliban's other weapon: the tacit cooperation of Pakistan. Officially, Pakistan committed itself on September 12, 2001, to rooting out al Qaeda and other Islamic militants within its borders. Every few months, starting from early in Bush's presidency, urgent missions would arrive in Islamabad and be whisked off to receive the ritual pledge of solidarity from Pervez Musharraf, the general who took control of the country in a 1999 coup. Their visit would often be preceded or followed by the capture of an al Qaeda lieutenant or a Taliban commander plucked off the streets of Peshawar or removed from a safe house in Karachi. But the fact remained that the Pakistani Army and Pakistan's Directorate for Inter-Services Intelligence, known as the ISI, had a relationship with the Taliban and other militants that stretched back decades as they fought common enemies—the Soviets and India.

The army and the ISI are overwhelmingly dominated by Punjabis, the ethnic group that has long held power in Pakistan. Before 9/11, Pakistan was among the few nations to recognize the Taliban government because the Islamic radicals served a useful purpose for Musharraf: They kept India out of Afghanistan and away from the long border the country shares with Pakistan. When Musharraf promised Bush, in the days after 9/11, that Pakistan would switch sides and fight the Taliban—and the al Qaeda forces they harbored—he knew that elements in his own intelligence service would refuse to go along. While Bush portrayed Pakistan as a "key ally" in a long war, the Pakistanis mastered a double game. Musharraf came to Washington to scare up additional billions in aid to fight terrorists (in the end Pakistan got about $10 billion for that work) while quietly arming and training the Taliban and other radical insurgent groups in an effort to gain greater influence over the tribal areas.

The Pakistani government isn't the first to have tried and failed to govern the tribal areas from Islamabad. The British did not do much better. They were overwhelmed by the 10,600 square miles of land, with its 12,000-foot peaks, a territory largely devoid of real roads. The British approach was to try to influence the area with "political agents" who, riding from one tribal area to another, negotiated with the *maliks*, the tribal chiefs. To the tribes, the border with Afghanistan is meaningless; their tribal boundaries are far more ancient than the Durand Line drawn by the British in 1893 to create a border between what were then India and Afghanistan.

Musharraf knew this history well, and knew the limits of Pakistan's influence. So while he told Bush whatever he wanted to hear—that Pakistan would root out al Qaeda—in fact his army had far more modest aims. One was simple: to keep the Pashtun secular nationalists, who long resented the central government in Islamabad, from being able to wield power in the area and challenge Punjabi authority. But the second aim was a long-term one: to keep India at bay. The Pakistanis are convinced that the Indians are seeking influence in Afghanistan because they want to encircle Pakistani territory. If Musharraf picked up a few bad guys along the way, and handed them off to the Americans, that was a political bonus. But it wasn't his plan.

It may take years to come to a full accounting of whether Bush was deceived by Musharraf or whether the president and his aides simply deceived themselves because they needed Pakistan so badly in the hunt for bin Laden and other al Qaeda leaders. "Did everyone know what game the Pakistanis were playing?" one top official who discussed the issue regularly with Bush asked in the summer of

2008. "Of course. People here weren't born yesterday. But they thought that over time, the Pakistanis could be brought around."

It is clear from interviews with officials who left the administration after the first term, however, that Bush had other choices than to rely so heavily on Musharraf's promises. In 2002 and early 2003, many of those officials told me, Washington could have sent troops into the tribal areas under the pretense of "hot pursuit" of bin Laden and his associates. At the time, though, we had neither the forces on the ground nor the mind-set to fight a long war. And Bush's reliance on Musharraf to wage the war for him turned out to be one of the biggest misjudgments of the war on terror. Bush would eventually come to realize that the Pakistani president commanded forces that were not only unwilling to take on al Qaeda and the Taliban in Pakistani territory, but were incapable of doing so.

"When two hundred of their guys were captured by twenty militants with a bunch of rusty rifles," one of Bush's aides said to me, "we should have realized this was simply not going to work."

But in a larger sense, America's failures in Afghanistan and the tribal areas of Pakistan between 2002 and 2008—more time than it took a previous generation of Americans to win World War II in the Atlantic and the Pacific—are a case study in the costs of strategic distraction. In the race to win in Iraq, we lost focus on hunting down Osama bin Laden and eliminating the Taliban. Moreover, while we dealt with Afghanistan and Pakistan as separate problems, defined by a line Sir Mortimer Durand had established over a century ago, the Taliban and al Qaeda acted as if the territory were a single tribal land—what some British officers called Pashtunistan. Until Bush's last full year in office, when he issued a series of secret "permissions" that finally gave the CIA—and some American Special Forces—greater leeway to attack inside Pakistan, the White House did not treat the area as a single battlefield. And it insisted, as it did time and again in Iraq, that we did not need a new strategy— until, of course, the day a new strategy was adapted. It was yet another example of the inability of the administration to change course when circumstances changed. Inside Bush's insular White House, a strategic change was often equated with weakness or viewed as an admission of error.

Instead, the administration mounted a public-relations effort that seemed disturbingly reminiscent of the "five-o'clock follies" in Vietnam exactly forty years before, the daily briefings filled with boundless optimism and reams of statistics about roads built and enemies killed. As in Vietnam, the statistics were designed to hide the larger truth and to distract attention from warnings being circulated inside the administration that laid out the very real possibility of failure in coming years.

Perhaps the starkest of those warnings came from a lively, red-faced Australian who had made his name running counterinsurgency operations for the Australian Army, David Kilcullen.

Blunt-spoken and razor-smart, Kilcullen had been hired by Condoleezza Rice to bring counterinsurgency expertise to the State Department. She had plucked him from the Pentagon, where he had helped rewrite the department's strategy for "long-duration unconventional warfare," which Kilcullen would say, with a disarming smile, "involves everything Americans are worst at," starting with patience.

Kilcullen knows his military history, and that education, combined with his penchant for calling it like it is, surfaced quickly. Visiting Kabul in the spring of 2008, Kilcullen found himself talking one night to Maj. Gen. Bernard S. Champoux, McNeill's skilled deputy chief of staff for stability. Champoux volunteered to Kilcullen that Afghanistan might be a classic case of imperial overstretch: America, he said, made "a similar error to the one Hitler made when he invaded Russia in 1941. He started one war before another one was finished."

"No," Kilcullen interrupted him. "It wasn't a similar error. It was the same error."

Back in Washington, Kilcullen took to calling Iraq "the secondary theater" in the war against terrorism. It was a line designed to tweak the dwindling few who still subscribed to Bush's view that Iraq was the "central front" in that war. To Kilcullen, Bush's line was self-justifying fantasy: Afghanistan and tribal areas of Pakistan were where al Qaeda and the Taliban lived and conspired, yet the United States had based one soldier in Afghanistan for every six it had in Iraq. (Bush's aides pointed out that it was bin Laden himself who called Iraq the place to battle the Americans, but once al Qaeda in Mesopotamia was weakened, that front clearly began to shift.)

In Kilcullen's view Bush's "central front" line was symptomatic of an administration that had never quite understood what it was up against. The United States, he told me later, had been "overconfident after the fall of the Taliban." Bush, Rumsfeld, and Rice had viewed the problems in Afghanistan chiefly through the lens of a giant reconstruction project. By the time it was clear that there was a fight on for the future control of the country, the United States simply no longer had the assets in place that it needed to win.

Worse yet, Bush's early willingness to believe that Musharraf would deal with al Qaeda and insurgent groups in Pakistani territory made success in Afghanistan all the more difficult. Similar warnings were being voiced privately in Washington. "People should know," Kilcullen told Rice in one meeting early in 2008, "that we are in danger of losing the war." Not immediately, he said, and not even dramatically. The scenario he laid out was one of simple disintegration, especially if the Northern Alliance—the Afghans with whom America teamed up to oust the Taliban—simply lost confidence in Karzai's government and took power. Then, he warned Rice, Washington could be left supporting an elected rump government in Kabul, while other parts of the country simply spun out of Washington's control.

Kilcullen was right: Bush's successors will be dealing for years with the consequences of massive misjudgments in Afghanistan. Confident to a fault that they were on a roll, filled with hubris about American military power, insufficiently interested in what it takes to rebuild countries from the bottom up, too eager to depend on Musharraf's promises, Bush and his team forgot their ultimate objective: the destruction of the Taliban and al Qaeda and an end to the sanctuary that Afghanistan provided. The money that ultimately flowed into Afghanistan came years late. By then the window was closing on efforts to convince Afghans there was an alternative to life under the Taliban and to an economy dependent on poppies. In 2008, polls still showed that Afghans overwhelmingly supported America's presence and hated the Taliban. But they were increasingly doubtful that America had the will to make a difference.

The opening of a new front in Iraq only exacerbated the problems of distraction and deception. As the second war went awry, the United States had to fight a holding action in Afghanistan until it could free up American forces in Iraq to return to the task that should have been addressed six years before.

But Afghanistan was also a symbol of something far more sinister; it became a cautionary tale of the dangers of democratic overreach. Bush and his advisers—chiefly Secretary of Defense Donald Rumsfeld—became emboldened by the swiftness of their initial success in toppling the Taliban. Almost immediately they began applying the same model to Iraq, even if it did not truly fit. Bush convinced himself and tried to convince the country that we did not need to choose between success in Afghanistan and "victory" in Iraq. We could have a liberated, democratizing Afghanistan, even while toppling Saddam Hussein. It was an argument designed to justify engaging in a new war before finishing the one already begun.

Tragically, it proved to be fiction.

In April 2002, five months after the American invasion of Afghanistan, James Dobbins, the administration's special envoy for Afghanistan, was a deeply frustrated man. An expert on nation-building who had been the Clinton administration's special envoy for Somalia, Haiti, Bosnia, and Kosovo, Dobbins had taken on just about every crummy job in American diplomacy and performed brilliantly. No one in the American government understood more deeply the complexity—and the daunting level of commitment and high-level attention by America's top leaders—that it took to rebuild failed states.

Yet as he looked at Afghanistan, he saw a Pentagon and a White House so focused on hunting al Qaeda that it was putting far too little effort into addressing the conditions that allowed the movement to flourish. Just as he was beginning to despair of the fate of his personal campaign to win a major commitment to the country and prepare the ground for a moderate, democratic government after years of Taliban rule, he received an unexpected call from President Bush's speechwriting office. The president, his caller said, was planning to announce a far deeper commitment to the effort to rebuild Afghanistan.

"They were writing a speech," Dobbins recalled later, and the speechwriters wanted to know, "Did I see any reason not to cite the Marshall Plan?"[6] The political advantages of wrapping Bush in the mantle of Gen. George C. Marshall, the savvy warrior whom history remembers as a great humanitarian, were obvious. The Marshall Plan, a centerpiece of the remaking of American foreign policy in the late 1940s, was exactly the historical analogy Bush loved to cite. When Marshall announced the plan at a Harvard commencement, the rebuilding effort in Europe was a mess; his speech marked the turnaround that remade the post–World War II world.

For his vision of how to blend hard power and soft, for his understanding that military victory is a point of departure rather than an endpoint in the most important confrontations, Marshall is legitimately considered a hero—no place more so than at the State Department he once managed. The elegant waiting room for visitors outside the secretary of state's office is called the Marshall Room and is decorated with Marshall's portrait, an engraving showing the campus of Marshall's alma mater, the Virginia Military Institute, and a copy of the Harvard commencement address. As secretary of state, Powell often directed his visitors to that wall. Marshall, after all, was the other four-star general who ended up as the country's chief diplomat. Powell was acutely conscious of the parallel.

What Bush's speechwriters saw as an inviting rhetorical analogy, Dobbins instantly saw as an opportunity. "I said, 'No, I saw no objections,' so they put it in the speech," he recalled with a big smile.[7] He was delighted that the White House had come around to his view—or, more accurately, would be putting words in the president's mouth that would commit the administration later, in the inevitable budget battles, to making good on Bush's promises.

On April 17, 2002, Bush traveled to the Virginia Military Institute and spoke before a backdrop of imposing buildings on the campus where Marshall had graduated 101 years before. "Marshall knew that our military victory against enemies in World War II had to be followed by a moral victory that resulted in better lives for individual human beings," Bush declared, his voice washing over the sea of young cadets. He called Marshall's work "a beacon to light the path that we, too, must follow."[8]

Bush knew all too well that the Afghans believed they had heard similar promises before, only to be left abandoned, chiefly by his father's administration after the Soviets left in 1989. That bright morning at VMI, the younger Bush vowed to avoid the syndrome of "initial success, followed by long years of floundering and ultimate failure."

"We're not going to repeat that mistake," he said. "We're tough, we're determined, we're relentless. We will stay until the mission is done." As the cadets cheered, Bush promised that the United States would rebuild roads, dig wells, reconstruct hospitals, reopen schools, and establish a stable economy, a revitalized army, and a democratic national government.

It was lofty oratory, but it was never matched by a deep financial commitment to Afghanistan's future. Marshall's project in the 1940s ultimately cost $13 billion, spread over seventeen nations, equivalent to roughly $90 billion in today's dollars. By comparison, just months before the speech, Dobbins had flown off to Tokyo to a donors' conference seeking commitments to rebuild the recently liberated country. He raised pledges of $5 billion, including an American commitment of a paltry $290 million, less than 5 percent of the total pledged. Worsening the embarrassment, the Iranians—who hated the Taliban—committed twice as much. The American contribution was so pitiful, Dobbins told Powell, that it amounted to about $20 for every Afghan man, woman, and child—a sixteenth of what the United States had spent, per person, in the first year of reconstructing Bosnia, and an eighth of what it had spent in Kosovo. "Both of those," he told me later, "were vastly richer societies that had been much less devastated by war." Powell responded "with an impatient shrug," Dobbins recalled, born of the knowledge that the administration was not planning to ask Congress for more money anytime soon.

"What the numbers told you was that this was an administration that simply still didn't believe in nation-building, and didn't even like the phrase," Dobbins told me years later. "So when they started talking about Marshall Plans, I grabbed at it."[9] For Bush, even uttering Marshall's name marked a momentous shift. After all, he was the man who had belittled "nation-building" while campaigning for president eighteen months earlier; Rice had memorably said she didn't want the 82nd Airborne Division walking children to kindergarten. When I interviewed Bush at Crawford before his first inaugural, I brought the subject up as we were hiking around the ranch. I reminded him that Gore had given us a lengthy interview during the campaign in which he described the Marshall Plan as a model for future American foreign policy. Bush had declined to be interviewed on his foreign policy views by the *Times*, but that day he suggested that Gore didn't understand the way the world worked.

"I just didn't know what Gore was talking about," the president-elect said, leaning up against his pickup. "That's just not what our military is for."[10]

But within a few months of taking office, Bush began to discover that his convictions collided with reality. In late July 2001, I covered Bush's trip to Kosovo, his first visit to the Balkans operation that, during the heated election campaign, he had argued was the kind of state-building exercise that should not be the responsibility of the American military. He was there for only a few hours, but it was long enough for him to discover that without the Americans there to provide security, there would be no hope of generating any economic activity or attracting outside donors, much less investors. "I remember riding in a helicopter with him during that trip," Rice told me when I went to talk to her about the lessons the president had learned in his early years in office. "And he said to me, 'We have to get something going.' And it was only the military that was around to do that."

The speech at VMI was little noticed in the United States; it was only half a year since 9/11, and the country still seemed to be in a daze. But Bush's words resounded powerfully in Afghanistan. By invoking the imagery of the famed Marshall Plan, Bush encouraged high expectations among Afghans, who envisioned cargo planes swooping in with food and equipment and massive projects that would create jobs. Afghanistan was, of course, a very different place from postwar Europe, proving the point (proved again in Iraq) that older models of national reconstruction rarely translate well to modern times. Afghanistan had never been a unified country; it was a patchwork of tribal loyalties. Unlike Germany or Japan, it had never had a strong central government. The British had come to endless grief trying to create one during their occupation of the country in the nineteenth century. Now Afghanistan ranked as the world's fifth poorest country. Life expectancy was forty-three years, and illiteracy rates were shockingly high. Because there was no industrial sector to rebuild, the drug trade seemed particularly attractive. If China's claim to capitalistic success was that it clothed the world, and if Japan's was its ability to churn out cars and computer chips, Afghanistan's niche lay in its role as provider of over 90 percent of the world's opium.

Despite Bush's promise in Virginia, in the months that followed his April speech no detailed reconstruction effort emerged from the administration. Nor was there an integrated strategy, one that would have combined military force with on-the-ground economic efforts, much less a plan to wean the country's farmers away from poppies. The blame for that clearly resided with Rice's National Security Council, which is responsible for coordinating the instruments of American power to make sure that the president's instructions are carried out. "There would be meetings, and a recognition that we needed a more comprehensive approach," one of Rice's closest aides said to me later. "Then we'd meet again in a few months, thrash out the same problem, come up with the same solution, talk about the same comprehensive approach, and little happened."

Within months of Bush's speech, the true problem became apparent: Afghanistan was already in the rearview mirror. The next objective was Iraq, and as one senior official told me a year later, "Either you are the number one issue or you are not. And Afghanistan was not."

Privately, some senior officials, including Rumsfeld, were concerned that Afghanistan was a morass where the United States could achieve little. Within hours of the president's speech, Rumsfeld announced his own approach at a Pentagon news conference. "The last thing you're going to hear from this podium is someone thinking they know how Afghanistan ought to organize itself," he said. "They're going to have to figure it out. They're going to have to grab hold of that thing and do something. And we're there to help."[11]

Even Rice was ambivalent about how deeply the United States should jump in. "My problem with nation-building is that it assumes that we build their nation, when in fact it is not the United States building Afghanistan as a nation," she told me in April of 2003. "It is Afghanistan building Afghanistan as a nation."[12]

The problem was that Afghanistan had never been a nation, in the Western sense. And the country was filled with people—starting with tribal leaders—who had little interest in creating one.

◆

EVEN IN A WHITE HOUSE thoroughly obsessed with preventing internal disagreements from becoming public for fear of feeding domestic criticism, there was no way to hide the struggle over what America's mission in Afghanistan should be. The issues went far beyond nation-building; they encompassed the bigger question of how to direct American power in the post-9/11 world. Both the national mood and the hubris of the moment seemed in perfect sync: America's focus was supposed to be on "draining the swamp," to use the phrase commonly heard in the West Wing at that moment. To Rumsfeld that meant getting out of Afghanistan as quickly as America had gone in; the objective, he argued, was to rid the place of al Qaeda, and that had been achieved.

As early as December 2001, however, Powell and Rice recognized the risk of that approach. Both made the case in NSC meetings that if America was perceived to be walking away, if it allowed Afghanistan to fracture anew, Bush would appear far more interested in starting war than in achieving lasting peace. But those discussions did not yield a comprehensive reconstruction plan. Instead they led to a drive to hold elections—the same instinct had led Bush to support elections in the Palestinian territories four years later, before any side was ready—and to promote the symbolism of change. A penchant for symbols of democratic progress also served to underlie Bush's frequent repetition of the fact that girls in Afghanistan were going to school for the first time since the Taliban had taken charge; it fit into the concept of a war of "liberation." (The images of elections and inclusive schools had the air of an ex-post-facto explanation; before 9/11, Bush never publicly mentioned the educational challenges facing young girls in Afghanistan, much less suggested he would go to war to get them into school.)

The clash of worldviews came to a head in February 2002 in the White House Situation Room. Powell, fearing that the interim government that the United States had installed was weak and increasingly isolated, proposed that American troops join the small

international peacekeeping force, called the International Security
Assistance Force (ISAF), patrolling Kabul. He believed that over
time Karzai, still an interim leader, could extend his influence beyond the capital.

"President Karzai wasn't able to extend the government's reach
much beyond Kabul," Powell told me. "The ISAF was initially only
there to protect Kabul." Powell had a clear model in mind: the 1989
invasion of Panama, when American troops spread out across the
country after ousting the Noriega government. It was an operation
Powell had been involved in day-to-day as the chairman of the Joint
Chiefs of Staff, and he knew what could be accomplished. "Obviously, Afghanistan and, for that matter, Iraq, are much larger than
Panama. But the strategy has to be to take charge of the whole
country by military force, police, or other means," he said.[13] Otherwise, he knew, it was only a matter of time before things began to
spin out of control and the Taliban would seek to fill the vacuum.

Powell's argument was based on studies headed up by Richard
Haass, his director of policy planning at the State Department, and
a veteran of Bush 41's administration. Haass had polled his European counterparts and told Powell he believed a force of 20,000 to
40,000 peacekeepers could be recruited, half from Europe, half
from the United States.

When Powell made his argument for sharing responsibility,
Rumsfeld shot back that the European countries would be unwilling to contribute more troops. And, Rumsfeld added, sending in
American troops to fill the void would only reduce pressure on Europeans to contribute and provoke the Afghans' historic resistance
to perceived invaders. Worse, he said, it would divert American
forces from hunting terrorists.

Others in the room feared that confusion would arise if European forces viewed their task as peacekeeping, while the American
military saw its job as fighting terrorists. "The president, the vice
president, the secretary of defense, the national security staff, all of
them were skeptical of an ambitious project in Afghanistan," Haass

said; "I didn't see support." Rice, despite having argued for fully backing the new Karzai government, told me in early 2007 that she had concluded that Rumsfeld was closer to right. "I felt that we needed more forces, but there was a real problem, which you continue to see to this day, with the dual role," she said.[14] The decision was to make Afghanistan a largely American project, with no joint international force.

Powell told aides he thought Bush was making a huge mistake and predicted that sooner or later Bush would be forced to send in a joint force. Within two years he proved correct, and Bush began to advocate for the inclusion of allied forces in the mission. At the time, however, Powell took the loss stoically. "He seemed resigned," Dobbins said later.

"I said this wasn't going to be fully satisfactory," Dobbins recalled saying to Powell. "And he said, 'Well, it's the best we could do.'"[15]

In the end, the United States deployed 8,000 soldiers to Afghanistan in 2002 with orders to hunt al Qaeda first and the Taliban second, and not to engage in peacekeeping or reconstruction. The 4,000-soldier international peacekeeping force already in Afghanistan did not venture beyond Kabul, a restriction that Haass warned in internal memos was a "prescription for failure."

He, too, soon proved correct. To have any influence in the regions beyond Kabul, Americans found themselves striking deals with local warlords, much as the British had done more than a century before. The Americans had little choice but to look the other way when their new Afghan allies decided that the best way to rake in cash was to restore Afghanistan to its role as the world's leading producer of poppies.

It would take years before the consequences of all of these decisions became fully apparent in Afghanistan; however, the appearance of quick success had an immediate effect in Washington. It sustained the illusion that Afghanistan was the template for America's future wars. "If the talented and experienced men and women at the top of the Bush administration could polish off the Taliban in a matter of weeks," Dobbins wrote later, "why shouldn't this same crack national security team be able to guide American policy to an equally easy and quick success in Iraq?"[16]

The true lesson of Afghanistan slowly emerged: While the United States wields the world's largest hammer, not every problem is a nail. By the second term, Bush and his top aides grew to understand that without a program for reconstruction, the gains the military had initially made in the opening days of the war would be lost. They stopped talking about regime change, and started talking about "building capacity" for countries to help themselves. But by that time most of the damage had been done, as Afghanistan began to retreat toward anarchy.

BY ANY STANDARD, the number of Americans initially focused on stabilizing Afghanistan was laughable. In the first year after the invasion, there were so few State Department or Pentagon civil affairs officials in the country that thirteen teams of CIA operatives, whose main job was to hunt terrorists and the Taliban, were asked to stay in remote corners of Afghanistan to coordinate political efforts. "It took us quite a while to get them regrouped in the southeast for counterterrorism," John E. McLaughlin, who was deputy director and then acting director of the CIA, told me after he had left government. "Everyone was begging them to stay. They had the relationships with the local leaders, and the cash."[17]

But the Bush administration had no intention of letting them stay; the CIA was never intended to be an aid organization. And by the middle of 2002 the American sense of victory was so robust that the top CIA specialists and elite Special Forces units who had helped liberate Afghanistan were already packing their guns. They were shipping out to Kuwait and other countries on the periphery of Iraq. George Bush had decided to trade a war of necessity for a war of choice, before the war of necessity had been won.

Years later, members of Bush's top national security team

would argue to me that they never robbed Afghanistan of resources in order to oust Saddam Hussein. "It didn't happen that way," Stephen Hadley, the president's national security adviser, insisted to me one early summer day in 2007, when I interviewed him about what had gone wrong in Afghanistan. Well prepared with his brief, he presented me with impressive-looking statistics that the White House rapidly ordered declassified to make its case that forces were "surged" into Afghanistan at key junctures even during the worst moments of conflict in Iraq. Hadley's numbers are undeniable, but they tell only part of the story.

Robert Grenier, the former director of the CIA's counterintelligence center, and a veteran of operations in South Asia, tells the other part—how assets critical to preventing the Taliban's return were siphoned off when the administration became convinced that knocking over Saddam Hussein's regime in Iraq would be only slightly more difficult than taking out Mullah Omar had been in Afghanistan.

In October 2002, Grenier walked into the makeshift Kuwait City headquarters of Lt. Gen. David McKiernan, the American general charged with planning the invasion of Iraq. Situated in a group of warehouses north of the city, the headquarters was a beehive of construction workers and heavily armed guards. Grenier and a half dozen other CIA operatives made their way to a secure conference room for a private meeting with General McKiernan.

It was already clear to both men that President Bush's ultimatum to Saddam Hussein to disarm meant war with Iraq was likely, if not inevitable. But Grenier was already worried about the effects in Afghanistan, where, he feared, intelligence about the Taliban and al Qaeda would suffer if resources were diverted to Iraq.

Grenier asked McKiernan what his intelligence needs would be in Iraq. The answer was predictable, Grenier recalled later at an outdoor café in Washington one warm afternoon. "They wanted as much as they could get," he laughed. "And they wanted it all moved there yesterday."

Afghanistan had become last year's problem. The complexities of invading Iraq were the issue of the day, and the CIA mounted a massive intelligence operation inside Iraq that was twice the size of its effort in Afghanistan in 2001, Grenier said.

But it came at a price. Throughout late 2002 and early 2003, the agency's most skilled counterterrorism and Middle East specialists and paramilitary operatives were rotated out of Afghanistan. "The best experienced, most qualified people who we had been using in Afghanistan shifted over to Iraq," Grenier said. "We're talking about fewer than twenty key people, but these were key people."[18]

In retrospect, the turnover of intelligence personnel greatly reduced the United States' influence over powerful Afghan warlords who were refusing to turn over to the central government tens of millions of dollars they had collected as customs payments at border crossings. It was the experienced officers, with long-standing ties to those warlords, who could make the case to the tribal leaders that their long-term interests lay in supporting a stronger central government in Kabul. But the replacement officers who showed up in Afghanistan, Grenier said, were younger agents, who lacked the knowledge and influence of the veterans who toppled the Taliban in 2001. "I think we could have done a lot more on the Afghan side if we had more experienced folks," he said. "If you don't have those relationships, your ability to influence goes down."[19]

But the turnover of intelligence officers was just the beginning. At the Pentagon's Central Command, headquartered in Tampa, Florida, which was running both wars, a senior official who played a key role in planning both missions, said that both the "white special ops" and the "black special ops" began vacating Afghanistan as well. The first are special operations teams like the Green Berets, known to generations of moviegoers. The second are the military's covert Special Mission Units, like Delta Force and Navy SEAL Team Six.

It was bad enough that their departure created a vacuum in Afghanistan that the Taliban, though bruised and battered, could begin to fill. What was worse is that these same Special Forces lost their focus on the biggest target of all: al Qaeda Central, just over the border in Pakistan.

In 2002, U.S. military officials pressed the Pakistanis to allow the elite American Special Forces to establish small, unobtrusive bases in the tribal areas to launch operations against bin Laden, his deputies, and the Taliban forces who were setting up a safe sanctuary just across the Pakistan border. Musharraf flatly refused. Instead, though, he agreed to allow the "black" Special Forces to join Pakistani units on specific raids into the tribal areas to root out al Qaeda fighters. This allowed Musharraf to retain control of all operations.

The arrangement never worked. To the American Special Forces, accustomed to working alone and in highly flexible, coordinated teams, the Pakistanis were more of an impediment than a help. Moreover, the Pakistanis had to deny publicly that any American military were on Pakistani soil, a lie that became obvious to tribesmen who spotted the Americans.

Within a year the whole arrangement collapsed, never to be revived. With the White House's attention now turned westward toward the war in Iraq, the pressure on Musharraf from Bush simply evaporated. With the Special Forces shifting to hunting down insurgents and al Qaeda associates in Iraq, both bin Laden and the Taliban had the freedom they needed to reconstitute small training camps and run increasingly bold operations into Afghanistan.[20]

It wasn't only the Special Forces that were suddenly scarce. So were the aerial surveillance "platforms" like the Predator, remotely piloted spy planes armed with devastating Hellfire missiles, which were increasingly being sent to Iraq. For years the U.S. Air Force wanted nothing to do with the Predator; in the traditional Air Force culture, it's only an airplane if there is a live pilot in the cockpit. The Predators seemed more like sophisticated toys—ungainly prop planes—that were controlled by young junior officers who trained through video games and operated the powerful equipment via a joystick in some trailer half a world away. ("Boys with toys" and "joystick jockeys" were the cleanest phrases the real combat pilots used to refer to these officers.) But by late 2001, those video gamers in the trailers started taking out al Qaeda and Taliban leaders as they moved in and out of houses or camps in the mountains of Afghanistan. The Pentagon was not getting credit for those kills because the majority of the planes were operated by the CIA. Now the Department of Defense suddenly wanted to take control of the new Predators rolling off the assembly line of General Atomics, the San Diego company frantically manufacturing the drones.

Predators were not shifted directly from Afghanistan to Iraq. But as new planes were produced, they were shipped to the Middle East, not to Afghanistan. In retrospect, that allocation was a huge mistake: The Predators are particularly effective at identifying targets in the sparsely populated mountains of Afghanistan. Satellites and reconnaissance vehicles work fine in Iraq.

"We were economizing in Afghanistan," said one senior official who received detailed intelligence reports from the flights. "The marginal return for one more platform in Afghanistan is so much greater than for one more in Iraq."

"If we were not in Iraq, we would have double or triple the number of Predators across Afghanistan, looking for Taliban and peering into the tribal areas" in Pakistan, where both Taliban and al Qaeda leaders were believed to be hiding, the official told me, unwilling to go on the record because he still held a senior military position. "We'd have the 'black' Special Forces you most need to conduct precision operations. We'd have more CIA.

"We're simply in a world of limited resources, and those resources are in Iraq," he added. "Anyone who tells you differently is blowing smoke."[21]

But in Washington, the downsizing seemed like the logical next step. "You have to remember that at least initially no one really planned to stay," said Lt. Gen. Karl Eikenberry, who served in Afghanistan twice, including eighteen months as the American commander. "There was no plan for an extended military presence. We were primarily focused on al Qaeda, and the Afghans soon realized this."[22]

Eikenberry was among the few with the experience and the rank to argue the case that Washington was missing an opportunity to build a bulwark against the Taliban and to keep the country from backsliding into anarchy. Whenever visiting dignitaries arrived, he took them on a tour of Afghanistan's missing infrastructure—the blown-up bridges, the nonexistent roads—and explained how it was keeping the economy from coming back to life.

"I remember Karl saying to me, 'If you give me the choice between another division and another big road, I'll take the road,'" Rice recalled later.

"The key question is, 'Is the government of Afghanistan winning?'" Eikenberry asked during a congressional hearing in 2007. "In several critical areas—corruption, justice and law enforcement, and counter-narcotics—it is not."[23]

But while Eikenberry converted many of his visitors, he ran headlong into the Rumsfeld Doctrine: The American military was there to liberate, not to build, particularly in a country with a centuries-old record of seeking to expel foreigners.

RICHARD NIXON had no real "secret plan" to end the Vietnam War when he took office in 1969, despite the strong hints during his campaign that he kept one in his jacket pocket. When he had to invent one, he came up with "Vietnamization," the turning over of security responsibilities to the Vietnamese. When George Bush had to invent one for Afghanistan, he came up with the equivalent—"Afghanization," though his staff knew better than to suggest he use the word. Instead, Bush talked specifics, such as the idea that Afghanistan would initially create a 70,000-member national army, with American help.

He repeated the promise in a series of Rose Garden press conferences with Karzai, dressed in his trademark karakul hat and capelike Afghan *chapan,* at his side. Over time, the promises expanded. Japan would disarm some 100,000 militia fighters. Britain would mount an antinarcotics program. Italy would carry out judicial reform. And Germany would train a 62,000-member police force.

On paper the vision looked great. In reality it was a disaster. There was no overall coordination. The dispersal of responsibility across many nations meant that no one was in command. "When everyone's in charge," Hadley lamented in one Afghanistan meeting, "no one's in charge." Moreover, Washington appeared to misjudge what the Afghans wanted and what they would tolerate. Lakhdar Brahimi, the United Nations special representative to Afghanistan at the time, said diplomats in Kabul found that Afghans, exhausted by years of internecine civil war with the Taliban, longed for outside help, even if it meant a foreign presence.

"It could have changed everything," Brahimi said during a trip to the United States in 2007, referring to a larger peacekeeping force. "The people of Afghanistan were all for it."

But the United States simply did not have the infrastructure for civilian reconstruction, and the Bush administration made no effort, until its second term in office, to build one. Sixteen months after Bush's 2002 "Marshall Plan" speech, the United States Agency for International Development, the government's main foreign development arm, had seven full-time staffers and thirty-five full-time contract staff members in Afghanistan. That's not much for a country the size of Texas. Most of the contractors were local Afghans, according to a government audit. Sixty-one of the agency's positions for Afghanistan were left vacant.

"It was clearly insufficient," said Robert Finn, the American ambassador to Afghanistan from 2002 to 2003. "Afghanistan has been funded at a lower level than any other postwar humanitarian crisis. . . . I said from the get-go that we didn't have enough money and we didn't have enough soldiers," Finn said. "I'm saying the same thing six years later."[24]

The numbers back him up. In the two years after the American-led ouster of the Taliban, Afghanistan received only $57 per capita in international aid, while Bosnia received roughly $679. Even the newly created state of East Timor, hardly a place of vital strategic interest to the United States, received about $233 in aid per person.

But the numbers are truly shocking when compared with the amount America spent in the early years in Iraq, a country that is geographically smaller and has a slightly smaller population. Of course, the reconstruction of Iraq was supposed to be self-financing because of the country's oil reserves and the cash they would have generated for the Iraqi government. Yet in 2004, a year after the ouster of Saddam Hussein, the United States allocated about $18 billion for reconstruction in Iraq over a period of several years. It is hard to come up with a comparable number for Afghanistan, but that same year about $720 million was allocated for Afghanistan, which had none of Iraq's petroleum resources. Put another way, the Bush administration got its aid formula backward. Afghanistan needed the help far more desperately than Iraq did.

The Afghans may not have known the numbers, but they saw the results. On the ground, Afghans, awed by American military power in 2001 and impressed by Bush's rhetorical commitment, expressed surprise when legions of American engineers failed to appear in Afghanistan in 2002. "It was state-building on the cheap, it was a duct-tape approach," recalled Said T. Jawad, Karzai's chief of staff at the time and Afghanistan's current ambassador to Washington, in the embassy that the United States renovated beautifully after the Taliban's fall. "It was fixing things that were broken, not a strategic approach."[25]

In separate conversations over the years, both Rice and Hadley acknowledged that the failure to build a civilian reconstruction effort ranked among the administration's biggest failings. "We have problems with capacity, and with execution," Hadley said repeatedly. Rice fumed to me in one interview that while Powell had talked endlessly about the need for such a capability inside the U.S.

government, "he didn't leave any." A year later she spearheaded the first effort at the State Department to establish a standby corps of experts who could help struggling nations build a legal system, schools, and a bureaucracy for revenue collection. But the reality remains that little was ready in time to help the Afghans.

FROM THE FIRST DAYS after 9/11, the public line about Pakistan was that its president, Pervez Musharraf, had undergone a religious conversion as the World Trade Center burned. He was now as passionate about counterterrorism as, say, George Bush. Or so the story went. Suddenly, the American president who couldn't recall Musharraf's name during the 2000 campaign declared that he and the Pakistani leader were like brothers. And Musharraf realized that if he played his cards right, he would not only get the United States to forget about the sanctions it had imposed on Pakistan after its 1998 nuclear tests, he would get billions in aid, too.

He was right.

Musharraf's strategy was on clear display when he showed up at the White House in February 2002. It was the first time he had been invited since he took power in the 1999 coup against Nawaz Sharif, and Bush went all-out to treat him as he would have treated Tony Blair or another longtime ally. The two leaders held a news conference in the Cross Hall, the long corridor on the first floor of the White House lined with portraits of recent U.S. presidents and adorned with a rich red carpet. Bush described Musharraf as a "leader of great vision and courage."[26] There was no mention of Pakistan's nuclear breakout, or of the investigations then under way into the nuclear dealings of A. Q. Khan, the Pakistani metallurgist, though Bush had been briefed on the investigations and the suspicions of Pakistani government complicity.

Just a day before the meeting, in a well-timed move, Pakistani authorities had nabbed Ahmed Omar Sheikh, a member of the militant group Jaish-e-Mohammed, in the city of Lahore. (He would be convicted later in the year for his involvement in the kidnapping and killing of Daniel Pearl, the *Wall Street Journal* reporter. Musharraf, however, told us that day that Pakistan was trying to negotiate Pearl's release, adding, "I am reasonably sure he's alive.")

In retrospect, there were signs of where this relationship was going. Musharraf was unwilling to hand over Omar Sheikh to American authorities; there were suspicions of the militant's connections to Pakistani intelligence services.[27] And Bush was unable to give Musharraf what he most wanted: an end to quotas on the import of Pakistani textiles and clothing. America was willing to do anything to help an ally, except for ending protective tariffs.

The courting of Musharraf accelerated. He was back in June 2003, for a session at Camp David, the first for any leader from South Asia, an honor considered even more prestigious than an invitation to the White House. Bush hailed the apprehension of "more than 500 al Qaeda and Taliban terrorists" in Pakistan, an impressive number tarnished only by the fact that new terrorists were being recruited just as fast. Bush repeated that "we will stay on the hunt" for al Qaeda leaders, and Musharraf told him there was "no doubt in my mind" that the Pakistani military would clean out the northwest territories and "will be able to locate any al Qaeda members hiding in this area."[28]

These assurances were just what Bush wanted to hear, and he declared Pakistan a "major non-NATO ally," offering Musharraf a $3-billion aid package. Bush's aides, not wanting to spoil the moment, waited until later to insist that the aid was contingent on Musharraf's efforts to curb terrorism, stop nuclear proliferation, and support democratic reforms in the country. "I'm not calling those conditions," a senior administration official told reporters at the time, "but let's be realistic. Three years down the road, if things are going badly in those areas, it's not going to happen."[29]

Three years down the road, things were going really badly in those areas. But by then the $3 billion in aid given had grown closer to $10 billion.

◆

While Bush was cheering on Musharraf, Bob Grenier was focused on Osama bin Laden and the other al Qaeda leaders believed to be living inside Pakistan's borders. Grenier was the Islamabad station chief for the CIA, leading the highly classified effort to track and kill bin Laden and his organization and their Taliban associates.

The search was not going well. While the United States talked about rounding up the Taliban, it was considered a second-order problem. "From our perspective at the time, the Taliban was a spent force," Grenier said, adding, "We were very much focused on al Qaeda and didn't want to distract the Pakistanis from that." A former American military commander in Afghanistan said that the Pakistanis quickly picked up on Washington's priorities. "They got the message. They knew that if they delivered a few al Qaeda guys—maybe the ones in the cities—we'd get off their case about the Taliban."[30]

Pakistani support for the Taliban was not new. Throughout the 1990s, Pakistan's intelligence services had backed the Taliban as a counterweight to an alliance of northern Afghan commanders supported by India, Pakistan's bitter regional rival. Pakistani officials saw Karzai, Afghanistan's new president, as pro-India as well.

Deciding that the Pakistanis would never act against the Taliban, Grenier urged them to focus on arresting al Qaeda members, who he said were far more of a threat to the United States. He knew that no matter what the Pakistanis promised about rooting out their onetime allies, they had no interest in doing so. "The results were just not there," he recalled. "And it was quite clear to me that it wasn't just bad luck."

But it took years for Washington to recognize the degree to which the Taliban were coming back, crossing from Pakistan into Afghanistan in small teams and killing American troops and aid workers, and acting as a support network for al Qaeda's leaders in Pakistan.

# CHAPTER 6

# THE OTHER
# "MISSION
# ACCOMPLISHED"

As THE FOCUS SHIFTED to Iraq in 2003, the U.S. Army needed its most experienced and well-armed troops heading to Baghdad—meaning that those sent into Afghanistan to train the new Afghan National Army were mostly reservists formed into small ad-hoc teams. Most of those courageous but inexperienced soldiers had never before left American shores; it would take time for them to understand what kind of army operations were needed in the unforgiving terrain of Afghanistan. Making matters worse, they were being teamed with experienced Afghan fighters and were expected to advise the Afghans on complex combat tasks that many of the reservists themselves had never performed. Not surprisingly, these deficiencies slowed the creation of the new Afghan force, a central part of the American effort to stabilize the country.

"Competing Iraq requirements almost certainly led to a decision to utilize reserve forces to perform the mission of training the Afghan National Army," one Pentagon official who was involved in the triage told me later. "There was a cost."

He laid out the math. In recent years, he noted, NATO and American forces have not even come close to providing the number of troops that, by their own estimates, are needed in Afghanistan. Given the size and population of the country, classic counterinsurgency doctrine would have called for a force of about 400,000. By 2006 or so, "we worked that down to about 160,000," General McNeill recalled as he neared the end of his time as commander in Afghanistan.[1]

But even that revised number was unattainable, owing largely to ballooning requirements in Iraq. By the end of 2007, there were 41,000 American and NATO troops in the country—more than half of them Americans—and maybe 60,000 Afghan soldiers and police. (The police were trained so poorly that many American officials said they should not be counted at all.) At best, some of McNeill's aides calculated, Afghanistan needed 60 percent more troops than it had in place to hold the country together. At worst, it needed 300 percent more.

The Army's math was different from Rumsfeld's math. The Rumsfeld Doctrine called for minimizing the American presence, not increasing it. That became clear during the spring of 2003, as Rumsfeld traveled to Afghanistan just as White House officials put together plans for President Bush to land on the deck of the aircraft carrier USS *Abraham Lincoln* and declare the end of major combat operations in Iraq.

Clearly, one couldn't make a declaration like that about Iraq unless there was a similar, if less dramatic, announcement about the other war that had been under way for a year and a half.

So on May 1, hours before Bush stood beneath the infamous "Mission Accomplished" banner, Rumsfeld held a press conference with Karzai in Kabul's threadbare nineteenth-century presidential palace. Seated at a table adorned with a bouquet of flowers and two small Afghan and American flags, Rumsfeld announced that major combat operations had ended in Afghanistan, too.

"We clearly have moved from major combat activity to a period of stability and stabilization and reconstruction activities," Rumsfeld said, as Karzai sat by his side. "The bulk of the country today is permissive, it's secure."[2]

The Afghanistan announcement was largely lost in the spectacle surrounding Bush's speech. But the declaration of relative stability in Afghanistan proved no less detached from events on the ground than Bush's premature victory lap in Iraq.

Three weeks after Rumsfeld's triumphant announcement, Afghan government workers who had not been paid for months held street demonstrations in Kabul. An exasperated Karzai threatened publicly to resign. In an angry speech at the country's supreme court, he announced that his central government had virtually run out of money because warlords were hoarding customs revenues. "There is no money in the government treasury. The money is in provincial customs houses around the country. Millions of dollars, hundreds of millions of dollars."[3]

Eighteen months after the fall of the Taliban, warlords continued to rule vast swaths of Afghanistan.

Rumsfeld understood Karzai's problem, but his focus had turned to a different issue—Iraq. Months earlier he had called on a trusted aide to oversee Afghanistan: Dov Zakheim, the Pentagon's comptroller. A slight, intense man, he was among the original "Vulcans," the foreign policy team set up for the 2000 campaign by Condoleezza Rice and named for the Roman god of fire, whose statue stands in Rice's hometown, Birmingham, Alabama. Zakheim, who was close to Vice President Cheney, came to the Bush administration a true believer. He left deeply disillusioned.

To Zakheim's surprise, Rumsfeld asked him to serve as the Pentagon's reconstruction coordinator in Afghanistan. It was an odd role for a comptroller, whose primary task is managing the Pentagon's $400-billion-a-year budget.

"The fact that they went to the comptroller to do something like that was in part a function of their growing preoccupation with Iraq," said Zakheim, who left the administration in 2004. "They needed somebody, given that the top tier was covering Iraq."

Zakheim quickly discovered that Afghanistan was the land of great promises and little follow-through. In January 2003, he traveled to the country with Paul Wolfowitz, then the deputy secretary of defense and one of the chief architects of the Iraq War. Wolfowitz's one-day mission to the country was meant to assure the Afghans that they would not be forgotten. The streets of Kabul were cleared for his visit, and he gave a speech in which he promised more help, more forces, more aid. "We are here to keep helping," he told Afghan Army recruits. "We are not walking away." And while it was no secret Washington was gearing up for war in Iraq, Wolfowitz insisted that Afghanistan would not suffer as a consequence. "We are regulating our deployments here based on the needs here in this country. Big enough to do the job, but no bigger than necessary, and we have more than adequate forces to do what's necessary."[4]

No one believed him—even some members of his own delegation. "Then we went back to Washington," Zakheim recalled, "and everything returned to normal—that is, very little action."

A MONTH AFTER Rumsfeld's announcement in Kabul, his aides presented a strategy to the White House aimed at weakening warlords and engaging in state-building in Afghanistan. In some ways it was the very approach Rumsfeld had rejected right after the invasion.

Pentagon officials said that Rumsfeld's views began to shift after a December 2002 briefing by Marin Strmecki, an Afghanistan expert at the Smith Richardson Foundation, who argued that Afghanistan was not ungovernable and that it could be turned into a moderate, Muslim state.

Strmecki delivered a private briefing on Afghanistan to the Defense Policy Board, a group of former government officials that advised Rumsfeld on defense matters. Richard Perle, a leading neoconservative who chaired the board, invited Strmecki to speak because he feared that senior American officials knew too little about Afghanistan.

"I was concerned that we really didn't understand it very well," Perle recalled. "And so I looked for people who did."

For two hours Strmecki told the likes of Henry Kissinger, former defense secretary James Schlesinger, and former House speaker Thomas Foley, among others, that Afghanistan was not an anarchic morass. The United States, he said, needed to better integrate Pashtuns—Afghanistan's largest ethnic group and historically the Taliban's base of support—into the country's new government and mount a "serious state-building effort" across Afghanistan. His analysis was, in essence, an effort to implement the policy Bush had announced in his April 2002 speech that had never materialized. Rumsfeld was so impressed by Strmecki's emphasis on training Afghans to run their own government—the solution Rumsfeld was looking for—that he hired him.

Soon Zalmay Khalilzad, an Afghan-American who was a senior National Security Council official and the administration's leading expert on Afghanistan, returned from Iraq. As the administration's special envoy to Iraqi exiles, Khalilzad had championed the invasion and had pushed hard for local empowerment in Iraq. He clashed frequently with L. Paul Bremer III, who had been made the head of the American occupation in Iraq. Upon Khalilzad's return to Washington in May 2003, Rice—who was still the national security adviser—asked him to develop a new American effort in Afghanistan with Strmecki.

In July, Khalilzad met privately with Bush and agreed to become American ambassador to Afghanistan. But he insisted on one condition: that the scope of the American effort there be vastly increased. Khalilzad knew that he needed support from the president if he had any hope of overcoming opposition from the Office of Management and Budget to increasing aid to Afghanistan.

"We had gotten the president to [agree to] a significant increase," Khalilzad recalled. "He said, 'You have it.'"[5]

Khalilzad had the sway within the administration he needed. He could get Rice or —if need be—Bush on the phone in short order. He had headed the Bush-Cheney transition team at the Defense Department and served as a counselor to Rumsfeld. During Bush's first term, he was the director of the National Security Council's

Office of Middle East and Southwest Asian Affairs. He may also have been the first Afghan George Bush ever really got to know.

"Zal could get things done," recalled Lt. Gen. David W. Barno, a former American military commander in Afghanistan.[6]

But it was now clear that the United States would need help from its allies. It went out to drum some up.

JUST TWO YEARS after the Taliban fell to the American-led coalition, a group of NATO ambassadors landed in Kabul to survey what appeared to be a triumph, a fresh start for a country ripped apart by years of war with the Soviets and brutal repression by religious extremists.

At the head of the pack was a youthful-looking, mustachioed American diplomat, R. Nicholas Burns, who led the crowd from Brussels as they thundered around the country in American Black Hawk helicopters. They had little to fear on the streets; with the Taliban routed, Afghanistan seemed eerily peaceful. The ambassadors casually strolled through the quiet streets of Kandahar. They sipped tea with tribal leaders and talked about roads and schools and how to close down the madrassas that turned out young extremists, teaching them both the Koran and the art of setting off car bombs.

Burns, always disposed to find the best news in dire places, told his tour group that Afghanistan's allergy to a foreign presence had not materialized; polls showed that the Afghans wanted Westerners to stay and their aid to flow to the far reaches of the country. The American-installed government of Hamid Karzai was still standing, even though, back in Washington, White House officials derisively called the smooth-talking, Westernized Karzai the "emperor of Kabul" because he was incapable of extending his power beyond the Afghan capital. As Burns and his fellow diplomats traveled around the country they saw that life was coming back, schools were opening, marketplaces were jammed. More important, a rudimentary democracy was taking hold—and the Afghans themselves appeared to be embracing it. It all played to Burns's argument: This was the time for NATO to embrace the Afghan cause. They could go into the country as peacekeepers, with little fear of taking the kinds of casualties that the European public could not stomach, while the Americans focused on the next hard target.

But privately, even Burns, usually the cheerful master of spin, was taken aback by assertions made in the briefing the ambassadors received that day at the United States Central Command's heavily guarded base. With exhaustive PowerPoint presentations ticking off one accomplishment after another, the ambassadors were reassured that the Taliban was a "spent force," so thoroughly destroyed it could never return.

"Some of us were saying, 'Not so fast,'" recalled Burns, who went on to become the undersecretary of state for political affairs, and inherited the fallout from that misplaced optimism. "I mean, we are dealing with Pashtun loyalties that go back centuries."[7]

Those loyalties, Burns knew, meant that al Qaeda and the Taliban had not been vanquished, they had merely relocated. Walking east, they retreated to their traditional refuge, the lawless tribal areas of Pakistan, high in the mountains along the unguarded border between the two countries. There they regrouped and retrained, as "guests" of the tribal leaders, many of whom sympathized with their cause, or whose sympathies could be bought.

But the military briefers seemed to be describing a dreamland in which the enemy simply evaporated. Burns said later that even then he did not buy the argument. "While not a strategic threat, a number of us assumed that the Taliban was too enmeshed in Afghan society to just disappear," he told me in the summer of 2007.*

---

* By 2008, it became clear to many in the U.S. government, and particularly in the U.S. intelligence community, that the Taliban could become a "strategic threat," dividing the country into several parts, leaving an American-backed "rump" government in an increasingly isolated Kabul.

Astoundingly, it took years for that skepticism to take hold back in Washington, and this painfully slow process was the root cause of what may have been the largest failure in strategic thinking, nation-building, and counterterrorism strategy after 9/11. The intelligence reports circulating through Washington between 2001 and 2003, I was told by senior intelligence officials, reported that the Taliban were so decimated they no longer posed a threat to either American forces or Karzai's government. Those assessments fueled the confidence—many who worked in the West Wing in 2003 now call it arrogance—that Donald Rumsfeld's "light footprint" strategy had remade the rules of modern warfare. It seemed possible to use superior American technology, intelligence, and covert forces to knock off a government and withdraw as fast as politically palatable, leaving the locals to carry on. The Powell Doctrine—the caution that a nation should go to war reluctantly but, once committed, must use overwhelming force—was all but declared dead. Rumsfeld's rules ruled.

When Khalilzad arrived in Kabul on Thanksgiving 2003, he brought nearly $2 billion in additional funding—twice the amount of the previous year—as well as a new military strategy and a bevy of private-sector experts known as the "Afghan Reconstruction Group" charged with intensifying reconstruction efforts.

They began an ambitious new reconstruction plan dubbed, with characteristic Bush White House enthusiasm, "Accelerating Success." Its centerpiece was exactly the kind of nation-building once dismissed by the administration. General Barno, commander of forces in Afghanistan from November 2003 to May 2005, breathed new life into eight military "Provincial Reconstruction Teams" responsible for building schools, roads, and wells and winning the "hearts and minds" of Afghans. The teams amounted to a much smaller version of the reconstruction forces that Powell had proposed eighteen months earlier.

By January 2004, Khalilzad and United Nations officials had crafted a new Afghan constitution. In September 2004, Khalilzad used the threat of American military force to persuade Ismail Khan, one of the country's most powerful warlords, to accept Karzai's order that he resign as governor of the western province of Herat. The following month, Karzai was elected president in a surprisingly violence-free campaign. At the White House, the biggest worry about Khalilzad was that he was proving more popular in Afghan opinion polls than Karzai himself.

"You know it's time to pull your U.S. ambassador," one White House official told me, "when his poll numbers are higher than the [host country's] president's." (In 2008, with Karzai's popularity plummeting, there were renewed rumors that Khalilzad would run for president. By then, Khalilzad was the U.S. representative to the United Nations, living in the ambassador's official residence in the Waldorf-Astoria Hotel in New York, and the prospect of taking the helm of a collapsing state may have seemed less than appealing.)

At the same time, NATO countries steadily deployed more troops into Afghanistan, and soon Rumsfeld—pressed for troops in Iraq—proposed that NATO take over security for all of Afghanistan. After initially balking, NATO officials began to negotiate.

By the spring of 2005, Afghanistan seemed to be moving toward the vision that Bush had promised to achieve. But then, fearing that Iraq was spinning out of control, the White House asked Khalilzad to become the new American ambassador to Baghdad. Soon, Afghanistan again paid the price for being a second priority.

Before departing Afghanistan, Khalilzad fought a final battle within the administration—one that revealed the depth of the divisions within the American government over Pakistan's role in aiding the Taliban. There was no subject more delicate as the administration tried to coax Pakistan's president, Pervez Musharraf, to cooperate.

In a farewell interview on Afghan television, Khalilzad noted that Pakistani journalists had recently interviewed a senior Taliban commander in Pakistan. He questioned Pakistan's claim that it did not know the whereabouts of senior Taliban commanders. It was an expression of skepticism forbidden in Washington, where the administration's position had long been that Musharraf was doing everything he could.

"If a TV station can get in touch with them, how can the intelligence service of a country, which has nuclear bombs and a lot of security and military forces, not find them?" Khalilzad asked.[8]

Pakistani officials publicly denounced Khalilzad's comments and denied harboring Taliban leaders. But, deliberately or not, Khalilzad had exposed the growing rift between American officials in Kabul and Islamabad. The diplomats and the CIA station in Afghanistan were becoming increasingly alarmed by the threat emanating from the Pakistani sanctuary. When their American counterparts in Pakistan downplayed that threat, Khalilzad's colleagues accused them of "drinking the Kool-Aid" and accepting Pakistani assurances that played down the problem.[9] It was the first shot in a battle that would rage for years.

"Colleagues in Washington at various levels—including the highest—did not recognize that there was the problem of sanctuary and that this was important," Khalilzad said later, measuring his words carefully because he was still serving in the administration, as the U.S. ambassador to the United Nations. "I favored a stronger effort clearly in Pakistan against al Qaeda, but also a strong effort on the Taliban issue."[10]

But with Bush increasingly preoccupied with Iraq, he expended little energy pressuring Musharraf to take action against the militants in the tribal areas. Personal phone calls to the Pakistani general, designed by Bush's aides to force Musharraf into action, backfired. Two former U.S. officials told the *Times* that they were surprised and frustrated when Bush repeatedly thanked Musharraf for his continued cooperation in the war on terrorism, rather than demanding swift action against al Qaeda and Taliban elements operating within Pakistan's borders.

"He never pounded his fist on the table and said, 'Pervez, you have to do this,'" recalled one former senior intelligence official who saw the transcripts of the phone conversations.[11]

It was a pattern I saw with Bush time and time again: He talked far tougher in public than in private, and was often susceptible to the pleas of other presidents and prime ministers that leadership is difficult, and that the rest of the world didn't understand the pressures of the top job. "It's classic Bush," I was told by one leading member of the Iraq Study Group who had examined some of these interactions. "Whether it's Maliki in Iraq or Karzai in Afghanistan or Putin in Russia, Bush always feels like he has to build them up—he's really allergic to acknowledging any real divergence of views."

It was not until 2006, after ordering yet another study on Afghanistan's future, that Bush began to press Musharraf hard on the Taliban. By then it was too late.

Despite Musharraf's assurances, the administration was concerned that the Pakistani military and intelligence service's historical ties to the Taliban had never been cut. The Pakistanis, one senior American commander said, were "hedging their bets."

"They're not sure that we are staying," he added. "And if we are gone, the Taliban is their next best option" to remain influential in Afghanistan.

So the Taliban leadership remained in hiding in Pakistan, waiting for an opportunity to cross the border. Soon they would have one.

IN SEPTEMBER 2005, NATO defense ministers gathered in Berlin to complete plans for NATO troops to take over security in Afghanistan's volatile south. It was the most ambitious operation in NATO history, and across Europe leaders worried about getting support at home. Then American military officials dropped a bombshell.

The Pentagon, they said, was considering withdrawing up to 3,000 soldiers from Afghanistan, roughly 20 percent of total American forces in the country at the time.

"It makes sense that as NATO forces go in and they're more in numbers," Gen. John P. Abizaid, the head of the United States Central Command at the time, said in an interview. "We could drop some of the U.S. requirements somewhat."[12] At the defense minister's meeting, Rumsfeld urged NATO countries to go beyond traditional peacekeeping, to mount combat operations, and eventually to take over security in eastern Afghanistan, the scene of some of the country's fiercest fighting.

"Over time, it would be nice if NATO developed counterterrorism capabilities," Rumsfeld said with characteristic diplomacy, "which don't exist at the present time."[13]

British, French, and German leaders immediately balked at the idea. The German defense minister, Peter Struck, said that shifting NATO's mission from peacekeeping to combat "would make the situation for our soldiers doubly dangerous and worsen the current climate in Afghanistan."[14]

In Kabul, the NATO takeover of the south and the proposed American troop reduction alarmed Afghan officials. Said T. Jawad, the Afghan ambassador to Washington, told me the proposed withdrawal was seen as the first stage of a long-term shift of American troops to Iraq.

"When there were indications the troop numbers might be reduced," said Jawad, "it raised a lot of concerns about whether the U.S. would stay."

NATO's secretary general, Jaap de Hoop Scheffer, protested to Rumsfeld that a partial American withdrawal would discourage others from sending troops. "I had a lot of telephone calls with him, making the case," de Hoop Scheffer told me in the spring of 2007, in his office in Brussels. "But have you ever tried arguing with Rumsfeld?"

In the end the planned troop reduction was abandoned, chiefly because Karl Eikenberry, the American ground commander at the time, and his team concluded that the Taliban were returning. In retrospect, it was Eikenberry who was the first to recognize how bad things were getting. He told Washington he needed to reinforce NATO efforts in the south and generate more combat power in the east to counter the Taliban. But the announcement had already sent a signal of a wavering American commitment. The warning sign was not missed by the people of Afghanistan, who feared that they would once again be forgotten by the Americans, as they had been after the defeat of the Soviets in the 1980s.

"They had been abandoned once," said Ronald E. Neumann, who replaced Khalilzad as the American ambassador in Kabul. "They are super, super sensitive about it happening again." Eikenberry put it more directly: "The Afghan people," he said, "still doubt our staying power."[15]

To sell their new missions at home, British, Dutch, and Canadian officials portrayed deployments to Afghanistan as safer and better than sending troops to Iraq. Other NATO countries, led by Germany and Italy, saw their mission in Afghanistan as traditional peacekeeping, and their national parliaments imposed restrictions to keep their forces out of combat missions in the volatile south and east. Those regions were to be left to the Americans, Canadians, British, and Dutch.

The White House meanwhile quietly reduced its financial commitment to Afghanistan. In December 2005, three months after the proposed troop withdrawal was announced, the Office of Management and Budget slashed aid to Afghanistan by a third.

I asked Rice and Hadley how they could make the case that they were more committed than ever to rebuilding Afghanistan, while cutting the funds for reconstruction. They argued that much of the money allocated to Afghanistan the previous year had not been spent, which was true. The Afghan bureaucracy was so inefficient that it could not spend what it had received.

"There was an absorption problem," Rice said.

But Americans in Afghanistan knew the danger that was created by the perception that American funding was being cut. Neumann said he had argued against the decision. Even so, a study by the Congressional Research Service concluded that American assistance to Afghanistan had dropped by 38 percent, from $4.3 billion in fiscal year 2005 to $3.1 billion in fiscal year 2006.[16]

Neumann said that Rice asked him to redirect $350 million in existing funds to meet "essential priorities." The result was that plans to expand the rebuilding of the country's power system, to extend agricultural development programs into drug-producing areas, and to increase the budgets of Provincial Reconstruction Teams were delayed.

By February 2006, Neumann was so concerned about the situation that he sat down in his office and composed a cable to his superiors in Washington. In a series of meetings with his staff and American military commanders over the previous several weeks, Neumann had come to the conclusion that the Taliban were planning a major spring offensive.

"I had a feeling that the view was too rosy in Washington," recalled Neumann, who retired from the State Department after serving as ambassador. "I was concerned."[17]

Neumann's cable proved prophetic. In the spring and summer of 2006, taking advantage of the ongoing transition in the south from battle-hardened experienced U.S. and coalition troops to newly arrived NATO forces, the Taliban carried out their largest offensive since 2001, attacking British, Canadian, and Dutch forces.

Hundreds of Taliban swarmed into the south, setting up road checkpoints, assassinating government officials, and burning schools. Suicide bombings quintupled, to 136. Roadside bombings doubled. All told, 191 American and NATO soldiers died in 2006, a 20-percent increase over the 2005 toll. For the first time it became nearly as dangerous, statistically, to serve as an American soldier in Afghanistan as it was in Iraq. (By the spring of 2008, it became far more dangerous to serve in Afghanistan, and after the "surge" in Iraq, American casualties in Afghanistan actually exceeded those in Iraq, even though there were a quarter of the number of American troops serving in the Afghan theater.)

Neumann said that while suicide bombers came from Pakistan, the vast majority of Taliban fighters in southern Afghanistan were local Afghans. Captured insurgents said they had taken up arms because the local governor favored a rival tribe, or because corrupt government officials provided no services, or because their families needed money. Ideology was not a major factor.

In retrospect, Neumann now believes the failure of the United States to support Karzai's fledgling government with serious reconstruction and large numbers of troops in 2002 and 2003 opened the door to the Taliban resurgence. Neumann credited the administration with eventually changing its approach, but noted that crucial time was lost and that the approach appeared episodic and driven from the bottom up. Given the rapid turnover of personnel on the ground, a steady top-down approach was required, but never materialized.

"The idea that we could just hunt terrorists and we didn't have to do nation building, and we could just leave it alone," he said, "that was a large mistake."[18]

The Taliban's spring offensive was successful not only in Afghanistan but in Pakistan, where pro-Taliban militants inflicted heavy casualties on the Pakistani Army in the tribal areas. The army was humiliated; if it couldn't take on these tribal groups, how could it hope to pose a deterrent to India?

Under pressure, Musharraf agreed in September 2006 to strike a "peace deal" with militant groups along the border with Afghanistan. The Pakistani leader had fallen under the spell of Gen. Ali Mohammad Jan Aurakzai, the commander of the Pakistani forces based in northwestern Pakistan. A tall, commanding figure who was raised in the tribal areas, he argued that the American warnings about new sanctuaries for al Qaeda and the Taliban were overblown. He told the *Times* that American warnings were based on "guesswork" and that his soldiers "found nothing" when they went to sites identified by the Americans. He told Musharraf that the most important thing was to avoid triggering a rebellion among the tribes. At one point in 2006

Musharraf brought Aurakzai to the White House for a meeting with Bush, where he made a detailed case that there was no problem in the region.[19]

Bush's counterterrorism team was horrified. "You just knew this was going to be a disaster," Fran Townsend, the head of the Homeland Security Council, said to me later. "But what could we do? Tell Musharraf he couldn't sign a truce inside his own country?"

The deal was simple: In exchange for Musharraf's agreement to remove troops and military checkpoints from the area, the local tribes would guarantee Taliban forces did not attack Pakistani soldiers. There was a vague agreement that the militants would not go into Afghanistan, but that was unenforceable. If the Pakistanis could monitor their borders, they wouldn't have needed a peace deal at all. Many U.S. officials were critical of the agreement, stating that the deal empowered the militants, allowing them to consolidate their position in Pakistan.[20] "They are taking territory," one Western ambassador in Pakistan reported. "They are becoming much more aggressive in Pakistan."[21]

The contentious issue of the peace agreements was also clearly visible during a private dinner at the White House attended by Karzai and Musharraf in September 2006. In the days before the dinner, Karzai had told a group of reporters at the *Times* that "the terrorism problem is in Pakistan, not Afghanistan," and accused Musharraf of turning his back on the problem. Then Musharraf got into the spat. Making the rounds on television shows to promote his forthcoming autobiography, Musharraf called Karzai "an ostrich with his head in the sand," accusing his counterpart of unfairly blaming the Taliban attacks on Pakistan.[22] Clearly this relationship was not working out the way Bush intended.

Now the two were sitting across the table from each other in the White House residence. Bush kept it small; Rice attended, but the idea was to get the two leaders to work together. Clearly, though, their relationship was ice-cold. The leaders avoided eye contact and refused to shake hands. Bush sat in between them, refereeing the meeting, which he later called, in a stretch, "a constructive exchange."[23] It wasn't. The two leaders went home, and cross-border attacks increased.

EVERY WEEK, according to intelligence officials I interviewed over the past two years, Bush began his meeting with the CIA director with a question about the hunt for bin Laden. And every week he got some version of the same answer: We're working on it, boss, but the trail is pretty cold.

In 2006, four years after the start of the war, and at the worst moment in Iraq, Bush came to the conclusion that Musharraf was never going to deliver. He signed off on a secret plan code-named Operation Cannonball, allowing the CIA to target al Qaeda operating in the tribal areas, specifically looking for bin Laden and Ayman al-Zawahiri, his deputy. U.S. intelligence officials, however, say that the operation was consistently undermined by disagreements within the Bush administration—and inside the CIA—over whether to take the risk of launching into the tribal areas.[24] There was a parallel debate among the CIA, the State Department, and the military's Joint Special Operations Command over how to get the job done, and how to manage the inevitable backlash when the wrong house was blown up, or American forces were captured.

The terrorist sanctuary in Pakistan was one of the hardest problems the Bush administration confronted. But like so many debates inside the Bush White House, this one never ended. Fran Townsend, who rose from a job at the Coast Guard to become Bush's most trusted adviser on homeland security, got a wake-up call about the magnitude of the problem one day in 2006 when she went to Fort Bragg, North Carolina, the home of the Joint Special Operations Command, the military's most secretive combatant command.

Townsend enjoyed her reputation as a renegade; there were not many short, female White House officials who were sent off for secret meetings with King Abdullah of Saudi Arabia and, in one confrontation that became the source of a lot of White House humor, a one-on-one with the Libyan strongman Muammar el-Qaddafi. Her diplomatic missions inspired a lot of resentment among the White House staff, but Bush trusted her, and the secret missions continued until she left in early 2008.

Townsend was too smart to ask permission before she took up Lt. Gen. Stanley McChrystal's standing offer to talk to the very unhappy Special Forces officers who had just returned from Afghanistan; she knew that Donald Rumsfeld, then about to get the ax as secretary of defense, would block the encounter. So without telling anyone she appended her drop-by at Fort Bragg to another, more innocuous trip.

"People will talk to me in a way they won't talk to a lot of others from the White House," she said to me one day after she had left the administration, "because I don't look quite so intimidating."

She started the session by telling the officers, "It is impossible to offend me." They took her at her word and, according to several who were present, years of frustration and anger poured out. As Townsend stood in the middle of a horseshoe-shaped conference table, one officer began with a simple demand: If someone asked her who was in charge of the search for bin Laden, what would she answer?

She said it was the CIA's job. But, she admitted, "they can't execute the mission" because they do not have sufficient paramilitary forces, "so they don't have this one by themselves." For that, the CIA needed the Special Forces—the elite group she was facing.

The officers responded that the search was being run by a two-headed hydra, each headed off in different directions. "What's the strategy to get these guys?" one officer demanded. "What's the campaign plan?" The reality, she had to admit, was that there was no real campaign plan, just a series of tactics and approaches that evolved over time. She asked them, "Why aren't you having this conversation with the CIA?" After she left, she called Stephen Kappes, the longtime director of operations at the CIA who returned in 2007 as the deputy director of the entire agency, a signal that long-trusted operatives were back in charge. Kappes was headed down to Fort Bragg for his own visit.

"Prepare yourself," she told him. "Brother, you are walking into a world of hurt."[25]

When she got back to the White House and reported that the men sent out to kill bin Laden thought there was no strategy, Steve Hadley had an urgent question for her: "What were you doing at Fort Bragg?"

IN JULY 2006, NATO formally took responsibility for security in the south of Afghanistan, and by the end of the year for the east, as well. To Americans and Europeans, NATO is the vaunted alliance that won the Cold War. To Afghans, it is little more than another strange new acronym. To the soldiers on the ground—and to the fractious politicians in Europe and the United States—one thing was obvious: NATO and the Americans never came up with a common strategy for winning in Afghanistan. By 2008, that division turned into a nightmare.

Like the Afghanistan War itself, the struggle between Washington and NATO started as a low-intensity conflict that quickly got out of hand. All through 2007, President Bush and Robert Gates, the former CIA director Bush turned to when Rumsfeld was fired in late 2006, escalated the pressure on NATO nations whose commitment to Afghanistan was about to expire. With the Taliban resurgent, Bush and Gates pressed them not only to stay, but to move their troops where they were most needed—to the south, where the confrontations were worst, but where the risks of casualties were also the greatest.

To make up for smaller numbers, Americans turned to their advantage: air power. When the fighting with the Taliban got intense, they called in airstrikes. Inevitably, a blunt instrument like air power causes major civilian casualties. When I visited NATO headquarters in the middle of 2007, one of those strikes had killed twenty-one civilians. And in the NATO cafeteria, where European officers balance espresso cups on their knees at 4:00 p.m.—creating the tableau of a force that doesn't quite look up to taking on the Taliban—there were complaints that the American tactics were turning the Afghans against the West. Still, as one senior NATO official said as the Americans were trying to smooth things over after the bombing that went bad, "Without air, we'd need hundreds of thousands of troops [in the country]."[26]

The argument is about far more than just a difference on proper tactics. At its core, the American mission in Afghanistan is one of counterterrorism. The Americans' first instinct is to hunt down the Taliban and eliminate them. The Europeans, in contrast, want to focus on reconstruction—the task they thought they signed up for when Burns persuaded them to come to Afghanistan. But by 2007, it became clear that those reconstruction projects could not proceed at a time when the Taliban were retaking villages and burning schools as fast as the West could build them. Trying to pressure the NATO allies to increase support for military operations, Gates, in testimony to Congress in December 2007, criticized the NATO commitment in Afghanistan. Voicing "frustration" at "our allies not being able to step up to the plate," he added that "I am not ready to let NATO off the hook in Afghanistan at this point." He ticked off vital requirements—about 3,500 more military trainers, twenty helicopters, and three infantry battalions.[27]

"Clearly, the Europeans do not see Afghanistan the way we do," said one former key commander of American forces. "They see it in terms of national reconstruction. We see Afghanistan as forward defense, and we are the only country willing to absorb significant casualties."

That difference of view reflects a badly divided command structure, one in which General McNeill commanded the NATO troops but not the Special Forces, or over the effort to build the Afghan forces who are key to any successful counterinsurgency. There is also no overall civilian responsibility for reconstruction—that is a job the Afghan government is supposed to be doing, but cannot.

"I never thought," McNeill said, "that I'd be wishing to create bureaucrats. But that's what I'm desperately wishing for."[28]

By the fall of 2007, the Bush administration came up with yet another plan to kick-start the reconstruction effort. Having given up hope that Karzai's government was capable of organizing the building of roads and schools and storage areas for farmers to bring their crops to market, they proposed creating an all-powerful czar who would manage the international effort on the ground in Afghanistan. And they had a man in mind: Lord Paddy Ashdown, a former commando turned British politician, who was widely credited for organizing efforts in Bosnia a few years before. Months of diplomacy went into getting the secretary general of the United Nations, Ban Ki Moon, to endorse the idea of a UN "coordinator" who could force countries to work together on the projects each was sponsoring.

By the end of 2007, an announcement seemed imminent. Karzai met with Ashdown during a trip to Kuwait in December and soon signed off on the whole idea. Not surprisingly, news of the upcoming announcement was leaked. And then trouble came: The press in Kabul, which often reflects the government's view, began comparing Ashdown to another famous Briton who showed up in Kabul: Sir William Macnaghten.

As historical analogies go, this was not a kind one. British schoolchildren learn Macnaghten's story as a cautionary tale in the cost of imperialist ventures: Sir William was murdered in 1841 in an uprising during the British occupation of Afghanistan. His body, minus the head and limbs, was hung from a pole in the bazaar. The following year the British withdrew from the country.

In the end, Karzai dragged his feet, and ultimately rejected the plan. In January 2008, meeting Rice and Gordon Brown, the British prime minister, at the annual Davos conference, he said that Afghanistan had "major problems" with bringing in a reconstruction czar. The problem was that Ashdown is British, and Karzai thought that the whole thing sniffed of British imperialism in a country that already had its share of colonial masters. Rice thought that Karzai feared that Ashdown would be far too powerful, a viceroy who controlled all the aid money, and therefore could make decisions for the Afghan government. Of course, that was part of the point. But when Karzai rejected the choice, the proposal died.

It didn't come as a surprise to anyone who had dealt with Karzai. While Bush publicly portrayed him as an indefatigable champion of democratic values, the rest of Bush's administration fumed that behind the sheen of Western urbanity, Karzai was a tool of the drug lords.

In 2006 and 2007, opium production mushroomed, and the country became the source of 93 percent of the world's heroin—not a statistic Bush was likely to cite in public. By some estimates, opium was now generating half of Afghanistan's GDP. Half of the production was in Helmand Province in the southwest, and it was no accident that the Taliban was strongest in the same place—they were being financed by the drug trade.

"Karzai was playing us like a fiddle," Thomas Schweich, a former State Department narcotics official, wrote in a *New York Times Magazine* article that also charged that the Afghan president's brother was in the middle of the trade. Schweich charged that when Karzai's attorney general gave the Afghan president a list of twenty corrupt officials, many with links to the narcotics trade, Karzai told him not to prosecute any of them. (Karzai insists he has fired many corrupt officials.)

Schweich summarized Karzai's strategy this way: "The U.S. would spend billions of dollars on infrastructure improvement; the U.S. and its allies would fight the Taliban; Karzai's friends could get rich off the drug trade; he could blame the West for his problems; and in 2009, he would be elected to a new term."[29]

Schweich's assessment may be too black-and-white; in a country plagued by corruption, Karzai was probably the best the United

States could do. But Schweich's description of the Bush administration's own failings are more damning than anything he could say about the Afghan president. The Pentagon, the State Department, and the Justice Department all had different philosophies about how to deal with the corrupting influence of the drug trade. When Schweich arrived in his job and asked for a copy of the interagency strategy to deal with the problem, he was told there was none. Once again, the Bush administration could not decide: As Bush left office, a semblance of a counterinsurgency strategy was coming together—but it differed from the strategy of our NATO allies.

UNTIL LATE 2007, Afghanistan was still what Gen. James Jones, a retired American officer and a former NATO supreme commander, called the "forgotten war." Washington was focused on the surge in Iraq. Afghanistan was the afterthought.

Across the border in Pakistan, the Taliban's resurgence became indistinguishable from al Qaeda's resurgence. Their relationship was a two-way street. The Taliban provided a safe haven and a support network; al Qaeda paid them in training, expertise, and financing. At least officially, the Bush administration denied that the situation in the tribal areas had spun out of control. So did Musharraf, who wrote in his autobiography, published in 2006, that "Pakistan has shattered the al Qaeda network in the region, severing its lateral and vertical linkages. It is now on the run and has ceased to exist as a homogeneous force."[30]

That was dubious spin when Musharraf wrote it. By July of 2007, it was farcical. That is when the American intelligence agencies released their assessment that the American strategy along the Afghanistan-Pakistan border had failed, partly blaming Musharraf's hands-off approach. "It hasn't worked for Pakistan," Townsend admitted to us. "It hasn't worked for the United States."[31]

The report confirmed the obvious: Bush and Musharraf might convince each other that the middle management of al Qaeda had been decimated, but the facts suggested otherwise. In plain language, the report concluded that al Qaeda had reorganized its command structure and was once again planning attacks against the United States. When I asked Townsend how Bush could keep arguing that Iraq was the "central front" in the war on terror—the front absorbing so much of our money, troops, and attention—she fell back to the argument that bin Laden had talked about Iraq as the central front, and therefore the White House had to do the same. Townsend, of course, did not believe that for a second—within the White House, she had been arguing for a far greater shift of resources.

Historians may argue for years whether a fuller commitment to Afghanistan could have prevented that safe haven from being formed across the Pakistan border. But many Americans with long experience in the region believe that President Bush's insistence that Iraq was the "central front" in the war on terror was more than wrong—it raised the cost of solving the problem later.

THE DEBATE over how the 2001 victory in Afghanistan turned into the current struggle is well under way.

"Destroying the al Qaeda sanctuary in Afghanistan was an extraordinary strategic accomplishment," said Robert D. Blackwill, who was in charge of both Afghanistan and Iraq policy at the National Security Council, "but where we find ourselves now may have been close to inevitable, whether the U.S. went into Iraq or not. We were going to face this long war in Afghanistan as long as we and the Afghan government couldn't bring serious economic reconstruction to the countryside, and eliminate the Taliban's safe havens in Pakistan."[32]

Between the summer of 2007 and the summer of 2008, a clear consensus emerged from my conversations with current and former officials: A consistent, forceful American effort could have helped to prevent the Taliban and al Qaeda's leadership from regrouping. But Bush himself, and those closest to him, could not bring themselves to that conclusion.

General Jones, the former NATO commander, said the invasion of Iraq caused the United States to "take its eye off the ball" in Afghanistan. He warned that the consequences of failure "are just as serious in Afghanistan as they are in Iraq."[33]

"Symbolically, it's more the epicenter of terrorism than Iraq," he told me. "If we don't succeed in Afghanistan, you're sending a very clear message to the terrorist organizations that the U.S., the UN, and the thirty-seven countries with troops on the ground can be defeated."

It is not that Bush did nothing to turn back the Taliban's advances. As part of the "surge" effort in Iraq in 2007, he ordered an increase in the number of troops to Afghanistan, and pressured the NATO allies to follow suit in order to prevent a resurgent Taliban from launching a spring offensive. By the end of 2007, White House officials insisted that the additional troops had succeeded; they pointed to evidence that attacks were beginning to recede. Once again it was wishful thinking.

But in an interview just days before Christmas that year, General Lute, the coordinator for Iraq and Afghanistan, freely acknowledged that to hold villages in Afghanistan, the United States and its allies needed far more. "We've seen what we can do with just an extra battalion or two floating around the south," he said. "But we're still retaking ground that we won weeks ago, or months ago, and then could not hold." He spoke almost exactly six years to the day since the Taliban was ousted. The United States and its allies had defeated both Nazi Germany and Imperial Japan in less time. Fighting wars of counterinsurgency, it turned out, was something even the world's greatest superpower was not prepared for.

It took years before it was clear to many in Washington that the premature declaration of victory over the Taliban, and the subsequent decision to move on to Iraq without looking back, amounted to one of the biggest miscalculations by the country's leadership in modern American military history. Washington had it backward. The Afghans were interested in seeing the United States stay; they had listened to Bush's Marshall Plan speech and assumed that cargo planes full of supplies would soon be arriving in Kabul, with aid to be disbursed throughout the country. An era of economic revitalization would follow, the way spring follows winter in the high passes. It never happened. By the summer of 2008, Condoleezza Rice was asking what had happened to the Provincial Reconstruction Teams she had created.

It is impossible to know how long American troops would have been required to stay in Afghanistan had Washington concentrated fully on finishing the task it started with such success. But since the Taliban has been allowed to regroup, and developed a symbiotic relationship with its al Qaeda neighbors and other insurgents in the tribal areas, it will take years, maybe decades, before America can leave without risk that the country could collapse, and revert to its pre-9/11 status as a Petri dish for terrorists.

As the 2008 presidential campaign heated up, Barack Obama argued that the central front in the war on terror was along the Pakistan-Afghanistan border, and in the towns in Afghanistan that the Taliban were retaking. Many of his supporters cringed whenever they heard Obama talk about increasing the American force in Afghanistan; after all, they had been drawn to him as the antiwar candidate. But Obama needed to provide his defense credentials, and for him Afghanistan was the right war.

For McCain it was more complicated. "I agreed with both General Petraeus and Osama bin Laden, who both said that Iraq was the central battleground in this struggle," McCain insisted. "And I also believe that Afghanistan is going to be a longer struggle in some respects."

As they were packing up to move out of the White House, the Bush administration recognized as well that America would be in Afghanistan for years—but Bush never acknowledged it. Instead, he talked about the big increase in troops that would be needed in

2009, after he left office. He was not interested in entertaining questions about why those troops were not sent years before. Stephen Hadley, who had argued so strenuously to me in 2007 that the White House had never held back on sending needed troops to Afghanistan, acknowledged that another big increase would be necessary after Bush left office. That was quite a shift for an administration that thought it had the war won in 2002.

Yet by the fall of 2008, the United States was still not deployed to face the threat. There were still four times more forces in Iraq than in Afghanistan. Violence was soaring. Some months the number of American casualties in Afghanistan exceeded the number in Iraq. The once-quiet streets of Kandahar, where the NATO ambassadors had once sipped tea with the tribal leaders, became the site of regular suicide bombings and a wave of kidnappings, aimed at further eroding public support in Europe for the NATO mission.

"When you look back on it now, it's blindingly obvious we never defeated the Taliban and we never finished the Afghan war," David Kilcullen told me one night after he had just returned from a long visit to Iraq—and on his way to survey the damage in Afghanistan. In six years, he said, "We just shifted our problem to the east," just over the Pakistani border.

"It sounds harsh," said Kilcullen, who left the State Department a frustrated man, "but that's what we accomplished."[34]

# PART III

## PAKISTAN

# "How Do You Invade an Ally?"

# CHAPTER 7

# SECRETS OF CHAKLALA CANTONMENT

We were compelled to show in May 1998 that we were not
bluffing, and in May 2002, again, we were compelled to show
that we do not bluff.

— Former President Pervez Musharraf, June 17, 2002,
quoted in a plaque on Khalid Kidwai's office wall

TO GET TO the headquarters of the blandly named Strategic Plans
Division, the branch of the Pakistani government charged with
keeping the country's growing arsenal of nuclear weapons out of the
hands of al Qaeda and its militant Islamist sympathizers, you must
drive down a rutted, debris-strewn road at the edge of the Islamabad
airport.

Stray dogs and the homeless wander along a street lined with
crumbling and collapsing houses, some of which are just piles of
brick with corrugated metal roofs held down by heavy stones.
Garbage piles up, uncollected, for months. In the distance you can
see the haze of exhaust that seems to hover permanently over the
nearest town, Rawalpindi.

Just past a small traffic circle, a tan stone gateway looms,
manned by a lone, bored-looking guard loosely holding a rusting
rifle. It marks the entry to Chaklala Cantonment, an old British

garrison from the days when officers of the Raj escaped the heat of Delhi for the cooler hills on the approaches to Afghanistan. Pass under the archway, and the poverty and chaos of modern Pakistan disappear.

Chaklala is the well-tended home of the country's military and intelligence services, a reminder that in Pakistan the bulk of power rests with those two institutions, sometimes operating with brutal efficiency, but just as often undercutting each other. Not surprisingly, both the army and the Directorate for Inter-Services Intelligence, known as the ISI, have reserved society's best privileges for themselves. Inside the gates, they live in trim houses with well-tended lawns. Business is conducted in long, low office buildings that look like a single-level motel, with a bevy of well-pressed adjutants buzzing around.

About three-quarters of a mile down the road within the walls of the garrison and barely marked, lies the small compound for Strategic Plans, where Khalid Kidwai keeps the country's nuclear keys—and watches for any sign that Pakistan might, for the second time in recent history, be vulnerable to another major breach of its nuclear secrets, another attack from within.

The reality of the Second Nuclear Age is that, in the end, what happens or fails to happen in Khalid Kidwai's modest compound on the edge of the Islamabad airport is far more likely to save or lose an American city than are the billions of dollars we spend each year maintaining a nuclear arsenal that will never be used, or the thousands of lives and hundreds of billions of dollars we lost in Iraq. Yet Pakistan's ability to control its arsenal ranks among the least understood, least discussed, and in many ways the scariest nuclear challenges facing the next president—and, if we continue to be lucky, presidents for years to come. For while there are reasons to worry about loose nuclear material in Russia—a situation that remains worrisome, but less worrisome than it was a decade ago—Pakistan is the only nuclear state with a powerful militant insurgency in its midst, one that clearly has aims to take over the country, and desperately wants to acquire the Bomb. It does not help matters that the government has veered between a dictatorship that has supported both the United States and the Taliban and a newly elected democratic leadership known chiefly for its corruption and ineptitude.

Kidwai is fifty-eight, a compact man with an arch sense of humor, often hidden beneath a veil of caution, as if he were previewing each sentence to decide if it reveals too much. He was installed in his post, perhaps the most sensitive in Pakistan, by Musharraf himself, and for the nine years of Musharraf's rule, the two men remained close. Their worldviews were shaped by the Pakistan Army. They also share the army's demeanor—a preternatural calm meant to convey to Pakistanis and the outside world that everything is under control, no matter how bad things get. In 2007, both shed their uniforms but held on to their civilian posts—Musharraf as president, Kidwai as keeper of the country's nuclear arsenal. Musharraf's luck ran out, however, in August 2008, when he was forced to step down.

But Kidwai has held on to his job—a fact that some insiders in Washington consider far more consequential to American interests than who is sitting in the presidential palace. Kidwai oversees the entire security structure meant to keep Pakistan's nuclear weapons and fuel out of the hands of outsiders—Islamic militants, al Qaeda scientists, Indian saboteurs, even American Special Forces teams that the Pakistanis fear are perpetually bobbing just offshore, refining their plans to snatch Pakistan's weapons if a crisis erupts. (It is not an entirely unwarranted fear.)

In Washington, American officials know Kidwai because he was on the receiving end of one of the most tightly held secret projects with Pakistan since 9/11: a classified, nearly $100 million effort, financed by American taxpayers, to teach Pakistan how to lock down its nuclear- weapons. Even though American officials had only Kidwai's assurances about how the money would be spent—auditors were prohibited by the Pakistanis, who refused to let foreigners into their most sensitive nuclear sites—Bush determined it was worth the risk.

The alternative was to do nothing to help secure an arsenal of upward of a hundred nuclear weapons, in the most volatile corner of the world. The program was one of the reasons that American officials insisted, during Pakistan's descent into chaos in late 2007, that they had no reason to doubt Pakistani claims that the nuclear infrastructure was secure.

Privately, though, they admitted they had plenty to lose sleep about. While there was little doubt the weapons themselves were relatively safe, there was plenty of reason to wonder about the security of Pakistan's laboratories, including the one still named for A. Q. Khan, years after the conniving metallurgist had been disgraced for his sale of Pakistan's nuclear secrets.

There was more—a threat whose severity President Bush and his top aides spent much of 2008 trying to assess. In the spring of that year, as Musharraf was losing his grip on power, an urgent new stream of reporting began coursing its way through the CIA, the Pentagon, and the White House. Al Qaeda and other militant groups were focusing anew on the Holy Grail that had eluded them before 9/11: stealing the secrets to the Pakistani bomb.

In the '90s, al Qaeda had fallen for at least one nuclear scam, buying up a box full of useless radioactive junk. Now there was evidence suggesting that al Qaeda and other terror groups were attempting to take a different road to the same destination. They were recruiting Pakistanis who had been trained in nuclear sciences and engineering abroad to try to figure out which ones might harbor sympathy for radical Islamic causes. According to an American intelligence report that was restricted to very senior officials in Bush's war cabinet, a few of those scientists appeared to be returning to Pakistan to seek jobs within the country's nuclear infrastructure.

By the spring of 2008, the entire top tier of the national security leadership in Washington had been briefed on the intelligence assessment. "I have two worries," one senior official who had read all of the intelligence with care told me, as the reports were circulating.

"One is [what happens] when they move the weapons. And the second is what I believe are steadfast efforts of different extremist groups to infiltrate the labs and put sleepers and so on in there."

Quietly, American intelligence officials alerted their Pakistani counterparts, including Kidwai, about the threat. But like the warnings of airplane plots prior to 9/11, none of it seemed "actionable": There were no specific names or places.

"This is all overblown rhetoric," Kidwai told me soon after we settled into the big white leather chairs in his spacious office inside the garrison, decorated with models of the missiles that can carry nuclear payloads to India and beyond. It was a Saturday morning, and things were quiet at the Strategic Plans Division. He had time to pace me through the layers upon layers of protections that he and Musharraf had pieced together as Pakistan moved from nuclear pariah to the world's eighth nuclear power.

"Please grant to Pakistan that if we can make nuclear weapons and the delivery systems," Kidwai said, gesturing to the models of the missiles and a photo of Pakistan's first nuclear test, a decade ago, "we can also make them safe. Our security systems are foolproof. This is what gives us the confidence that what happened before with Dr. A. Q. Khan—it could never happen again."[1]

"WHAT HAPPENED BEFORE" is the greatest known breach of nuclear security in the atomic age, a breach the Pakistanis calmly denied for years was happening at all.

Apart from the country's founder, Mohammed Ali Jinnah, who died in 1948, Pakistan may have no more revered hero than Khan, now seventy-two and in remission from prostate cancer. It was Khan—metallurgist, egoist, first-class self-promoter—who crowned himself "Father of the Pakistani Bomb," a title to which others could rightfully lay equal claim. Most Pakistanis, however, do not care about the shameless self-promotion, or even about the brazen crimes Khan committed as he sold the fruits of Pakistan's nuclear program around the globe. In Islamabad, some taxi drivers still keep a picture of him dangling from their rearview mirrors.

For the roughly 160 million citizens of Pakistan, the popular narrative recalls how Khan, through a mix of stealth and savvy, figured out how to even the score with India and Western powers by turning a poor, fractious country into a nuclear player by the late 1980s, a decade before its nuclear test. Since that test, Pakistan has made the leap from international outlaw to an accepted, acknowledged nuclear power that the world must respect and fear. Even today, one widely read Urdu-language newspaper in Islamabad runs a daily feature about how many days Khan has been kept under house arrest, albeit in luxurious incarceration, and berates the government for failing to free him.

That protest may soon prove successful: In the summer of 2008, a Pakistani court relaxed some of the restrictions on Khan, though it ordered him to stop talking about his past. No doubt that gag order came as a relief to many Pakistani politicians and military officers, who are a lot more concerned about what Khan says than about what he does. They have reason to worry. Tired of his incarceration, embittered at Musharraf for pardoning him and then imprisoning him, perhaps emboldened by the sporadic protests suggesting *he* should have been elected Musharraf's successor, Khan had begun hinting that he was getting ready to talk. Specifically, he threatened to talk about who inside the country's power structure had been aware of what he was doing, and who was complicit. For example, he said in one conversation, there was a shipment of centrifuges—the giant machines that spin at supersonic speeds, enriching uranium into fuel—that he sent to North Korea when Musharraf was still chief of the army.

"It was a North Korean plane, and the army had complete knowledge about it and the equipment," Khan said. Did that mean Musharraf, America's ally, knew? "It must have gone with his consent," Khan responded, offering no evidence.[2]

Musharraf, of course, denied knowing anything, and in a lengthy interview in 2005 he told me that he had courageously taken on Khan. But whatever the truth, Khan brilliantly exploited his hero status, creating a culture of deference and secrecy that completely enveloped him and the bomb project into which Pakistan poured its sparse treasure. He was protected by a political and military elite that desperately wanted the bomb and were happy not to ask questions about his deal-making or demand to know how a Pakistani bureaucrat on a government salary could afford a house in Islamabad's best neighborhood and properties abroad. Their deliberate absence of curiosity gave Khan the opportunity he sought.

In the 1980s, when Pakistan already possessed a crude device but was still a decade away from testing it, Khan began to build a multinational network—stretching from Kuala Lumpur to Dubai and Capetown—that packaged and sold the nuclear technology he had accumulated throughout the years. Over time, this illicit project went far beyond selling the designs for uranium enrichment technology that Khan himself stole from Europe decades ago for Pakistan's own indigenous weapons program.

Khan was once at the center of almost every major nuclear flashpoint the United States faces today. It was Khan who sold Iran the uranium enrichment equipment and designs that put it within reach of a bomb and on a collision course with the West. It was Khan who sold the North Koreans those centrifuges, which they thought they needed to explore a new path to making weapons, after their first efforts—producing plutonium from an aging nuclear reactor— were shut down by the Clinton administration in the mid-1990s. And it was Khan who not only delivered the Libyans more than $100-million worth in centrifuges but threw in a bonus, wrapped inside the plastic bags from the dry cleaner near his house: the nearly complete blueprints for the bomb China set off in the mid-1960s. After a brief standoff in Tripoli between American officials and international inspectors over who should hold on to the confiscated designs, they were flown back on a special flight to Dulles Airport and stored in a secure underground room in the Energy Department, off the National Mall in Washington, as investigators tried to figure out who else had gotten access to the plans.

It turned out Khan had other designs as well. Deep in his computer systems he hid other, far more sophisticated blueprints. To the investigators who uncovered them long after Khan was already under arrest, the designs appeared to be for the Pakistani bomb. To this day, even while publicly celebrating the shattering of the Khan network as a rare coup for the intelligence community, investigators around the world are struggling to understand who else bought these far more complex plans, the recipe for the Pakistani arsenal. As I traveled the world exploring potential national security crises, the Pakistani bomb designs that got away elicited the longest silences, the most artful evasions, and, among those willing to talk, the most concern.

ASTOUNDINGLY, Khan's perfidy unfolded within miles of Kidwai's headquarters. Khan Research Laboratories, where the power-hungry scientist built his empire and shipped out his equipment, is just down the road from Chaklala Garrison. From the highway you can't miss the laboratory's entrance: It is marked by a replica of a Pakistani missile, one of many government-financed monuments to the accomplishments of a man still considered a hero by most Pakistanis. On the other side of the garrison lies the airstrip Khan turned into his own personal FedEx hub, where a mix of charter planes and Pakistani Air Force cargo craft—provided to the country by the United States—were used to ship Pakistan's nuclear centrifuges and other equipment to clients who paid him hundreds of millions of dollars. (The exact amounts have never been made public.) To this day, the Pakistani military swears they had no idea what Khan was doing—an assertion American and British investigators have found difficult to believe.

Venture a few miles beyond the gates into the chaos of

Rawalpindi, and there are constant reminders of why the world fears what could happen if Pakistan melts down. As al Qaeda and the Taliban have seen their chance to destabilize Pakistan, Rawalpindi has become an assassin's playground. Twice it was the site of efforts to blow up Musharraf's motorcade, a plot later tied to both al Qaeda and members of Pakistan's own military. By 2007, extremists had turned their sights on Benazir Bhutto. They attacked her and her followers on the day she returned to Pakistan to run against Musharraf. She survived. But it was only a matter of time, and in late December 2007, as she emerged from a decrepit park where she had just addressed thousands, they succeeded. The second attack, a mix of bullets and a suicide bombing, was as messy and chaotic as the country. It was a moment of raw violence that echoed Pakistan's history: The park Bhutto had spoken in was named for the country's first prime minister, Liaquat Ali Khan, who was assassinated fifty-six years before, just a few hundred yards away. (In one of those bizarre twists of history, the doctor who tried, unsuccessfully, to revive Bhutto at Rawalpindi's main hospital was the son of the doctor who tried, unsuccessfully, to revive Liaquat Khan.)

Those assassinations were products of different but linked conflicts that rip at Pakistan's core. Liaquat Khan was assassinated by a Pashtun separatist, in retaliation for the prime minister's insistence that Pakistan must extend its writ of control over the restive tribal lands along the border with Afghanistan. A century and a half ago, those same lands were a hotbed of opposition to the British. Today they have become the new sanctuary of al Qaeda, the Taliban, and a second generation of militants like Baitullah Mehsud, who has been accused by both the Americans and the Pakistanis of dispatching Bhutto's assassins. Three months after her death, the Pakistanis I met near the park believed—rightly or wrongly—that she was killed in part because she was an American puppet who talked of targeting those militants, and even of letting international investigators interview A. Q. Khan, something Musharraf had strictly forbidden.

Even Musharraf, who was denying charges that his government had failed to protect his rival, couldn't bring himself to fake much regret about how she met her end.

"She was very unpopular with the military. Very unpopular," he said a few weeks after her death. She was seen, he said, as an "alien" by Islamic leaders, flaunting the degree to which she was "a nonreligious person." And she forgot the first rule of Pakistani politics: "Don't be seen as an extension of the United States. Now I am branded as an extension," he said, "but not to the extent she was."[3]

Whatever its motivation, Bhutto's assassination reinforced the sense in the West that Pakistan remains one anarchic turn away from spinning out of control. The summer before her death, there had been the bloody shoot-out with militants at the Red Mosque in Islamabad, the sudden appearance of suicide bombers in the heart of the capital, followed by the power struggles on the streets between Musharraf's forces and lawyers seeking the restoration of judges that Musharraf had dismissed for challenging his power. Taken together, all of these events raised fundamental questions few in Washington wanted to discuss publicly: Could a modern nuclear state lose control of its arsenal? Could another A. Q. Khan or, worse, Islamic fundamentalists gain access to nuclear designs or fuel? And if the worst case came to pass, was there anything we could do?

THE MAN WHO THINKS about these questions every day is Rolf Mowatt-Larssen, a former CIA officer who helped crack the Khan network and confidant of the former director of the agency, George Tenet.

These days Mowatt-Larssen has moved into the center of Washington—the National Mall, ground zero if trouble breaks out—working from an office within a secure vault in the basement of the Energy Department. The department is responsible for developing and maintaining the country's nuclear stockpile, and its intelligence division, which Mowatt-Larssen runs, has access to the government's best technical expertise on what it takes to make a bomb, and how to keep someone from getting what they need to build one.

In the corner of his office, where many people would keep a potted plant, Mowatt-Larssen keeps a centrifuge standing against the wall—one of Khan's, given to him after the Libyans surrendered their purchases from the Khan network. It is a reminder, one he sees every time he looks up from his computer, of how easy it is these days for shadowy networks to deal in the technology that was once the sole property of nations. Mowatt-Larssen is paid to design the worst-case scenarios about how quickly a country or a terror group could move from centrifuge to bomb—and then to test those assumptions against the fortunate reality that it's all harder than it looks.

But he also digs deeper, into the statements and philosophy of Islamic radicals, and sometimes comes out in some interesting places. I asked him about the assumption, taken as an article of faith among many that if al Qaeda ever bought or made a nuclear device, it would use it immediately.

"I don't think we know if that's true," Mowatt-Larssen told me. "There would need to be some religious rationale first," he argued, especially now that an alternative narrative has broken out in the Islamic world, one in which al Qaeda's tactics are creating a backlash that could be undermining its own goals.[4]

He described to me the struggle al Qaeda went through to devise the proper religious justification for obtaining and using a weapon that might kill the faithful along with the infidels. The high-water mark of that effort may have come in 2003, he noted, when al Qaeda obtained a fatwa from a sympathetic Saudi cleric, Nasir bin Hamid al-Fahd, who argued that while the use of nuclear or biological weapons by infidels would be unlawful, it was permissible by those defending the Muslim faith. Saudi authorities, as part of their effort to stamp out the al Qaeda forces that have tried so hard to oust the al Saud family, forced him to appear on television later that year to recant some of his rulings.

But Mowatt-Larssen is convinced that al Qaeda would have pressured a cleric to make such a ruling only if it thought it needed a religious justification for future actions. From his basement office, he monitors not only the movement of nuclear materials, he monitors the movement of Islamic opinion. An ideological war has broken out among Islamic militants over the question of whether Islamic law allows the kind of violence that made al Qaeda famous. There are some signs Ayman al-Zawahiri, bin Laden's second in command, may have held back on a chemical weapons attack a few years back because he feared the backlash.[5] But no one is willing to count on Zawahiri's sense of restraint.

Instead, war planners in Washington focus on capabilities, and that is where Pakistan—and Kidwai's operation—become the central concern. Pakistan is the place where a fractious and corrupt government, an abundance of weapons, nuclear fuel and designs, and fatwas like al Fahd's all coexist within a few hundred square miles around Islamabad. And so, very quietly, because the backlash by the Pakistanis would be so severe, Mowatt-Larssen has tried to test the question of what happens if suddenly those weapons are in play.

That journey has led his intelligence operation inside the Energy Department, along with colleagues at other intelligence agencies, the Pentagon, and Special Forces commands, to conduct a series of what they benignly call "tabletop exercises" in which a chunk of nuclear material is suddenly assumed to be missing somewhere in Pakistan. Virtually every time, the scenarios end in a murky sea of ambiguity. Top officials in Islamabad and Washington can't get a clear picture of what happened, or of what's happening next, much less decide what to do about it. And by the time a clear picture does emerge, it is too late to do much except panic.

"The fear is that sometime in the next few years, someone is going to have to wake up the president and tell him that we think— we don't know, we think—that ten Pakistani weapons are missing, and we can only suspect who has them," said David Rothkopf, a former Clinton administration official who wrote one of the leading studies of decision-making within the National Security Council. "But it doesn't play out like it does in the television shows. Not only can't you order a preemptive strike, you don't know where to strike. Or even what's really missing. It's the classic post–Cold War nightmare."

Ashton B. Carter, another former Clinton administration official, has taken the scenario one step further for Harvard's Preventive Defense Project: He has assembled government officials to play out the scenario the "day after"—that is, the day after a weapon goes off in an American city.

"There's a 90-percent chance it will come out of the old Soviet arsenal or out of Pakistan's program," says Carter. "And once you figure out which one it came out of, what do you do? Launch a nuclear strike against an ally for something the president of the country probably didn't know was missing? When's he's still got a closet full of nuclear missiles? Not going to happen. And so that leaves the only other option: Find a way to lock it down now."

CARTER IS RIGHT: When the biggest threat looks more like loose nukes that escape Pakistan than launched nukes out of Russia, all the old tricks for avoiding Armageddon don't work. Our nuclear arsenal has become the Maginot Line of the age of terror: big, scary, and fundamentally useless as a deterrent. It was designed for a different age, for weapons that came streaking into the United States from silos in the Soviet Union, tracked every step of the way on a giant monitor deep in the mountains of Colorado. However, if a bomb gets out of Pakistan, it's unlikely to be on a missile, and it won't be showing up on that screen.

Every television producer worth an Emmy Award figured this out years ago, spawning the dozens of movies and series in which bad guys get a load of uranium or plutonium, and the only way to stop it is to send Jack Bauer into their basement. The drama hinges on whether the traffic is so bad on the Los Angeles highways that he'll arrive too late. By comparison, going around the world trying to fix every decrepit nuclear storage site, building double fences and training local police to use radiation detectors doesn't make for very exciting television.

Apparently, it turns out not to make for very exciting policy, either. Wherever I have traveled around the world—talking to American intelligence officers in Pakistan, military officials who patrol the Pacific, or the Homeland Security officials who spend their days thinking about attacks on the nation's capital—they all say the same thing: As the situation in Iraq worsened, the post-9/11 efforts to create a multilayered defense against a domestic WMD attack waned, even though Bush and his aides readily acknowledged that no terror group on earth could pose an existential threat to the United States unless they obtained a nuclear or biological weapon.

The United States spends a little more than a billion dollars a year locking down nuclear material outside the United States—not a small amount of money, but only a tenth of what we spend on missile defense, a technology that assumes the next attack on the United States or its allies will come streaking across the sky the old-fashioned way.

It is not that nothing is being done—there are new bureaucracies, chiefly the behemoth born of 9/11, the Department of Homeland Security. But the easy fixes are over, and the hard work of investing in a truly multilayered defense against nuclear and biological attacks lies ahead.

"Look, I don't think you are going to see someone drive a commercial airliner into buildings again. It could happen, but I think we've sealed that up pretty well," said Adm. Timothy Keating, who headed the newly created "Northern Command," the military command set up specifically to coordinate the military response to another 9/11. (He is now in charge of all U.S. forces in the Pacific.) What worries Keating is that the United States may once again be experiencing a failure of imagination, this time about a nuclear weapon flown into the country "on a private G-5 [Gulfstream V] aircraft, for example, or the ease of a biological attack. I worry about that, even if you have to say it is unlikely."[6]

It is only one of the huge loopholes left in America's defenses. "It amazes me," said John F. Lehman, a Republican and secretary of the navy under Ronald Reagan, who looked at this issue as a member of the 9/11 Commission. In December 2005, a year after the commission issued its findings, its members reconvened to issue a report card on how well the Bush administration and Congress did at sealing up the huge vulnerabilities discovered during the investigation. The report card was a sea of C's, D's, and F's, including a D for one of the most important recommendations: a "maximum effort" by the U.S. government to secure the world's nuclear weapons. The report concluded that "countering the greatest threat to America's security is still not the top national security priority of the president and Congress."

I ran into Lehman in May 2008, when he was actively advising John McCain and asked if he had seen any improvement. "No," he said. "It's gotten worse." Our investment in real defense, he noted, defense against the single weapon that gets smuggled into a city in the United States or another city around the world, remained pitiful. Our strategy for dealing with Pakistan and its weapons was in disarray, to be generous. The result is that the United States has stumbled along with no real plan, just a series of largely disconnected, underfunded programs.

To his credit, Bush started one truly great innovation in this area. It was largely the invention of Robert Joseph, who in Bush's first term drove the White House to focus far more on "counterproliferation" (actively intervening to destroy or seize weapons) than on "nonproliferation" (keeping countries from going nuclear). Conservatives and liberals have been in an endless debate about which one is a smarter approach; the reality is that both are needed, simultaneously. No future president, Democrat or Republican, will ever have the luxury of picking one or the other.

Joseph's creation was called the Proliferation Security Initiative, and it involved informally signing up countries to intercept nuclear or biological shipments. Joseph deliberately steered clear of treaties or negotiated agreements "because they take ten years to happen," he once told me. Instead, he focused on the laws each country already had on the books and pressing leaders to view those authorities more broadly. So far, more than seventy countries have signed on, some with more enthusiasm than others, and periodically members of the group hold exercises to board ships or intercept airplanes, demonstrating that they are serious about working together.

There are holes in the system: Pakistan refused to join, fearing it would be a target rather than a partner. South Korea initially refused to join, fearing it would anger the North, but eventually joined in 2009. And enough countries signed up that once a shipment of missiles to Syria or centrifuges to Iran are detected, there is an international procedure for stopping the ship or plane, especially if it stops for refueling.

That marks a huge advance. Until the Bush administration pressed countries to sign up, there was no effective way to halt such shipments. But by definition, the Proliferation Security Initiative is a backup measure that involves chasing down materials once they are en route to another country. It depends on superb intelligence and quick response. You cannot count on either.

That is why cutting off new supplies of nuclear fuel is so important, and fleetingly it seemed that Bush would be serious about getting something done. In 2004—right after the Khan network was broken up—he went to the National Defense University in Washington to lay out a seven-part plan to limit trade in nuclear material, calling for a halt on such shipments "to any state that does not already possess full-scale, functioning enrichment and reprocessing plants." Of course, the language created a double-standard: Countries such as Iran would be prohibited from making nuclear fuel, even though they are signatories to the Nuclear Non-Proliferation

Treaty. Any of America's friends who are already in the business—Japan or European countries, even nuclear renegades such as Pakistan—would be allowed to continue.

Some of Bush's closest allies began objecting. Canada and Australia, two countries that contributed critical forces in Afghanistan and Iraq, argued that they wanted to start their own enrichment operations to extract additional revenue from the uranium that they mined. Soon Bush simply stopped talking about his plan. It disappeared from the agenda at international meetings. Like Bush's speech about a Marshall Plan for Afghanistan, or a national effort to rebuild New Orleans, his main proposal to limit the amount of nuclear fuel produced in the world fizzled.

Then Bush did something that made things worse: He struck a deal with India that would allow the country, for the first time, to get civilian nuclear technology from the United States. For decades, such trade has been illegal because India never signed the Nuclear Non-Proliferation Treaty—one of only three countries that refused. (Pakistan and Israel also never signed, and North Korea quit the treaty in 2003.) American law made it illegal for any American firm to help India's civilian nuclear power program. For years the Indians had lobbied in Washington to get the ban lifted, arguing that the world's most populous democracy deserved better from the United States.

Eventually, that logic won out. In his second term, looking for a way to deepen the relationship with India—partly as a hedge against a rising China—Bush agreed to negotiate a deal that would allow American firms to export technology to India—worth billions—along with nuclear expertise. But the negotiations went terribly for the United States. Bush and his chief negotiator, Nicholas Burns, were never able to extract a promise from the Indians that in return for American assistance they would stop producing weapons-grade nuclear fuel and stop expanding their arsenal. Desperate for a deal, Bush signed anyway.

Of course, every kilogram of nuclear fuel that the United States sold the Indians to use in their power plants freed up some fuel to make more weapons. Pakistan, of course, vowed that if the Indians built more weapons, so would they. Bush, in short, accelerated the arms race in South Asia.

"This took stupid to new levels," a senior American military official in Islamabad said to me in the spring of 2008. "We're going into the Paks every day and warning, 'Look, you have to lock up your weapons and all your fuel, because the more there is, the better the chance that one day you are going to wake up and discover Osama's got some of it.' And they say, 'That's your problem. You're helping the Indians, and wasn't it Bush who said *we* are America's great ally against terrorism?'

"Who are we kidding?" the senior military official asked. "Musharraf? Ourselves?"

The result is that Kidwai sits in his office overseeing two separate missions. One is to plan Pakistan's nuclear future, as it keeps building more and better weapons. The other is to convince skeptical visitors that what happened a few years ago could never happen again—even if Pakistan goes up in flames.

KIDWAI'S PROBLEM is that every time he tries to convince the world that in Pakistan everything *is* locked down, people familiar with the country's history have the same reaction: We've heard it all before.

When the *Times* published its first lengthy investigative piece about Khan's activities in January 2004, a Pakistani government spokesman reflexively denounced the article as "a pack of lies." A month later, Khan was forced by Musharraf to "confess," though he never said exactly what he was confessing. He was never charged, never tried, and never convicted. He was simply pardoned and put under house arrest—the best way to keep the details of how he raided Pakistan's nuclear secrets out of the press. When the CIA or international investigators had questions for him, they had to route them through the Pakistani government. The answers they got back, one of the top investigators said to me one day, "are the answers the Pakistanis want us to hear."

Today Kidwai argues that the Khan era is over and the West just does not recognize the progress the Strategic Plans Division has made. Though he will not go into details, he nods in silent agreement when asked if American experts are correct in assuming that Pakistan stores its missiles separately from its warheads, and its warheads separately from their nuclear triggers, making it more difficult for terrorists to acquire all the components they need.

He keeps a PowerPoint presentation at the ready in his conference room to show how 2,000 scientists with "critical knowledge" of nuclear technology are constantly monitored, vetted, and subjected to psychological profiling. In recent years the monitoring has extended to retired members of the program to make sure that, in addition to their pensions, they don't collect a little something extra from a richly endowed Islamic militant group in return for their expertise.

Both in public and in private, White House officials say they are impressed with what the Pakistanis have done, and they hint with knowing smiles that they know more about the status of Pakistan's weapons than they can say. Nonetheless, dig a little deeper and one quickly discovers doubts about Kidwai's confidence that "it could never happen again."

Put plainly, most senior American officials who track nuclear issues think Kidwai is under such pressure to put the best possible face on Pakistan's nuclear security that he glosses over the most potent threats.

As the 2008 intelligence reports that shot through the top of the administration indicate, analysts worry most about Pakistan's nuclear laboratories, particularly the old Khan laboratory. The labs have always been a black hole for American officials, a no-go zone. There, and at a competing weapons development facility run by Pakistan's Atomic Energy Commission, work is under way to speed the production of a new generation of bombs, smaller weapons utilizing plutonium. With each succeeding generation of nuclear weapons development, there is more and more knowledge circulating about how to build a bigger bomb with less material. And while you can lock down weapons with codes and fences and guards, locking down expertise is a lot harder.

Working in some secrecy, the Bush administration attempted, laudably, to help Musharraf with the nuts and bolts of nuclear security. The effort was contained in a highly classified program that started in the months immediately after 9/11, when people began to realize that the terrorist attack, horrific as it was, could have been a lot worse.

The problem is that, years later, no one is sure how well the program is working. Like everything else that has happened in six years of an uneasy alliance between America and Pakistan, the effort to secure the weapons has been undercut by mutual distrust. Publicly, American officials almost never talked about Pakistan's nuclear weapons program. Privately, many inside the White House were obsessed with it. Once, early in 2007, Bush mused openly about his fears regarding the Pakistani intelligence service. He said he believed the ISI never really cut its "old school ties" with the Taliban.[7] Months later, as Pakistan appeared on the verge of political meltdown and Musharraf was slipping toward irrelevancy, one of Bush's nuclear experts acknowledged to me that "if the place falls apart, all the assurances we've been given about the safety of the weapons are worth squat." (Others, notably Bush's national security adviser, Stephen Hadley, disagreed.) The fact is, the Bush administration didn't know what would happen to the nuclear weapons if Pakistan dissolved into chaos, and neither will Obama's.

YET EVEN IF the United States had its priorities in order, securing the world's bomb fuel and loose weapons would not be easy, as I learned after visiting Kidwai. In the new nuclear age, our allies—the Pakistanis chief among them—distrust our motives just as our enemies did during the Cold War. And so, when he heads to work inside Chaklala Garrison these days, Kidwai has several preoccupations. One is stopping the outsiders who might attack Pakistan's nuclear facilities, a group that includes everyone from the Indians to al Qaeda to brutal new tribal leaders such as Baitullah Mehsud, the thuggish militia leader whom the CIA believed ordered the Bhutto killing. The second is stopping insiders who might be planted in the program to seize part of Pakistan's arsenal, or maybe just its bomb-making secrets. But his third problem is us.

Kidwai is nothing if not a realist. He knows that Washington's offers of technological aid are both a blessing and a threat. He has no doubt that the United States has developed extensive contingency plans to seize or neutralize Pakistan's nuclear weapons if it fears that terrorists might get to them. The truth, American officials tell me, is that those "plans" are still more like hopes. "It would help," one official said, "if we knew where the damn stuff was."

The result of these deep mutual suspicions is that the United States knows little about what's happening inside Pakistan's nuclear complex. "It scares the hell out of me," said a senior Bush official who spent a lifetime studying the Soviets. "Every morning I could see what was happening inside the Soviet nuclear system. I've never had a morning when I could see inside Pakistan's."

That explains why Kidwai and his Strategic Plans Division have grown ever more central to Washington's strategy, however incomplete, about what to do if the only nuclear-armed nation in the Islamic world begins to slip over the precipice. For all the public talk about democracy and development, about the need to foster moderation in Pakistani society, in the end it is the security of that arsenal that captivates Washington's attention.

KHALID KIDWAI is only a few years younger than Pakistan itself, and he has spent much of his life trying to create pockets of order in a nation to which order does not come naturally.

In his youth, Kidwai was protected from these Hobbesian elements of Pakistani life. He grew up in a world of Urdu literature and poetry. The enemy was India, not forces within Pakistan itself.

His father, Jalil Ahmed Kidwai, who lived to be ninety-two, was one of the country's best known authors and critics, whose studies of Indian, Pakistani, and Western literature are still the stuff of Ph.D. dissertations. His mother was a school principal in Karachi, the now-violent port city on the Arabian Sea where the family moved during the turbulence of the partition from India in 1947. The central question on the minds of most Muslim exiles at this time was whether Pakistan could withstand India's onslaughts, and it did not take long for the young Khalid to settle on his dream: to fly in the Pakistani Air Force, the most romantic branch of the armed forces of a new nation that needed to be able to strike deep into India if it was to survive.

At age twelve, he passed the exam for the Air Force–sponsored school in Sargodha, the site of the country's largest air base. "I wanted to make it as a pilot," he told me, "and it was the fastest way." Three years later, as a tenth-grader, he got a firsthand view of what war with India would look like. On September 6, 1965, he and his classmates were hurriedly sent home; war had broken out, and the students were in the bull's-eye. The next day Indian warplanes attacked the Sargodha base, but to little effect. When the students fled, most of the Pakistani aircraft based there were quietly moved elsewhere.

Sargodha remains a defining part of Kidwai's life, largely because much of Pakistan's nuclear arsenal is stored there or nearby. But Sargodha also is the place where his early dreams were dashed. When he graduated, Kidwai received the disheartening news that he would never become a pilot; a mild disorder with his eyes disqualified him. "My next obvious choice was the army," he said, and like many in his generation of military men in Pakistan, he stayed on, enjoying the professional pride and the security blanket it provides.

In 1971, as a young second lieutenant, Kidwai was suddenly in the thick of two vicious wars. The first was the civil war with what was then called East Pakistan, today known as Bangladesh, during which he was promoted to captain in an artillery regiment. On November 23 of the same year, war broke out again with India, and Kidwai was captured and held as a prisoner of war for two years in Allahabad, India. It was an experience he is reluctant to talk about.

After his release, the army made sure Kidwai was exposed to the two countries with which Pakistan had its most crucial relationships: the United States and Saudi Arabia. In 1979, he was posted to Fort Sill, Oklahoma. For a newly married young officer, still in recovery from his years in prison camp, it was a jarring exposure to a world that could not have been more different from his own.

Fort Sill is the last of the old Indian forts, created by a hero of the Civil War, Maj. Gen. Philip H. Sheridan, to finish off the Comanche, the Apache and others threatening the Western settlement of the country. Geronimo lived there, along with more than three hundred other Apache prisoners of war, and died there a century ago. But by the time Kidwai arrived, Fort Sill had long since reinvented itself as the U.S. Army's artillery school and a place where young officers of allied nations came for training. It offered a program—later suspended during America's effort to isolate Pakistan following its nuclear tests—that allowed Americans to get to know a rising generation of Pakistani officers. And it gave Kidwai an appreciation of the United States that is still somewhat rare among the Pakistani elite. He talks longingly about life in Oklahoma's wide-open wheatfields, of traveling through Colorado and Texas, and even of witnessing the awesome power of a tornado that wiped out a whole neighborhood of Lawton, Oklahoma, where he and his new wife were living. But what really struck him was the warmth of the local families who sponsored them, despite the paucity of Muslims in Comanche County.

It was also at Fort Sill that he caught his first whiff of the role of nuclear weapons in the modern military. The artillery school at the fort prepared American officers for Cold War operations in Europe and regularly drilled them on the procedures under which tactical nuclear munitions might be used to fight off a Soviet force invading Western Europe. For Kidwai, this seemed something of a remote subject; India had just tested its first bomb, and Pakistan was still far from obtaining a nuclear deterrent. But the subject intrigued him—chiefly because whenever the nuclear training became intense, the brass at Fort Sill found something else for the foreign officers to do.

"We'd be sent off for trips to Washington or someplace," Kidwai recalled with a laugh, "so that we were out of earshot."

As he worked his way up the Pakistani Army's rigid promotion system, he found himself posted next to Saudi Arabia. There he gained a view of a very different kind of ally for the Pakistanis—a Sunni nation so awash in oil money that it could pay Pakistan handsomely to help defend the country.

For roughly two years Kidwai lived along the Jordanian border, while his wife learned Arabic by socializing with ladies from the region. By May 28, 1998—the day on which Pakistan's power and Kidwai's life would change dramatically—he was back in Pakistan, based just south of Lahore, an eager brigadier general just days away from his promotion to major general.

Even today, you can see Kidwai's pride in the scope of Pakistan's accomplishment that day as the Chagai Hills shook from Pakistan's first underground nuclear test. His country had done more than answer India's challenge; it had built the ultimate deterrent. Along the way, Pakistan had overcome a series of halfhearted efforts, led by the United States, to cut off its nuclear supplies and dissuade it from building its own bomb.

Year after year Pakistan lied to Washington when confronted with all-but-definitive evidence that it was constructing a weapon. When Washington could no longer overlook the obvious, Pakistan simply endured the resulting economic sanctions, even though the country's economy was flat on its back. It all seemed worth it, Pakistani officials have told me, after that first test detonated without a hitch. Then, just for good measure, the military detonated five more tests over the next few days, with Khan present at the last test to accept the kudos, even though others had been the ones to design the weapons.

Kidwai told me there was a special satisfaction in the fact that Pakistan had conducted six successful tests in those mountains. "That was one-upsmanship," Kidwai said, smiling proudly as we looked at a photograph of one of the tests hanging on his office wall. "India had conducted only five." Underneath the photographs, Kidwai keeps a small fragment of the Chagai mountain under glass, displayed like a moon rock at the Smithsonian. The explosion had turned it bright white.

Kidwai professes not to have known in advance about the tests. "I had no clue," he said, "because I was not a part of the nuclear establishment at that point." In fact, the tests were so sensitive that very few in the upper echelons of the military were clued in that tests were on the way. But it was no secret that the army, the keeper of the weapons and the institution with the executive authority over their use, was determined to demonstrate that Pakistan had the bomb and would never give it up, no matter what the diplomatic and economic costs.

India's test had given the army, and Khan, the political cover they needed to demonstrate their technical accomplishment. Each got something out of the show. Pakistani authorities could claim that they were merely responding to a provocation from the Indians, who had gone first, in hopes they would escape sanction. But the Pakistanis also relished the opportunity. "You have to understand there were huge sensitivities," Kidwai said. "There is a history of the world trying to roll it back, to stop us, to get us to give it up." Khan cemented his role as a national hero, and soon his laboratory was swarming with North Koreans, clearly interested customers.

The Clinton administration was helpless, but made one last, halfhearted effort to force Pakistan to stuff the genie back into the bottle. Angry because he had put his credibility on the line in pressing

Prime Minister Nawaz Sharif not to conduct the tests, Clinton imposed heavy sanctions on both India and Pakistan, as required by a law called the Glenn Amendment, designed to make any new nuclear power pay a price for conducting a nuclear test. Clinton declared that Pakistan had missed a chance to "improve its political standing in the world," and said both India and Pakistan had to "take decisive steps to reverse this dangerous arms race."[8] Six billion dollars in aid was canceled, and lending from the World Bank and the International Monetary Fund was delayed.

While they protested, both Indian and Pakistani officials knew that nothing lasted forever—especially sanctions. In fact, just after September 11, 2001, three years after the tests, the Bush administration suddenly concluded it needed Pakistan as an ally in the war against the Taliban and al Qaeda. The sanctions were lifted overnight. The message to the rest of world—Iran included—was clear: Hang tough, proceed with your nuclear ambitions, and sooner or later the West will need you badly enough to accept you as another nuclear power.

No sooner had the radioactive and diplomatic dust settled from the test site than Kidwai was called in by his boss, the chief of the army staff, Gen. Jehangir Karamat. A former armored corps commander and staunch nationalist, Karamat was a veteran of both Indo-Pakistani wars, in 1965 and 1971. He had commanded the Pakistani troops in Saudi Arabia, and tangled with Prime Minister Nawaz Sharif over his insistence that the military be given a clear role in running the country. He told Kidwai that he had to put everything else aside for an urgent project: to come up with a system to protect Pakistan's new atomic weapons from all enemies—the Indians, the West, and especially the angry Americans.

Together, Karamat and Kidwai knew speed was of the essence. If the West thought that Pakistan had a few weapons in its inventory, and no system to keep them safe, Pakistan's leaders feared they would come under even more pressure to "roll back" the program and give up the handful they had manufactured. The only way to resist that pressure, they knew, was to create a large arsenal fast and to hide it away in tunnels and caves where neither the Indians nor the Americans could seize or destroy the warheads.

Moreover, Islamabad needed to convince the world it could become a responsible nuclear power that was just as capable of securing its weapons as the Russians, the Chinese, or the Israelis. That was where Kidwai and his team came in.

Kidwai is the first to concede that he came to the job with zero expertise. Apart from his limited exposure to nuclear artillery issues at Fort Sill, he had no real experience in the subject. He had no scientific background in the design or manufacture of nuclear weapons, or in the mechanisms to lock them down. He had never studied deterrence theory. None of this seemed to matter. He was considered a quick study and, most important, a loyalist. By October 1998, he had developed the rudiments of a plan, and he presented it to Musharraf, who was just months away from taking over the country in a military "counter-coup" against the prime minister he detested, Nawaz Sharif.

But as Musharraf later told me, he and Kidwai quickly came to realize that the greatest danger to their plans for nuclear control lay not in New Delhi or in Washington. It was a short walk down the road, at the Khan laboratory. They just didn't know what to do about it.

ABDUL QADEER KHAN had not been present at the creation of the Pakistani nuclear program, but he insinuated himself into it with astounding speed.

Pakistan's quest had begun more than two decades prior to India's first nuclear test in 1974. Long before coming to power as Pakistan's military leader, Benazir Bhutto's father, Zulfikar Ali Bhutto, had dreamed of a Pakistani nuclear weapon, arguing that "all wars of our age have become total wars." He toured the Muslim world to raise money. He stopped in Iran, Saudi Arabia, and eventually Libya, to see

Col. Muammar el-Qaddafi, who harbored similar dreams. Soon the money began to flow, a reported $100 million from Qaddafi. The Saudis are also believed to have donated heavily, but to this day top American officials say they have never seen definitive evidence about what they got in return. It didn't take a nuclear scientist to figure out their potential motives: Worried about the Iranians, the Saudis are presumably eager to have access, if needed, to what some call "the Sunni bomb."

The Indians, however, had a head start. In May 1974, with Indira Gandhi as a witness, they had conducted their first nuclear test. The Indians called it a "peaceful explosion," but because the test was conducted within a hundred miles of the Pakistani border, the message was short of subtle. "I never really understood what kind of 'peaceful explosion'—a nuclear explosion, how can it be peaceful?" President Pervez Musharraf said to me during a conversation in 2005. To Musharraf, a young officer rising through the army ranks at the time, the Indian test left Pakistan so vulnerable that "our strategy of minimal deterrence was undermined, was compromised." It did not take long, he said, before "we decided that we had to go nuclear."[9]

Years later, Benazir Bhutto recalled during a conversation in London that her father was overcome with shock and shame when he first heard about the Indian test. He said privately to her, and then publicly, that "we will eat grass, but we will build the bomb."[10] For a desperately poor country, making the declaration and accomplishing the goal were two very different things. Bhutto was told that designing a bomb was not very hard. Coming up with the fissile material to make one was an entirely different matter.

The message raced through the military. It was then, in a case of spectacular timing, that Khan wrote a letter offering up his services from the Netherlands, where he was working at a European consortium that produced centrifuges for uranium enrichment. His offer quickly reached the upper echelons of the Pakistani military. "For Pakistan after 1974 there was nothing more important than the bomb," Talat Masood, a retired senior general in the army told me one evening as he was serving coffee in his living room.[11] Khan was soon back home, his files stuffed with stolen production documents. Soon he had his own lab, which he modestly named for himself.

"The two laboratories, the Khan Research Lab and the Pakistan Atomic Energy Commission, were given an unprecedented level of freedom and resources considering the poverty level of the country," Masood told me. "All the security around them was not to make sure that they didn't abuse the authority; it was to protect what they were making."

While the Pakistanis saw the bomb program as part of their epic competition with India, to the rest of the world it marked the fruition of John F. Kennedy's prediction that many more states would soon become nuclear powers. Suddenly, the great powers— the United States, Russia, Britain, France, and China—no longer held a monopoly on nuclear weapons. India's "peaceful explosion" and Pakistan's reaction were bound to change the world. They did, but not in the ways many anticipated.

Year after year, as American presidents and Pakistani prime ministers came and went, intelligence agents from the United States and Europe watched as Pakistan slowly gathered all the elements it needed for a bomb. High-performance metals from Europe and nuclear triggers from the United States, at least until the operation to send them through third countries to mask their true destination was shut down, were being shipped to Pakistan. Though American intelligence agencies missed it at the time, there was also the nearly complete bomb design from China, the one that ended up in Libyan hands decades later.

Yet over the years Democratic and Republican presidents had averted their eyes from the overwhelming evidence being gathered by the CIA. The reason was simple: Washington needed Pakistan in the war against the Soviets in Afghanistan and later to support the forceful removal of the Taliban. To declare publicly that Pakistan was building the bomb would have required Washington to cut off aid to the country, something the White House believed it could not afford to do. So, in time-honored tradition, it fudged the evidence, neither denying nor confirming in public the proof it had in hand.

For its part, the Pakistani military—and Khan in particular—operated with equal secrecy. Before her death, Benazir Bhutto insisted that when she became prime minister in December 1988, her own commanders refused to discuss the project with her. The army chief, she said, had told her, "There's no need for you to know." He was clearly concerned that she would give in to pressure from the Americans, her patrons.

But to the CIA, Bhutto looked too weak to confront the Pakistani Army on a major issue of national security. To make the point that they knew what Pakistan was up to, Bhutto was escorted in June 1989 to CIA headquarters in Langley, where she was presented with a full American mock-up of the Pakistani bomb and warned that the United States was following every step. She realized from that experience, she argued later, that she was being kept in the dark about the state of the weapons program. But she also contended that the Americans were helping her come up with subterfuges that would enable all sides to talk around the truth. "We were told that if we wanted to keep the aid" from the United States, she said in 2005, Pakistan should simply avoid assembling all the parts into a completed weapon. "When is a chicken a chicken?" she asked in the same interview, describing this diplomatic sleight of hand with a smile.

While Washington was quietly teaching Bhutto the art of nuclear ambiguity, it was missing the big turn in Khan's program. He was double- and triple-ordering critical parts for Pakistan's program, then repacking and selling some of the parts and the technology. "He knew there was no accountability in the system," Talat Masood recalled. "And why should he? He was at the center of attention, he was highly egotistical, he was highly ambitious," later making it clear he thought he should be running the country.

He was also somewhat delusional about Pakistan's own capabilities. General Masood remembered confronting Khan about the security of missiles he was buying for the Khan laboratory. Khan insisted he was building the Ghauri, one of Pakistan's first nuclear-capable missiles, from his own parts and designs. "It was ridiculous, because everyone knew we were buying these from the North Koreans, and we had to be giving them something in return." Khan, he noted, soon wanted to produce conventional weapons as well—anti-tank missiles, shoulder-fired antiaircraft missiles—which investigators believe he wanted to trade for nuclear technology. But he may also have simply wanted to sell them.[12]

During her exile in London, Bhutto insisted that she never knew that Khan was seeking to profit by selling Pakistan's technology. But she said she had "noticed a big change between Khan in my first term and Khan in my second term." In her first term, she said, he had been "very nationalistic, very proud" as he marched in and out of meetings declaring that he was the man who would match India, bomb for bomb, missile for missile. Clearly he had more influence over the program than she did: Bhutto claimed that during her two terms as prime minister, she was not in command of the nuclear weapons program. The first time she was removed from office, in 1990, she claimed she was a victim of a "nuclear coup," triggered in part by her insistence that she had the right to convene the National Command Authority, the government organization set up to decide Pakistan's nuclear doctrine and control all major decisions about its nuclear weapons—including when to use them.

When she returned to power in 1993, she once again found herself unable to extend her reach over the nuclear program, or so she said. Meeting Khan again, she recalled, she saw a changed man: the nationalism had given way to a more religious tone.

"I had noticed that he had become more Islamist," she said. Khan kept talking about his mission to create an "Islamic bomb" that would match the "Jewish bomb." In retrospect, he may have simply been creating a rationale for spreading the technology around the world, one more publicly acceptable than pocketing tens of millions of dollars in profits.

Bhutto laughed when she heard the Pakistani government's claim that top officials did not know that Khan had shifted gears and begun selling his technology. "I do not buy this theory that Khan did everything on his own," she said. "But maybe it suits Mr. Musharraf to say Khan did everything on his own."

It also suited her to blame Musharraf, the rival she was trying to take down. When it came to aiding and abetting Khan, however, her own hands were not entirely clean. On a visit to North Korea in the 1990s, according to accounts provided by Khan's associates and by American intelligence officials, Bhutto reportedly brought back to Islamabad some North Korean missile designs that would enable Pakistan to ensure that its nuclear weapons could reach deep into India. North Korea later got uranium enrichment equipment, according to statements Khan made after his arrest in 2005. It is still unclear what was quid and what was quo. Until her death, Bhutto remained maddeningly evasive about her role in the exchange.

IF THERE IS a single story out of the Khan laboratories that sends a shiver down the spines of American officials, it is the tale of Sultan Bashiruddin Mahmood.[13]

Until 1999, when he was quietly removed from the Khan laboratories, Mahmood was one of the scientists who worked in utmost secrecy on the gas centrifuge program that Khan stole from the Netherlands and brought back to Pakistan. Mahmood then moved on to the country's next huge project: designing the reactor at Kushab that was to produce the fuel Pakistan needed to move to the next level—a plutonium bomb.

Mahmood grew up in India, and, after the 1947 partition, moved to a village outside of Lahore, where his family lived in poverty. He was among the lucky few who won a scholarship to college and, by the 1960s, found himself in Manchester, England, working on a degree in nuclear engineering.[14]

He returned to Pakistan after six years of study and quickly became a student of the intersection between fringe science and the Koran. He wrote *The Mechanics of the Doomsday and Life after Death*, a book arguing that in parts of the world where morals degrade, disaster strikes. Though he was acknowledged as a highly capable engineer and scientist, over time his colleagues began to wonder if Mahmood was playing with less than a full deck. He talked often of his fascination with sunspots, and his next treatise was an extensive essay in Urdu about the role sunspots played in triggering the French and Russian Revolutions, World War II, and uprisings against colonial masters around the world.[15]

"This guy was our ultimate nightmare," an American intelligence official told me in late 2001, when we first wrote about Mahmood. "He had access to the entire Pakistani program. He knew what he was doing. And he was completely out of his mind."

While Khan appeared to be in the nuclear-proliferation business chiefly for the money, Mahmood made it clear to friends that his interest was religious: Pakistan's bomb, he told associates, was "the property of a whole Ummah," referring to the worldwide Muslim community.[16] He made no secret of his goal: He wanted to share nuclear technology with anyone who might speed "the end of days," which he said would pave the way for Islam to rise as the dominant religious force in the world.

Eventually his religious intensity, combined with his sympathy for Islamic extremism, scared Mahmood's colleagues. In 1999, just as Kidwai was beginning to examine the staff of the nuclear enterprise, Mahmood was forced to take an early retirement. At a loss for what to do, he set up a nonprofit charity, Ummah Tameer-e-Nau, ostensibly designed to allow him to send relief to fellow Muslims in Afghanistan. It turned out that the ones most interested in Mahmood's efforts were Osama bin Laden and his deputy, Ayman al-Zawahiri, the former surgeon from Egypt who had become the chief operational officer of al Qaeda.

In August 2001, as the September 11 plotters were making their last preparations in the United States, Mahmood and one of his colleagues at the charity, Chaudiri Abdul Majeed, met with bin Laden and Zawahiri over the course of several days. Years later, what exactly transpired in those meetings remains a mystery. There is no doubt that Mahmood and Majeed talked to the two al Qaeda leaders about nuclear weapons, and there is no doubt that al Qaeda desperately wanted the Bomb. George Tenet, the CIA chief, recalled later that reports of the meeting were "frustratingly vague," but included an account of how a senior al Qaeda leader displayed a canister that may have contained some nuclear material, and there was talk of how to design a simple firing mechanism.[17] What no one knew is whether this session was just about bin Laden's wish list, or whether al Qaeda had a plausible plan to obtain a nuclear weapon.

Either way, the flood of intelligence that poured into Washington in the days after 9/11 set off a panic that the attack, horrific as it was, might be just a start. Mowatt-Larssen, the longtime CIA nuclear expert, now at the Energy Department, was given perhaps the most daunting job at the agency in the aftermath of 9/11: to make sure that al Qaeda did not have a worse weapon at its disposal. "The worst nightmare we had at that time was that A. Q. Khan and Osama bin Laden were somehow working together," recalled Mowatt-Larssen. "There were all these connections, and connections to the Libyans," who reported to the British and others that they had been approached by bin Laden's group with offers to sell a weapon.

In retrospect, this was the moment when Bush began to shape his foreign policy demands that foreign leaders make countering terrorism their highest priority, a loyalty test that was understandable at the time but eventually came to skew, and often undermine, America's interactions with the world. When Colin Powell landed in Pakistan in mid-October 2001, Ground Zero was still smoldering, the American invasion of Afghanistan was looming, and Powell needed to bring answers back to Washington—fast. Publicly, Powell's trip was designed to stress a new era of cooperation with Musharraf and "to demonstrate our enduring commitment" to "a great Muslim nation."[18] But its true purpose was to offer more help to Pakistan in controlling its own arsenal and to confront the Pakistani leader with evidence to force him to detain Mahmood and Majeed, and allow the CIA to question them.

Facing no alternative, Musharraf had the two arrested six days later. But after a cursory interrogation—the suspects were permitted to go home at night—they were released. Then, in November 2001, Tenet and Mowatt-Larssen briefed Bush and Cheney about the campfire meeting with bin Laden. For the first time, Mowatt-Larssen recalled, "we were looking at the idea of terrorists looking at full strategic weapons, the kind of weapons only states had." The evidence suggested, but did not prove, a connection between al Qaeda and the Khan network, perhaps with the involvement of the Libyans. This collaboration among nuclear aspirants later proved to be less than met the eye. But at the time it could not be dismissed. Bush and Cheney found the prospect so alarming that they told both Tenet and Mowatt-Larssen to head for Islamabad immediately to confront Musharraf about the meeting with bin Laden. Within hours, Tenet and Mowatt-Larssen were on an aging Boeing 707, used decades before as *Air Force One,* and the next day they were ushered into Musharraf's office.

"The reaction was interesting," Mowatt-Larssen recalled later. "Musharaf's first words were 'Men in caves can't do this.'" He told Tenet and Mowatt-Larssen they were looking for nukes in all the wrong places; why didn't they focus on Russia and the former Soviet Union? After an hour of intense conversation, Musharraf came around and ordered the two rearrested. But while the Americans could join the interrogation, he said, Pakistan could not acknowledge their presence. Musharraf could not be perceived as caving in to U.S. demands.

At first Mahmood denied ever meeting the al Qaeda leaders. Then he failed a series of polygraph tests, administered by Americans who had slipped quietly into the country. Eventually he and Majeed were confronted with evidence showing that they had promised to help bin Laden build a weapon. Gradually their memories improved. Mahmood described the meetings, bin Laden's persistent questions about what it would take to obtain a bomb, and his explanation that building the weapon would be a lot easier than obtaining the right kind of fuel. Bin Laden, he reported, asked, "What if we already have the material?"

Bin Laden's single previous effort to obtain that material turned out to have been a failure. The al Qaeda leader apparently fell for a scam out of Uzbekistan that provided him with some mildly radioactive material that might have been of use in a dirty bomb, but not in a nuclear weapon. (During their visit, Mahmood and Majeed were reportedly shown a canister by a senior al Qaeda leader that they were told contained some nuclear material, but it seems likely it was low-level stuff, perhaps the expensive fruits of the Uzbekistan rip-off.)[19]

Under interrogation, Mahmood and Majeed said the conversation left them with the impression that al Qaeda already had a nuclear program under way, albeit a haphazard one, in which desire outstripped supplies of fissile material and expertise.

The interrogations of Mahmood and Majeed were deeply unsatisfactory. For all his desire to give jihadists a power akin to Pakistan's, Mahmood was a specialist in the fuel-production side of the business, enriching uranium and making plutonium. He had no access to nuclear material and had never designed a bomb. Mahmood's son, talking to reporters later, said that his father had explained to bin Laden that there was nothing easy about building a bomb and that al Qaeda would first have to obtain nuclear fuel.

Still, for the CIA, fresh from the failures leading up to 9/11, it was scary stuff. Tenet's description of the evidence to Bush and Cheney prompted the vice president to mumble his "1 percent" rule: that even if the chances of a nuclear 9/11 were only 1 percent, the possibility had to be eliminated as if the evidence were overwhelming. Tenet later argued that Cheney's statement was "misinterpreted" as a policy to pursue all threats, no matter how remote, as if they were certainties. But Cheney was right about one thing: Nuclear terrorism is different. It is, as Tenet wrote later, one of the few attacks terrorists could mount that would "change history."[20]

In the end, Mahmood and Majeed were never prosecuted because the Pakistanis did not want to risk a trial in which the country's own nuclear secrets could come out, much less broadcast the carelessness that had allowed one of their former scientists to meet unnoticed with bin Laden. Today, Mahmood is back home, under tight surveillance that seems intended more to keep him a safe distance from reporters than to keep him away from extremists.

Kidwai insists that Pakistan's investigations have concluded only that Mahmood and his friends engaged in "some sort of discussions" about how to make nuclear weapons and that bin Laden "perhaps showed some interest" in how to build them. Mahmood had probably drawn basic sketches of a nuclear weapon, he said, but they were crude drawings, more like something you would scribble on a napkin, than a detailed plan. Kidwai dismisses the whole matter as the misadventures of a wayward scientist.

In Kidwai's telling of events—a version of the story that is a lot more benign than the version heard in Washington—"nothing went anywhere." He clearly wants this episode to be dismissed as revealing bin Laden's wish list, a list that he argues was never fulfilled. "It's over," he insists.

Still, one of his deputies acknowledges that the meetings with al Qaeda "will haunt us for many years" because they will fuel suspicions around the world that Pakistan is unable to control its most precious asset: the nuclear knowledge that exists inside the heads of its scientists and engineers.

◆

THE TERRIFYING PART of Mahmood's story is not just what transpired around the campfire, but rather that the meetings happened
at all. They took place three years after the Strategic Plans Division
came into existence, and demonstrated the huge vulnerabilities in
the Pakistani nuclear infrastructure.

By Kidwai's count, there are roughly 70,000 people who work in
the country's nuclear complex. Roughly half of those are involved in
the technology of the program, including 7,000 to 8,000 scientists.
Of those, Kidwai estimates that about 2,000 are "hard-core nuclear
scientists and engineers" with critical knowledge of how to build a
weapon. They are the focus of the Strategic Plans Division's personal reliability program, an effort that Kidwai characterizes as a
screening program for the medically unfit and psychologically unreliable. Intelligence experts in Washington describe the program in
far starker terms, saying they hope it weeds out religious zealots,
Taliban sympathizers, al Qaeda spies, and the economically desperate, ensuring that they are not in the ranks of Pakistan's nuclear
hierarchy.

The differences in description are worrying, though the simple
explanation may be that Kidwai does not want to admit that there
are elements of Taliban and al Qaeda looking to get inside the nuclear program. When I asked one of Kidwai's Americanized aides to
describe the program, he said, "We're looking for the fundos [funda-
mentalists], and that is not always easy to figure out."

At its heart, the personal reliability program is about what we
would call domestic spying: Kidwai has created his own intelligence
service, so that he does not have to rely entirely on the ISI, an agency
that is believed to be infested with Taliban sympathizers. The intelligence arm of Strategic Plans monitors everything from bank
transactions to religious habits to the political persuasions of the
country's nuclear engineers. When Musharraf was still at the height
of his power, an engineer was dismissed, allegedly because he was
overheard speaking ill of the president and his policies.

But the truth is that weeding out "fundos" in Pakistan is hard work. Unlike Mahmood, they do not necessarily publish bizarre theories. Pakistan is, after all, an Islamic state, and it would be a dangerous leap to assume that any fervent Muslim would sell out the country's nuclear arsenal. (In fact, one retired Pakistani general told me that A. Q. Khan would have likely passed the personal reliability test with flying colors, unless his overseas bank accounts were monitored.) Like the borders between Pakistan and Afghanistan, the line between religious fundamentalism and militant fundamentalism is hard to draw.

A visit to Pakistan's leading university campuses reveals that something has changed. A decade ago, most young women walked the campuses with their heads uncovered. Not today. "I look out at my classes today, and among the women I can't see many of the faces," Pervez Hoodhboy, one of the lonely critics of the Pakistani nuclear program, told me when I visited him at his office at Qaid-e-Azam University in Islamabad in the spring of 2008. Intense and prone to question authority, Hoodhboy is chairman of the physics department.

"That was rarely the case before," he said, showing me a photo of some of the women in his class twenty years ago who were dressed in blue jeans.

A craggy-faced scientist who spends most of his time sparring with Pakistan's religious and nuclear establishments, he has the air of a rebel resigned to the fact that he will always be regarded as an outcast in his own country. Almost alone, he has argued that Pakistan's nuclear weapons program has made the country less safe. His critics, including Kidwai, tend to cast him as the physicist who cried "fundo" once too often. But Hoodhboy has a good record of documenting undercurrents of Pakistani society that the government, in its effort to portray a moderate face to the world, would rather suppress.

His argument is simple: As the nuclear program attracts new, young talent, it will be next to impossible to weed out militant fundamentalists. What's more, the country is turning a blind eye as fundamentalism is taught in the schools—not just in the religious madrassas, but in the public and private schools that educate the rest of the population. To prove his point, Hoodhboy showed me pictures he has collected from a schoolbook used by both regular schools and the radical madrassas to teach the Urdu alphabet. To American eyes, it is more than a little shocking. The problem isn't the words; it's the pictures.

Take the word *collision*, which is pronounced *tay* in Urdu. The illustration? A picture of two airplanes flying into a burning World Trade Center. "Of all the pictures of a collision that you could find," Hoodhboy told me, "it's curious that they use that one in the textbook."

Naturally, members of Musharraf's government have assured visiting Americans that the textbooks are being cleaned up and that sections advocating jihad are being deleted. Hoodhboy makes a persuasive case that the changes have largely been for show. What's more, a $100-million government project for "madrassa reform" was killed after it met with enormous objections from the religious establishment.

And the problem is not limited to basic readers for first-graders. Leafing through today's high school textbooks is a little like reading Japanese textbooks about World War II, the ones in which the Rape of Nanking is still described as an event that may or may not have happened. In Pakistan's case, the textbooks say little about Afghanistan or the brutal rule of the Taliban; they skip right ahead to Iraq, arguing that Americans occupied the country to seize territory and oil. Some suggest Washington has designs on the rest of the region. However twisted, it is a storyline that George Bush made far easier to sell.

THE PANIC IN WASHINGTON about what al Qaeda sought from Pakistani scientists led to a sea-change in the American approach to the country: Instead of sanctioning Pakistan for possessing nuclear weapons, America began paying Pakistan to lock them down. It was a program shaped by the very public efforts to lock up nuclear weapons and material in the Soviet Union. Washington boasts about that project, but to this day officials go silent when asked about the parallel program in Pakistan, for fear of destabilizing the government.

Bush never engaged in the issue prior to 9/11. But after the attacks, the administration began acting like parents who discover, belatedly, that one of their kids has been having sex: It dropped the lectures about the virtues of abstinence and started talking about safety.

When Colin Powell traveled to Pakistan in October 2001, one of the real purposes of what he called one of his "general-to-general" conversations with Musharraf was to impress upon him that whatever Pakistan was doing to secure its arsenal, it wasn't enough.

Powell knew what he was talking about: As a young Army officer in Germany during the Cold War, he was a "nuclear weapons employment officer," which meant, he told me, that "I knew how to sit down with various maps and charts, and describe where to put a nuclear weapon and what it would do to the enemy." It was an experience that also gave him a hands-on sense of how easy it might be, in a moment of chaos, to lose track of where a weapon is located.[21]

He told Musharraf it was urgent that he accept American help in locking down his program. Powell knew that back in Washington, where paranoia about a second attack was through the roof, one nightmare scenario after another was being played out. In some, bin Laden exploited connections or bribed someone to get his hands on a real weapon. In others, the ISI—long sympathetic to the Taliban—helped its friends get their hands on the one weapon that could stop the coming American-led invasion.

"There were a lot of people who feared that once we headed into Afghanistan, the Taliban would be looking for these weapons," one senior official involved in the effort told me.

Musharraf later had another interpretation of events: The Bush

White House thought he was at high risk of being killed or deposed, and they feared a free-for-all for the weapons. In his memoir, *In the Line of Fire*, Musharraf recalled being "put under immense pressure by the United States regarding our nuclear and missile arsenal."

"They were not very sure of my job security, and they dreaded the possibility that an extremist successor government might get its hands on our strategic nuclear arsenal. Second, they doubted our ability to safeguard our assets." [22]

But when I talked to him in 2005, Musharraf argued that he could not afford to appear to be giving in to American pressure. Any hint or rumor that he was allowing American hands to be put on Pakistan's one great source of power would be a death knell for any Pakistani leader.

"This is an extremely sensitive matter in Pakistan," Musharraf said. "We don't allow any foreign intrusion in our facilities. But, at the same time, we guarantee that the custodial arrangements that we brought about and implemented are already the best in the world." [23]

Kidwai was even blunter. "Powell made the offer, and we had no problem in agreeing to examine that," he recalled. "But we were highly sensitive to the local sentiment that the slightest interaction with the Americans would be seen as a sellout."

The result was that Bush and Powell boasted in public about their efforts to secure nuclear weapons and materials in Russia, and ordered enormous secrecy around the parallel effort in Pakistan. They never spoke about the program in public. The budgets, though modest, were highly classified.

When I began asking around the White House about the program, the president's national security adviser, Stephen Hadley, asked me to come to his office to hear his arguments for why the *Times* should not publish stories about the program. Premature publicity, he argued, could undermine the effort to secure the weapons at a time when many of them had probably not been properly locked down. Moreover, he said, the revelation could galvanize opposition to President Musharraf and fuel the argument that he was an American lapdog.

Hadley's first argument, that a story would aid terror groups, convinced the *Times*'s editors to delay publication until the protections were better established. (At the same time we told the administration that we do not withhold stories simply because they would prove embarrassing to American or foreign officials.) Ultimately the story was held for three years, until the chaos in Pakistan in the fall of 2007 urgently raised the question of whether the nuclear stockpile might be vulnerable during a potentially violent overthrow of Musharraf. (When I told the White House that the events in Pakistan were leading the paper to revisit our earlier agreement to delay publication, Hadley withdrew his request, and within days the *Times* published many of the details in a front-page story.)*

Yet when the program began, Powell knew there were risks that if the secret of the American aid to Pakistan was kept too close, India might be tempted to act on its own to destroy or seize Pakistan's nuclear stockpile, thereby sparking another conflagration. So in the fall of 2002, at a time of renewed tension between India and Pakistan, Robert D. Blackwill, the U.S. ambassador to India, got an urgent message one weekend from Powell. He was to go to see the prime minister of India, Atal Bihari Vajpayee, immediately. A phone call would not do, nor could it wait until Monday. He was to read Vajpayee a brief statement explaining that the United States

---

* By the time the paper published the story, many of the details had begun to leak out. In 2005, President Musharraf acknowledged in an on-the-record interview with us that he had received "international" help in securing the weapons, and the following year the Pakistani authorities gave a few more details to the local press in an effort to dispel rumors, which were never confirmed, that American personnel were involved in guarding Pakistani military sites. By the time of the 2007 instability in Pakistan, which appeared to threaten Musharraf's hold on power, the administration apparently decided that the secrecy around the program was impeding its ability to assure Americans that it had a plan in place to deal with the risks. "I think at this point," one senior administration official said to me, "it's better that we make clear that we have attempted to help Pakistan through its security problems."

was providing assistance to the government of Pakistan to help secure the country's nuclear weapons. Blackwill was given explicit instructions to answer no questions, to leave no paper with Vajpayee,
and to insist on total secrecy.

"It was pretty comical," Blackwill recalled later about the instructions. Vajpayee's foreign policy advisers would not allow the
aging prime minister to be completely alone with the American ambassador, especially one with Blackwill's fearsome reputation and
skills. Blackwill lived within the letter of his instructions and left no
paper—but, at the insistence of the Indians, he allowed them to take
extensive notes on what was said. Years later, the Indians remain
unimpressed about what the United States accomplished. "We look
at Pakistan's nuclear facilities harder than anyone else does, because we have the most to lose," one high-ranking Indian general
told me during a briefing on the country's military posture in New
Delhi in April 2008. "Frankly, we have no confidence much has
changed. Do you?"

In fact, at the end of Bush's term, the American officials who
know the most about Pakistan's program are not as confident in
private as they sound in public. For obvious reasons, Washington's
official line is that the nuclear program is now secure. As long as the
military—meaning Kidwai and the Strategic Plans Division—have
ultimate control over the weapons, the constant chaos in the political leadership is unlikely to pose a threat, they insist. "It's a very professional military," one senior American official told me during the
worst of Pakistan's internal upheavals, in November 2007. "But the
truth is, we don't know how many of the safeguards are institution-
alized, and how many are dependent on Musharraf's guys."[24]

That fear of new leadership helps explain why Washington
clung to Musharraf for so long, even to the point of appearing less
than enthusiastic about the rise of a democratically elected government. "The nightmare scenario, of course, is what happens if an extremist Islamic government emerges—with an instant nuclear
arsenal," Robert Joseph, who helped design much of the American

program to lock down the nuclear weapons, told me as Musharraf appeared on the edge of ouster in 2007.[25] But even after that fear passed—the Islamic parties did poorly in the elections in early 2008, even in the regions of the country where they have the strongest presence—there was plenty of reason to worry about what could happen in a time of political chaos.

In the 1990s, A. Q. Khan thrived in part because he knew that a Pakistani government distracted by its own leadership struggles would not be paying attention to his business dealings. His relationship with Iran flourished in the chaos that followed the death of President Muhammad Zia al-Haq in a plane crash in 1988. (Zia is buried outside a spectacular mosque that is just down the block from Khan's house.) The first deliveries of centrifuges to Iran took place as Benazir Bhutto was trying to secure her power. The deals with North Korea and Libya happened amid the political jockeying that brought Nawaz Sharif to office. A study of the Khan network published by the International Institute for Strategic Studies in London concluded that "the diffusion of domestic political power among the troika of the president, the prime minister, and the army chief obscured the command and control authority over the covert nuclear weapons program."[26]

Kidwai insists none of this could happen again; a decade after Pakistan's nuclear tests, the National Command Authority, he says, is far better established. He is almost certainly correct, though when I was in Pakistan in April 2008, interviewing members of the newly elected government, two top officials who were part of that command authority said they had no idea what it involved. "I haven't been briefed yet," one confided to me. "I'm not sure what my role is supposed to be." When I related this conversation to a top American official in Washington who asked me, on my return, what I had learned about the security of the Pakistani nuclear program, he grimaced and said, "Now you know what we've been dealing with for five years."

In fact, despite their public enthusiasm about Kidwai's program, American officials cannot say precisely what has been accomplished.

That is due partly to Pakistan's paranoia about not letting foreigners know where their weapons are, or exactly how they are protected. When a delegation of Americans went to Islamabad in the spring of 2007 to ask for more transparency concerning how American money was being spent, they were sent home empty-handed.[27]

By any measure, the American aid devoted to locking up the world's most dangerous weapons in one of the world's most volatile countries is pocket change. The Pakistan program amounted to less than $100 million over five years, the equivalent of six hours or so of operations in Iraq in 2008. If Americans got to hold a referendum on which was more directly related to their security—ending the internal fighting in Baghdad or securing the weapons closest to al Qaeda's camps—it seems pretty clear how they would vote.

But as in most things in life, when it comes to preventing nuclear Armageddon, money isn't everything. There are, for example, nuclear rules—rules that are never posted, but that are supposed to be understood by all sides in a conflict. Even during the depths of the Cold War, there were rules in place that gave the Soviet premier and the American president some confidence that they knew how the other would act. Sometimes those rules stretched nearly to the breaking point, most notably during the Cuban Missile Crisis. As the Cold War dragged on, however, predictability became the greatest assurance of safety. We knew how far we could push the Soviets; they knew how far they could push us.

Only now are those rules beginning to be established between Pakistan and India. What is terrifying is that such rules will never exist between Pakistan and its newest enemy, the militant groups within Pakistan that see the country as their most promising target for takeover.

The absence of rules worried American officials during the tense months in 2001 and 2002 when it appeared, for a while, that the conflict between India and Pakistan could go nuclear. The incident that precipitated the hostilities was an attack on the Indian parliament in December 2001, just as the United States was consumed by the September 11 attacks and the invasion of Afghanistan. The attacks were the work of two terror groups within Pakistan, Jaish-e-Mohammed and Lashkar-e-Taiba, though there have always been suspicions that some elements of Musharraf's government may have been complicit. The crisis that followed led to the mass mobilization of the Indian Army, and a corresponding reaction in Pakistan. Colin Powell remembers scrambling to organize allies so that some foreign minister or world leader was visiting both New Delhi and Islamabad just about every week to talk both the Indian and Pakistani leadership down from their thinly veiled threats to use nuclear weapons. Musharraf was a particular worry because he was publicly warning that "we have means" to defend the country even if the Pakistani soldiers massing along the border were dwarfed by India's forces.

"We had sort of a duty roster out there for who is going tomorrow to keep these clowns from killing each other," Powell told me in a conversation six years later. He recalled phoning Musharraf from Paris, with Bush sitting at his side, during a trip the president was taking through Russia and Europe. Powell's worry was that some hotheaded Pakistani field commander would take Musharraf's threats too literally.

"I called him from our embassy in Paris," Powell recalled, warming to the tale. "I said, 'Mr. President, how are you?'"

"'Ahh, Mr. Secretary, how are you?'" Powell said, imitating Musharraf's distinctive accent.

"I said, 'Well, I'm fine—umm, can we do general-to-general?' And he said, 'Of course, my friend.' And I said all this talk about nuclear weapons or 'means' has got to stop. I said I was trained in this stuff and I know what it does and what it doesn't do and I also know that in this century no civilized person could ever think of taking such an existential step that has not been taken since 1945.

"'It can't and won't happen,' I said, but I told him, 'General, you are scaring the crap out of everybody, so you've got to cool it.' And he laughed and he said, 'I understand.'"

Both sides stood back. They took a breath. They put their nuclear weapons back in their holsters—if they'd ever actually taken them out. (Kidwai argues that no weapons were moved during the crisis, though some American intelligence officials have their doubts.)

The very fact that Powell had to intervene, however, underscored the fact that Pakistan and India had never established "redlines." Without them, the Pakistanis could not warn their commanders what kind of action might provoke a nuclear response by India. The Indians did not know what kind of action could trigger enough panic in Islamabad that they would roll out their arsenal.

It is worrisome because in the scenarios that American officials play out in private, militants might deliberately provoke another India-Pakistan crisis by launching a spectacular terror attack in India. At first it might seem as if the goal was to blow up the nascent peace process that has restored calm on the subcontinent. The real objective, however, may be darker: to provoke a conflict that would tempt Pakistan to move its nuclear weapons into place. That is when the arsenal would be most vulnerable, particularly if the Islamist groups are aided by insiders.

"Farfetched?" one senior American strategist said to me in 2008. "Maybe, but in Pakistan maybe not."

When American officials "wargame" the next step, they ask the question, Would the Pakistani government tell Washington if one of its weapons was lost? American officials don't want to have to depend on Kidwai or his successor to pick up the hotline to deliver the bad news and to ask for a little help. For one thing, there's no hotline to pick up. For another, injured pride would likely trump prudence.

SO FAR, the American role in securing Pakistan's arsenal has been limited largely to training the people who, in turn, train the Pakistanis who operate or guard the country's weapons. American legalities—and paranoia on all sides—have prevented the United States from taking the next step: sharing the sophisticated electronic technology that for decades has successfully kept American weapons safe.*

The training has largely taken place at Sandia National Laboratories in New Mexico, where many of the government's nonproliferation and nuclear-detection technologies are developed. Roughly 200 Pakistanis have learned the basics of protecting a nuclear arsenal at this facility. Most of this instruction was hardly rocket science. The lectures included how to build double fences, how to install security systems and motion sensors, and how to use night-vision goggles and radiation-detection devices. When it became clear that the Pakistanis had put a lot less effort into acquiring the right protective hardware than they had put into building a giant new reactor to produce plutonium, the United States paid for much of the safety equipment, shipping some of it directly to the Pakistani military. As soon as it was delivered, however, it disappeared into a black hole: The Pakistanis were not about to reveal where the warheads and missiles were stored.

Nonetheless, Hadley argues that even if you cannot verify the results, the American program is worth every penny. "I think it's exactly the kind of thing that the American people want us to be spending our money on," he said one day in his office. "They just want to know the weapons are safe." Now, with American support, Pakistan is supposed to be building a training center outside Islamabad to conduct the same training on Pakistani soil, but it is years delayed.

Hadley was less eager to discuss the administration's internal battle over whether to provide Pakistan with a far more advanced technology for securing weapons—something the nuclear experts

---

* During my visit to Pakistan in April 2008, Kidwai and other officials raised with me the issue of the series of cascading errors that led the U.S. Air Force to unknowingly fly a bunch of nuclear weapons on a B-52 bomber across the country in August 2007. There they were left at Barksdale Air Force Base in Louisiana for thirty-six hours with none of the special security required for nuclear devices, a point the Pakistanis enjoy making whenever the United States portrays them as vulnerable to "losing" a weapon.

call PALs, or "permissive action links," a series of codes and hardware protections that make sure only a very small group of authorized users can arm and detonate a nuclear weapon.

PALs are a leftover from the Cold War, designed to make sure
some rogue sergeant in a silo didn't wing a weapon toward Moscow.
It may be more important in the Second Nuclear Age than it was in
the first. When countries with little or no experience with nuclear
weapons suddenly find themselves stacking them up in tunnels
and caves, it would be nice to know that a terrorist who procured
one could not simply set the timer and walk away.

In the American version, PALs hinge on what is essentially a
switch in the firing circuit that requires the would-be user to enter a
numeric code that starts a timer for the weapon's arming and detonation. If the sequence of numbers entered turns out to be incorrect
in a fixed number of tries, the whole system disables itself. It is
pretty similar to what happens when you repeatedly type the wrong
passcode into an ATM machine, and the machine eats your bank
card. But in this case, imagine that someone trying to use your
stolen card entered the wrong code one time too many, and a series
of small explosions was set off to wreck the innards of the bank machine. That's what happens to an American warhead—it is rendered
useless. And in the American design, the system is buried deep inside
the weapon so that no would-be terrorist could get inside to disable
the safeguard system.[28]

In an age of nuclear peril, it seems that this is precisely the kind
of technology you would want to spread around the world to your
friends, especially to friends who are better at building nukes than at
figuring out how to keep them from going off. But nothing is that
simple.

After Powell's trip to Pakistan, a study provided to the White
House concluded that giving PALs to the Pakistanis would violate
both international and American law. After all, Pakistan was the ul-

timate nuclear outlaw: The country developed its arsenal covertly, never signed the Nuclear Non-Proliferation Treaty, and refused to allow investigators to question the greatest nuclear smuggler in history. Under U.S. law, Washington could not legally transfer nuclear technology to the Pakistanis, even if it was technology to make their weapons safer. Period. Ordinarily, one would not expect that to impede the Bush administration: In almost every other element of the war on terror—interrogating of suspects, setting up secret prisons, and inventing rules for military tribunals—the Bush administration rarely slowed down for legal niceties. But in this case they did.

To experts such as Harold M. Agnew, a former director of the Los Alamos weapons laboratory, where most of the United States' nuclear arms were designed, the rules restricting the transfer of PALs are lunacy. They seem like a holdover of old-think, when one of the biggest fears was that we not teach other nations too much about how we secure our own weapons.

"Lawyers say it's classified," Agnew told my *Times* colleague Bill Broad. "That's nonsense. We should share this technology. Anybody who joins the club should be helped to get this. Whether it's India or Pakistan or China or Iran, the most important thing is that you want to make sure there is no unauthorized use. You want to make sure that the guys who have their hands on the weapons can't use them without proper authorization."[29]

Unfortunately, the Pakistanis suspected that the United States had more in mind than just nuclear safety. Any PALs offered up in a FedEx box from Washington, they figured, would come with a secret "kill switch" that would allow someone deep inside the bowels of the Pentagon to track or disable Pakistan's nuclear assets. They were undoubtedly right.

Kidwai insists that he solved this problem by sending Pakistani engineers off to develop what one could only call "Pak-PALs," an indigenous version of the American system. He told me that it was every bit as safe as the American version.

No one will talk about what role, if any, the United States played in designing this system. But history provides a possible clue. Back in the early 1970s, the United States faced a similar problem with a country that produces cheese the way Pakistan produces radicals: France. Worried about protecting the French arsenal, the United States began a series of highly secretive discussions with French scientists that amounted to a game of "twenty questions," though in Washington-speak it was termed "negative guidance." The process was detailed in a 1989 article in *Foreign Policy* by Richard Ullman.[30] According to that account, the French described their approach to building and securing a warhead, and the American nuclear scientists gave guidance about whether they were going off track. Just think of a blindfolded kid trying to pin the tail on a donkey, as everyone else shouts, "You're getting warmer."

At this party, however, Washington was selective about who was allowed to play. When the race was on to secure Russia's arsenal, the United States hurried the declassification of limited information about American warheads so that it could be shared. China was another story: The Clinton administration determined that sharing PALs would be too risky, even though China was a signatory to all the right treaties. Officials feared giving the Chinese too many insights into how American systems worked, and it feared the backlash of seeming to sell another piece of critical technology to Beijing.

In the case of Pakistan, we may know how well Kidwai's "indigenous" PALs system works only after something happens. "Among the places in the world that we have to make sure we have done the maximum we can do, Pakistan is at the top of the list," John McLaughlin, who served as deputy director of the Central Intelligence Agency during the investigation into A. Q. Khan, told me one afternoon in his small office at Johns Hopkins University. "I am confident of two things," he added, "that the Pakistanis are very serious about securing this material, but also that someone in Pakistan is very intent on getting their hands on it."

Naturally, no one in the U.S. government will say much of anything in public about what they know about Pakistan's arsenal, and even in background conversations top officials in the White House, the Pentagon, and the Energy Department are elusive. But, just as Kidwai fears, hardly a few months go by in Washington without someone conducting simulations of how the United States should respond if a terror group infiltrated the Pakistani nuclear program or managed to take control of one or two of its weapons. In these exercises, everyone plays to type: the State Department urges negotiations, while the Special Forces command loads its soldiers into airplanes. The results of these simulations are highly classified, for fear of tipping off the Pakistanis about what the United States knows or doesn't know about the location of the country's weapons. But as one frequent participant put it to me, "most of them don't end well."

The problem with these exercises is that in the end the participants are never convinced that they could tell an American president, with confidence, that they know where all of Pakistan's weapons are—or that none are in the hands of Islamic extremists.

"It's worse than that," a participant in one of the simulations told me. "We can't even certify exactly how many weapons the Pakistanis have—which makes it difficult to sound convincing that there's nothing to worry about." Kidwai turned silent when I pressed him on the question of the size of Pakistan's arsenal. But it is clear that the number keeps changing because the country is upgrading its weaponry, building new, more efficient, plutonium-core weapons.

IN THE TOWER housing the International Atomic Energy Agency's offices in Vienna, the A. Q. Khan affair is not "closed," despite Kidwai's protestations. There are many unanswered questions remaining about his network, and one looming one. Who else possesses the design for Pakistan's bomb?

The question came up in earnest around 2006, when investigators in both the United States and Europe finally cracked the hard drives on Khan's computers, recovered from Bangkok, Dubai, and other locales where the Khan network was active.

The biggest trove was found in the computers that belonged to the Tinner family in Switzerland—the engineering specialists to whom the CIA had turned, and paid upward of $10 million, to provide information and help sabotage nuclear equipment going to Iran.

When Swiss police raided the Tinners' offices and seized their computers, they found the Khan network's most important documents. There was a vast amount of material—orders for equipment, names and places where Khan's associates operated, even old love letters. There were several terabytes of data, a huge amount to sift through.

"There was stuff about dealing with Iranians in 2003, about how to avoid intelligence agents," said one official who had reviewed it. "But then we got the new stuff—things that the local police had missed, maybe because it was encrypted."

In 2008, announcing that the files had been destroyed by the Swiss government, Pascal Couchepin, the Swiss president, said they included "detailed construction plans for nuclear weapons, for gas ultracentrifuges for the enrichment of weapons-grade uranium, as well as for guided missile delivery systems."

The most important of those plans was a digitized design for a nuclear bomb. But this was not the same design that the inspectors had seen before, the one the Libyans turned over on giant sheets of blueprint paper. Those sheets, while helpful to anyone building a weapon, "were more like an appetizer," said the official who had seen both. This was the main course.

The plans were far more sophisticated than what had emerged from Libya. There were "timers and triggers in the design," one investigator said. "Clearly someone had tried to modernize it, to improve the electronics. There were handwritten references to the electronics, and the question is, who was working on this?"

The design was not complete; it would have little value to a terrorist with no experience, but could have been quite helpful to a state, such as Iran, seeking to build an arsenal. The more that investigators examined the design, the more it became clear it was Pakistani.

It is unlikely that the work itself was done by A. Q. Khan. He was never a bomb designer. Instead it appeared to be a weapon design he had access to, and when the IAEA passed questions to Khan about whether this design had gone elsewhere, his response, one official told me, was "I cannot exclude the possibility."*

The concern that raced through the upper echelons of the IAEA was that copies of this new design resided on the hard drives of several computers. It was impossible to know how many times it may have been copied.

The Swiss themselves were nervous about holding on to the bomb design—as became evident as a great drama played out between the Swiss and the CIA. The CIA did not want the Tinners prosecuted—not only would prosecution hurt the effort to recruit new nuclear spies, it would force the agency to acknowledge that the Tinners had worked for Washington. Moreover, at a moment when anti-Americanism in Pakistan was running high, the revelation that the bomb design was Pakistani would create even greater tension and undermine the effort to get the Pakistanis to cooperate. Eventually, the Swiss were persuaded to destroy all the material—even if it meant killing off any prosecution of the Tinners.[31]

Back in Washington, news of the new, more sophisticated de-

---

* These statements by Khan have to be treated with considerable skepticism. Questions aimed at Khan were forwarded by the IAEA and the CIA after he was put under house arrest in 2004. The Pakistani intelligence services say they brought the questions to him, and then delivered his answers back to Washington or Vienna. But neither agency had much understanding of how the questions were translated, or whether Khan's answers were edited by Pakistani authorities before they were returned to avoid statements that might contradict Pakistan's official line—that he had no access to weapons designs, and that no other Pakistani officials knew what he was doing.

sign was closely held. One senior official I went to interview was happy to talk about the American effort to secure Pakistan's weapons. But when I started inquiring about the plans on the Khan computers, he hesitated. "I can confirm that they were there—we helped crack the code," he said. "But beyond that, it's one of the few things we simply can't talk about." When I asked about it at the White House and the upper echelons of the State and Defense Departments, some officials grimaced, others said they had never heard about it.

The design suggests that Khan was branching out, offering to sell not only the centrifuges to make bomb fuel but the blueprints to do something with it. "This looks to me like it was a cohesive plan," one IAEA official said. When I asked Kidwai about it, he clearly knew about the discovery, but he waved away its importance. "What we've seen is incomplete," he said. Anyway, he added, he did not believe that Khan would have had access to complete bomb designs, because they were done in a competing laboratory.

THE MAN WHO knows the answers to these questions is A. Q. Khan himself, and he isn't talking.

Except, of course, when the subject turns to regaining his freedom. Then he becomes garrulous. It didn't take long after the installation of a new government in Pakistan, in April 2008, for Khan to break his silence. With the rise in nationalistic fervor in the country—and the sense that it was time for the Americans to stop pushing Pakistan around—he saw a chance for his release.

"I saved the country for the first time when I made Pakistan a nuclear nation and saved it again when I confessed and took the whole blame on myself," he told a reporter one evening in a telephone call.[32] His family was pressing to allow him to have visitors and travel outside the house on Hillside Avenue, suggesting not so subtly that if the new government did not end his four-year-long home sentence, he might be tempted to talk about who else in the government was involved in his activities.

Appearing on television, the country's new foreign minister, Shah Mehmood Qureshi, said the time had come to restore Khan to a position of respect. "Yes, I don't want to see his movement restricted," he told a Pakistani television station one day when I was reporting for this book in Islamabad. "He is a Pakistani, a respected Pakistani; I think that he should be allowed to see his friends, to go for a drive, to have a meal at a restaurant. I see no reason why he should be deprived of that; on the other hand we have to be concerned about his security and his health."[33]

In private, though, Khan was beginning to express to a few associates some second thoughts about his life's work. In January 2008, he wrote to one colleague that his desire to develop his nuclear expertise came from what he called the "traumatic" moments of his early life. He recalled traveling from Bhopal to Karachi with his family in 1947, amid horrific violence between Hindus and Muslims. He described the 1971 war in which Pakistan gave up "East Pakistan"—the war in which Kidwai was taken as a POW—which he termed a "disgraceful and humiliating surrender."

"I got scared Indira Gandhi would go for the final kill," he said. But in his old age, he had begun to discover that he empowered the army to rule over the country forever. "I never dreamt or thought of the disgraceful way the army would control the country under its boot," he said. "They are here to stay on top of us for all time. I had thought that I was doing a patriotic service. Now it looks like it was a mistake."[34]

He ended the letter with a half-sentence: "No use of self-pity."

# CHAPTER 8
# CROSSING THE LINE

TEN DAYS AFTER Benazir Bhutto was killed on the streets of Rawalpindi, America's two top spy chiefs boarded a CIA plane for the grueling, fifteen-hour flight to Pakistan. They carried aboard a portfolio of fresh intelligence about the man they believed killed her, and a dire warning to Pervez Musharraf that his government was the next target.

The very fact that the "two Mikes," as they are called in the intelligence world—McConnell and Hayden—were traveling together made this an unusual mission. Bush had come to depend on his morning intelligence briefings, with their "threat matrixes" and accounts of overnight captures or action in Iraq, and his aides believed he was vaguely uncomfortable whenever his director of national intelligence and the CIA director were out of Washington at the same time.

But Pakistan was headed into a downward spiral that left them little choice. Hayden and McConnell thought that this was Musharraf's last chance, his last opportunity to take on the militants in the tribal areas and to defuse the protests in the streets. The gravity of the message, they hoped, would be reinforced by the rank of the messengers.

The trip was a blitz—more than 16,000 miles round trip for a stayover in Islamabad that lasted less than a day. But they were able to fly completely under the radar. If anyone saw them get off the CIA's unmarked plane—highly unlikely given the secrecy and security surrounding their visit—they would have looked like two graying executives arriving to sell airplane parts or consulting services.

McConnell looks like George Smiley in a John le Carré novel. He measures each sentence carefully, as if weighing what his audience already knows and what it is cleared to know. He speaks in a light Carolina drawl with an intense demeanor leavened by a flash of ironic humor.

Hayden, by contrast, is a sprightly, balding former Air Force general, with a down-home demeanor rooted in his youth in a hardscrabble area of Pittsburgh. Hayden also ran the NSA—after McConnell—and with mixed results. Known as a skilled bureaucratic infighter, he won battles over funding and shook up the place. He courted reporters by inviting them into Fort Meade, home of what was once known as "No Such Agency." But his signature program, Trailblazer, which began in 2001 as part of an effort to improve the agency's ability to sort through a haul of 650 million messages a day, cost hundreds of millions of dollars and suffered long delays. His critics used it to question his management skills; his advocates maintained that he woke the agency from its post–Cold War stupor. In the Bush years, he emerged as the defender of the post-9/11 warrantless wiretapping program—the administration dubbed it the "Terrorist Surveillance Program" once its existence was exposed—and was left to explain why the administration simply ignored legal requirements that it found inconvenient. Away from the cameras, he was far more down to earth than might be expected of an Air Force officer turned spy chief.

"He's Type A, but Mike's far more likely to find the humorous or the ridiculous in whatever problem we're tackling," one of his colleagues told me. "And he's often the first one to say, 'You know, there are some problems that all the covert action in the world won't solve.'"

Pakistan was one of those problems. Since 2001 Musharraf had been the master of promises, most unkept. One day he was vowing to send 100,000 troops into the tribal areas to root out what he called "miscreants," a politically less loaded term than "terrorists." The next day he was pronouncing that seeking Osama bin Laden was Bush's problem, not his, while quietly assuring Bush in private phone calls that his statements were all about quieting domestic criticism while sending crack counterterrorism teams into the mountains to bring him bin Laden's head. In 2002, Musharraf made a huge show of arresting 2,000 suspected militants, many of whom had trained in Taliban camps that Pakistan had sponsored. After he had milked the arrests for publicity, he quietly ordered all of the prisoners released. He was, as McConnell and Hayden often commented to each other, the master of the double game.

Inevitably, the game turned against him. Many of the same militants Pakistan had once supported to fight the Soviets, and secretly funded to blow up Indian troops in the disputed areas of Kashmir, were now taking aim at the Pakistani government itself. To them, Musharraf was an American lackey who had sold Pakistan's soul, its sovereignty and, if you believed the rumors, maybe control of its nuclear weapons to the Americans. In a country where conspiracy theories are served up with dinner, others thought he had been duped, falling for a secret plot between India and the United States to disarm Pakistan, then destroy it.

To the Americans, this view of Musharraf was not only incomprehensible, it was laughable. Musharraf appeared so busy balancing competing interests to stay in power that he was ignoring the storm gathering around him. As they flew to Islamabad, McConnell and Hayden debated how to convince Musharraf that he could not survive unless he took the war to the militants. They pored over the evidence they were prepared to show him, largely intercepts of conversations among the insurgents in the northwest territories. Cell phone conversations convinced them that the man who had ordered Bhutto's death was Baitullah Mehsud, a thuggish militant who had established the Tehrik-e-Taliban just weeks before Bhutto's death in an effort to create an umbrella organization for the "Pakistani Taliban."

That was only the opening page of the portfolio. McConnell and Hayden planned to lay out for Musharraf what Hayden later termed a map of the "nexus between Pashtun extremism and the growing attacks on Pakistan." They brought evidence of how attacks originating from the safe haven of the tribal region had "gotten worse, progressively worse." The warning to Musharraf was stark: This was an all-out war between Pakistan and the militants, and Pakistani forces had to get into the fight.

As always, Musharraf was a cipher. He knew what his visitors wanted to hear and sounded as if he were in complete agreement. Hayden later told associates that Musharraf was under no illusions. After all, this was a man who had survived at least two assassination attempts. He was finishing our sentences, Hayden said when he returned to Washington. He got it.

McConnell wasn't so sure. He thought Musharraf was still living in a state of denial, unaware of the dark clouds headed for Islamabad.

WHAT MUSHARRAF did not know during his meeting with McConnell and Hayden—or, at least, what he was not explicitly told—was that Bush was out of patience and secretly preparing for a major change in American strategy. Only days before their trip, after considerable debate within his national security team, Bush secretly began to lift the restrictions that greatly limited CIA operations inside Pakistani territory. It was the first of a series of decisions—none ever announced publicly or even acknowledged in my conversations with administration officials, except by knowing looks or their requests that not too many details become public, for fear of the backlash in Pakistan.[1]

Bush did not issue a new "finding"—the legal document, which

the White House would have to report to Congress, that permits
the CIA to conduct a new covert operation. Instead he loosened restrictions on an existing finding, one issued just days after 9/11.
Using that method, he did not have to notify Congress of a new approach.

Until the early days of 2008, the CIA Predator aircraft that hov-
ered off the Afghan-Pakistan border could strike targets inside Pakistan only under the most restrictive conditions. The plane's
operators—7,000 miles away, flying the drones from video consoles
in Nevada—could not strike without knowing exactly who they had
in their sights. There had to be a full assessment of the potential
"collateral damage." You could not hit a basement full of terrorists
if above them was a living room full of kids. The list of acceptable
targets was small—a short list of top al Qaeda operatives, starting
with bin Laden himself.

Now, in a process that had taken months, Bush had expanded
what Hayden and McConnell called "the permissions." He simply
lowered the standard of proof needed before the Predators could
strike. For the first time the CIA no longer had to identify its target
by name; now the "signature" of a typical al Qaeda motorcade, or of
a group entering a known al Qaeda safe house, was enough to authorize a strike. Moreover, the agency and Special Forces were
given permission to go after a wider group of al Qaeda members.
The list of targets was expanded to about twenty. And they could
make use of a specially modified version of the Predator—designed
for precision strikes. It could drop a ton of guided bombs and missiles, all from a pilotless "hunter-killer drone" that had bulked up
to the size of a small fighter aircraft. It was a drone on steroids at
50,000 feet.

One of his top national security aides referred to the choices
presented to Bush as "a Chinese menu of other options" that would
gradually allow the CIA greater latitude. "It's risky," the aide said,
"because you can make more mistakes—you can hit the wrong
house, or misidentify the motorcade."

By the time Bush was done making his menu selections, it was clear that a new front was opening in the war along the Afghanistan-Pakistan border. Bush's decision was enveloped in enormous secrecy because Musharraf had warned of a huge backlash if Americans were ever caught operating in sovereign Pakistani territory—something he publicly insisted he would never permit. Of course, he knew the United States was already in Pakistan, with two small CIA "forward operating bases" deep inside Pakistani military facilities. But the bases were tiny, and the American faces could be easily explained away as military advisers. Now, Bush was greatly upping the ante. This would turn out to be only the first in a series of escalating "permissions" as the White House became convinced that the Paksitani government was both unwilling to deal with the Pashtun militants in the tribal belt and incapable of doing so. "It was born of sheer frustration," one of Bush's top aides said to me. "It was clear that the chaos settling over the country would continue, and maybe worsen."

He paused. "The problem of Pakistan comes down to this: How do you invade an ally?"

IT QUICKLY TURNED OUT that McConnell and Hayden were talking to the wrong man. Pervez Musharraf still *looked* as if he were leading Pakistan. He was as charming and witty as ever, with all the characteristics that had led Bush to invest too much confidence in him. He had been able to talk general-to-general with Powell. He could spin out a democratic vision for Pakistan that appealed to Americans. But at home his magic had long since worn off. And it took Bush far too long to understand that Musharraf was yesterday's dictator.

Bush's dependence on Musharraf was understandable, up to a point. Since the Pakistani's shotgun transformation into an American ally in the hours after the 9/11 attacks, he seemed like the kind of leader Bush was looking for, a wily pragmatist, a survivor who understood where his interests lay. But, over time, Bush came to believe too much of his own public praise for Musharraf. Out of optimism, out of necessity, out of an absence of other options, Bush clung to the hope that Musharraf was a fierce warrior against terrorists of all stripes—a perception Musharraf fostered early in the "war on terror" by handing over some al Qaeda members.

The intelligence reports Bush and the rest of the national security team received each morning—and Hayden's own presentations in January 2008 to Bush's national security team—told a very different story. In the weeks after Bhutto's assassination, a flurry of new assessments on the deepening crisis in Pakistan concluded that it was unlikely that Musharraf, the man in whom Bush had invested America's entire Pakistan strategy and with it the battle against the Taliban and al Qaeda, could remain in power for long. The general, Hayden reported, had started losing control in the summer of 2007, with the standoff and shootout with militants who seized the famed Red Mosque in Islamabad. By August, Rice was often on the phone with Musharraf—twice a day, in one case—urging him not to impose martial law, a step that would almost certainly require Washington to denounce him for backing away from the democratic reforms he had long promised. Then came the fall of 2007 and a succession of political crises, as Musharraf attempted to kneecap a growing democratic movement by arresting protesting lawyers instead of using his time and resources to hunt down terrorists.

Rice and her deputy, John D. Negroponte, who had recently returned to the State Department after an unhappy year and a half as America's first director of national intelligence, tried to help save Musharraf from himself. They worked behind the scenes to engineer Bhutto's return to Pakistan and urged a "power-sharing" agreement between the plotting Bhutto, whom they distrusted, and Musharraf, whom they viewed as his own worst enemy. They knew it was a marriage made in hell, between two politicians whose hatred of each other went back years. But the hope was that the deal would take the passion out of the anti-Musharraf protests and buy some time. Washington could point to a democratic transition, and still have Musharraf at the other end of the phone. It was, in short, an unstable, long-shot political deal dressed up as a strategy.

The first assassination attempt against Bhutto occurred hours after she stepped off her plane for her first return to Pakistan in eight years. During the election campaign—which Musharraf permitted to go ahead, under tremendous pressure from the United States—she drew huge crowds, but the danger was palpable every day. It was only a matter of time before the inevitable suicide bomb exploded, or a shot rang out from the crowd. Even before she was struck down, Islamabad was rife with conspiracy theories, fanned by Bhutto's supporters, that Musharraf was deliberately withholding the kind of protection she needed. That charge was never proven, and she would not have trusted his guards anyway. Musharraf insisted that he offered protection, but after her assassination in December he shrugged and all but said she had it coming.

In December, as the negotiations over power-sharing took place behind the scenes, Bhutto argued with visiting American officials that they were making a huge mistake in betting on Musharraf. "Mr. Ambassador," she said, drawing out every word in a telephone conversation with Negroponte, "don't you think it is time for him to go?" Her motives were transparent, and Negroponte was more amused than convinced. But at the White House, in corridor conversations, some officials were beginning to question whether their critics were right. They had bet on one horse for seven years, and now he was lame.

Musharraf's party was crushed in the elections, which were held more than a month after Bhutto's killing. "From that moment he was toast," one of Bush's cabinet members said a few months later. Bush had to welcome the arrival of democracy, but with the new era came a powerless, bitterly divided government. It pitted a former prime minister, Nawaz Sharif, whom Musharraf had thrown out of power and sent into exile in a coup in 1999, against Bhutto's widower, Asif Ali Zardari, who had evaded or defeated corruption charges on several continents.

By the time I arrived in Islamabad in April 2008 to survey the damage, Musharraf's star was fading (He canceled an interview, and his spokesman, a burly ex-general who seemed unable to accept reality, explained one night that Musharraf was "the only one who can command this country, but he can't be talking about it.") Having finally fulfilled his promise to retire from the army—and thus give up his most powerful role—Musharraf watched his authority ebb each day. "Without the uniform, he is nothing," a senior general in the army, suddenly able to express his contempt for his ex-boss, told me late one afternoon at army headquarters. "He is just Bush's instrument, and the instrument is no longer sharp."

By late spring, Bush realized that seven years after he had begun assiduously courting a Pakistani leader whose name he famously could not remember during the 2000 campaign, Pakistan was, in essence, being governed by no one. The newly elected civilian government was manned by the powerless, the corrupt, and the incompetent. The military was the only institution holding the country together, but for once it was staying out of politics. For the militants in the tribal areas, it was a dream come true. Pakistan was becoming a failed state, and the militants and the Taliban were speeding the process with regular bombings, kidnappings, and assassinations.

But admitting the obvious—that al Qaeda, the Taliban, and the militants had more running room than ever—was painful for an administration that was beginning to understand how much its preoccupation with Iraq had cost elsewhere. Just how painful became clear when Ted Gistaro, the National Intelligence Officer for Transnational Threats, gave a speech in the doldrums of August 2008, that stated the obvious: In the year since the formal intelligence estimate concluding that al Qaeda had reconstituted itself in the tribal areas, al Qaeda had "maintained or strengthened key elements of its capability to attack the United States in the past year." Its hold on the tribal area was stronger than ever, Gistaro said, and "it now has many of the operational and organization advantages it once enjoyed across the border in Afghanistan, albeit on a smaller and less secure scale." Al Qaeda had "replenished its bench" of midlevel operatives, Gistaro explained, and deepened its alliances with the Taliban and other militants. Al Qaeda was more dynamic than ever, he argued, because it had "developed succession plans, [and could] reshuffle leadership responsibilities, and promote younger commanders with years of battlefield experience to senior positions."[2]

Fortunately for Bush, so much of official Washington was elsewhere because of the summer holiday and congressional recess that few noticed the conclusions. Some administration officials pushed back gently, telling members of Congress they thought the situation had been overstated. But the White House had long since pulled the plug on Bush's regular speeches proclaiming victory against al Qaeda, speeches in which he usually cited statistics about how many of bin Laden's lieutenants had been killed, and how the organization's middle management had been wiped out. The speeches were now painfully easy to ridicule.

IF ANYONE NEEDED evidence that the reality on the ground was even worse than the formal assessments, it could be found near the Pakistani border, in the city of Kandahar, once the center of Taliban power in Afghanistan. That was, of course, the city where Nick Burns had taken the NATO ambassadors in 2003 to convince them that Afghanistan was becoming more peaceful, and that NATO should send in forces. It was the place where they sipped tea with tribal leaders. And while Americans rightly regard Pakistan and Afghanistan as separate countries, to the Taliban and other Pashtun tribal leaders, it is all one friendly, familiar piece of territory. To them, the border, formally known as the Durand Line, is just a Western invention, an invisible boundary named for a long-dead Brit. It is meaningless to them; it only means something to the American military and NATO, for whom it has long been a wall over which they could not pass.

On the evening of June 13, 2008, a white fuel tanker truck pulled up near the gates of Kandahar's biggest prison. The driver hopped out of the cab, laughed, and ran off. In a flash, the few guards at the gate recognized what was happening and opened fire on him, but they missed—killing the son of a shopkeeper nearby instead. Within seconds a rocket-propelled grenade hit the tanker, setting off the fuel, killing the guards, and blowing a huge hole in the entryway to the prison. Just blocks away, the Afghan police didn't move; they, too, figured out what was happening and were too frightened to help. That left ten guards—several of whom were already dead—to fight off a wave of about forty invading Taliban. The undermanned NATO outpost in the city, consisting almost entirely of Canadian troops who had already suffered heavy casualties, were off dealing with roadside bombs that had been set off just a half hour before, in what appears to have been an effective diversion. By the time they figured out what was happening, it was over.

Investigators later determined that of the 900 prisoners who escaped that night, slightly more than a third were hardcore members of the Taliban.[3] Still, six years after the American-led invasion, the prison had no blast walls, not even a barrier at the front gate. "This has been car-bomb central for years," one senior administration official said to me after accounts of the prison break started leaking out. "We're pouring hundreds of millions of dollars of aid into the place. And we can't figure out how to build a blast wall?"

But it wasn't just the wall that was blown to pieces that night; so were the last remnants of credibility of the Karzai government. "What astounded me," said Vikram Singh, a former Defense Department official who traveled to Afghanistan in the summer of 2008 and met with tribal leaders in Kandahar, "was how little control Karzai's government had beyond the capital." Roads that were rebuilt with international funds, and hailed by Bush in speeches, were now unsafe even during the day. Singh quickly concluded that driving from Kandahar to Kabul would be suicidal for a foreigner.

Even one of the provinces adjacent to Kabul was under de facto control of the Taliban, giving the capital a feeling of constant siege.

The spring brought a grim new turning point: American casualties in the country exceeded those in Iraq—even though the American force in Afghanistan was a fifth of the size of the U.S. force in Iraq during the "surge." NATO forces became a regular target of suicide bombers and militant attacks; in August one battle involving 100 insurgents cost the lives of ten elite French paratroopers.

The Taliban and the insurgents had seen their window of opportunity. Despite the commitment of European leaders to stay in the fight, most NATO countries had ignored Bush's call for them to provide more troops. While several thousand additional American troops were arriving in Afghanistan as reinforcements, Bush was a lame duck, conducting one "strategy review" after another—an odd exercise in the last months of an eight-year-long presidency. The next administration would undoubtedly start with its own such review—and it would be months before a new national security team would be ready to adopt a strategy. And as long as the Americans could not cross the border into Pakistan, the Taliban knew that they had little to fear, save the occasional Predator overhead.

In the summer of 2008, just before the seventh anniversary of the attacks that started America's war in Afghanistan, Barack Obama, Senator Jack Reed of Rhode Island, and Senator Chuck Hagel, who was retiring after two terms as a Republican senator from Nebraska, visited Afghanistan. I saw Hagel a few days after he returned, and we talked about the military assessments he had received.

"It's never looked worse," Hagel, a Vietnam veteran, said to me. Then he stopped and corrected himself. "It's never looked worse since September 10, 2001."

IN LATE MAY 2008, McConnell made a secret trip to Pakistan—his fourth or fifth since becoming the director of national intelligence, trips that seemed to blur together in his head. But this one was dramatically different from the rest—and ended up driving the push in the last days of the Bush administration to greatly step up covert action across the border into Pakistan.

Pacing quickly through his usual rounds of meetings with Musharraf and a raft of intelligence officials in Islamabad, McConnell and his small entourage found themselves in a conference room with several military officers, including a two-star Pakistani general.

One officer was talking to another participant in the meetings as if the American intelligence chief—the visiting dignitary for the day—wasn't in the room. Not surprisingly, he was being pressed about Pakistan's strategy in the tribal areas, and he was "reluctant to start," one of the participants in the conversation recalled. "But once he got into it, he couldn't contain himself."

The officer began making the case that the real problem in the tribal areas and in Afghanistan was not al Qaeda or the Taliban, or even the militants who were trying to topple the Pakistani government. The real problem was Pakistan's rival of more than sixty years, which he said was secretly manipulating events in an effort to crush Pakistan and undo the 1947 partition that sought to separate the Islamic and Hindu states.

"The overwhelming enemy is India," the Pakistani officer told the general. "We have to watch them at every moment. We've had wars with India," he said, as if anyone in the room needed reminding.

The Pakistani two-star described President Karzai's cozy relationship with the Indians, seeking investment and aid. With alarm, he talked about how the Indians were opening consulates around the country and building roads. What the rest of the world saw as a desperately needed nation-building program, the Pakistanis saw as a threat. He wasn't alone in that view; conspiracy theories about India's activities in Afghanistan are a daily staple in the Pakistani media.

As the officer talked, he became more and more animated. "The Indians will surround us and annihilate us," he said, knowing that

McConnell was hearing every word. "And the Indians, in their surrounding strategy, have gone to Afghanistan." Those newly built
roads were future invasion routes, he seemed to suggest, without
ever quite saying so. The consulates were dens of Indian spies. The
real purpose of the humanitarian aid to Afghanistan was to run
"operations out of Afghanistan to target Pakistan."

The conspiracy theory deepened. "In the long run, America will
not have the stomach to bear the burden of staying in Afghanistan,"
the officer continued, still seeming to ignore the presence of the
American intelligence chief. "And when America pulls out, India will
reign. Therefore the Pakistanis will have to sustain contact" with the
opposition to the Afghan government—meaning the Taliban—"so
when the Americans pull out, it's a friendly government to Pakistan."

"Therefore," the officer concluded with a flourish, "we must
support the Taliban."

That last statement stunned McConnell. For six years the
American government had paid upward of $10 billion to the Pak-
istani government to support its operations against al Qaeda and
the Taliban. Bush and his aides knew—though they never admitted—that much of that money had been diverted to buying equipment for the Pakistani military to bulk up against the Indians.
What was sold to Congress as "reimbursements" were actually
being used to buy new airplanes and new artillery. The equipment
would be enormously useful in stopping an Indian invasion force,
but was useless in battling terrorists in caves. Now a Pakistani officer, in his fury and frustration, was openly admitting what the Pakistani government had officially denied, that it was playing both
sides of the war, the American side and the Taliban side. In return
for the American billions, Pakistani forces or intelligence operatives
occasionally picked off a few al Qaeda leaders (though even that
had slowed to a trickle). But they were actively supporting the Taliban and even some of the militants in the tribal regions. In a world
of fungible money—that $10 billion in American aid was paid

straight to the Pakistani treasury—it was almost as if the American taxpayers were making monthly deposits in the Taliban's bank accounts. Some in the Pentagon objected but were overruled.

None of this was really a surprise—except to the American people, who were regularly told by President Bush that Pakistan and its leadership were a "strong ally against terror." Even some of Bush's aides cringed when he uttered those words. "It was like hearing him say 'Victory in Iraq,'" one told me after leaving the White House. "He thought that to publicly acknowledge the muddled complexity of it all was some kind of admission of defeat."

Even inside the White House, some officials admitted to me that the "reimbursements" to the Pakistani military were just this side of fraud. They had been paid out even when Musharraf had announced he was pulling back from the tribal areas because of a "truce" he had agreed to with tribal leaders. When Congress threatened to link the "reimbursements" to the Pakistani military's performance, one American general summarized his reaction this way: "It's about goddamn time."

Bush knew the truth: Intelligence reports written over the past five years have all documented the ISI's support of the Taliban—something Bush had admitted to me and other reporters. He knew, of course, that even Musharraf had little interest in sending his army into frontier territory, where, as Bush once put it to an aide, "they get their asses kicked every week." Every military professional who returned from Islamabad came back with the same report: Seven years after 9/11, 80 percent of the Pakistani military was arrayed against India. McConnell himself, returning from one of his trips, noted that there is only one army that has more artillery tubes per unit—everything from old cannons to rocket launchers and mortars. It is North Korea's, he said. It was a telling statistic. Artillery tubes weigh tons—and are useful only in holding back Indian hordes as they come across the plains. They are useless against terrorist enclaves in the mountains.

Overhearing the two-star's rant about India was not the only rude surprise McConnell experienced on this trip. He had brought with him the chart he used in the White House Situation Room tracking the number of attacks inside Pakistan over the past two and a half years. One of the charts showed that about 1,300 Pakistanis had been killed in 2007, chiefly from suicide bombers, about double the number in 2006. (The figures didn't include Pakistani troops killed in various clashes against militants.) He told Musharraf and Gen. Ashfaq Kayani, the smooth-talking, American-trained head of the Pakistani Army and former chief of the ISI, that the casualty numbers were on track to double again in 2008. Then he described the interviews that Osama bin Laden and his deputies had given, declaring their intention to topple the Pakistani government. You're aware of these casualty numbers and what bin Laden said, of course, McConnell asked. He got blank stares. They told him they had not heard about bin Laden's statements.

"It was news," McConnell reported to his colleagues later. "I talked to the highest levels of the Pakistani government and it was news. They just weren't tracking it." It astounded him that officials in Washington and at the American embassy in Islamabad might be keeping more careful tabs on the rising number of attacks than were Musharraf or Pakistan's new crop of democratically elected leaders. Were they ignoring the obvious, or were they just denying they knew about it, part of the deceptions within the deceptions as they supported both sides in the terror fight?

When McConnell returned to Washington in late May 2008, he ordered up a full assessment so that he could match what he'd heard from a single angry officer with the intelligence that had poured in over the years. His question was a basic one: Is there what McConnell called an officially sanctioned "dual policy" in Pakistan? That was a polite way of asking whether the leadership of the country—including Musharraf and General Kayani—had been playing both sides of the war all along?

It did not take long for McConnell's staff to produce the answer. Musharraf's record of duplicity was well known. While Kayani was a favorite of the White House, he had also been overheard—presumably on telephone intercepts—referring to one of the most brutal of the Taliban leaders, Maulavi Jalaluddin Haqqani, as a "strategic asset."[4] (A quarter-century ago, Haqqani was an American asset as well, when he organized Mujahideen fighters from several nations to attack the Soviets during the occupation of Afghanistan. In the real-life version of *Charlie Wilson's War,* Haqqani was the classic local ally of convenience.)

McConnell took the formal assessment to the White House, concluding that the Pakistani government regularly gave the Taliban and some of the militant groups "weapons and support to go into Afghanistan to attack Afghan and coalition forces." This was not news to many in the administration, but McConnell wanted to have it down on paper. The assessment was circulated to the entire national security leadership, and to Bush, who was still giving public speeches praising Musharraf as a great ally.

"It wasn't news to him," said one of the officials who briefed Bush and watched his reaction to McConnell's assessment. "And he always says the same thing: 'So, what do you do about it?'"

By the summer, Bush answered his own question. For the first time in a presidency filled with secret unilateral actions, he authorized the American military to invade an ally.

This was a different kind of invasion than the type Americans were used to seeing on CNN during the Bush years. This was not Iraq or Afghanistan; Bush did not want to topple a government, control any territory, or search for any weapons of mass destruction. (Though in Pakistan he could have actually found some.) He certainly did not want to give threatening speeches or send a big force into a sovereign state, a mistake that would help create a new generation of pro-Taliban sympathizers. Worse yet, if the Americans did anything obvious, it would lead to a huge confrontation with the Pakistani military. The new government would have no choice: They were about to issue articles of impeachment against Musharraf, accusing him of acting as Bush's toady, too eager to fight in what millions of Pakistanis called "America's war."

Yet Bush knew that if he waited for the new Pakistani government to act on its own, he would likely leave office at noon on January 20, 2009, with Osama bin Laden still a free man, whole cities in Pakistan on the verge of falling to the Taliban, and the border territory with Afghanistan a mountainous amusement park where all of America's greatest enemies could gather to share the rides.

What Bush, Hadley, Rice, Gates, and the military had in mind were operations that were entirely covert and, if everything went well, completely deniable: quick attacks by Bush's favorite branch of the military, the Joint Special Operations Command, over the border into Pakistani territory. There they would do what JSOC had done so effectively against al Qaeda in Iraq: hit a house full of suspected terrorists, kill the occupants, grab the cell phones and computer hard drives, and exploit the information inside them instantly. If the intelligence led to another nearby safe house, or a cell phone that could be traced, that would be hit the same night, if possible.

There was a problem, however. Bush always assured the Pakistanis, particularly in public, that American ground operations on their territory would happen only with advance consultation with the Pakistani military, and, when possible, American and Pakistani troops would operate together. It sounded like one of those great partnerships with a "major non-NATO ally," which was still Pakistan's official status. In reality, those joint operations had been rare, and almost never satisfactory for either side. The Pakistanis resented the American military presence. It was embarrassing to have them on Pakistani soil, and it didn't help that they were equipped with the latest in everything, including the newest night-vision goggles and communications devices. The Pakistanis weren't just on a different wavelength, they were stuck in a different technological age.

For their part, the Americans were always vaguely suspicious that the Pakistani military was tipping off targets in advance. The military-to-military relationship was increasingly sour. But it was a love fest compared to the animosities between the CIA and their intelligence counterpart in Pakistan, the ISI. "By summer there was a sense inside the CIA that the ISI is absolutely in complete coordination with the Taliban," said one senior official who was in the middle of the debate. Still, Hayden knew he had to tread somewhat carefully; the CIA depended heavily on the ISI for its information about militants in Pakistan, and that was not likely to change.

By late June, however, evidence began to arrive to back up the CIA's hunch. The National Security Agency intercepted messages indicating that ISI officers were helping the Taliban plan a big bombing in Afghanistan. The target was unclear. "It read like they were giving them the weapons and the support," said one senior official who had been read into the intelligence. The decision was made to send Stephen R. Kappes, the deputy director of the CIA and a veteran of the CIA station in Islamabad, to present the Pakistani leadership with the evidence and demand a cessation of the connections to the Taliban. Kappes made the trip, but arrived too late. On July 7, India's embassy in Kabul was bombed, killing fifty-four people, including India's defense attaché to Afghanistan.

"It confirmed some suspicions that I think were widely held," one State Department official who dealt with Afghanistan told my colleague Eric Schmitt. "It was sort of this 'aha' moment. There was a sense that there was finally direct proof."[5]

By the time Kappes arrived in Pakistan to "put demands on the table," according to a senior administration official, Bush had already begun to act. He decided he had to go well beyond his decision in January to loosen the reins on the CIA. Now he lowered the barriers even further. "We got down to a sort of 'reasonable man' standard," said one official. "If it seemed reasonable, you could hit it." All notions of "advance consultation" with Pakistani authorities were scrapped. Now they would just be informed of a strike—preferably a few seconds before it happened.

That was only the start. For the first time Bush was going to put the American military into the fight inside a sovereign nation that was also an ally. And for the first time he approved lists of militants who could be targeted by either the CIA or American military commandos—lists that went far beyond the ranks of al Qaeda.

Haqqani topped the classified list, because he was identified as an "al Qaeda associate." So was Baitullah Mehsud, the accused killer of Bhutto. The list went on. Mullah Omar, the one-eyed Taliban leader who had managed to escape during the 2001 invasion and was still actively plotting the Taliban's return to Afghanistan, made the list. Gulbuddin Hekmatyar, a former warlord and Mujahideen leader who once fought the Soviets and now is designated a "global terrorist" by the United States. A range of lesser-known militants. It was a huge decision, and among the most tightly held in the U.S. government, because the potential for backlash was so great. In legal terms, some inside the administration noted, it would be as if the president sent American commandos—not just stealthy CIA operatives, but platoons of night fighters with big guns—into Berlin or Paris to root out groups plotting to bomb an airplane. Suddenly a flurry of memos was ordered up, seeking authority for the military to act, not just as a temporary adjunct to the CIA, but in its own right. White House officials developed a new definition of "anticipatory self-defense" that justified the violations of Pakistan's sovereignty. To some, especially in the State Department, where the few officials who knew about Bush's decision were queasy about it, the secret decision was akin to Nixon's decision during Vietnam to conduct a "secret war" in Cambodia, where the Vietcong had found sanctuary.

It also presented enormous legal problems. While the CIA could operate inside Pakistan with a proper "finding," authorizing the military to do so was far trickier. For weeks lawyers argued about how they could expand on the authorizations that allowed the military to conduct a "war on terror" across the border into a country that was an ally, but has publicly barred the military from entering. Inside the White House, Bush's choices seemed stark:

send in American forces or continue to suffer an escalation of the violence against coalition forces in Afghanistan, and an increase in the risk posed by al Qaeda and the Taliban from their safe haven in Pakistan. Opinions were written and put in the file.

Many elements of the decision, and the legal logic behind it, remain secret to this day. Presumably they will be reviewed—and perhaps rewritten—by the Obama administration. But in deciding to loosen the reins on JSOC, for the first time since 9/11, Bush expanded the list of targets in the region far beyond al Qaeda.

"The briefings all made clear that there were three insurgencies under way in the tribal belt, not just one," said one official who participated in the debate. "There was al Qaeda—Osama and his buddies, plotting away, and we were no goddamn closer to them than we were in 2001. There was big-T Taliban, the guys going into Afghanistan to attack us and attack NATO. And then there was the little-T Taliban that was headed for Pakistan's capital itself—those are the guys living in the hope that some day they could take over the whole state, nukes and all."

Bush had decided, in essence, to go after all three. The war for Afghanistan had spread over the border into the tribal regions of Pakistan and North and South Waziristan, a huge piece of land (imagine the dimensions of Massachusetts, but the topography of Switzerland). Bush just didn't want to tell the Americans or the Pakistanis he was fighting there.

IN JULY 2008, with Musharraf losing power daily, Prime Minister Gilani arrived in Washington for his first visit. Because of Kappes's secret trip to Islamabad only days before, he knew he was going to come under intense pressure for a plan to defeat the militants—something he was completely incapable of doing. But he knew better than to show up without a gift.

So he arranged for one. He planned to tell Bush that he had sent forces into the tribal areas to clean out a major madrassa—one well known to American intelligence officers—where hardline ideology and intolerance were part of the daily academic curriculum. There were roughly 25,000 private Islamic schools around Pakistan, though only a small number of them regularly bred young terrorists and sent them out to attack Americans. Musharraf, naturally, had promised time and again to close the worst of the schools—and, as my colleague Dexter Filkins put it, "never took the slightest steps to do so."[6] Though Gilani never knew it, Bush was aware of this gift in advance. The NSA was already picking up intercepts as the units that were getting ready to hit the school called up to the tribal areas in advance, to warn them what was coming.

"They must have dialed 1-800-HAQQANI," said one person who was familiar with the intercepted conversation. According to another, the account of the warning sent to the school was almost comical. "It was something like, 'Hey, we're going to hit your place in a few days, so if anyone important is there, you might want to tell them to scram.'"

But leave a few weapons around, Haqqani's operatives were told, so that it would not look as if the Pakistani Army had come up with nothing. They needed a few trophies to bring back. "Oh, and they warned them that there would be a lot of smoke bombs and stuff, but they shouldn't worry too much."

When the "attack" on the madrassa came, the Pakistani forces liberated a few guns and hauled away a few teenagers. Sure enough, a few days later Gilani showed up in the Oval Office and conveyed the wonderful news to Bush—the great crackdown on the madrassas had begun.

The officials in the room did not want to confront Gilani with the evidence that the ISI was involved—that would require revealing sensitive intercepts, and they simply did not trust Gilani to stay quiet. They were even hesitant to tell the man they viewed as really running Pakistan: the army chief, Gen. Ashfaq Kayani, in whom the administration had invested almost as much confidence as they once showered on Musharraf. Kayani had been trained in the

United States years before, and American military leaders knew him, and respected him. But he also used to run the ISI, the organization that they believed was aiding the Taliban. Presenting the latest evidence to Kayani might not prove all that fruitful, one of Bush's aides told me. Kayani "would shake his head and tell us he'd try to learn about who at the ISI was doing this kind of thing—as if he hadn't been the head of the ISI for the previous few years."

So instead of confronting Prime Minister Gilani directly with the evidence that he knew the raid on the madrassa was a sham, Bush simply told him, in effect, that he'd heard that some of these raids and arrests amounted to less than met the eye. Gilani looked at him, seeming not to understand at first. Later I asked a senior official who participated in the meeting, was Gilani clueless about what the military and the ISI were doing?

"Well, yeah," he said. I told him I'd heard that the meeting with Gilani had been disastrous, that Bush had quickly dismissed Gilani as a sophisticated politician, but powerless. The aide thought about it, and added, "I wouldn't call it the president's worst meeting with a foreign leader ever."

When they were finished discussing the depth of Pakistan's economic crisis, and aid the United States might pump into the economy, Bush escorted Gilani out to the South Lawn to repeat the same words he had often said with Musharraf at his side—that Pakistan was a "vibrant democracy." Twice Bush repeated the line that the United States "respects" Pakistan's sovereignty. He made no mention, of course, of his decision to order American Special Forces to enter Pakistani territory. Perhaps for fear of their differences becoming too obvious, they took no questions, and Bush sent the new Pakistani leader packing after lunch. But the next day Gilani showed up at the Council on Foreign Relations forum in Washington and seemed to be living in a different world.

With Bush-like optimism he said, "Pakistan is back," and predicted that "soon you will see a lot of investors coming to Pakistan." When he was asked why his own government had such trouble hunting down militants, he argued that they were enjoying secret successes. They were pushing Taliban and other militants out of their safe haven. He didn't say where they were going, but it seemed evident the answer was Afghanistan. Officials in the audience looked at each other in wonderment, because they knew the Pakistani Army had barely been in the region.

Someone asked him about reining in the ISI, and he responded, "It is under the prime minister," an assertion that turned out not to be true. "Therefore they will do only what I want them to do." The crowd—a pretty sophisticated audience of Washington insiders, some of whom had been posted to Pakistan or just finished reading intelligence about it that morning—just looked at one another and shook their heads.

BY THE END of the summer of 2008, the secrecy Bush had tried to wrap around his January and July orders began to unravel. Since the beginning of the year there had been twenty or so Predator strikes—more than in the previous two or three years combined. The "black" Special Forces, newly liberated from the restrictions that had bound them before, began looking for targets ripe for a cross-border raid, the kind of raids that had been conducted every day in Iraq and Afghanistan. Under the new operating rules, there was no prior consultation with the Pakistanis, or even warning. The idea, said one of the planners, was that the attacks would be "not deep, not frequent, and not very loud." But that turned out to be impossible to engineer, and an early raid provoked yet another crisis, threatening whatever was left of the shredded American alliance with Pakistan.

The inevitable collision came on the night of September 3, 2008. A unit of Navy SEALs was helicoptered to the Afghanistan-Pakistan border, just opposite the town of Angor Adda, in South Waziristan. That town, and several around it, were believed to be the base used to launch several attacks against American and NATO forces.

Equipped with night-vision goggles and operating in almost

total silence, nearly two dozen SEALs hiked several miles through the mountains, to a small house that they believed was used as an al Qaeda gathering point. They could have hit it, of course, with a missile from a Predator. But the purpose of Bush's new order was to unnerve the terror groups and to exploit whatever information the Special Forces could grab—hard drives, cell phones, anything that would crack the network of al Qaeda, the Taliban, and other militant fighters. "What we learned in Iraq is that we have to act less like the army and more like 'CSI,'" said one general who was trying to apply the lessons of one conflict to the other.

When they attacked the house, there was a brief but furious firefight. Everyone inside—probably a dozen or so, including a young woman and her baby—were killed in a matter of minutes. What surprised the SEALs was the arrival of another group of well-armed militants, apparently from a nearby house, who showed up as reinforcements. They were also killed. Then American helicopters dropped in, no longer worried about blowing the element of surprise, and swept the SEALs out of Pakistan and back to their base in Afghanistan.

As the sun rose, and villagers ventured out of their houses to count the dead, it was obvious to all that Bush had opened a "third front." America was now five years into a war in Iraq and seven years into a war in Afghanistan. But it was just beginning to engage in ground warfare—as opposed to just missile strikes—on sovereign Pakistani territory.

"It was a little louder than we would have liked," said one senior official who analyzed the first fruits of Bush's new thrust. "There was a hell of a firefight. We wanted to send a message that would really disrupt the network—that you better post guards, you better stay away from the border, you better not sleep in the same house two nights in a row. But it kicked up a hell of a storm, and that's always a problem."

Suddenly the Pakistani newspapers were filled with tales of the raid, with disputes about how many people were killed, and rumors about who had been inside the house. In fact, none of the occupants appeared to be high-level al Qaeda, which prompted one former top strategist for Bush to ask me, "Is this worth it, if you Talibanize 166 million people, and you don't come up with one dead al Qaeda guy you can name?" Bush's answer was clear: It was worth it if America could begin closing down the sanctuary during his presidency. Otherwise, his aides were convinced the Afghan war would be lost. It was only a matter of time.

ON A SATURDAY in mid-September 2008, just days after Zardari had finally been inaugurated as president and had delivered his first address to Parliament vowing a national debate about how to fight terrorism, the entire Pakistani cabinet gathered for dinner in the prime minister's residence. The ritual was well known to Zardari; he had lived in this privileged corner of Islamabad when he was the deal-making First Man of Pakistan, and Benazir Bhutto was the country's embattled prime minister. It was back then that he got his nickname "Mr. Ten Percent," a derisive moniker referring to his sticky fingers, which one American diplomat said "understates his skills at corruption by about twenty percent."

At least he knew how to work a deal. As president, Zardari had Musharraf's old title but none of his old authority. He was ignored by the army, and derided by the intelligence services. His only secure hold was on Benazir's old party. That day, in his first address to Parliament, he had sounded all the right notes, vowing in his speech to eliminate extremists and—the words Washington was waiting to hear—to stop terror groups from using Pakistani soil to attack "other countries."

Yet Zardari knew the risks of appearing to do the bidding of the Americans. Zardari was not about to make the Musharraf mistake.

But he was not off to a good start. As Musharraf left, the country was headed over a financial cliff; foreign exchange reserves had shrunk to just under $6 billion, and the country only had about $3

billion available to pay for oil—which Pakistan had always subsi-
dized—and food. The reserves were dropping at the rate of $1.25 bil-
lion a month. Saudi Arabia, which had always stepped into save
Pakistan from the brink, was unwilling to announce a major concession on the price of oil, or allow deferred payments for the 100,000
barrels that Pakistan imported every day from its fellow Sunni nation. An inspection team from Moody's, the international credit
rating company, had just been in town, and when they left they cut
Pakistan's credit rating to "negative." At a time of a financial crisis in
the United States, which was radiating outward, it was almost impossible to imagine who would throw Pakistan a lifeline.

THE DINNER that night for the cabinet was supposed to be held at
the Marriott, a luxury hotel just a few hundred yards from the
prime minister's official residence. It was the meeting place of Islamabad's elite; you could sit in the broad lobby or the dining
room and see everyone—CIA agents and their counterparts from
the ISI, expatriates who could afford the ridiculous prices, government ministers, and financiers. But recently the hotel had been
making Americans uneasy; it was a huge target, and many of the
rooms looked directly out on the street. While there were barriers in
front of the hotel, security officials had long worried that it was
vulnerable—it was big, American, near the center of political
power, and, worst of all, barely set back from a busy road. The place
should have been on high alert, especially after a steady stream of
intelligence reports assessed that militant groups that had already
succeeded at killing Zardari's wife might be planning to mark his
inauguration with another spectacular attack.

Now the inauguration was over, and the Pakistani guards
around the hotel had returned to their usual sleepy routines. The
army troops dismantled their barriers and departed. As evening fell,
the policemen along the main roads of Islamabad, a low-rise, wide-
open city, were sitting on their haunches along the road, enjoying

The chief inspector at the International Atomic Energy Agency, Olli Heinonen (left), stayed with the agency rather than give up a car he loved. For the past four years, he has slowly tightened the noose on the Iranians, pressing its nuclear negotiators, including Javad Vaeidi (right), to explain documents that strongly suggested Iran was designing a nuclear warhead. © *Dieter Nagl/AFP/Getty Images*

President Mahmoud Ahmadinejad (right) gave voice to rising Iranian nationalism and used events like this one—a tour of the centrifuges built at Natanz to enrich uranium—to make Iran's nuclear progress seem irreversible. *Courtesy of Iran's Presidency Office/European Pressphoto Agency*

Defense Secretary Robert Gates (center), the former CIA chief, was the anti-Rumsfeld and shook up the Bush administration with his calls for putting more attention and money into diplomacy. Visiting Afghanistan in January 2007, he conferred with Lt. Gen. Karl Eikenberry (far right), the first American commander in Afghanistan to sound the alarm that the resiliency of the Taliban had been underestimated.
*Defense Dept. photo by Cherie A. Thurlby*

David Kilcullen (far right), a blunt-talking Australian counterinsurgency expert, tried to sound the alarm that Afghanistan was on the path toward breakup when he served as an adviser to Condoleezza Rice.
*Defense Dept. photo by Spc. Chris McCann*

An Afghan soldier with a rocket-propelled grenade, near Kandahar, where a major prison break showed the helplessness of the Afghan government. © *Philip Poupin/Redux*

An Afghan policeman looking across the Helmand Valley, the center of Afghan drug production. © *Cathal McNaughton/AFP/Getty Images*

Mike McConnell (left), the director of National Intelligence and Michael Hayden, the director of the CIA, traveled together to Pakistan in a vain effort to convince President Pervez Musharraf that if he did not clear militants out of the tribal areas, the United States would.
© REUTERS/Larry Downing

As frustrations mounted over the inability of the Pakistanis to attack targets in the tribal areas in 2008, the Bush administration sent in more unmanned drones, equipped with missiles, for precision-guided attacks over the Pakistani border. *U.S. Air Force photo by Staff Sgt. Jeremy T. Lock.*

President Bush, meeting here in the Oval Office with President Pervez Musharraf in 2006, believed in the Pakistani leader for too long. Musharraf was forever promising stepped-up military action in the tribal areas. McConnell later determined that Musharraf was part of the "dual policy" in which Pakistan's leadership financed the Taliban, even while fighting it. *White House photo by Eric Draper*

A. Q. Khan, the man who built the world's largest nuclear black market network and sold technology to Iran, North Korea, and Libya, remains a hero in Pakistan today, even after he was placed under house arrest in response to American pressure. Pakistan has never allowed him to be interrogated by American officials.
© *Usman Khan/AFP/ Getty Images*

The bombing of the Marriott Hotel in Islamabad in September 2008 left no doubt that the war for control of a nuclear armed nation of 160 million had arrived in the capital. "This is the home game," a top White House official declared the next month after visiting Islamabad.
© *Farooq Naeem/AFP/Getty Images*

Chris Hill, a man born to negotiate, was actually conducting two high-stakes talks at once: one with the North Koreans at the Six Party Talks, and one back at the White House, where he was constantly in a struggle with Vice President Cheney's office. © *Andrew Wong/Getty Images*

Kim Jong-Il's stroke in the summer of 2008 raised the question of who is really in charge in North Korea. In 2006 he took one of his "inspection tours" of defenses along the border with South Korea.
© *Pierre Bessard/REA/Redux*

One of the grainy photos of the Syrian nuclear reactor—built with North Korean help—that the head of the Mossad, Israel's intelligence agency, brought to Stephen Hadley, Bush's national security adviser. Hadley and American intelligence officials were surprised: They had seen the building, but missed its significance. A few months later, in September 2007, the Israelis destroyed the nuclear facility despite Bush's objections.
*Central Intelligence Agency*

Bush's relationship with Russia's prime minister, Vladimir Putin, changed radically. They went from holding laughing joint-seminars with students in Crawford and St. Petersburg to this finger-pointing encounter at the Beijing Olympics in August 2008, just as Russia was invading Georgia.
*© Anatoly Maltsev/AFP/Getty Images*

When Hu Jintao, China's president, lit the Olympic torch—designed by engineers at Lenovo—on March 31, 2008, he was also trying to put down a rebellion on the streets of Lhasa, the largest city in Tibet.
© *Feng Li/Getty Images*

A presidency beset by international crises, incompetence and plummeting public approval ended with disaster at home: a stock market crash of proportions not seen since the days of the Great Depression. Bush seemed sidelined by the events; the nation had stopped listening to him.
© *Spencer Platt/Getty Images*

the traditional breaking of the fast during Ramadan. Everyone was out of position, just as the Taliban knew they would be.

So there was just a stunned silence when a huge dump truck careened around the corner and crashed into the hotel's front gate. At first nothing happened. Guards came out to investigate. It was a few moments before the 1,300 pounds of TNT and RDX, mixed with aluminum oxide, exploded in a fireball that took out the whole front of the building, killing more than 60 people and injuring more than 250. The fire grew so large and hot it could be seen for miles. At the prime minister's residence, the cabinet could feel the explosion, and then could hear, in the distance, the cries of the injured and dying.

It was the biggest terror attack inside the Pakistani capital, and no one thought it would be the last. Within days Pakistani authorities said they thought the huge explosive load had been assembled right near the capital, undetected. But they had no real suspects—it could be any of a half-dozen militant groups, they told Washington. The American embassy in Islamabad—which already had the fortress look of the castle of a Medellín drug lord—told its employees to work from home if they could, and closed its visa section, erecting the final wall between Pakistan and America. Lawyers and business executives who had stayed through the Musharraf years, and had taken to the streets to protest in favor of democracy, talked about moving away. One of the major newspapers in the capital, one that usually supports Zardari, surveyed the collapsing economy and the rising threat, and concluded that the new government was "confronted with a general breakdown of the state." With that bombing, there was no doubt Pakistan had become the central front in the war against the extremists. "We have to stabilize Iraq, because if we don't, there's no hope of creating a model for the Middle East," one of the members of the U.S. joint chiefs told me not long after the bombing. "But what's going on in Pakistan is, to my mind, going to be the number-one crisis for the next president—Bush's truly unfinished business. Because we've never seen a nuclear state implode before, and that's the threat that comes right here," he said, pointing to downtown Washington.

But as Bush left office, America and Pakistan were no closer to a common strategy than they were on September 12, 2001. Bush had utterly failed to convince the Pakistanis that they were fighting a war for their own survival. The Pakistanis were still, in Musharraf's words, "tightrope walking." Publicly, that meant giving the United States just enough help to keep the aid flowing, without making Pakistanis think that they were fighting "America's war." In reality, it meant supporting both sides of the war—so that Pakistan was positioned to ally itself with the winner, whether that was Washington or the Taliban. This was no alliance. It was a huge diplomatic failure. And what was left was the only country in the world where Islamic militants, nuclear weapons, and a failing government all were thrown together into a bloody and chaotic mix.

THERE ARE SOME bitter lessons in America's failed alliance with Pakistan.

The first is obvious: We left Afghanistan far too early and focused on the sanctuary in Pakistan far too late. Once we diverted intelligence assets and forces to Iraq, we missed the key signals of the mounting insurgency—and willfully ignored the obvious evidence that the Pakistani government was not capable of or interested in dealing with the problem. And like so many problems that Bush pushed off, this one became a full-scale crisis by the time he decided to deal with it.

The second was almost as obvious: Bush invested far too much confidence in his personal relationship with a single strongman, exactly the mistake that he rightly criticized Bill Clinton for making in dealing with Russia during the Yeltsin years. Perhaps it was unavoidable for much of the Bush presidency; the political opposition in Pakistan was so muffled that it would have been hard to reach out. But when Musharraf began to lose power, Bush and his aides

could not imagine Pakistan without him, and so they were far too
slow to show that they were on the side of those seeking a democratic nation. "It gets pretty embarrassing when our guy is spending
more time beating up lawyers in the streets than beating up al
Qaeda," Nick Burns acknowledged to me during the unraveling of
Musharraf's government in late 2007. This was symptomatic of
Bush's style of governing: He was intoxicated with the value of picking up the phone and having a leader-to-leader talk, arguing that it
enabled him to get through layers of bureaucratic obfuscation, to
cut deals that only presidents can make. With some allies, that
might have been correct. With Pakistan, it revealed a misunder-
standing of Musharraf and the games he was playing. Until the last
eighteen months of his presidency, Bush appeared to believe what
he said publicly about Musharraf, when he would walk him out to
reporters at Camp David and pump him up as a man committed to
democracy and a stalwart fighter against terrorism. He was neither.

"I just don't think the president saw it for the longest time," one
of his former aides who handled the war in Afghanistan told me
after Musharraf was forced out of office. "He loves being able to
pick up the phone and call. But he just couldn't bring himself to
lower the boom," the aide said, speculating that he feared it would
jeopardize the relationship, and leave him with nothing.

No one understood this better than Pervez Musharraf himself.
"He became the master of telling Bush whatever Bush wanted to
hear, and then going back home and telling the Pakistani military
what it wanted to hear," said Vali Nasr, a scholar at Boston University who was well plugged into this relationship. "I think the Pakistani military was never on board. Not on September 12, 2001, and
not at any point after that. They hedged their bets. They are obsessed with the thought that Afghanistan will become a client state
of India," and surround Pakistan's borders. "So they are more interested in counting Indian consulates in Afghanistan than they are in
counting terrorist training camps in the tribal areas."

Bush's biggest mistake, however, was his failure to use all the elements of American soft power in Pakistan—especially because he was unable, or unwilling until the end of his presidency, to employ much hard power. With Congress's acquiescence, the administration pumped roughly $1 billion a year into Pakistan to pay for counterinsurgency operations that mostly never happened. Everyone knew it; the Pakistanis were not fooling Washington. Washington was fooling itself.

For all his talk about his determination to fight the war on terror, Bush never came face to face with the strategic choices he had to make. Early in his presidency he established some basic truths in his mind: Pakistan was his ally, Iran was his enemy, and the "central front" of the war on terrorism was in Iraq. Every few months there would be "strategy reviews" and new papers issued, but each came to the same conclusion: that the Pakistanis needed to be pressured to win this war on their own. Only rarely in those reviews did the reality bubble to the surface—that many senior Pakistanis viewed the United States and India and Afghanistan as something of an Axis of Evil of its own, plotting Pakistan's downfall. The Pakistani establishment believed that by allying with Bush in the week after 9/11, they were buying security. By the time Bush left, they felt more insecure than ever.

There are some problems without a solution, and this may be one of them. But a few steps seem worth trying. Tying American military aid to real performance is one. Spending at least as much, or maybe more, helping to build Pakistani schools and to bring roads and hospitals into the tribal areas, is long overdue. Until Pakistanis of all stripes are invested in American-backed projects, they will not be invested in American-style success. The stategy will have to be implemented delicately, and no doubt the projects themselves will become targets for militants.

Eventually Bush edged toward that thinking. When I visited Pakistan, the American ambassador, Anne W. Patterson, was enthusiastically promoting a new plan to spend $750 million in the tribal areas on development projects—over the next five years. It struck me as way too little, way too late—and still just a fraction of what we were paying the Pakistani military to fight for our side, while they secretly supported the other side.

I asked Ambassador Patterson why it took until 2008, seven years after 9/11, to get projects going to build schools and roads, especially in the one corner of the world where we are in a desperate battle for the minds of impoverished teenagers weighing the lure of the West against a life as a militant.

She paused, clearly wanting to speak her mind. "Well," she said, "the important thing is that we are doing it now."

Sooner or later the United States is going to have to talk to some elements of the Taliban. During Bush's last months in office, Bob Gates admitted as much, saying "there has to be ultimately, and I'll underscore *ultimately,* reconciliation as part of a political outcome of this." The British came to the same conclusion in 2008. But getting there would require a new president in Washington. As Gates knew, negotiations are not what Bush had in mind when he declared "with us or against us."

IN OCTOBER 2008, at the very end of Bush's presidency, his staff held a task force meeting at the White House every day to conduct yet another Afghanistan-Pakistan review. The whole exercise had an air of unreality to it: "Whatever we decide to do is going to get rewritten by the next president in three months," one of the members of Bush's review effort said to me one day.

The review would allow Bush to argue that he had left his successor with a workable plan. If Obama failed to execute it—well, that wasn't in Bush's control.

But very little was. The Pentagon told the review panel that few troops—maybe a combat battalion or two—would be available for service in Afghanistan; most were still tied up in Iraq. The intelligence agencies told the panel to brace itself for a 40 percent increase in violence. A new National Intelligence Estimate circulating through the administration warned that Afghanistan was in a "downward spiral" and that corruption inside the Karzai government was accelerating the problem.[7] Reading between the lines, the document was a sweeping indictment of a White House that waited too long to respond to warnings, that poured too many resources into Iraq, and that still was too slow in turning around the strategy.

"It's taken them a long time to realize it," said Hank Crumpton, the man who had led CIA operations in Afghanistan after 9/11, and operated along the fuzzy border with Pakistan. "But now they know it's pretty grim."[8]

Grim indeed. The final review, when completed, concluded that Pakistan was the real prize for al Qaeda—not Iraq, not the greater Middle East, not the ability to terrorize Europe. "For al Qaeda, Pakistan is the home game,"one of the members of Bush's review panel concluded. It is territory that al Qaeda and its associates know intimately. At the end of Bush's term, al Qaeda clearly had its best shot ever: The Pakistani economy was collapsing (the country was so close to defaulting on its debt that it sought a bailout from the International Monetary Fund), the government was more unstable than ever, the anger at American Predator strikes was at an all-time high. The effort to bring new aid into the tribal areas had barely gotten off the ground.

The review concluded that in the end, the United States has far more at stake in preventing Pakistan's collapse than it does in stabilizing Afghanistan or Iraq. If only Bush's aides had come to that conclusion in 2002, before the United States turned its sights on Saddam Hussein.

WITH AFGHANISTAN and Pakistan in simultaneous meltdown, President Karzai came to Washington at the end of September 2008. He was in his traditional robe, his handshake was still firm.

Urbane as always, he brushed off any questions about the attempts on his life, as if that was just part of everyday life.

When we talked, he made the case that if Bush wanted to win through unilateral action, he simply acted too late. In the one country where Bush needed to take early, strong action against terrorists, the man who said "bring 'em on" had hesitated. It was un-Bush-like, he seemed to suggest.

"If someone in those territories in Pakistan . . . makes a statement saying he will send people to kill Americans in Afghanistan and to kill Afghans in Afghanistan, what do you expect us to do?" Karzai asked. "Sit and wait for him to kill us? Or defend ourselves?" He was sounding a lot like Bush circa 2002, when the preemption doctrine was issued.

But then his tone turned. "Now, here is the delicacy of the matter," Karzai went on. "How do we do it? Do we interpret his statement as the statement of a few people? Or of the community? Or the statement of a terrorist network? The right thing would be to differentiate a terrorist network from the community that they have taken hostage. To help the community liberate themselves, and to isolate these elements."

This was something, he suggested, that couldn't be done with Predator hits. Even nighttime raids were problematic—yes, the Special Forces could come in at night and kill twenty people in a firefight, but that often just Talibanized the young men in the community. It had to be done by negotiation.

"Let me tell you a story," he said, and related a conversation with an Afghan relative, who had been talking to some teenagers who were being raised in Taliban-controlled territory. (Karzai himself doesn't get out much, for obvious reasons.)

"They talked a bit about travel, and about New York, and one of them said, 'Yes, I would like to bring bombs to New York and blow it up.' Now, these are teenagers—teenagers! Teenagers should think about New York and how exciting it is, all that neon, all that action, and just want to be on its streets." Seven years after the invasion that threw the Taliban out of power and put the smooth-talking Karzai in the president's palace, he was suggesting that in our bigger effort, we are failing. We are left with a generation, he said, whose first thought about New York is still a burning desire to annihilate it.

# PART IV

## NORTH KOREA

# THE NUCLEAR RENEGADE THAT GOT AWAY

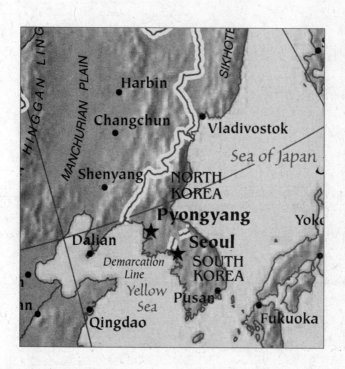

# CHAPTER 9

# KIM JONG-IL 8,
# BUSH 0

THE ISRAELI F-15S crossed into Syria soon after midnight on September 6, 2007, screaming undetected across the desert, headed for a target deep in the Euphrates Valley. They traversed two-thirds of the country, barely setting off the air defenses that the Syrians had paid Russia millions to construct.

In minutes they swooped over the tiny town of al-Kibar and left a pile of concrete, rebar, and rubble on the eastern banks of the Euphrates River. They had splintered apart a baseball-diamond–sized building that the Syrians had been working on, in deepest secrecy, for more than six years. The jets then disappeared over Turkey, dropping their empty fuel tanks as they circled back to their bases. Operation Orchard, as the Israelis had code-named it, was executed so quickly that the Syrians needed time to figure out what had happened to their prized project in the desert, much less what to say about it.

To no one's surprise, the Syrians' first instinct was to lie. At first a government spokesman would acknowledge only that some Israeli planes had pierced Syrian airspace and fled. A few days later Bashar al-Assad, Syria's brutal but inexperienced ruler, told an interviewer that the planes had hit some empty buildings on a military base. He waved the whole thing away as a wasted mission, an act of folly rather than of war. But satellite images suggested otherwise: They showed Syrian bulldozers swarming over the site, racing to bury all remaining evidence of what had once stood there. Within seven weeks the site had been scraped clean, and a new building appeared on the footprint of the old, to make it far more difficult for international inspectors to collect evidence of what had been there weeks before.

As questions mounted, the Israelis hinted they had hit something really big, something "nuclear related." Then, uncharacteristically, they shut up. Spinning tales, some Israeli officials told the British press the attack they launched that night was wrapped in such a blanket of security that the pilots themselves did not know where they were headed until they were aloft. That was nonsense. The mission had been discussed for months and planned down to the last precision-guided weapon. But the story about the pilots was part of an elaborate smokescreen that the Israelis spewed out as Jerusalem and Washington tried, each for its own reasons, to keep secret the intelligence about what had stood on that desert site.

For a while, they succeeded. In a series of secret conversations, Bush and Prime Minister Ehud Olmert had agreed that any public discussion of the strike—and the nature of the target—could force Assad into a corner. "There was a sense," Defense Secretary Robert Gates told me months later, that "if you play this wrong there could be a war between Israel and Syria. That was the central worry."[1] But the Americans had another concern, on the other side of the world. The airstrike, it turned out, was about a lot more than destroying the crown jewel of a covert nuclear program in Syria.

It was also about North Korea.

What the Israelis had targeted was a nearly completed nuclear reactor built by North Korean engineers in one of the most stunning examples of proliferation in the nuclear age. For six years American spy satellites had watched the mysterious building rise in the desert and analysts had spun out theories about what it could be—everything from a covert nuclear facility to a water treatment plant. The Syrians had disguised its purpose by building it in plain view with no barbed wire, no military guards. Around 2002, they even erected a benign-looking, square industrial wall and roof over the entire site to hide the telltale shape of a reactor.

The deception worked for years. The Americans were suspicious, but they failed to discover the real purpose of the project. Then, one day in late April 2007, Meir Dagan, chief of the Mossad, Israel's legendary intelligence service, called the White House from Israel and asked for an urgent meeting with President Bush's national security adviser, Stephen Hadley.

On a Wednesday morning in early May 2007, he slipped unnoticed through a White House gate and was ushered into Hadley's large corner office of the West Wing, diagonally across from the Oval Office. The curtains were drawn, as always, so that passersby entering the West Wing from the White House driveway—or reporters walking to the briefing room—could not see visitors. But in this case the precaution may not have mattered; Dagan is not widely recognized in Washington.

The Israeli spy chief had brought with him a file folder full of photographs. But Dagan's pictures were different from the overhead satellite images that analysts across Washington had been trying to decipher. Thanks to the work of Israeli agents, Dagan spread out a treasure trove of photos taken from inside the facility, inside the curtain walls that satellites could not penetrate. What they showed solved the mystery of al-Kibar.

Hadley had known Dagan, the son of Holocaust survivors, since Bush's first term. The two men were close to the same age, and each was a quiet, behind-the-scenes insider who sat atop the national security apparatus of his nation. When Hadley had been a young member of the National Security Council staff and a midlevel Defense Department official in the early 1970s, Dagan had been running a special antiterrorist unit in the Gaza Strip that reported directly to Ariel

Sharon, the gruff Israeli general. By 2002, Dagan had ascended to head the intelligence organization that was constantly on alert to detect threats to Israel. Hadley, the quiet, orderly lawyer, was already deputy national security adviser, working out of a shoebox-size office right next to national security adviser, Condoleezza Rice. He joked that he was the "invisible guy in the boring suit standing by the lady in *Vogue*."

Hadley moved into Rice's job, and her office, when she became secretary of state at the beginning of Bush's second term. Now, sitting by Hadley's orderly desk, the burly Israeli intelligence chief talked him through each of the photos, some taken three or four years previously, apparently by a Syrian who had been "turned," or paid handsomely for his snapshot collection. Hadley recognized instantly the obvious signs that the Syrians were building a nuclear reactor, probably for weapons production. There were no electrical lines leading in or out of the facility, nor any of the other telltale signs of a reactor built for the purpose of generating energy.

Then Dagan pulled out his trump card: a photo of two men standing by a car near the nuclear complex. On the right was the head of the Syrian Atomic Energy Commission, Ibrahim Othman. On the left was a man Dagan identified as Chon Chibu, a North Korean who managed the production of fuel at North Korea's main nuclear weapons site at Yongbyon.

In fact, to the American intelligence analysts who were looking at the same pictures, passed on by their Israeli counterparts, the images seemed familiar. Very familiar. The innards of the reactor building bore a striking resemblance to the reactor at North Korea's main nuclear complex half a world away, where the country harvested the plutonium that built its small nuclear arsenal. Even the windows and doors were in the same places. For twenty years analysts had gotten to know Yongbyon intimately: It was number one on the list of potential bombing targets in North Korea, and more recently it was the same reactor that the Bush administration was trying to cajole, bribe, and corner the North Koreans into closing down.

"A carbon copy," one official who had reviewed the intelligence told me. "You looked at it and said one thing: 'Shit, the Koreans have been screwing around more than we knew.'"* It was the first hard evidence that North Korea—the broke, desperate, isolated kingdom of Kim Jong-Il—had found a way to bring in millions of dollars in hard currency by selling its most valuable skill, the manufacturing of nuclear bomb material.

The North Koreans and the Syrians appear to have been working together on the project for the better part of a decade, perhaps back to the end of the Clinton administration. Yet apart from vague suspicions that the two countries were working on something together, perhaps even something nuclear, the American intelligence community never put it all together.

"This would be a scene from Monty Python if it wasn't true," observed David Rothkopf, who wrote the definitive history of the National Security Council. "In 2003 you had all these war planners gathered in the Situation Room planning to bomb Saddam for nuclear facilities that didn't exist. They're all staring at maps, but it's of the wrong country. Right next door, two of the most spied-on countries on earth are building a reactor."

"And did we know about it?" Rothkopf asks, shaking his head. "Now that's what I call an intelligence failure."

The events in Syria underscored the real nature of the North Korean threat—and it wasn't the threat that the Bush administration fixated on from the time its band of hawks, regime-changers,

---

* It took five weeks after the Israeli raid to break the story of what the Syrians had built—and even that story elicited no public response from the administration. (David E. Sanger and Mark Mazzetti, "Analysts Find Israel Struck a Syrian Nuclear Project," *The New York Times*, October 14, 2007, p. 1.) Within days, commercial satellite photographs of the site began to appear, showing what the buildings looked like before the attack, and the Syrian effort to bulldoze the rubble and hide the evidence. The CIA released some of the Israeli photographs of the inside of the reactor in April 2008.

and neocons took office. Throughout much of Bush's first term, both the president and his aides raised the specter that North Korea could unleash an attack on Seoul or Tokyo and, someday, if it made its missiles a bit more reliable and accurate, on the West Coast of the United States. Their motives were pretty transparent: A North Korea with nuclear weapons and long-range missiles was the poster child for the need for missile defense. Donald Rumsfeld himself had made that case in a lengthy study published two years before he became Bush's defense secretary.*

It was a pretty far-fetched justification. Kim Jong-Il may be strange, but he isn't stupid, and he knows that any direct attack would result in the obliteration of his lucrative family business: the North Korean state. The real risk was that in his desperate search for hard currency Kim would sell his country's only marketable expertise—how to make bomb fuel—or, worse, that he would sell whatever excess fuel he had lying around. The North Korean threat was about proliferation, not missiles.

Yet until North Korea's nuclear test in October 2006, President Bush never explicitly warned the North Koreans about the consequences for the country if it was ever caught proliferating. What Bush didn't know until nine months later was that Kim Jong-Il had been crossing the proliferation red line for years in Syria, undetected by American intelligence agencies that had been looking at all the right buildings but were unable to figure out what was happening inside. The Syrian case was, as one senior intelligence official told me later, "the Iraq mistake in reverse." In Iraq, he said, the agency had connected dots that were not there and sent up warnings of a revived nuclear program that no longer existed. In Syria, it failed to put the pieces together until the Israelis arrived with the crucial bits of the puzzle. Adding to the embarrassment, the whole project was happening less than a hundred miles from the Iraqi border.

---

* Known popularly as "The Rumsfeld Commission," the group was formally titled "The Commission to Assess the Ballistic Missile Threat to the United States."

Hadley was taken aback by Dagan's evidence but hardly shocked that North Korea would take such a risk. For years he had been reviewing intelligence reports about North Korea's highly profitable sales activities in the Middle East. But as he told me in 2002 when we first discussed the possibility of North Korean nuclear proliferation to terror groups or the states that sponsored them, all the evidence in hand concerned North Korean sales of missiles, which can deliver ordinary explosives or something more fearsome. Syria, Iran, and Pakistan had been eager buyers. But when Hadley secretly ordered a study of whether the North Koreans could be supplying Iran or others with nuclear technology, the answers that came back amounted to nothing more than scores of pages of ambiguous evidence.

"We've had lots of suspicions," Hadley once told me as we flew together on a small plane that took him on one of his low-profile trips to Russia, "but no solid evidence."

Until now.

As Hadley thumbed his way through the Israeli evidence with Dagan at his side, he knew what was coming next: It was only a matter of time before Olmert, seeking to restore his reputation after being humiliated in the battle for Lebanon the previous summer, would demand that the United States destroy this reactor in the desert, or stand back while Israel took care of the problem itself. There was a famous precedent: the Israeli attack on an Iraqi reactor a quarter-century before. America joined the condemnation of that strike at the time and ended up thanking the Israelis years later.

Hadley immediately sent Dagan across the river to Langley, Virginia, to show his portfolio of pictures to Hayden, the director of the CIA. The next day Hayden used his regular Thursday briefing to describe to Bush the detailed Israeli intelligence. Bush quickly ordered that the CIA coordinate the analysis and that the agency's reports be restricted to a handful of officials. Even before the analysis came back, he had Rice and Hadley engage the Israelis, in hopes of dissuading them from immediately launching an attack that his entire national security team feared could set the region aflame.

Bush administration officials have never acknowledged publicly that they debated whether the United States should take out the North Korean–Syrian project. But in interviews, two senior officials told me that Bush seriously considered ordering an American military strike on the reactor. Not long after Dagan's visit, the Pentagon developed a detailed plan for a lightning strike—similar to the one that Israel ultimately carried out.

"It was discussed, in the Oval, more than once," said one senior administration official who participated in the drafting of option papers and the subsequent deliberations. "The thinking was that if we did it instead of Israel, there was less of a risk of it turning into a broader Middle East war."

Bush's top aides declined to discuss how close the United States came to striking Syria. But Hadley told me that in his mind, the reactor did not meet the standards of the "Bush Doctrine" for a preemptive strike. The CIA declared that because so much was missing at al-Kibar—including the equipment needed to convert reactor waste into bomb fuel—the United States could prove only that Syria was developing the *capability* to build a bomb, not that it was intending to produce one. It was exactly the kind of parsing of the intelligence—facts versus assessments, capabilities versus intentions—that never took place prior to the invasion of Iraq. In this case, post-Iraq caution had kicked in, and the intelligence agencies, aware that they could not survive a second big mistake, made clear to Bush that what they could prove was very different from what they suspected.

Based on the evidence at hand, the official said, "we had low confidence that it's part of a weapons program." And in the end, Bush decided he could not order another military strike on a state he accused of possessing a program to build weapons of mass destruction. Despite his repeated insistence in recent years that invading Iraq was the right decision, he had learned a bitter lesson.

Instead, he and Rice pressured the Israelis to agree to a different approach—diplomacy with deadlines. "We had an alternative plan," Condoleezza Rice later told me, "that involved going rapidly to the

United Nations, exposing the program, and demanding that it be immediately dismantled."[2] The thinking was that while Iran had the money and the clout to resist such pressure, Syria did not.

To the Israelis, it was a remarkable turnabout. The administration that justified its invasion of Iraq on the grounds that Saddam Hussein's weapons programs posed an imminent danger was now arguing for a more patient, diplomatic approach—despite the fact that the Syrian reactor project was far more sophisticated than anything Saddam had under way in 2003. "It was laughable logic," a senior Israeli official told me later. "Whatever happened to the George Bush who said that after 9/11, we could not let threats fester?"

Olmert was unmoved. Diplomacy at the United Nations, he and his top aides responded, mirrored how the world had been reacting to Iran's nuclear program. The result, he argued, had been nothing short of disastrous: The Iranians had only sped up. Syria would not be allowed to go down the same road, Olmert declared. Moreover, his deputies argued that it was far safer to strike the plant before it was loaded with nuclear fuel. Striking it later risked spreading radioactive material in a dust cloud that could be carried over neighboring countries.

Bush's aides could not argue with that logic—after all, it echoed their own justification for the preemptive strike on Iraq. But they suspected that Olmert, already under investigation for taking campaign donations illegally, may have seen merit in rallying the country around a strike. "They thought this was Osirak all over again," one senior American official told me later. He was referring to Iraq's first large nuclear reactor, started in the late 1970s when Saddam Hussein had visions of making Iraq into a nuclear power. And it was also the site of one of Israel's finest military moments, a daring raid in 1981 that left the reactor a pile of smoldering pieces, infuriating Saddam and setting back his effort to obtain the plutonium he needed to make a weapon.

Olmert must have remembered well what Osirak did for the reputation of Menachem Begin, the take-no-prisoners prime minister whose reelection resulted partly from the sheer daring of that surprise strike on Saddam's nuclear plant. In Syria, Olmert had a chance to steal a little of Begin's magic. He had taken office only when Ariel Sharon was suddenly disabled by a horrible stroke. He had no military credentials and was still reeling from Israel's botched confrontation with Hezbollah the previous summer. The credibility of Israel's deterrent capability had been damaged by its tepid and ineffective actions in Lebanon. For Olmert, more was at stake than simply stopping a Syrian nuclear program in its infancy. He had to, in the words of one of his top aides, "restore our deterrent capability—and send a message to the mullahs."

"We had post-Iraq syndrome," one senior American official told me later, summarizing the furious debate between the two capitals, "and the Israelis had preemption syndrome."

After arguing with the administration over the summer, Olmert approved a plan for the attack. Though they had debated the issue tirelessly with Rice, Hadley, and Bush himself, in the end the Israelis did what they wanted to do from the start. They were careful not to inform Washington of the precise timing so that both nations could claim, with technical accuracy, that the Americans had not known about the attack in advance. Back in Washington, the president who had once sworn to act decisively against "the world's worst dictators" seeking "the world's worst weapons" fell into a deep public silence after the Israeli strike. At a press conference a few days later, he refused three times to answer questions about the attack.

Hadley, in New York at the end of September for the opening of the United Nations session, visited the editorial board of *The New York Times*. He was asked if he wanted to go off the record to explain what had been blown up that night in the desert and whether it indicated that the wave of proliferation long feared in the Middle East might finally be upon us. He looked at his questioner, Bill Keller, the *Times*'s executive editor, and paused. Then he looked around at the rest of us—editorial writers, columnists, editors, and reporters gathered in a glass-wrapped room in the *Times*'s new headquarters overlooking midtown Manhattan. He knew that a team of reporters was working on breaking the story of what exactly the Israelis had hit in Syria, and he wasn't about to help.

"Off the record?" Hadley said drolly, breaking into a smile. "The president has spoken on this. Off the record, no comment."[3]

BY THE END of its eight years in office, the Bush administration tried to portray its encounters with North Korea as evidence that George Bush had learned the art of patient diplomacy—and had been rewarded with success. That argument was half right. There was a huge change of approach between the first term and the second. But the mistakes that Bush made with North Korea in his first few years in office ended up haunting him for the rest of his term, leaving Obama with a far more complicated nuclear standoff. By the time Bush started backpedaling, it was simply too late: North Korea had accumulated all the weapons fuel it needed, and did not appear about to give it up.

The first term was dominated by Dick Cheney and his cadre of regime-changers, determined to push the government of Kim Jong-Il over a cliff. At every step of the way, teaming up with Rumsfeld, Cheney did all he could to ensure that negotiations with North Koreans were doomed to fail, down to banning negotiators from shaking hands or partaking in toasts with their North Korean counterparts.

Not surprisingly, these calculated insults and the first-term negotiating tactics did not succeed in bringing about a crashing end to Kim's regime. Cutting off banking relationships and using covert action had not worked either. During Bush's second term, humbled a bit by the realities of what was unfolding in Iraq, and recognizing that neither the North Koreans nor their weapons were going away, the administration resorted to the traditional approach for dealing with small hostile states: actual negotiations. Condoleezza Rice, her perspective on diplomacy altered a bit by her new role as secretary of state, brought in a seasoned negotiator, Christopher Hill, who wanted a deal—too much, in the eyes of his critics. Together, he and Rice conspired to cut Cheney out of the picture. When Rumsfeld was fired, his replacement, Bob Gates, generally sided with Rice and strengthened the State Department's approach within the administration.

Not wanting to involve the United States in another military conflict, Gates knew that negotiations had to be pursued. "Bob's view," one of his top aides said, "was that he was brought into this job to solve three problems—Iraq, Iraq, and Iraq—and he doesn't need a crisis in Asia."

But Hill recognized that during the first term Bush had dug himself into a hole. On Bush's watch, the North Koreans had built up an impressive arsenal. They had gone from an unconfirmed one or two weapons to eight or twelve; no one knew for sure. They were unlikely to give it all up for any price.

So Hill did the best he could with the hand he was dealt. He got Kim to agree to the shutdown of the Yongbyon reactor, the same reactor the Syrians were trying to replicate, thereby ensuring that the arsenal would not get significantly larger. One day in the summer of 2008, the North Koreans even blew up the cooling tower of their reactor. Hill had choreographed the whole thing, including a near-simultaneous announcement by Bush that he would start the process to take North Korea off the list of countries that support terrorism, thereby clearing the way for more economic interchange with North Korea than at any other time since the armistice that ended the Korean War. In Bush's last months, to no one's surprise, the whole deal constantly appeared on the verge of unraveling.

Nonetheless, Bush's announcement was a stunning reversal for a president who had essentially declared that he would deal with the North Koreans only after they gave up their weapons and closed their gulags. Just how stunning was evident to anyone who ran into Cheney. A few days before the deal was announced, he was asked about the impending agreement at an off-the-record briefing in the

Old Executive Office Building, just across the street from the West Wing. He froze, according to four participants who had been engaged in the half-hour-long question-and-answer period.

Then he snapped, "I'm not going to be the one to announce this decision. You need to address your interest in this to the State Department." Done taking questions, he immediately left the room.[4]

A few days later I asked Rice about this incident during a conversation in her office. She smiled broadly, and said nothing.

THE MESSAGE the Bush administration hoped to send out by reaching the deal with North Korea was clear: North Korea is run by a bizarre despot, but it is on the road to disarmament. It is a country tamed, if not yet defanged.

The truth was a lot more complicated. Few despots had benefited more from Washington's distraction during the Iraq War than Kim Jong-Il. In early 2003, the North threw out international inspectors and, in full view of U.S. spy satellites, took the last steps needed to convert spent reactor fuel into material for six to eight bombs. That was the critical moment if the Bush administration was ever to intervene, diplomatically or militarily. It did neither.

January through March 2003 were the crucial months when the White House was rolling out a detailed strategy to convince the world that Saddam Hussein had to be confronted, immediately. It could not be bothered with WMD on the other side of the globe. When the *Times* published front-page stories describing, contemporaneously, the nuclear weapons fuel that was being produced half a world away while Bush was headed to Iraq, Rice and other administration officials complained that we were focused on the wrong story. It was Saddam, living in a more dangerous neighborhood, who posed the far more potent threat. In 2008, when I reviewed this history with a key member of Bush's national security team, he appeared to have forgotten that these two events were playing out simultaneously.

"What month was this?" he asked.

"This was February of '03," I said. There was a long pause, and then he said: "Had a few other things on our mind. . . . We missed a couple of things."[5]

It turned out that missing "a couple of things" had real consequences. North Korea became the nuclear renegade that got away.

Within three years, Kim Jong-Il had conducted North Korea's first nuclear test in an effort to shout to the world that even a broke, backward country could play in the nuclear club. Today it looks as though that test was more akin to a lab experiment than a bomb, which explains why it ended in a fizzle, not a boom.* But it was enough of an explosion for Kim to send the message that he had sufficient nuclear material to slip to a terrorist group and the technology to show them how to make at least a crude bomb. It was convincing enough to move the administration toward diplomacy. But by that time a problem the White House had ignored for most of the first term, North Korea's expanding nuclear program had grown infinitely more complicated.

After six wasted years, Bush deserves credit for some modest progress. Getting North Korea to dismantle its reactor was something Clinton never accomplished—even if Bush left office with the North Koreans threatening to rebuild it. But Bush's inattention during the first term—or rather his obsession with Saddam's phantom programs rather than Kim's real ones—left his successor to face the hardest part of the Korea problem: persuading a desperately insecure regime to give up its arsenal. To the North Korean leadership, these weapons are the last thing keeping the country from being rolled over by its richer, fast-growing neighbors who have come to view the North the way wealthy New Yorkers view blighted, crime-ridden parts of the city: Wouldn't it be a lot nicer as an office

---

* In their declaration accounting for nuclear materials in the spring of 2008, the North Koreans said they used two kilograms of plutonium to conduct the test. That is too small an amount to make a weapon, and, if accurate, would explain why the explosion was less than a kiloton.

park? "If you were Kim," asked Art Brown, the former top CIA officer who handled North Korea issues for decades, "would you give up the only thing that has protected your regime from collapse?"

Even the hawks who wanted to push North Korea over the brink, causing its regime to collapse, believe that the White House lost its focus. "If you are looking for the place where Iraq really distracted them, where we really paid the price, it was North Korea," Robert Joseph, a former undersecretary for arms control and international security and one of the creators of the squeeze-them-until-they-expire approach, told me one day over coffee, months after he had left the State Department in disgust. He had walked out after writing a letter to Condoleezza Rice, his longtime friend, arguing that by negotiating with North Korea and providing them with a million tons of oil and lifting sanctions, she and Bush had flipped 180 degrees, and now were propping up an odious regime. On that point there is little dispute. The administration spent the first term praying for North Korea to implode. When that failed, it spent the second term trying to get back the weapons built during the first term.

It's questionable whether Joseph's strategy of "tailored containment" of North Korea, which Bush partially embraced, would ever have brought the country to its knees. Every American president since Harry Truman has dreamed of watching the North Korean regime collapse on his watch. Every single one left office frustrated and disappointed. When Clinton signed a deal in 1994 that ended the first North Korean nuclear crisis, many in his administration whispered that the North Korean regime would collapse before the United States, Japan, and South Korea had to make good on their part of the bargain: building "proliferation-resistant" nuclear reactors for the country. Clinton's chief negotiator, Robert Gallucci, warned his colleagues not to bet on North Korea's demise.

For all his combative rhetoric and withering criticism of his predecessor's Korea policy, Bush fell into the same trap as the most optimistic of the Clintonites. And when the hated regime declined to collapse, the president who vowed never to "tolerate" a nuclear North Korea had little choice but to cut a deal.

To broker that deal, Bush had to walk back from his insistence that the North Koreans come clean about Syria and about what they did with a pile of equipment they bought from A. Q. Khan that could give them a second pathway to a bomb.

"I'd say the score is Kim Jong-Il eight, and Bush zero," Graham Allison, a Harvard professor and author of one of the leading studies on nuclear terrorism, told me in April 2008 after the CIA made public the photos of the Syrian raid and evidence. "If you can build a reactor in Syria without being detected for eight years, how hard can it be to sell a little plutonium to Osama bin Laden?"

# CHAPTER 10
# CHENEY'S LOST WAR

TWENTY YEARS AGO, after settling into a six-year assignment as a foreign correspondent in Tokyo, I turned for the first time to the question that seemed to be gripping Asia: How did the North Koreans plan to survive in a world in which every sign pointed to their imminent demise?

On the other side of the world, the Berlin Wall was falling. The Soviet Union was showing the first signs of dissolution. No one yet dared to think about a world in which the Cold War was over. But in South Korea in the 1990s, debate was breaking out—prematurely, it turned out—about whether it would be a wonderful thing, or ruinously expensive, to reunify a peninsula that had been divided since the end of World War II.

In a desolate site northwest of Pyongyang, next to the bitterly cold, badly polluted Kuryong River, the North was constructing its survival strategy. It was called Yongbyon. Barbed wire and antiaircraft guns surrounded a nuclear complex into which the country had poured its scarce treasure for three decades. Inside the gates, a huge facility had gradually taken shape: a nuclear reactor, a "reprocessing facility" where bomb fuel could be made, and an even larger reactor under construction, though never finished.

It was all in open view, but it never became the center of American attention until the late 1980s, when spy satellites began to track more closely the operation of the smaller, five-megawatt reactor, in an attempt to determine when its fuel was being unloaded. By the early 1990s, the CIA and experts at the Energy Department had calculated that during one of the reactor's shutdowns, North Korean engineers had extracted enough spent fuel to make one or two bombs. "We just didn't know what they had done with the fuel, or if they had actually manufactured weapons," recalled Joseph Nye, who ran the National Intelligence Council early in the Clinton administration. "It was more like educated guesswork."

Either way, the production of bomb-grade plutonium marked the culmination of a forty-year quest by the country's quixotic founder, Kim Il Sung. In 1950, at the age of thirty-eight, Kim took the huge gamble of invading the South. He caught both his enemies and his patron—China—completely unawares. The move, both bold and foolhardy, became part of the legend—and the mythology—surrounding the Great Leader. But it was also the moment when he learned the negotiating power bestowed upon those who wield nuclear weapons.

In that desperate winter of 1950, with Chinese troops pouring over the border to help beat back the forces that Gen. Douglas MacArthur was landing at Inchon, Harry Truman warned that he would take "whatever steps are necessary" to stop the Chinese from wiping out South Korea. As America faced the prospect that it might lose the first hot war of the Cold War, the warning was repeated in various forms. The threat seemed entirely plausible: After all, Truman was the man who unleashed the Bomb against Hiroshima and Nagasaki, and he said he'd never lost a night's sleep about the decision because it saved the lives of countless American soldiers preparing to invade Honshu, Japan's main island.

As Kim later learned, MacArthur requested permission to use America's nuclear arsenal against targets in both China and North Korea. MacArthur's request was denied, and he was famously relieved of duty not long afterward. But through the negotiations that led to the armistice, American officials hinted strongly that if diplomacy failed, the nuclear option was on the table.

When an uneasy peace fell over the Korean peninsula, Kim vowed never again to face a superpower without the ultimate weapon. His determination only accelerated in the 1960s, after he concluded that the Russians had rolled over rather than confront the United States during the Cuban Missile Crisis. He decided they could not be counted on to come to his aid if he once again entered into conflict with America. For a poor country surrounded by much bigger powers, North Korea saw the Bomb as the ultimate insurance policy. In this calculation, Kim was ahead of his time—ahead of Israel and India, ahead of Pakistan, and ahead of a brutal Iraqi named Saddam Hussein. He was decades ahead of the Iranians. It was a survival insight that he no doubt passed down to his son, who at the time was more interested in foreign movies—and the starlets who appeared in them— than in nuclear weapons.

Within three years of the end of the Korean War, Kim was sending scientists to the Soviet Union for training in nuclear physics.* By the early 1960s, Yongbyon began to take shape, and the Soviets delivered a research reactor in the mid-sixties, when American attention was focused to the south, in Vietnam. By the mid-1970s, Kim was determined to build a much larger reactor, the one that decades later became the model for Syria's facility. Based on a declassified British design called Calder Hall, it ran on natural uranium—raw fuel the North Koreans could mine from their own territory. And every time the reactor was reloaded, North Korean scientists would receive a load of spent fuel that could be reprocessed into enough plutonium for roughly half a dozen bombs.

In a harbinger of events years later involving Iraq, Washington let its attention lapse as the North Koreans put together their bomb factory. Vietnam preoccupied Johnson and Nixon; in recently declassified notes from a meeting between Nixon and South Korean

---

* There are many accounts of the early days of the North Korean nuclear program; for one of the most concise, see Joel Wit, Daniel B. Poneman, and Robert L. Gallucci, *Going Critical: The First North Korean Nuclear Crisis* (Washington, D.C.: Brookings Institution Press, 2004), ch. 1.

President Park Chunghee, there is discussion of the Chinese and Soviet nuclear programs—but none of the North's nascent effort. Then came nuclear advances by Israel, Pakistan, and India. Yet, month by month, the expansion of Yongbyon was being recorded by American spy satellites.

Even through most of the 1980s, when it became clear that the North was close to obtaining bomb fuel, there was virtually no public discussion of North Korea's nuclear ambitions. The Reagan administration pressured the Soviets to get Kim to sign the Nuclear Non-Proliferation Treaty, and he did in 1985. The signature meant nothing; the North dragged its feet on an agreement that would have brought inspectors into the country, and the United States protested little. By the time Washington woke up, the North was well on its way to a bomb and not about to turn back.

When word of the Yongbyon nuclear complex finally moved from classified intelligence reports to the front pages, no one seemed to know what to say about it. The Chinese were silent; North Korea was hardly at the top of the agenda for leaders in Beijing still reeling from the Tiananmen protests. The Soviet Union, which had given Kim much of the technology to help build Yongbyon, was on the brink of collapse and desperately interested in opening up trade with the South. Quickly it became clear that the Soviets were unsentimental about their old Stalinist ally; visiting delegations of Russians might be comfortable in Pyongyang, but in South Korea they had access to Hyundai cars, Samsung electronics, and working capital. Quick to calculate their own interests, they threw their diplomatic energy into the other side of the Demilitarized Zone, the line that marked the makeshift border between the North and the South.

The South Koreans were alternately panicked about North Korea and, less vocally, proud of its nuclear accomplishments. Many in the South Korean government were still bruised by the United States' swift action to stop their country from building a nuclear weapon of its own in the mid-1970s. More than a few South Korean officials conceded to me in the early 1990s—usually over

Korean *shochu*, a popular after-work beverage—that they were impressed that their starving cousins had used their wiles to develop a bomb. "It will be ours one day," one South Korean official told me, looking forward to the time—which he optimistically thought was not too far away—when the North collapsed and South Korea could inherit a unified, nuclear-capable peninsula.

It was symbolic of the confusion of those days that in April 1991 the South Korean defense minister, Lee Jong Koo, said his country might be forced to mount a commando raid against Yongbyon if the North Koreans persisted in pursuing the Bomb. When his threat was reported by the South Korean press, he withdrew his statement, although not before North Korea denounced it as "virtually a declaration of war." He may well have been the last senior South Korean official to give voice to the thought that the North Korean threat had to be neutralized, not tolerated.

In a harbinger of things to come a decade later with his son, George H. W. Bush was distracted by another problem—Iraq. In 1990, as the intelligence on Yongbyon was beginning to pour in, the elder Bush was far more focused on how to push the Iraqis out of Kuwait. Saddam, he argued, in language the younger Bush would come close to adopting, was "worse than Hitler." Kim Il Sung had almost certainly killed more people and built more gulags. But the elder Bush didn't have much to say about him.

The assumption at the time was that North Korea was a problem that would solve itself. Surely a broke, corrupt, and brutal dictatorship simply couldn't survive when Communist regimes were collapsing everywhere. After all, the Cold War was over in Europe; how long could it persist in Asia?

The assumption was that the clock was ticking and that the failed regime was on its deathbed. Adm. Timothy J. Keating, current commander of U.S. Pacific Command, recalled a Pentagon meeting in which the chairman of the Joint Chiefs of Staff and the directors were sitting around the table when Vice Adm. Denny Blair, then the Joint Staff's director, entered with a sandwich-size plastic bag full of grain. Blair put it down, and when it was his turn to speak, he pointed out that this was all the average North Korean citizen got to eat every day.

"So this was ten years ago," Keating recalled, "and we all thought, 'This can't last.' I get ten times that much for lunch."[1]

I, too, was persuaded by that narrative. When I got to North Korea for the first time on a ten-day trip in 1992, everything I saw reinforced the view that collapse was imminent. I underestimated the ability of the regime to hang on. The real lesson of that trip was that Kim was a little like a crazy relative who had locked himself up in a rundown house in an otherwise upscale neighborhood. He had wrapped the house in barbed wire, put missiles on the roof, and designed a brilliant survival strategy: If the rest of the neighbors didn't bring him oil, gas, and take-out food, he would blow the place sky-high. The amazing thing was that it was working; the neighbors didn't want any trouble.

The trip was a special tour organized for Japanese and South Korean businessmen, ostensibly to attract investment into a corner of North Korea that had been closed to foreigners for decades. Our destination was the Tumen River, a bleak, all-but-forgotten corner of Asia where Russia, China, and North Korea meet. In a desperate effort to keep the North Koreans engaged in the world, the United Nations was exploring a project to build a megaport there, figuring that the North Koreans would warm to the vision of all the cold cash that could be generated by exporting goods from all three countries to Japan and beyond.

Journalists were invited along after it became clear there weren't enough participants crazy enough to shell out $5,000 for ten days in the workers' paradise. Since we rarely got to go into North Korea at all, and never into that part of the country, a group of us based in Tokyo at the time grabbed the ticket.

We flew in on a chartered North Korean jet, one that seemed in such disrepair that the Russians must have sold it to the North because it no longer met Aeroflot's strict safety standards. We were immediately shuttled over to the Koryo Hotel, the rooms of which were designed and extensively bugged for Westerners. The biggest risk at the Koryo was eating the food; fortunately, the restaurant was out of almost everything on the menu.

My first night, one of the two state-run television stations carried excerpts of a rare speech by Kim Jong-Il, the bizarre "Dear Leader." He had just turned fifty, and this outing was part of the long process of grooming him to take over from his father. My minder, a young North Korean who had diligently studied English at university, translated as the Dear Leader extolled the glories of the workers' state and denounced the "flunkyist attitudes" of the United States. It wasn't exactly Khrushchev's "we will bury you" speech, but we got the point. When it was over, I had a chance to survey Pyongyang from my hotel room. The capital of the country that was going to bury us was pitch dark—there wasn't enough electricity, my guide explained, to keep it lit at night.

When we started meeting with government officials the next morning, there were a few moments of candor, in which the country's leaders began to admit to a little nervousness that after the collapse of the Communist world, maybe it was time to get with the capitalist program—to a point. "There are only a few countries following the socialist ways," Kim Dal Hyon, the deputy prime minister, told us soon after we arrived on the broad, empty streets of Pyongyang. "We are one of them. But we want to develop our technology."

Then, conceding that he needed some foreign capital to make this dream work, he added, "It is for our own survival. The world is changing."[2]

The world may have been changing, but Pyongyang wasn't. The few cars that shuttled us around looked like North Korean knockoffs of Mercedes. (Naturally, our hosts insisted they were products of North Korea's mighty auto manufacturers. I learned later that they were constructed from kits the North Koreans had purchased in Germany years before and, by most accounts, never paid for.) We were escorted to the usual tourist sites: the mind-boggling gymnastic displays, the huge statues commemorating how Kim Il Sung—who was still alive during our tour—had fearlessly battled Japanese occupiers. We visited schools where children were taught that the United States had started the Korean War by invading the North. Another school, a government showcase for foreigners, included an empty classroom full of Japanese-made personal computers, advanced science laboratories equipped with up-to-date microscopes, and a room for driver's education, complete with a Chinese car and a screen projecting scenery racing by on the road. The only hitch was that almost no one in Pyongyang could afford a car.

The propaganda was more cutting-edge than the infrastructure. The pyramid-style, 105-story Ryugyong Hotel, designed to be the tallest in Asia, sat half finished, towering over the city. It was out of plumb, and construction had halted. It seemed like a symbol of the country. Things got worse as we headed north on an aging train, moving at about ten miles per hour because the trackbed had barely been improved since the Japanese left the country, in something of a hurry, after the defeat of their Empire.

From the windows of the train and then from tour buses—we had to carry our own fuel, because there was no place to fill up—we witnessed a country at a standstill. Factory smokestacks were visible in the distance, but not a single one had smoke emerging. At ports where we stopped, fertilizer rotted in the rain. At night the streetlights were off. Old women pulled plows across the hard earth; there was no livestock to do the job. The few ships in the docks were rusting, and dockworkers were scarce. They were greatly outnumbered by the soldiers who, armed with World War II–era rifles, kept us from wandering anywhere near the handful of workers. Who could blame them? That year malnutrition was widespread, with many people not getting their full allotment of 4.4 pounds of red meat and chicken per month. The regime had just adopted a new slogan: "Let's Eat Two Meals!"

◆

WE ARRIVED AT the Tumen River basin to find a rusting port near the common border with Russia and China. The North Koreans thought that the strategic location—and its proximity to Japan—made it the ideal trading hub for Northeast Asia. In a perfect world, they would have been right. But tens of millions of dollars, if not more, were needed to dredge the port and upgrade its corroding infrastructure.

That was, in fact, the long-term plan of the United Nations, which saw the river basin as a place to demonstrate to the North Koreans that there were opportunities for profit if they engaged constructively with the outside world. The North Koreans were intrigued. But every time we asked for specifics about what kind of help the North was seeking, we tripped into the country's bipolar foreign policy: One minute, North Korean officials were talking about the need for major investment, the next they were delivering lectures on why the country could exist just fine in splendid isolation. This usually involved a lecture on the success of *juche*, Kim's ideology of self-reliance. *Juche*, they said, explained why North Korea was still around while the rest of the Communist world had fallen.

If so, we asked Kim Dal Hyon, why look for foreign investors?

"Some people think that this is contradictory with the philosophy of independence," Kim shot back, "but this is not so. We have long encouraged foreign investment. But we have been isolated by the world community because of pressure from some world superpowers." The Tumen project, it turned out, was a joke, a desperate effort by the UN to keep engaged with the North Koreans. The region had been declared a special economic zone and "free trade area" by the North Koreans in the hope of attracting Japanese, Chinese, and Russian investors. But the river had silted up years before and was far too narrow and shallow to handle seagoing freighters. Japanese executives who toured the region found that very little of the infrastructure had improved since some of them had left, as youngsters, when the Japanese occupation ended in 1945. "The river is too narrow to carry ships," one executive of a major trading house said. "They are wasting our time."

Of course, North Korea wanted an end to isolation on its own terms. It wanted to ensure that its radios could receive only two stations—both government-run—so that its people heard only about the glories of living north of the Demilitarized Zone and about the Hobbesian nightmare of the South. Most important, the state wanted to shield North Koreans from a vision of the South's wealth— the gleaming towers, the new cars, the satellite TVs and cell phones.

The few North Koreans we could actually talk to with some degree of candor understood the harsh truth: Forty-five years after the end of the Korean War, North Korea had been virtually abandoned by its longtime allies. Some food and fuel still flowed, but not the way they did throughout the Cold War, when the United States supported the South, and the Soviet Union and China vied to prop up the North. Naturally, this was a subject that North Korean officials did not want to discuss.

But no one could fool Li Song Pil, the spry stationmaster on the North Korean side of the Tumen. Li was able to measure the country's isolation with statistical precision. A few years before, he told me, six or seven freight trains crossed the river every day. Now, he said, "sometimes we see one. Sometimes, nothing comes."

Later that year, China—the country that had sent more than a million troops swarming over the border more than forty years ago—invited South Korea's president at the time, Roh Tae Woo, to make an historic first trip to Beijing. Roh brought what the Chinese wanted: news that South Korea's trade with the Chinese would double to $10 billion. South Korean–owned electronics factories and clothing plants dotted Guangdong Province, the manufacturing hub of China that has sprung up from the rural landscape over the past twenty years. The South Koreans were there in search of low-cost labor: Had the Korean Peninsula been unified, there is little doubt that many of those factories would be in the North today, not in China.

Just before he left office, I went to see President Roh, a surprisingly mild-mannered former general who became the first truly freely elected president of South Korea—before his time was tainted by the kind of scandals that seem to engulf every South Korean president. He had grown up a Cold War hawk. Yet he told me with confidence that the North's "determination to develop nuclear weapons has become weaker." And he believed that North Korea was about to crumble under the pressures mounting against it.

"North Korea is much more isolated this year than it was last year," he told me. "Their economic situation is deteriorating, and their people are suffering from the lack of food. They have decided they must gradually open up. They have no choice. The waves of liberalization are rolling in."

Like almost everyone else at that time, he turned out to be a tad too optimistic (but not as optimistic as his successor, Kim Young Sam, who showed up in Washington in 1995 and told President Clinton that the North Korean government would collapse in three months). The South Koreans thought they would be spending the last years of the 1990s and the first years of a new century managing reunification. It was not to be. The Tumen River remains as silted up today as it was the day we visited; the UN program exists largely on paper. The rusting rail lines are fifteen years further into decay.

There has been some modest progress—a rail line now runs through the DMZ, connecting the South to an impressive-looking joint economic zone that was the main experiment in North–South rapprochement. But when South Korea's new president was sworn in early in 2008 and took a far harder line, the North announced that their South Korean brethren working in the economic complex should pack up and get out. South Korean presidents have traveled to Pyongyang to meet Kim Jong-Il, but it has always been on North Korea's terms—and the first visit was lubricated by huge hidden payments to the North Korean regime to make the meeting happen at all.

It is easy for outsiders to forget that for all their common roots, North and South Koreans remain virtual strangers to one another.

They have grown up in different worlds, fought a war against each other, and rebuilt vastly different societies. One ranks among the most plugged into the Internet age; the other rarely sees images of the rest of the world. If reunification happens, it will be far harder to achieve than anything the Germans confronted. That fact has been driven home to South Korean negotiators who, when visiting Pyongyang, have opened their hotel-room doors to long-lost relatives. Some received a tearful embrace. Others got lectures on the wonders of the Great Leader's and Dear Leader's rule.

It is no surprise that when you find South Korean politicians or business executives in a candid mood, or in one of Seoul's gaudy nightclubs, they explain that they are in no rush for reunification. What they want is managed collapse, something that would let them use North Korea as a low-cost manufacturing center but keep its millions of hungry and poor on the other side of the DMZ.

Such views reflect a huge shift in thinking that has gradually taken hold in South Korea over the past twenty years: As the country has prospered and gained confidence, the fear of a North Korean attack or invasion has completely eroded.

For thirty years after the 1952 armistice, the South's politics were driven by the urgency of countering a potential North Korean threat. That fear supported three decades of military strongmen. But the country's migration toward democracy in the mid-1980s began to change that dynamic, and today most South Koreans—especially the younger generation—regard the North less as a menace than a deeply estranged branch of the family, headed by a crazed uncle. Donald Gregg, who served as the CIA's station chief in Seoul at the height of the Cold War and returned later as American ambassador to Seoul, told me he felt the change in the mid-1990s. "There is already a subliminal feeling of victory in the air—that unification will come, and it will come on the South's terms," he said. "That is an enormous change."

As this new attitude took hold, the South Koreans began to experience an exhilarating freedom. In a country pressed for living space, huge housing developments were built between Seoul and the DMZ—once the buffer zone where the South Korean and U.S. armies planned to repel an invasion. Now that invasion force would have to navigate backyard barbecues. In April 2008, when the North threatened to take "preemptive action" if a new government in Seoul pressured it too much, the South Koreans shrugged off the threat and went back to work. They'd heard it all before. The moment passed like a summer storm.

That was the good news. The bad news is that after several decades, reunification—the polite word for what would happen after the North collapses —looks no closer than before.

In my last months stationed in Asia, in the spring and summer of 1994, North Korea and the United States came as close to the brink of war as at any other time since the end of the Korean conflict. Most Americans were blissfully unaware. At the key moment in the crisis—a moment that former President Jimmy Carter defused with a trip to see Kim Il Sung—O. J. Simpson was in his low-speed chase along the California freeways, so captivating the world that even one of South Korea's top diplomats put aside his fear of incipient Armageddon to call me in my hotel room in Seoul.

"David," he asked, "are you watching CNN?"

"No," I said. "What did Carter and Kim agree on?"

"I've got no idea," he said. "No one's called. I'm watching O. J.!"

What was unfolding in North Korea was the first nuclear crisis of the post–Cold War era. Both the actions and the compromises made in those days, it turns out, set the stage for the proliferation disaster that followed during the Bush administration.

In late 1993, the North Koreans prepared to take their first load of fuel out of their big reactor at Yongbyon, fuel that would enable them to extract enough plutonium to build eight to twelve bombs. The United States pressed the North Koreans to allow inspectors to watch the process and to "seal" the fuel so that it could never be turned into weapons. This encounter was the first test of whether

Kim Il Sung would abide by the Nuclear Non-Proliferation Treaty he had reluctantly signed nearly a decade before. Kim refused, and threatened to use a huge loophole in the treaty—any country that signs can simply ditch the whole thing with ninety days' notice—to proceed with his plans to make his bombs.

Back in Washington, the Clinton administration determined that they could never allow Kim to turn that plutonium into weapons. American troops stationed throughout Asia, along with Japan, would have been placed in jeopardy. Defense Secretary William Perry ordered an updating of OPLAN 5027, the operations plan for defeating a North Korean attack, as well as an update of the contingency plan for destroying the reactor at Yongbyon.

Perry later wrote that the reactor attack plan was presented "to a small, grim group seated around the conference table in my office."[3] The operation was to be quick and smooth, executed entirely from the air, with little risk that Americans would be injured. Because the nuclear plant was so remote, North Korean casualties would also have been low. "Without question," Perry concluded, "it would have achieved its objective of setting back their nuclear program many years."

But no one could predict Kim's reaction and whether it would lead the North Koreans to attack the South. The Americans knew they could not protect Seoul from the thousands of rockets and missiles that would rain down on the city from dug-in sites in the mountains just north of the DMZ. American military planners knew that by the time they took out those sites, there would already be hundreds of thousands of casualties in Seoul. The North Koreans sensed their leverage. When Clinton publicly started talking about the next step—getting the United Nations to impose its first economic sanctions on North Korea—Pyongyang responded with a familiar line: It would turn Seoul into "a sea of flames."

Clinton and Perry feared where this might be going, and by mid-June they were preparing for the possibility that the Korean War was about to be refought. They moved antimissile batteries to South Korea and shipped over chemical weapons suits to protect American soldiers. Seeing every sign that the North Koreans were getting ready to move their spent fuel off to a "reprocessing facility" where they would produce the plutonium, Perry recommended a major reinforcement of troops on the Korean Peninsula, in case the North Koreans sensed what was coming and staged a preemptive attack on the South.

"I was getting ready to recommend the military strike on Yong-byon," he later told me, if that step were needed to stop the nuclear fuel from being moved. "I don't know what the president would have chosen to do." Neither did Clinton's other advisers, who say the president was happy to have Perry out in public hinting at how the United States would respond—even though he had not committed to a plan himself. "No one ever had to make that decision, and we'll never know what Clinton would have done," Jim Steinberg, later the deputy national security adviser, told me.[4]

In June 1994, Jimmy Carter intervened. He headed to North Korea on his own, convinced the Clinton administration was on a collision course with North Korea. While Clinton asked his aides to brief Carter in advance, their wariness of Carter soon turned to fury. Here was classic Carter, they thought, inserting himself into a world conflict, with maximum publicity and minimum coordination with the White House. Carter spent two days with Kim Il Sung, floating in Kim's yacht, eating *bolgolgi*, a spicy beef dish, and other Korean delicacies, and engaging in the kind of direct conversation that the U.S. president had shunned. The North Koreans loved it; they craved nothing more than recognition as a significant world player. Here they were dealing directly with an American president, albeit a former one.

The two men arrived back on land with what they described as an agreement for the international inspectors to stay at the plant, but contained nothing about restarting the reactor. Both countries pulled back from the brink of confrontation.

I met Carter a few days later, during a stopover at the ambassador's residence in Tokyo. (Conveniently, the ambassador was Walter Mondale, Carter's former vice president.) After Carter relayed the tale of his negotiations, and tweaked the Clinton White House for its failure to engage in direct negotiations, I asked him how the eighty-year-old Kim looked. "Healthy as a horse," Carter said. "He told me he planned to rule North Korea for ten more years."

It is a good thing Carter chose a career in politics, not medicine. Within a month, the "Great Leader" was dead. But because Kim had put his imprimatur on the negotiations, they became the last bit of his legacy. In a frenetic three months, Robert Gallucci, a wry, veteran American diplomat, came up with an "Agreed Framework" that required the North to freeze activity at its reactor. It held together, barely, through the rest of the Clinton administration. Activity at Yongbyon remained frozen. The IAEA's inspectors lived at the plant, monitoring the activity and making sure that the spent fuel rods stayed in a cooling pond. That was the insurance policy that the fuel would not be used for weapons. In return, the United States agreed to provide fuel oil to the North Koreans—a deal that helped the shaky regime of Kim's son, Kim Jong-Il. Japan, South Korea, and the United States agreed to begin slowly building two light-water nuclear reactors that ran on fuel that could not easily be turned into weapons.

There was a proviso: The North Koreans had to ship out of the country all their spent nuclear fuel before the key elements of the nuclear power plants were delivered. Many wondered whether they would ever comply. The fuel was North Korea's greatest bargaining chip, and as long as it was in the country, they could throw out the inspectors and race for the bomb. But if the North Koreans chose that course, the world would see, and U.S. officials concluded, would have time to respond.

Gallucci said later he simply was not able to negotiate a deal that called for them to surrender the fuel sooner. "That would have been terrific," he said. "Unfortunately, they simply weren't going to do it."

At the time, George W. Bush was busy with other things: He was just settling in as governor of Texas, and only Karl Rove was thinking of him as a future president. Even during the presidential campaign of 2000, Bush said little about North Korea beyond the hard-line talking points about defending the United States that are the staple of presidential campaigns. In the months before he left office, Clinton tried, and failed, to take the next step with North Korea. He sent Secretary of State Madeleine Albright to Pyongyang to talk about a new agreement that would curtail North Korea's missile activities and get the country off the government's list of state sponsors of terrorism. There were hints of an eventual peace agreement to formally end the Korean War. Today the trip is often remembered for scenes that Albright had a hard time living down later, as she sipped champagne with Kim Jong-Il and watched the country's famous circus. Clinton himself desperately wanted to travel to North Korea before leaving office, but his advisers warned that without a prenegotiated agreement about what the North Koreans would give up, he might only embarrass himself in his last days in office.

In retrospect, the North Koreans should have taken whatever deal they could have gotten. While they haggled and bet that whatever Clinton offered would still be on the table when the next president took office, many of the hardliners who were members of the "Vulcans," the group that soon-to-be national security adviser Condoleezza Rice gathered to tutor George W. Bush on foreign policy, already had the 1994 agreement in their sights. Cheney and Rumsfeld in particular thought it was a symbol of American weakness. They focused on its biggest flaw: Although it committed the North Koreans to eventual disarmament, it left Kim Jong-Il in possession of a stockpile of nuclear fuel. With that the North Korean leader could trigger a crisis at any time, throwing out the inspectors and threatening to build bombs. The Vulcans began to argue that Clinton had given away the store while keeping an evil regime alive by providing it with oil. They didn't yet have a concrete plan to kill off the regime. But they were working toward a new slogan: "We don't negotiate with evil, we defeat it."[5]

When Bush came to office, no one could have blamed him for thinking that Kim Jong-Il's economically incompetent and politically isolated regime could be pushed into the dustbin of history with just one strong shove.

But in their headlong drive for regime change, Bush and his top aides forgot that triggering a country's collapse is a goal, not a strategy. If it had been easy to engineer North Korea's demise, Truman or Eisenhower would have done it a half century ago. It turns out that the North Koreans have suffered deprivation for so long that a little bit more—another turn of the economic screw—was a drop in the sea of misery. Most presidents since have tried some uncomfortable mix of containment and engagement, hoping to lure the North Koreans out of their paranoid shell. None of these approaches worked either.

Bush tried something a little different: a mix of deeper isolation and more-strident name-calling. Meeting a group of senators in 2002, Bush referred to Kim Jong-Il as a "pygmy"; with his top aides, he compared him to a "spoiled child at the dinner table" who throws his food on the floor when he doesn't like what he is being served.[6] Even in 2005, when the administration was beginning to recognize that sometimes you need to talk to odious regimes to get your message across, the president called Kim a "tyrant" during a news conference, and referred to the "concentration camps" he kept in North Korea. Every time he uttered words like that, it made the hardliners—and many others who detest Kim, which is a pretty large group—feel better. Predictably, though, it ultimately proved a little embarrassing to Bush—particularly at the end of 2007, when he was forced to come around full circle, writing a personal letter to Kim urging him to abide by the agreement to declare all of his nuclear holdings and disarm, and vaguely hinting at all the good things that would come North Korea's way. ("We got him to resist the temptation," one of Bush's Asia hands jokingly reported, "to begin the letter 'Dear Evil Pygmy.'")

It took me a long time to understand that the running arguments inside the Bush administration over how to deal with this starving, fundamentally desperate state were symbolic of a presidential predilection that escaped most public discussion: paralyzing indecision. Too often "the decider" never decided. He let arguments about whether to use bigger sticks or tastier carrots go on for years, unresolved. He desperately wanted to be remembered as the president who set people free from awful regimes. When it became clear that the North would not collapse on his timetable, he would turn halfheartedly to diplomacy, but he had to be dragged every step of the way. Meanwhile, others in the administration tried to undercut the process.

The internal rift at the White House over how to deal with North Korea—whether isolation would speed the collapse of the regime or negotiations could ever change its behavior—started in the first weeks after Bush's inaugural. But rather than get resolved in a year or two, the division simply grew bigger and bigger, until the administration was daily operating at cross purposes.

The debate started in early March 2001, when the new administration was barely forty days old. Newly minted national security adviser Condoleezza Rice had a small group of us into her office to preview Bush's first meeting with President Kim Dae Jung of South Korea, who the year before had won the Nobel Peace Prize for his efforts to open a dialogue with the North through what became known as "the Sunshine Policy." I had known Rice for a few years before she signed up with Bush, and talked to her frequently during the transition. She had always impressed me as the ultimate pragmatist—someone less interested in ideological point-scoring than in finding ways, great and small, to shape the global chessboard. But something had changed.

For the first time I heard a tone of moral certainty in her voice, a certainty that if Clinton or Kim Dae Jung had shown enough toughness, America would not now be facing blackmail by a two-bit regime.

I asked her about Paul Wolfowitz's blistering complaint that the Clinton policy toward the North had amounted to bribery, paying the country in monthly doses of oil and food to keep their weapons program suspended.

Clinton had thought he had bought time, Rice responded. But he'd received nothing but empty promises, she argued, because North Korea had given up nothing—starting with the spent fuel from its reactor. "The problem with what the Clinton administration did is that it was all front-loaded," she argued that afternoon. "The North Koreans got everything up front—the food, new nuclear reactors—and nothing came out of the country."[7] Rice insisted that everything the United States was doing with North Korea at the end of the Clinton administration would halt, while a "total review" of the policy was under way.

Unfortunately, no one told the secretary of state. Even as we met with Rice, Powell was telling reporters across town that he hoped to "pick up where President Clinton and his administration left off."[8] He was quickly taken to the woodshed—not for the last time—and said later that "I got a little too forward on my skis." As Bush and Kim Dae Jung met in the Oval Office the next day, Powell was sent out to eat his words from the previous day. He told reporters that North Korea was "a threat" and that if anyone had the idea "there are imminent negotiations about to take place" with North Korea, "that is not the case."[9] He and his staff did the best they could to repair the breach. But the discord was just beginning.

Behind the scenes, the battle lines were already sharply drawn. Cheney, Wolfowitz, and their staffs looked for new ways to choke off North Korea, while Powell, Armitage, and others looked for ways to engage it. Michael Green, a young aide to Rice who later became Bush's senior director for Asian affairs at the National Security Council, was caught between the opposing forces. "We wasted a lot of time consumed by making sure that whatever we did, it was the opposite of what Clinton did," he told me in 2007. It was an opportunity that did not come back for seven years. The Clinton negotiation on North Korea's missile capability fell by the wayside. So did the discussion about what it would take to get North Korea off the State Department's list of nations that support terrorism. By the time Bush got back to those subjects, North Korea had all the plutonium it needed.

THE LONG WAR between the engagers and the isolators lasted much of the year.* Then the 9/11 attacks pushed North Korea into the background; it reappeared briefly during the 2002 State of the Union speech, when Bush famously declared it part of the Axis of Evil. (A senior White House official told me days after the speech that North Korea was included largely because "we needed one non-Islamic nation" in the triumvirate.)

But it quickly became apparent to everyone that all the talk about reversing eight years of what they saw as Clintonian appeasement was not matched by a credible plan to bring down Kim's reign of terror. The Bush team could change policy, but it couldn't change geography. Seoul, the capital of South Korea, was still only thirty-five miles from the North Korean border. In tour after tour of the border area, a succession of American commanders in South Korea had told me that if war broke out, there was no way to stop the first rounds of mortar fire that could destroy one of Asia's most vibrant cities. No one doubted that the United States and South Korea would ultimately win any conflict, but at huge human cost.

---

* John Bolton, the unapologetic hawk who worked in Powell's State Department but was working for the Cheney camp, argued in his book that Rice wanted Steve Hadley to "go to Pyongyang to talk to Kim Jong-il directly," but that Powell did not want the National Security Council directly engaged in diplomacy. John Bolton, *Surrender Is Not an Option* (New York: Simon & Schuster Threshold Editions, 2007).

Even North Korea hawks, like Bob Joseph, said the risk was just unacceptable. "Now that would be a disaster," he said to me once when I asked him about taking military action against North Korea's nuclear sites.

I suspect that the recognition of that reality, as much as anything else, explained why the neocons, the hawks, and the ideologues were so quick to turn their attention to deposing Saddam Hussein instead of Kim Jong-Il. Quite simply, Saddam had no way to strike back. Kim did. Iraq looked easy. North Korea didn't.

BUSH MADE TWO disastrous errors when dealing with North Korea. First the administration ripped up the 1994 agreement—flawed as it was—without thinking about Plan B, how it would respond when North Korea began making new bomb fuel. Then, when Kim Jong-Il threw out international inspectors on New Year's Day in 2003 and announced he would turn his stockpile of spent fuel into bombs, the administration that prided itself on clarity and toughness said nothing. It failed to draw any red lines, and failed to make it clear that North Korea would pay a huge price if it attempted "nuclear breakout." The result was that while North Korea fabricated the fuel for six or eight nuclear weapons, and boasted about it, Bush essentially averted his eyes and focused only on Iraq.

Bush's mistakes began in the fall of 2002. In October, in the same week that Congress authorized Bush to use force against Iraq—the vote that John Kerry, Hillary Clinton, and others would come to regret—the assistant secretary of state, James Kelly, was sent to Pyongyang on what was publicly described as the opening of a face-to-face dialogue. The public line was that he was bringing a "bold initiative" to offer to the North Koreans.

That was true, but hardly the whole story. Over the summer, more evidence had flowed in that North Korea was buying equipment for a secret, undeclared program to enrich uranium—an alternative path to a bomb. The CIA had tracked shipments from Russia of aluminum tubes, not unlike those they thought Saddam was buying, which they alleged were for manufacturing the rotors that are the critical working part of a modern gas centrifuge. But the tubes were not the only evidence. There were close to a hundred other items related to the uranium enrichment that analysts had followed. Some of them came aboard a cargo plane commandeered by A. Q. Khan.

If the intelligence agencies' evidence was right, then it was the proof the hardliners were looking for that North Korea was cheating on the 1994 accord it had signed with the Clinton administration. For Cheney, John Bolton (who was undersecretary of arms control and international security at the time, before being sent to the United Nations), and Wolfowitz, among others, this was the chance they were looking for to ditch the 1994 "Agreed Framework" and cut off the delivery of fuel oil to the North.

Through no fault of his own, Kelly's encounter with the North Koreans—in which he conveyed the accusation, but not the evidence—triggered a cascade of events that made a bad situation far worse. Rather than deny the evidence, as Cheney and others had anticipated, the North Korean officials spat back that they had the uranium program "and more."

The translation of the exact response has been in dispute for years, but in reading the transcript it becomes clear that the North Korean responses are dripping with sarcasm. It appears as if, by seeming to confirm the uranium effort, they were mocking the American intelligence.

Kelly might have defused the situation by proposing a path to resolving the issues, but his instructions gave him no leeway. An old-timer among Asia hands, he was known more for his easygoing personality than for his diplomatic creativity. He also had little clout inside the administration and was forever being hamstrung by precisely written instructions about what he could and could not say.

In Pyongyang that October, he was prohibited from describing the evidence of North Korea's cheating, much less turning over sanitized intelligence reports that would make clear they had been caught in the act. (Some of the early evidence came from South Korean intelligence agencies, though Seoul later forgot that inconvenient fact when they accused the Americans of poisoning relations with the North by using the new evidence to blow up the 1994 agreements.)

There is little doubt that the North Koreans bought A. Q. Khan's wares; Khan himself has described some of the transactions when he was questioned, on behalf of the CIA and the IAEA, by Pakistani investigators. (In July 2008, Khan spoke publicly for the first time about sending centrifuges to North Korea. He told the AP, "It was a North Korean plan, and the [Pakistani] army had complete knowledge about it and the equipment.")[10]

The question is whether they had figured out how to make it all work. In the overheated atmosphere of 2002, before the embarrassment of Iraq, the CIA assumed that once North Korea had the means to enrich uranium, it would master the art quickly. George Tenet, then the agency's director, told Congress that North Korea could begin producing uranium for a weapon by "the middle of the decade," and Hadley made the same case to me at the end of 2002. After Iraq—and after Rice and Hadley made a trip to the CIA to reexamine the evidence—that assessment changed. But it was not until early 2007 that the intelligence community publicly backed away from Tenet's declaration, telling a surprised Senate Armed Services Committee that they could only conclude "at the mid-confidence level" that the program was still active at all.[11] In short, it is unclear whether the North Koreans have ever mastered the process. That should be no surprise: It baffled the Libyans, who gave the whole thing up, and the Iranians endured years of setbacks before they figured it out.

The discovery of the uranium program and Kelly's encounter with the North Koreans was kept secret for weeks. The reason, it turns out, was the administration's obsession with Iraq. Congress was in the middle of the Iraq War authorization, and as a senior administration official said to me later, "We didn't know how much traffic the system could bear." So they kept the account of Kelly's trip quiet until one afternoon when both the *Times* and *USA Today* caught wind of what was happening.

As soon as we published our stories, Bush declared that the United States had caught the North Koreans "cheating," but there was no strategy to deal with the North's reaction other than to blow up the 1994 deal. A few days later in the fall of 2003, in a previously scheduled trip, Bush entertained President Jiang Zemin of China at the ranch in Crawford. Bush had almost no rapport with the elderly Chinese president, but this was a ceremonial farewell visit for Jiang, who was giving up the presidency.

The story the White House spun out years later is that the meeting was the beginning of a diplomatic push to split the Chinese away from the country it had supported for years. As Rice later recalled, "Jiang Zemin basically says, 'Yeah, that North Korean nuclear program, that's really a problem for you.' And the president says, 'No, I sit in the United States of America heavily armed. . . . This isn't a problem for us. This is a problem for you, because it's your region that's going to have to react to a North Korean nuclear weapon,'" implying but not quite saying that Japan would go nuclear next.

"That got Jiang Zemin's attention," Rice maintained.

Although Bush often cited this meeting as an example of his diplomatic prowess, the fact remains that China's main concern was in maintaining the status quo, creating just enough of a negotiating process to prevent Bush from taking military action. The Chinese were less interested in a nuclear-free North Korea than in keeping the United States out of their neighborhood. (Still, hope sprung eternal in the hearts of the hawks: In April 2003, just days after Saddam's statue was ripped down in Baghdad, Rumsfeld circulated a classified Pentagon memorandum arguing that the United States should team up with China to oust North Korea's leadership. Powell and his allies quickly declared the idea fatuous.

Triggering chaos in North Korea and risking a huge flow of hungry North Koreans streaming over the Chinese border was the last thing the Chinese leadership wanted.)[12]

The administration quickly leaned on its allies to cut off fuel oil shipments to North Korea, still being provided under the 1994 accord. Kim's order that the international inspectors living at Yongbyon must leave the country was the inevitable response. The North Koreans publicly declared that they would use the 8,000 spent fuel rods that the inspectors were watching to make bomb fuel.

It was exactly the threat North Korea had made years before, leading Clinton and Perry to prepare to reinforce American troops on the peninsula. But in interviews, key members of Bush's national security team said they were only vaguely aware of that history, including the warnings to the North about what might happen if they produced bomb fuel.

Whatever the state of their knowledge, Bush had no moves in his back pocket. When American satellites saw trucks pulling up along the frozen ground of Yongbyon that winter to haul away the cache— enough for eight to twelve nuclear weapons—Bush said nothing. It was not as if any of these events was a secret. The *Times* and other newspapers were publishing front-page stories about the removal of the fuel. But in late January 2003, just as Bush was receiving intelligence briefings about what the North Koreans were doing, he held a lengthy press conference with Prime Minister Tony Blair of Britain that was all about the threats Americans faced from weapons of mass destruction—in Iraq. The North Koreans understood perfectly: As long as American troops were headed for the Persian Gulf, Bush would be unable to back up diplomacy with a credible military option.

Still, Gen. Richard Myers, the chairman of the Joint Chiefs of Staff, who had once served as the commander of American forces in Japan, felt honor-bound to brief Bush one day on his military options. He told Bush that there was a well-developed plan to take out the North's nuclear facilities, and it had been updated since Perry refined it eight years before.

"It wasn't an appealing option at all," Myers said later. "We could handle the attack. It's the response that was the nightmare."[13] Their conversation was short. Bush wanted to know how the movement of troops toward the Middle East—where they would be massing in preparation for the Iraq invasion—was going.

A few months after the Iraq invasion, Condoleezza Rice argued that a Saddam Hussein with no nuclear weapons was more dangerous than a nuclear-armed Kim Jong-Il.

"Saddam lives in a worse neighborhood, David," she insisted, after I pressed her on the question of why the administration shouted so loudly about Iraqi weapons that, by that time, it seemed obvious would not be found. She seemed to shrug off the North's moves to churn out plutonium as fast as it could. "The North Koreans are surrounded by friendly or stronger powers," she said, adding that China in particular would be far more successful at containing the North's ambitions than the United States ever could.

She was right—if the fear about North Korea was that it would rekindle the Korean War by attacking the South or American troops. That was the conservative orthodoxy dating back to the Rumsfeld Commission, when North Korea became the poster child for missile defense. Rumsfeld also envisioned protecting the United States against Saddam's Iraq, and against Iran and Syria. "Concerted efforts by a number of overtly or potentially hostile nations to acquire ballistic missiles with biological or nuclear payloads pose a growing threat to the United States, its deployed forces, friends and allies," the report concluded.[14]

In reality, North Korean missiles raining down on Los Angeles or Tokyo seemed like a pretty dubious scenario. Kim Jong-Il might be bizarre and paranoid, but he had a strong interest in personal survival. Shooting a missile, particularly a nuclear-tipped one, would not constitute a very smart strategy if Kim wanted to rule to a ripe old age, as his father had done. In a nuclear exchange, North Korea's leaders would have the life expectancy of fireflies. They knew it, and the Bush administration knew it.

The real worry was that the North would sell its expertise or its nuclear fuel. Powell said so explicitly, in a series of conversations we had about North Korea as his frustration built with the administration's refusal to enter into real negotiations. The North Koreans were not suicidal enough to attack, he said. But they were poor enough to sell anything to anybody with enough cash. And their best customers lived in the same bad neighborhood that Rice kept talking about.

"You can't eat plutonium," Powell would often say in public. In private, he would add another line: "But you can sell it to get something to eat."

The fixation on Iraq had another strange effect. It led a president who never shied away from delivering an ultimatum to Saddam Hussein to balk at the idea of drawing "redlines" that the North would step over at its own peril. So Bush never told the North Koreans that there would be a huge price to pay for turning its spent nuclear fuel into plutonium for bombs. I once asked Hadley why an administration that prided itself on speaking so clearly, without diplomatic obfuscation, refused to draw redlines when it came to the North.

"They would just walk right up to them, and past them," he answered. "That's what the North Koreans do. And then what?"[15] That was the administration's central dilemma: It wanted to crush North Korea, but it did not want to wield bigger sticks for fear of a confrontation, or offer bigger carrots for fear of appearing to sell out.

But in the run-up to Iraq, Bush and Rice turned to a new argument: Toppling Saddam would have a "demonstration effect." Kim and his ilk around the world would likely be so intimidated by the show of American force that they would change their ways, for fear of being next.

"You heard this all the time," Michael Green told me later. "This was going to get Kim's attention, and bring the Iranians in line, too." Green says he believes that the theory was right, to a point, and immediately after the Iraq War there were signs that

North Korea was intimidated. Kim dropped out of sight for a couple of months; there was speculation that he was concerned he might be next on the hit list. But when America began to get bogged down, the leverage evaporated.

Although it's impossible to read Kim's mind, the lesson he appeared to draw from the Iraq invasion was that Saddam miscalculated when he took on the United States without a nuclear weapon to back him up. Whatever Kim's inner thoughts, his actions made it pretty clear he would not make the same mistake.

The administration began to understand this effect shortly after the invasion, when a senior North Korean defector who had escaped to South Korea, Hwang Jong Yop, visited the United States. A rail-thin man who was suspicious to the point of paranoia, he seemed a bit taken aback as he was escorted into the White House complex. Even to hardened White House officials, it was a little like an alien from space landing on the South Lawn, only to be invited in for tea to explain Martian society.

But when he sat down with Michael Green and Bob Joseph, two senior officials who often battled each other on how to deal with North Korea, Hwang was pretty clear about what was coming next. He said that in the leadership meetings he attended, North Korea's elite was determined to drive toward a nuclear test, come what may. Green and Joseph pressed to find out what it would take to disrupt this plan or to persuade Kim Jong-Il that it was in his long-term interest to give up the weapons.

This time it was Hwang's chance to look at the Americans as if they were aliens.

"Why would he?" he asked.

With the benefit of hindsight—after North Korea conducted its nuclear test—Green had to agree with Hwang's assessment. "There were signs that Kim Jong-Il intended to do this all along," Green said after he had left the administration. "And then we gave him his opportunity."

By the time Americans were settling into the Green Zone in Baghdad in the summer of 2003, the North Koreans had already harvested enough fuel for the arsenal they long desired. By American standards, the North Korean arsenal was tiny. But it was enough to test one bomb, to hide the rest, and to rattle the Americans by threatening to sell the surplus.

# CHAPTER 11

# "EVERYTHING IS APPOMATTOX"

By MID-2003, the level of distrust between Pyongyang and Washington reached heights unseen since the worst days of the Cold War.

The North Koreans convinced themselves that Bush and Cheney had targeted them for the next invasion, which made them desperate to exaggerate their nuclear skills, betting that the Bush administration would not risk a demonstration of what North Korea called its "deterrent." Cheney and his staff undermined every move toward reopening real diplomacy, using every opportunity at National Security Council meetings to remind the participants that the North Koreans were liars and cheats, as if anyone in the room had any doubts. Every time Powell or his deputy and close friend, Richard Armitage, hinted at the possibility of direct negotiations, or even talks on the sidelines of negotiations with several other nations, they got a lecture about the dangers of playing into Kim's hands the way Clinton did, and perpetuating an evil regime.

Astoundingly, "the decider" never stopped this internal war. The result was paralysis. Every step toward dialogue was undercut. The hardliners inside the administration were frustrated that Bush was halfhearted in his commitment to end tyranny in North Korea. Those who favored negotiations knew that until Bush was willing to dangle clear benefits in front of Kim, there would never be progress. The North Koreans seemed to sense that there was only one way to get Washington's undivided attention: Stage a large explosion.

INTO THIS IDEOLOGICAL stalemate stepped a Polish-born nuclear physicist more interested in North Korean stocks of plutonium than in Washington's stocks of venom. He ended up playing a crucial role in measuring the first and moderating the second.

Siegfried S. Hecker is a legend in the nuclear world: At sixty-four years old, his wiry build, boundless enthusiasm, and shock of white hair reminded many who knew him of the delightfully mad scientist in *Back to the Future*. But Hecker is anything but mad. He was the former director of the Los Alamos National Laboratory, where America built the first atomic weapons. It was a position first held by J. Robert Oppenheimer, who guided the Manhattan Project before his career was ended by the ugly politics of anticommunism during the Cold War.

Not surprisingly, Hecker knew his way around nuclear weapons and their building blocks. And he knew what it took to lock up the world's most dangerous materials. Over the previous decade he had made more than thirty visits to the former Soviet Union to help them secure their nuclear arsenal. And in late 2003, he was invited by the North Koreans to visit the Yongbyon nuclear facilities as part of the first American delegation to enter the complex since the international inspectors were ousted. The reason for the invitation was simple: North Korea wanted to prove its boast that it had turned its spent fuel into bomb-grade plutonium.

The delegation to Pyongyang had been organized by John W. Lewis, a professor at Stanford University who had traveled to North Korea nine times to conduct unofficial talks in hopes of finding the kind of common ground that the two governments clearly could not. In diplomatic lingo, these were called "track two" dialogues because they were unofficial, binding no one—making them a safe place to try out ideas with no commitments.

Hecker knew his role would be to cut through the grandiose North Korean claims. The North Koreans understood the significance of Hecker's visits. If they couldn't convince Hecker they had mastered the art of making a bomb, they couldn't convince anyone. They knew that Hecker would be reporting back to Washington—both in public testimony and in private assessments to the CIA and the national laboratories, the repository of American expertise on nuclear proliferation.

Kim Kye-gwan, North Korea's vice minister of foreign affairs and the delegation's principal host, told the group that he hoped their visit would "contribute to breaking the stalemate and opening up a bright future."

"We will not play games with you," he said.[1]

One official who traveled with Hecker on subsequent visits told me that Hecker was the perfect personality to deal with the North Koreans—nonconfrontational and able to treat the North Korean engineers as equals. "They talked about reprocessing nuclear fuel the way a bunch of baseball fanatics might talk about the strategy for pitching in a tough game," the official said. "Sig knew how to put the North Korean engineers at ease, and get them to open up—and probably reveal more than they knew they were revealing."

On January 8, 2004, the North Koreans took Hecker and the rest of the delegation through the major facilities, including the control room of the five-megawatt reactor that had produced North Korea's bomb fuel. They visited the "spent fuel pond" to look at what wasn't there anymore—the rods that would be turned into bomb-grade material. Eventually they settled into a cold conference room, where the North Korean officials lectured anew about their "deterrent." Hecker challenged them: Where was the evidence?

The North Koreans responded with an offer: "Do you want to see our product?"

"You mean the plutonium?" Hecker replied.

The official nodded.

"Sure," he said.[2]

The North Koreans returned with an innocuous-looking metal case and put it on the conference table. Inside, they claimed, was a sample of the plutonium reprocessed from the spent fuel that the international inspectors had guarded. There, sitting in something the size of a breadbox, was a chunk of what this whole argument was all about—the material that the North Koreans believed was the only thing that stopped the United States from pushing the country into the sea.

The North Koreans removed a wooden box containing two glass jars, one that they said contained plutonium oxalate powder and the other plutonium metal. The other members of the American delegation began to back away, suddenly deciding this would be a fabulous moment for a bathroom break, or a brisk stroll around the nuclear plant. Hecker chuckled when he saw them head for the exits, then checked the screw-on metal lids of the containers to be sure they had been taped shut.

"You want them taped," he said, because even a modest seal protects against most of the harmful radiation.

He had no instruments with him, so Hecker was relying entirely on his experience. He instantly recognized the green color of the oxalate, knowing that was the hue plutonium took on after it was exposed to air. This looked like the real stuff.

But Hecker wanted to be sure. He asked his North Korean hosts to return with the samples and a pair of gloves. He wanted to hold the material in his hands.

What they came back with were a pair of latex gloves, similar to what supermarkets sell for doing dishes. With a gloved hand Hecker picked up the jar of plutonium metal, wanting to get a feel for its density and its ability to shed heat, the two telltale signs that this was the real deal. The container was reasonably heavy and slightly warm. But he could not conclusively identify the contents of either jar without more-rigorous testing.

Later Hecker told Kim Kye-gwan what he had found and that he could not report back, with certainty, that the North Koreans had the material they claimed.

"I understand," Kim said: "I would like you to make this report to your government. Don't add anything and don't subtract anything."[3]

Within days Hecker was in Washington, and his message was clear: Whatever the Bush administration thought it was doing by ignoring the North Korean threats, it now appeared that the country could, at a minimum, produce bomb fuel. That did not mean they could make a bomb. But they had succeeded at the hardest part of the job. The rest was just a matter of time.

IN THE SUMMER of 2004, with American troops tied up half a world away from the Korean peninsula and the insurgency in Iraq heating up, the White House press office called me one hot August day. After ducking a *Times* interview for nearly three years, the president had decided one was in his interest, especially in light of his ongoing reelection campaign against Democratic senator John Kerry. I was told to show up on short notice in Farmington, New Mexico, where Bush was traveling the state with Rudy Giuliani, the New York City mayor who was already test-driving a presidential run of his own.

Bush was speaking at a rally in the local sports stadium on the edge of the flat, dried-out town. My colleague Elisabeth Bumiller and I were supposed to meet Bush in an unusual venue for a presidential interview: a cinder-block locker room under the stadium. The only daylight was from a few high-up casement windows. It was the only room the Secret Service thought was truly secure.

The only way to enter the locker room was to wind through the men's room. We made our way down the concrete stairs, and ahead of me I saw a parade of women—Elisabeth, Condoleezza Rice, Karen Hughes—troop past the white urinals to get to the dressing room, where someone had laid out a conference table covered with the kind of blue plastic tablecloth you would use at a summer picnic.

"You know, David," Rice said to me after walking briskly past the urinals, "I've gone many places with the president before, but I don't think I've been through a men's room." Bush himself was deeply amused. "I bet *The New York Times* is accustomed to better surroundings," he said with a smirk. Clearly he had never visited our newsroom.

The jocularity was a prelude to Bush's extraordinary assertion of confidence about how Iraq would unfold. By this time it was clear that inspectors would never find weapons in Iraq, undermining his argument about why action had been urgent. But Bush would not discuss that topic, and acknowledged only the most minor of mistakes: American forces in Iraq, he said, had won too quickly—allowing Saddam's Republican Guard to melt into Baghdad's neighborhoods and come back as guerrilla fighters. It was, he said, a miscalculation; he was clearly in denial about how much worse the situation could get.

When the subject came to North Korea, Bush wanted to show he was no cowboy, that he had endless patience for negotiation.

I reminded the president that early in 2002 he had declared he would never "tolerate" a nuclear North Korea. Yet wasn't that exactly what was happening? Hadn't Kim Jong-Il correctly calculated that he could amass his weapons fuel without fear of American action? After all, Bush had done nothing to stop him.

"Does 'tolerate' mean to you that you won't condone it, or does it mean you'll set some deadlines?" I asked him.

"It means we'll try diplomacy as a first resort," Bush shot back, seeing where this conversation was headed. I tried again; after all, I noted, when minimal diplomacy had failed with Iraq, he had turned to deadlines and force.

"Well, I don't think you give timelines to dictators and tyrants," Bush said, glossing over the fact that he had just given exactly that to Saddam—a timeline to disarm or face invasion.

◆

BY THEN, years of covering the White House had led me to understand that this was classic Bush. He knew the principles that mattered to him: an America that looks and acts strong, that presses for individual liberty, a country devoted to seeking and unseating evil around the world. But grand principles are quite different from a grand strategy. And the Bush White House confused the two, time and again. In Afghanistan and in Iraq, the White House proved far more interested in the tactics for knocking over odious regimes than in rebuilding their countries.

It was not until the second term that it began to sink in among Bush's advisers that if you are not going to go to war with all your enemies, and if they are not going to cooperate by imploding, talking to them is one of the few options left. Inside the White House, Bush's top aides, including Rice, knew the biggest obstacle to getting that process going was finding a way to get Bush to suppress— or at least temporarily forget—his own strident, moralistic talk.

Rice began the process with historical analogies, making the point that while Stalin wasn't exactly a Boy Scout, Roosevelt and Truman had met with him, even while he was sending people to the gulags.

Many aides around Bush recognized the dangers of the president's inability to separate his emotions about Kim from the practical realities of dealing with a crisis spinning out of control. The question, as one of his top advisers said to me one evening in 2006, is "How do you get the guy to change his mind?" Then he stopped, and answered his own question:

"You do it bit by bit. So slowly that he doesn't have to admit to himself that what he did last year is the polar opposite of what we've got him doing this year."[4]

◆

On the morning of July 4, 2006, as Bush celebrated the nation's independence with Airborne and Special Forces troops at Fort Bragg—a place he could always count on for a warm reception—North Korea was preparing for a fireworks display of its own. In June, intelligence satellite photographs had revealed that the North Koreans were fueling up missiles on their eastern coast. But this was not an ordinary test to demonstrate Kim's pique: the North Koreans appeared to be preparing to fire a Taepodong-2, an intercontinental missile. The Bush administration could not afford to brush this off as mere saber-rattling. It was one thing for Kim Jong-Il to send short-range missiles crashing into the Sea of Japan. It was quite another to demonstrate the ability of a charter member of the Axis of Evil to strike Japan or, eventually, the West Coast of the United States. For an administration that had trumpeted the need for missile defense—and had begun deploying the first interceptors at a base in Alaska—the question of whether the United States could knock the North Korean missiles out of the sky became a test of American credibility.

Inside the Pentagon, there was talk about whether Kim was testing the United States to see just how deeply it was distracted by Iraq. So quietly, without saying anything in public beyond a warning from Rice that a launch would be a "provocative act" that would be treated with the "utmost seriousness,"[5] Bush and Rumsfeld ordered the military to blow the North Korean missiles out of the sky—or at least to try.

The man put in charge of the effort was Adm. Timothy J. Keating, at the time commander of U.S. Northern Command. When I went to visit him in May 2008—after he had settled into a vast office overlooking Pearl Harbor in Hawaii, as the new American commander in the Pacific—Keating told me that for six weeks in early summer 2006 the military had prepared to launch ground-based antimissile interceptors from Vandenberg Air Force Base in central California and from Fort Greely, the Army launch site in prime trout-and-salmon fishing territory about 100 miles southeast of

Fairbanks, Alaska. The idea was to blow up the Taepodong over the Pacific, demonstrating that America's missile defenses were a real first line of defense against rogue states.

It was a huge risk. Tests of the missile defense system had often ended in embarrassing failures, even when highly choreographed. The United States had never launched antiballistic interceptors against an actual hostile target. But to Rumsfeld and other enthusiasts of missile defenses, there might never be another opportunity as good as this one. American satellites knew North Korea's exact launch site. There was only one Taepodong to target—no swarms of missiles that could overwhelm the primitive American system. The North Koreans didn't have the sophistication to spew out chaff and decoys that could fool the antimissile interceptors.

For weeks Keating and others debated whether to demand that the North Koreans declare their intentions. They thought about saying to Kim's government, "'We know you've got it on the rails, we are assuming you are preparing to shoot, tell us what's in the nose cone,'" Keating said. "We weren't sure. Was it a dummy load, was it another satellite that would broadcast the Great Leader's musings, or was it a weaponized warhead? Didn't know. So we were prepared to assume the worst; hence, we were prepared to launch missiles."[6]

On the morning of July 4, Keating was stationed at Northern Command headquarters, chiefly to help monitor the launch of the *Discovery* space shuttle. Just minutes after the shuttle's takeoff, the North Koreans began firing. A short-range Scud-C missile was launched at 2:33 p.m. Eastern time, followed about a half hour later by another short-range missile. They seemed like the prelude to the main event. Keating was on an open line with Rumsfeld, who did not know he was in his last months as secretary of defense.

Once the Taepodong left its launchpad, Keating and Rumsfeld would have between five and twenty minutes to decide whether to launch interceptors to take it out. The open line was crucial because every second would count. Satellites detected the North Korean launch at 4:01 p.m., but Keating and Rumsfeld never got to test their prized new system. Forty-two seconds into flight, the Taepodong broke up, either because of a launch failure or because the North Koreans aborted the flight.

"It came apart," Keating recalled with a laugh.

Keating told me he was confident that had the Taepodong headed across the Pacific, the new American system would have knocked it out. But we'll never know: North Korea's own embarrassment short-circuited any demonstration of what Americans bought for all those billions spent on missile defense.

The White House used the incident to make the point that, like Kim in his elevator heels, the North Koreans wanted to appear taller than they were. "The Taepodong was obviously a failure," Hadley told reporters later that evening. "That tells you something about capabilities."[7]

Bush tried to seize the moment, once again, to drive a wedge between North Korea and China. He called Hu Jintao, the Chinese president. As if Hu needed a reminder, he noted that the Chinese had sent a mission to North Korea to urge them not to conduct the test, only to be ignored by the tiny country that relied on China for its survival.

"I told him, 'Mr. President, this is a terrible day for China,'" Bush recalled in February 2007, in a conversation with a number of reporters. "'You warned the North Koreans and they ignored you. And I can tell you, Mr. President, I know that you think I'm a great friend of the Japanese, and I am. But if the Koreans go ahead and test a nuclear bomb next, no one may be able to stop them from building their own nuclear arsenal.'"

It was a pretty transparent effort to split the Chinese away, and no doubt Hu was pretty angry at the North Koreans. But as Bush recounted the story, I couldn't help thinking that China has had a lot of truly terrible days—the collapse of dynasties, invasion by the Japanese, the Rape of Nanking, horrific natural disasters. A failed missile launch into the Pacific by a wayward, impoverished, wacky neighbor might not rank among them. The incident demonstrated once again the divergence between Beijing's interests and Washington's. The Chinese feared pushing the North Koreans too hard. The Americans wanted to push them over the brink.

BUSH WAS RIGHT about one thing: North Korea's nuclear test was next.

Everyone saw it coming. Starting in September 2006, two months after the failed missile tests, there was all kinds of activity around a tunnel in North Korea that American spy satellites had monitored for years. It wasn't the first time. In September 2004, Rice told me at the end of an interview on another topic that the United States had seen indications of a possible test, which she thought was being timed in an effort to influence the presidential election, then less than two months away. At the *Times*, we confirmed the administration's account pretty quickly. (One of the wonders of the modern age is that commercially available satellite photography gives anyone access to images of a quality that only the intelligence agencies had a decade ago.) But the movement of trucks and the running of cables out of the mountainside cave subsided as quickly as they had appeared.

Two years later it seemed the North Koreans were intent on the real thing. On the night of October 9, 2006, just as I was cleaning up from a late dinner in our kitchen, a senior American official called me at home.

"The North Koreans just called the Chinese, and the Chinese called our embassy in Beijing," the official said. "They said they are going to blow the thing off in half an hour. And that was fifteen minutes ago."

We quickly cleared out the front page. And sure enough, around 11:36 a.m. Pyongyang time, the U.S. Geological Survey picked up a 4.2-magnitude quake on the Korean peninsula. If the Koreans had not provided their warning to the Chinese, it might have been interpreted as just a mild tremor. But the epicenter matched perfectly with the test site, in North Hamgyong Province. Minutes later North Korean officials made public what everyone suspected: They had "demonstrated" their nuclear deterrent.

But that may have been different from actually detonating a nuclear bomb. To this day there is still an argument over whether what the North Koreans lit off that day was a real weapon. The blast wasn't much more impressive than the Taepodong launch. It was nearly a dud, and many suspect it wasn't a real bomb at all, but just a small, controlled nuclear explosion. The yield was below a kiloton, far less than a tenth of the power of the bomb dropped on Hiroshima. (The North Koreans later reported that they used roughly two kilograms of plutonium, a comparatively small amount.) However, it was enough to allow the North Koreans to claim that they were now the ninth member of the nuclear club—which was all they were hoping to achieve.* They were clearly betting that sooner or later the world would regard them the way everyone seems to regard Pakistan—as a new nuclear weapons state that will never give up all of its atomic treasure.

Bush did not want to give Kim the pleasure of seeing the United States overreact. But he couldn't ignore the event, either. So he went downstairs in the White House, stood in front of a painting of George Washington, and finally issued a specific warning to the North Koreans—a warning that Bob Joseph and others had urged him to issue years before. Looking grim, with Rice standing just off to the side, he declared that "the transfer of nuclear weapons or material by North Korea to states or non-state entities would be considered a grave threat to the United States, and we would hold North Korea fully accountable for the consequences of such action." Naturally, no one wanted to say what "fully accountable" meant.

---

* The other eight include the five existing nuclear powers at the time of the signing of the Nuclear Non-Proliferation Treaty, the United States, Russia, China, Britain, and France. Israel, Pakistan, and India have never signed the treaty, and all have substantial arsenals, though Israel continues the charade of never formally confirming the weapons that it has now possessed for more than three decades.

In Bush's statement lies the kernel of a new American nuclear strategy, one that would threaten, ambiguously, retaliation against any state that is the source of nuclear material used in an attack by terrorists or another country. But that opens a host of complications that Bush did not want to deal with at the time—including the question of whether the United States could use nuclear weapons against a country that, knowingly or unknowingly, provided nuclear material or know-how to someone else.[8]

Naturally, the test touched off another titanic battle within the administration. The hardliners saw it as the moment to unify the world to choke off the North Koreans, who had clearly overplayed their hand. This time, the Chinese were truly angry. They condemned the North's nuclear claims as a "flagrant" violation of international norms and suddenly cut off trade across the North Korean border—not for long, as it turned out, but long enough to get Kim's attention. Rice and Joseph traveled to Asia, reassuring the Japanese that America's nuclear umbrella covered them. Rice talked tough, saying that the North would be confronted with sanctions "unlike anything that they had faced before."[9] Five days later the UN Security Council passed a resolution imposing the toughest international sanctions on North Korea since the Korean War by barring the transfer of materials that could be used to make weapons of mass destruction—transfers that were already largely controlled—and, more important, by authorizing all countries to inspect cargo coming into and going out of the socialist state. (There is no evidence anyone has done so.)

The resolution only passed, however, after the Security Council explicitly withdrew references to the possible use of force, a sticking point for Russia and China.[10] It was another legacy of Iraq, preventing Bush from using truly coercive diplomacy.

While Bush won the diplomatic wrangling, history would record that North Korea proved its nuclear capability and built the bulk of its arsenal on his watch. It is hardly a milestone he is eager to acknowledge; to this day the United States does not officially describe North Korea as a nuclear weapons state. "Nobody accepts that they're a nuclear power," Rice insisted a few weeks after the tests, as China announced the urgent resumption of talks. The North Koreans, she said, "can say it all they wish."[11]

Understandably, Bush and Rice did not want to give the Koreans the status they desperately sought. But the genie was out of the bottle. If the North Koreans had not exploded an actual weapon, they had proven they have the material and the knowledge for the basics of what it takes.

"The administration will continue saying that a nuclear weapon in North Korea is unacceptable, but in fact they are beginning to accept it," Scott D. Sagan, co-director of Stanford University's Center for International Security and Cooperation, told me shortly after the test. "The administration is switching from a nonproliferation policy to a deterrence and defense policy. It is a form of containment rather than a form of nonproliferation."[12]

The fact that North Korea had gotten away with it was obvious to other powers, starting with Iran. Kim had endured sanctions, yes, but nothing that threatened North Korea's existence.

"Think about the consequences of having declared something 'intolerable' and, last week, 'unacceptable,' and then having North Korea defy the world's sole superpower and the Chinese and the Japanese," Graham Allison of Harvard said to me shortly thereafter. "What does that communicate to Iran, and then the rest of the world? Is it possible to communicate to Kim credibly that if he sells a bomb to Osama bin Laden, that's it?"[13]

AFTER THE NUCLEAR TEST, something truly curious happened in Washington. The Cheney forces—those arguing for deeper isolation of North Korea in hopes of triggering the end of the regime—were vanquished. The administration had been shocked out of its complacency that the North Korean problem would somehow take care of itself while Bush focused on Iraq. Suddenly, talking to Kim Jong-Il sounded like a pretty bright idea.

In the first Bush term, it is likely that Bush would have responded to the test with crushing sanctions, and perhaps activated a long-dormant Pentagon plan that would have put a naval blockade around the country, reminiscent of the one Kennedy threw around Cuba at the height of the Cuban Missile Crisis. But with Iraq in crisis—Bush had already secretly concluded that the United States was at risk of losing against the insurgency—a confrontation in the Pacific did not seem viable. So Rice argued that the administration should capitalize on the international reaction and open real diplomacy with the North Koreans. As one participant in the National Security Council meeting where this was first discussed recalled later, "Cheney looked like he was going to be ill."

In the summer of 2008, Rice recalled that at that meeting, "we had to make a choice once the nuclear test had taken place. Were we just going to use the Security Council resolutions to tighten the screws and try and force some kind of North Korean behavior, or were we going to give them a chance and try to reopen the diplomatic track?"[14]

Rice said she argued for diplomacy and got a lot of push-back from the administration's hardliners. (When I asked her who took the opposing side of the argument, she said, "I'll just let you guess.") Her argument was not an easy sell. Every public statement made over the past six years pointed to a strategy of isolating the North.

"We could have taken maximum pressure against them," Rice recalled. "It wasn't a crazy argument. . . . They've done this, they've ticked off the whole world, they've shown that they're dangerous, just squeeze them."

Publicly, Bush insisted he would only talk to the North Koreans with all of its neighbors present at the table—the "Six Party Talks" that involved all of North Korea's immediate neighbors in Asia and the United States. He would not reward them, he insisted, with one-on-one talks that would allow the North to play the different countries against one another.

"Now all of a sudden people are saying the Bush administration ought to be going alone with North Korea," Bush said at the time.

"But it didn't work in the past is my point. The strategy didn't work. I learned a lesson from that and decided that the best way to convince Kim Jong-Il to change his mind on a nuclear weapons program is to have others send the same message."

But by January 2007, an enterprising diplomat who had made his name negotiating with Serbian killers was meeting one-on-one with the North Koreans. Among the critics of the Bush administration's handling of North Korea in its first term, none had been more vociferous than the American ambassador to Poland, Christopher R. Hill.

He had no problem with the decision to present the North Koreans with evidence they were cheating on their nuclear freeze. But it was a terrible idea, Hill thought, to issue ultimatums without thinking through the next steps of the chess game. It was typical, he said, of an administration that viewed all negotiations as essentially unwise, because sooner or later Washington would get taken to the cleaners by foreigners.

"These assholes don't know how to negotiate," Hill told a small group of friends and colleagues in 2007. "Everything is Appomattox. It's just 'Come out with your hands up.' It's not even really Appomattox, because at the end of Appomattox they let the Confederates keep their horses."

Hill's interest in Korea dated back to his days as a young foreign service officer, when he served in the fortresslike American embassy in downtown Seoul. He got a kick out of dealing with the South Koreans, with all their bluster and insecurity, born of 2,000 years of being used as pawns in power struggles between the Chinese and the Japanese. But once he broke their code, he found them fairly easy to handle on the other side of the negotiating table. Yet every morning when he picked up the papers, he told friends, he was astounded by how the Bush administration had botched its dealings with the South Koreans, a critical treaty ally. There had to be a better strategy concerning how to deal with what Hill, in wry moments, liked to call "a diddly-shit little country like North Korea."

Eventually he couldn't take it anymore. He shot off a cable to Powell and his deputy, Armitage, offering to help. "I said to Powell, 'If you can find a way to get a guy from Poland to Korea, I think I can help you there.'" Soon Hill found himself back in Seoul, this time as the American ambassador, with the job of trying to smooth things over between Bush and a South Korean government that wanted to buy off the North Koreans, not confront them.

Hill was born into diplomacy. Though he was raised in Little Compton, Rhode Island, some of his earliest memories are from Belgrade, where he was a five-year-old running around the embassy where his father worked as an American diplomat. These were the days of Tito's Yugoslavia, a place of harsh authoritarianism, but one of the few corners of Eastern Europe where things worked. His early years gave Hill a love of the Balkans that would test his talents as a negotiator long after Tito was gone.

Hill went on to Bowdoin College and then the Peace Corps, which sent him to Cameroon. It was perfect training for Hill: a country of 250 different tribes, with ethnic and cultural differences as confounding as the unpaved roads. His first tasks were modest. "I conducted audits," he remembered in late 2007, "running around the country on my Suzuki 125."

One day he drove the Suzuki to the port city of Douala, where he took the foreign service exam in an American consulate so small that it was staffed by only two diplomats. By the fall of 1977, he was following his father's footsteps into the foreign service—and he found himself right back in Belgrade.

He quickly became one of the State Department's rising Eastern

European experts, serving in Poland from 1983 to 1985. Then he moved to South Korea for three years as an economic officer, just as the country was moving toward democracy. He returned to the States and worked for Stephen Solarz, the New York congressman famous for his travels around the world—including North Korea. Upon his return to the State Department, Hill worked on the Poland desk, just as Poland erupted in the first big Eastern European uprising against the Soviet behemoth. Then the Berlin Wall fell. "I thought that history was over," Hill recalled.

It was just beginning to get interesting. Hill went on to Albania to open an American embassy there. Then it was back to Washington with a new administration under Bill Clinton. Hill found himself working for the brilliant, egotistical Richard Holbrooke, who was assistant secretary of state for Europe. Holbrooke took him on his nonstop adventures trying to patch together the Balkans, an effort that ended up in the Dayton Accords, negotiated on an air base in Ohio.

It was there that the thin, intense Hill demonstrated what he's best at—driving a bargain, giving a little to get a little. His saving grace was that his intensity was masked by a sardonic humor that made him completely capable of commenting, as if he were an outsider, on the absurdity of his mission.

In the Balkans talks, there were moments when he would watch Slobodan Milosevic, the brutal Serbian leader, growl and argue during the big negotiating sessions at Dayton. Later, if he could get him alone, Hill would demand, "What the hell was that about?" and frequently he got an actual answer. Gradually he channeled Milosevic, one of the world's most detested tyrants, toward a messy deal that ultimately saved lives.

There were two big lessons in the Milosevic experience that shaped Hill's negotiating style—and ultimately put him at war with the neoconservatives who thought he was selling America out to the North Koreans. "The first was that this knee-jerk view that you can't negotiate with dictators is garbage," Hill told me as we sipped coffee one warm spring day in Washington. "My view is that you can—especially if the dictator is surrounded by more powerful nations." The second lesson was that having twenty people around the table doesn't work. You get things done one on one, when there is less chance of a loss of face.

When Holbrooke took him to Macedonia during the negotiating process, the country's president, Kiro Gligorov, an aging, white-haired veteran of the wars against the Fascists, had one request: that he leave Hill in town as the ambassador. And so a midlevel career foreign service officer got his break; he was able to jump the queue for ambassadorships. But until Bush came to Poland, Hill's next ambassadorship, Hill had barely met the Republican president. They hit it off, not least because Hill is almost as passionate about baseball as Bush is.

Hill, however, is part of the State Department's deep bench of Red Sox fans. That cadre of diplomats raised Bush's hackles. He didn't mind the team; it was simply that the Red Sox fans around him, particularly at the White House, reminded him of the stereotypical elitist New England eggheads whom he rejected so virulently as he moved from Andover to Yale to Harvard Business School. Nicholas Burns, who became undersecretary of state, recalled nearly blowing a job interview with Bush by describing his enthusiasm for Boston's heroes. Hill got into such an argument with Bush over the 2007 World Series that Rice feared he was about to get the president off track on North Korea.

"You would see him roll his eyes when the subject of the Red Sox came up," one witness to these encounters said. "It was this look of 'not another one.'"

It was after Bush's trip to Poland that the deal was sealed to send Hill to Seoul. But he quickly learned that there was only so much the United States ambassador could do to patch up the fractured relationship. Seoul and Washington were on entirely different paths: Every time Washington tried to turn up the pressure on Kim Jong-Il, the South Koreans sent food, cash, or new investments that nullified the effort. In Bush's mind, the South's strategy was simply one of appeasement: It was building railroad lines across the DMZ and putting together joint ventures inside North Korean territory, essentially under North Korea's control. There were offers to provide the North with huge amounts of electricity and, of course, food aid. To the South Koreans it was an investment in the future: Because they did not feel truly threatened by North Korea, they wanted to manage the problem—and reduce the cost of eventual unification.

Washington's most successful effort at getting Kim's attention came when it choked off a tiny bank in Macao, where the North Korean leadership both laundered its money and kept the leadership's personal accounts. "I knew we were finally getting their attention," Bush told me once, "when President Roh came and complained that we had to stop. That was the first time I thought we were really getting to the North Koreans."[15] The battle over the bank also cemented animosity between Bush and Roh, whose approach to North Korea was partly repudiated when he left office in 2008, and was replaced by a much harder-line South Korean government that was more on Washington's wavelength.

Hill recognized that if the South Koreans didn't have a negotiating strategy, neither did Bush. The Six Party Talks were a sound innovation, because they put the burden on the Chinese and others to solve the problem. But as a practical matter, they often amounted to diplomatic farce: Each of the six countries had about thirty diplomats in the room, meaning that all the participants were reduced to posturing, knowing that every word uttered was heard by roughly 180 people. The scene was made worse by the seemingly endless pauses for translations. A series of giant "tulips" ran down the length of the negotiating table, and they would light up when every translator was done. Hill used the downtime to read box scores from the latest Red Sox games. As he said to friends, "I'm supposed to negotiate a nuclear deal with a bunch of white plastic tulips?"

The first instructions he had been given as a negotiator told him not to smile at the North Koreans, not to shake hands, and not to join in any toasts. "They showed," said Hill, "a complete lack of understanding about how the world works."

Over time, though, he managed to break every one of the rules. Though Bush had banned any direct bilateral talks with the North Koreans during the first term—after all, the place was run by a dictator—Hill pursued exactly that kind of contact. He lobbied ceaselessly to visit Pyongyang, usually to Rice's exasperation. Hill knew that with the North Koreans, you not only had to talk face to face— you had to be in their face. Though Bush insisted during the first term that the North Koreans would have to abandon their weapons before he would negotiate, soon Hill was giving a little to get a little.

"There's nothing we're doing," he told me at the end of the summer of 2007, "that anyone who has haggled for some vegetables in a Korean market won't recognize." Of course, vegetable-market diplomacy was exactly what Bush had rejected during the first term. Hill had to make up for lost time.

TO DO SO, Hill and Rice mapped out a strategy in late 2006 to circumvent Cheney. When a chance to reopen negotiations with North Korea cropped up in early 2007, Rice cut the deal directly with Bush; Cheney learned of it later. But the next steps would be harder: forcing North Korea to make good on its pledge to declare all of its nuclear facilities, equipment, and stockpiles and then permanently disable the Yongbyon plant. The last step would be the most difficult—getting the North Koreans to turn over their existing fuel and bombs, their only leverage with the world.

By the summer of 2007, Hill had succeeded in getting Yongbyon shut down. In fits and starts, after receiving plenty of oil and promises, the North Koreans started taking pieces apart. It was the most progress anyone had made in years.

In the fall, after the Yongbyon facility had been shuttered, Hill went to the White House for a lunch with Bush. They met in the Oval Office, then moved to the adjacent private dining room. Bush's mind was already on the next step, persuading the North Koreans to surrender the bomb fuel they had made on his father's watch, and on his own.

"What's it going to take to get them to give this up?" he asked Hill. Hill said he didn't know yet what the price would be, or even if it would prove possible. But it won't be cheap, he told the president. He said Bush might soon have to consider taking the North off the list of state sponsors of terrorism, a huge symbolic gesture toward reaching an accord with a regime Bush hated. And if the North complied with the rest of its commitments, the United States would also have to get around the Trading with the Enemy Act, a World War I–era federal law that had been used since the 1950s to try to choke off dealings with the North.

Cheney sat in on part of the meeting, brooding but saying nothing. What Hill was describing were steps Cheney had fought, behind the scenes, for years. During the first term, he had repeatedly stepped into the Oval Office at key moments to undercut the negotiators, or at least tie their hands with specific instructions that were likely to blow up negotiations. But he had lost Rumsfeld as an ally and no longer had his acolytes in key departments. Rice had outmaneuvered him, using her direct lines to Bush to argue, at the beginning of 2007, that he had no other choice than to talk to the repulsive dictatorship and offer specific rewards in return for each step of compliance. It was, in short, the opposite of the strategy she had laid out for me so confidently in her office in March 2001, when she said, simply, "We ought to look for ways to weaken the regime," making it clear that North Korea would not be rewarded until it gave up everything.

If Cheney was fuming, he was too smart to show it or to interfere; he almost never directly engaged with Hill. (Nor did he ever engage with Nick Burns, the Iran negotiator.) But with many of his back-channel approaches cut off, he was reduced to insisting that the North Koreans be forced to come clean on issues that they were almost certain to lie about—how much plutonium they had made, where it was, what had happened to the highly enriched uranium project they bought from A. Q. Khan, and, above all, what they'd built for countries like Syria.

Hill doubted that the North Koreans would be willing to talk about their Syrian adventure, he told Bush, but he assured him that the United States would insist that it be part of the declaration.

"Good job," Bush said at the end of the session—his favorite form of faint praise. (He often directed this compliment to foreign leaders at the end of press conferences; while he may have intended it to be folksy, one fumed to me later that Bush's comment was "the most patronizing line I ever received in public life.")

Everyone in the room, especially Hill, knew that this was the easy part. In the end, Bush and his team would be judged by a single standard: whether North Korea possessed fewer nuclear weapons and fuel than it had when Bush came to office, and whether the country was less capable of selling its nuclear products around the world.

Bush's own former aides knew it was a test Bush would fail. One of the president's former North Korea hands told me he feared that "when the administration is over, the North could have more weapons and find itself under fewer sanctions than ever." That, in the end, would describe Bush's Korea legacy.

At Yongbyon, Hill discovered the dirty little secret about why the North Koreans had been so willing to close and then dismantle their giant nuclear facilities: They were a rusting, radioactive junk-yard. "Kind of like a Cuban '56 Chevy," Hill said. "It could run for-ever. But if it ever stopped running, good luck to anyone who wanted to get it started again."

Out of money, the North Koreans had stopped maintaining the facility soon after the inspectors were thrown out in 2003—even though they were actively building a sister plant in Syria, half a world away. The deterioration was so great that the five Americans charged with supervising the dismantling included a doctor who was constantly checking for leaking radiation. The North Korean workers did not even have basic safety equipment; the United States had to insist that the North Koreans slow down on unloading fuel from the shut reactor to avoid an environmental disaster.

When it came time to cut the giant cooling loops of the reactor—a major step in making sure that it could not be turned on again without significant work—the North Koreans simply let the giant metal parts fall to the ground, where they now sit, rusting. Critics of the deal noted that to put the reactor back together, the North Koreans would simply have to lift the parts in place with a forklift and weld them back in place.

"The good news," Hill cracked one day, "is that they don't have any forklifts."

Certainly the mood was improving. The North Koreans had invited the New York Philharmonic to Pyongyang, and Hill helped make the visit happen. Rice was in South Korea the day before the first concert, and Bill Perry, the former defense secretary, went to her hotel room and urged her to travel to the North and attend the concert—she was, after all, a masterful pianist. "It's not the right time, Bill," Rice told him, eager to avoid replicating Albright's embarrassing trip to Pyongyang at the end of the Clinton administration.[16]

Dismantling Yongbyon, it turned out, was a lot easier for the North Koreans than owning up to the past. They missed their deadline for submitting a declaration of what they produced, and they refused to explain what happened to all that uranium enrichment equipment that A. Q. Khan told his interrogators he had sold to the North Koreans. One day, though, the chief North Korean negotiator, Kim Kye-gwan, offered to show Hill and his team the tons of aluminum tubes they had bought from Russia, a purchase that was one of the tip-offs that the North Koreans were trying to build centrifuges for enrichment.

◆

"THEY ARE NOT being used for uranium enrichment," Kim insisted. Soon Hill's aides were in a military factory two hours from Pyongyang examining the tubes, spread out on a large table. The North Koreans insisted the tubes were for a conventional weapon, a rocket launcher. One of Hill's senior aides brought the tubes back home—stuffing them into the luggage on a commercial airliner. It did not take long for government laboratories to report that they had detected traces of highly enriched uranium on the outside of the tubes. Whether that meant they were used for nuclear work, or just near some equipment used for nuclear purposes, was unclear.

As Hill squeezed the North Koreans for more, they eventually turned over 18,000 pages of operating records of the Yongbyon facility, intended to back up their declaration of how much plutonium the country had produced. It took teams of translators and experts months to sort through all the records, and even then there were the usual suspicions that the North Koreans might not have reported everything truthfully. Then it turned out that the operating records, like the Russian tubes, were tainted with trace amounts of uranium— "pixie dust," Hill insisted, half in jest—which North Korea could not easily explain. That fed suspicions that there was a secret uranium-enrichment program under way that the North Koreans might also be forgetting to mention.

But when it came to answering questions about Syria, the North Koreans simply shut down. They refused to talk about it. They told Hill that they were not currently helping any foreign countries build nuclear facilities, and would not in the future. Beyond that, Las Vegas rules applied: Whatever happens in Syria stays in Syria.

In the end, George Bush, the man who demanded that the North Koreans would have to tell all, accepted a meaningless statement in which the North Koreans acknowledged the American concern about proliferation activities—and admitted to nothing. But Bush badly needed a political win, and in late June he announced that he was starting the process to take the North off the list of state sponsors of terrorism. "The United States has no illusions about the regime in Pyongyang," Bush said, insisting his actions would have "little impact on North Korea's financial and diplomatic isolation." It almost seemed as if he were apologizing to the Cheney forces, or at least trying to placate them. He never mentioned Chris Hill's name.

"This is action for action," Bush insisted. "This is 'we will trust you only to the extent that you fulfill your promises.'" It was much more. As Bob Joseph noted, "the North Koreans actually got more than they did under Clinton," and Bush had control of neither the plutonium nor the weapons.

Bush did get something. The next day, June 28, 2008, the North blew up the cooling tower at Yongbyon. CNN was invited to record the event. Back in the United States, the image created a public impression that the North Korean nuclear crisis was somehow over. Of course, it was not: By late August, Bush had postponed taking the North off the terrorism list until Kim agreed to a series of intrusive inspections. With its usual mix of paranoia and bravado, the North declared that "the U.S. is gravely mistaken if it thinks it can make a house search in our country as it pleases, just as it did in Iraq."

With their classic flare for brinksmanship, the North Koreans tore the seals off their reprocessing facility and announced they would resume making bomb fuel. (Getting the reactor started would be a much more complex task—if they could manage it at all.) In short, they threatened to wreck the one diplomatic accomplishment Bush could claim at the end of his second term. As temper tantrums go, this one was pretty effective. Hill was sent back to Yongbyon and came up with a compromise that he sold—just barely—back in Washington. With Bush's approval, Rice signed the document that deleted North Korea from the list of state sponsors of terror. In return, the North Koreans agreed, vaguely, to allow some inspections outside of the Yongbyon nuclear complex. But it was unclear where, and the text of the agreement was not specific. For example, there was no permission to visit the site of the 2006 nuclear test or any of the many military facilities that intelligence agencies believe are involved in the nuclear program. All future access beyond Yongbyon would have to be negotiated by the next administration. Rice spent time on the telephone with her Chinese counterparts, extracting their agreement to press the North Koreans to make good on the pledges.

It was exactly the kind of agreement Cheney had spent the first half of the administration killing off. John McCain, in the midst of a presidential campaign that was going badly, expressed enormous skepticism. The Japanese—America's greatest ally—denounced it as a sellout, because it did not force the North Koreans to account for the Japanese nationals they had kidnapped and taken to the North years ago. (The outrage was fueled by a statement by the North Koreans that in the years since their kidnappings, the Japanese hostages had all died.) For the Bush administration, which had come to office declaring that it would never sign any agreement that was not "complete, verifiable, irreversible denuclearization," it was a bitter pill—an accord that was incomplete, partly verifiable, and probably reversible. Michael Green, Bush's former Asia aide, told the *Washington Post,* "There is a real danger that Pyongyang will pull a bait-and-switch now that the sanctions have been lifted."

For the next administration, the problem could be compounded by a power struggle to succeed the country's leader, Kim Jong-Il. In August, 2008, just before the last act in the nuclear negotiations with the Bush administration, Kim reportedly suffered a stroke. China flew in doctors to perform emergency surgery. By the time Hill arrived back in Pyongyang, rumors abounded about Kim's condition. The Chinese were saying little; the North Koreans were saying less. Hill feared that if Kim's illness proved long, it would freeze talks: after all, no one got fired—or shot—in North Korea for taking the hardest possible line.

In the long run, Hill told friends, North Korea was clearly a doomed, failed state by every measure. In the short term it had cards to play, from a hand they greatly strengthened during Bush's presidency. In Bush's time, North Korea produced so much nuclear bomb fuel that the chances of disarming the country diminished greatly, while the potential costs of disarmament rose exponentially. We didn't just lose our leverage with the North Koreans. We handed them our lever.

THERE ARE MANY lessons to take away from Bush's disastrous encounter with the North Koreans. First among them is that once countries believe that Washington has locked them in its gunsights—particularly bankrupt, corrupt little dictatorships—no one should be surprised if they race to get a nuclear weapon. This is the post–Cold War curse. Perhaps nothing could have deterred Kim Jong-Il from finishing the project that his father started. Certainly nothing could have stopped him from planting the seeds of nuclear ambiguity—keeping the world guessing about whether he had one or two weapons.

But after Saddam Hussein fell, Kim understood that he needed something more. He needed an arsenal big enough to convince the Americans that invading his country would be a lot riskier than invading Iraq. He needed an arsenal large enough to leave open the possibility that he might sell a few weapons on the black market. In short, he needed real nuclear deterrence.

Condoleezza Rice has argued that Kim Jong-Il didn't pass that threshold on Bush's watch, suggesting to me that they would need twenty or more weapons to have a convincing arsenal. I suspect they have plenty now to do the job, which is why they were willing to begin auctioning off their nuclear plant, piece by piece.

While the Bush administration liked to talk about North Korea, Iran, and other nuclear threats in the same breath—just a bunch of like-minded nuclear crazies—in fact they were very different cases. Unlike Iran, North Korea has neither the power to send the price of oil skyrocketing nor the ability to inflame the Middle East. North Korea wants to survive. Cash is the key to that survival—that's why they sold their know-how to the Syrians, and it is why they extracted commitments for oil out of American negotiators. The good news is that the North Koreans can be bought.

Eventually, Bush came to recognize that negotiations were his best bet. There is no other explanation for his willingness, late in the second term, to drop all the talk about running North Korea over a cliff. Bush, to use Hill's analogy, eventually discovered he was in a Korean vegetable market. By the time he stopped swaggering and began haggling, it was too late. North Korea had already produced its weapons, and the price tag for buying back that arsenal could be astronomical.

Yet Obama probably will not have a choice. If he fails to strike a deal to buy back the plutonium or the weapons, he will be dealing with a country that could, at any time, sell its wares. If he buys them back, he will be accused, chiefly by the hawks, of giving in to nuclear blackmail. And he will never know if he bought all of them—or if North Korea kept a few in reserve.

There is another lesson in the Korean fiasco—a lesson about the limits of American power. After Iraq, even the new American president will have a far harder time issuing a credible threat that he may resort to military force if diplomacy fails. Yet even the world's sole superpower does not control enough economic levers by itself to squeeze a tiny, destitute dictatorship. If we did, the odious regimes in Zimbabwe and Sudan would have disappeared long ago.

AS BUSH'S TERM came to an end, a group of top experts on Asia— some inside the government, some from the intelligence agencies, some outside experts and government officials—got together at the National Defense University to play a mind game: What would happen if everyone's wish came true, and North Korea collapsed? Where would its weapons and nuclear fuel end up?

The answer was pretty sobering: No one could be sure where the weapons were, and many believed they could find their way into the hands of renegade elements of the North Korean military. Others thought they would be sold on the black market by entrepreneurs seeking to capitalize on the chaos. "Biggest goddamn mess you ever saw," one of the participants said. "The Chinese, the Americans, the South Koreans—they are all trying to find the nukes. No one knew where to start looking, much less what to do."

The truth is that even though we have been watching North Korea since the earliest days of the Cold War, we're as much in the dark about the country's leadership today as we were at the outbreak of the Korean War in 1950. But we have more leverage than ever before—all of Asia wants this problem to go away. Bush capitalized on that by bringing all the neighboring countries into the talks with the North. And that alone may be the best argument for engaging with the North Koreans, with an energy the Bush administration could not muster.

The first Bush term was a demonstration of the dangers of thinking the United States alone has the power to bring a regime, even a weak one, to its knees with economic pressure. Unless the rest of the world is willing to help, that strategy is bound to fail. Cheney, of all people, should have known that. In his days as a CEO he made a compelling case about why unilateral economic sanctions do not work.

The lesson of the second term is that sometimes even the best diplomatic efforts can't turn back the clock. Had Bush tried old-school horse-trading early on, had he entered negotiations with North Korea with confidence, and had he focused on the countries that really had nuclear capability, it's possible—even likely—that Kim never would have amassed a small but potent arsenal.

Bush's aides all dispute that conclusion; Kim, they say, was unstoppable. We'll never know. But the Bush legacy is that he took a messy, dangerous problem and made it worse.

# PART V
## CHINA

# New Torch,
# Old Dragons

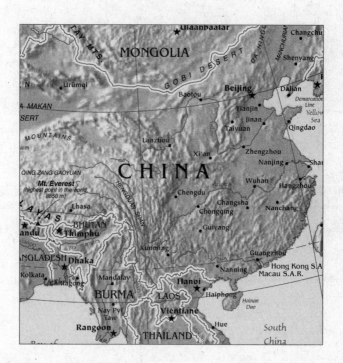

# CHAPTER 12

# GENERATION LENOVO

Do not fear going forward slowly; fear only to stand still.
—Chinese proverb

ON A BRISK Monday morning on the last day of March 2008, President Hu Jintao of China emerged from the high walls of Zhongnanhai, the eerily quiet leadership compound next to the Forbidden City in Beijing, for what should have been a moment of unfettered national joy: the lighting of the Olympic torch.

Like most grand, choreographed political events in the Chinese capital, this one was scheduled to take place in the center of Tiananmen Square, the place where Mao had announced the creation of the People's Republic, where the home of the National People's Congress, the Great Hall of the People, stands, and where, in 1989, tanks and troops brutally faced down pro-democracy demonstrators. Just days before the start of the Games, Tiananmen had been awash with thousands of tourists enjoying unusually clear spring days. Both the Chinese visitors from the provinces and the foreigners who were flooding the city were taking one another's picture in front of Mao's portrait and lingering near the Olympic countdown clock, which ticked away the milliseconds until the opening ceremonies began, scheduled for the auspicious date of 8/8/08, at 8:08 p.m.

Even those who lined up for this most somber of Chinese rituals—the fast walk through Mao's mausoleum to view the embalmed founder of the People's Republic, who resembles a ghoulish waxy replica of himself at Madame Tussauds—were jovial and happy. "Olympics a great thing!" one Chinese villager told me and one of my sons a couple of days before the ceremony, as we shuffled along in the line to see Mao. "China is back!"

More than a billion Chinese seemed to agree. They knew that by hosting the Olympic Games China could declare an end to 150 years of perceived humiliation, years in which Beijing's national power ebbed while Hong Kong and other lucrative trading ports were surrendered to the British and the Americans. This disgrace was followed by the worst subjugation of all, a brutal occupation of the country by the hated Japanese, historic rivals in the centuries-old struggle for domination of Asia. But the Olympics also marked a final burial ritual for the Chinese Revolution. Mao's Communist vision had been embalmed with him long ago, of course, replaced in the 1980s by such slogans as "To Get Rich Is Glorious." Over the past two decades the government edged toward its own national variant of this Chinese paean to individual accomplishment: To restore Chinese influence around the globe is glorious, too.

Yet for Hu Jintao that morning in Tiananmen, the lighting ceremony was far from joyous, and the tension was evident on his face. For three weeks Hu and his colleagues inside Zhongnanhai had been preoccupied by what Chinese leaders viewed as a mortal threat to the state—one that came from within.

In Tibet, the "autonomous region" that had been brought under Chinese Communist control during the 1950s, a group of monks and other dissidents were staging a brilliantly timed protest. For decades the Chinese government had attempted, with considerable success, to dilute Tibetan culture, limit religious freedom, and flood the region with ethnic Han Chinese—all part of an effort to tamp down separatist sentiment in the region. There had been violent protests in Tibet before. As a relatively young Communist Party chief in the region in 1988, Hu Jintao himself gained the attention of the party leadership when he successfully engineered a crackdown on a Tibetan protest and imposed martial law.

This time, however, martial law wasn't an option. The Tibetans had timed this uprising for maximum embarrassment of the Chinese leadership. Seven years before, to win the bid to host the Olympics, Beijing had agreed to vaguely worded commitments to improve its behavior on human rights. Everyone knew those commitments to the International Olympic Committee were unenforceable; no matter what the Chinese did, the Games would go on. But some Tibetans were clearly trying to goad Hu and his associates to initiate mass arrests—or worse—that would prove the emptiness of their promise. The protesters wanted to present Hu with the ultimate bad choice: Let rebellion spread, or risk a televised, or cell-phone-recorded, crackdown that would make a mockery of all of China's pre-Olympics propaganda about the country's "peaceful rise."

Already the grainy images on the Internet of burning vehicles and reports of how many protesters died—the government said 19, the Tibetans said 140—were prompting a few world leaders to hint that they might boycott the opening ceremonies, which were just months away. The Chinese government wasn't helping its own cause. In Beijing a few days before the torch lighting, the language the government used to describe the Tibetan protesters seemed as though it could have been written by Mao's speechwriters. They were "splittists," the government said—a phrase meant to evoke the centuries-old fear of the country being torn apart and weakened. But the toughest words were reserved for the Dalai Lama, long in exile in India. The Chinese described him as micromanaging the whole uprising. He was "a jackal in Buddhist monk's robes, an evil spirit with a human face and the heart of a beast," the government claimed. It went on, "We are engaged in a fierce battle of blood and fire with the Dalai clique."[1]

This wasn't exactly in the script for the run-up to the Olympics.

Instead, it was a raw display of power by an authoritarian regime that had changed less than it wanted the world to think. It was an ugly scene of Old China impinging on the manicured, Olympics-ready look of New China. So by the time Hu finally appeared that Monday morning, Tiananmen Square had been cleared of all those happy tourists looking for the countdown clock. Only those specifically invited could get inside the security cordon: Chinese leaders, prominent business tycoons, the acrobats, and the Chinese children in matching Olympic outfits chosen for their uniformly adorable look. The few Tibetans in the square were part of a group of ethnic-minority dancers. Just in case their cousins tried to crash the party, the subway entrances and side streets were cut off by paramilitary police.

A press release issued to foreigners declared that the torch lighting in the square had been marked by "long ovations," a curious claim since the release was handed out an hour before the event began. But for the Chinese leadership there was only one measure of success that morning: making sure that the picture of Hu Jintao lighting the torch would be beamed out to television broadcasters around the world without a single voice of dissent echoing in the distance. None was heard. That would change as soon as the torch relay sprinted into a world beyond Chinese control.

THE TORCH LIGHTING was supposed to represent the triumph of New China over Old China. Behind the fireworks—both the real ones and the electronic simulations that enhanced the effect on television—the Chinese hoped the Games would speed China's transition toward a new era devoid of Mao's revolutionary fervor and filled with a renewed sense of nationalism and pride.

Beijing's timing seemed nearly perfect. China was awarded the Olympics just after the turn of the millennium, at a moment when its historic rivals—the Japanese—were in economic and political retreat throughout Asia. Then came 9/11 and America's distraction in Afghanistan and Iraq. A new generation of Chinese leaders, led by Hu Jintao, the economic technocrat with an authoritarian edge, saw in these events a huge opportunity.

Hu had been something of a mystery to the world when he first became the general secretary of the Communist Party in the fall of 2002. He seemed mild-mannered, partial to speeches that were boring and colorless even by Chinese standards. But George W. Bush had welcomed his arrival. As Condoleezza Rice conceded to me soon after Hu took power, Bush and the aging Jiang Zemin, the Chinese president who preceded Hu, "never had much in common, and could never get a real conversation going." Hu and Bush were of the same generation and could talk business, she thought. As another of Bush's top China hands told me after sitting in on many conversations between the two presidents, "When he first arrived, Hu looked to us like a technocrat who was only focused on economic growth. And he is—if you can imagine a progressive, economically literate technocrat who must have read a lot about Stalin."

But Hu could never have anticipated that China's great rival for influence in the Pacific would distract itself for seven years on the other side of the earth. Then a decade after the Asian financial crisis, the tables turned. The United States, its investment houses reeling, its property market in a free fall, found itself more dependent than ever on Chinese capital. China was bound to gain leverage as it became richer. But no one on either side of the Pacific could have imagined the speed at which fortunes would reverse.

Today the Chinese sense that they rank among the biggest winners of the Iraq War. First they avoided getting sucked in. Then they saw an opportunity in our preoccupation in the Middle East. While we armored Humvees to survive roadside bombs, they were building a new generation of factories to survive the next era of global competition, creating jobs for tens of millions of young people pouring out of the countryside every year. While we spent $800 billion in a war with an indeterminate strategic end, they built a gleaming new airport in Beijing and a magnetic levitation train in Shanghai. "You gave us enormous running room," one academic who is close to Hu said to me in Beijing, as Olympic fever spread.

The Chinese are a long, long way from becoming a superpower. There is too much poverty, too much illiteracy, and too little rule of law to see that day on the horizon. But they used our distraction in Iraq to fashion a sphere of influence unlike any they have enjoyed for hundreds of years. Chinese foreign aid financed the building of a new capital in East Timor, putting one of Asia's newest nations in China's orbit. China's state-run firms have invested in big energy projects in Indonesia, and struck deals in the Sudan and many other countries in Africa that they hope will provide them with exclusive access to oil. From their trade surplus, they built a "sovereign wealth fund" to invest around the world, just as oil-rich states have invested their windfalls.

None of this happened under the radar. Washington was aware of it all, but never really grappled with its strategic implications. That was fine with the Chinese leadership. You can imagine what Hu Jintao wanted to say to George Bush: "Someone has to democratize the Middle East, and we can't think of anyone better than you. Keep at it, and let us know how you are doing in fifteen or twenty years."

Fifteen to twenty years is China's target. During that time its economy is expected to rival Japan's in size. Meanwhile, what better way to keep the Americans out of the way than to have them mired on the slow-growth side of the world—and preoccupied with the prospect of another act of terrorism?

This is the new, unspoken China Doctrine: Keep the Americans busy—somewhere else. It is not written down anywhere, but it's visible on skylines across Asia and it serves as the subtext of every conversation with Chinese business executives and government leaders.

It is a doctrine fueled by a robust economic strategy, borrowed from Japan after its own Olympic coming-out party forty-four years ago. Following the path carved by Sony and Honda, Hu Jintao's China intends to shed, ever so gradually, its reputation as the world's lowest-cost producer, while quietly moving up the ladder as a technological innovator, where the greater revenues lie.

How Obama handles a rising China is likely to prove far more important in the long term than how he organizes our departure from Iraq. For two administrations now, Washington has been engaged in a circular debate over whether Beijing is a "strategic partner" or a "strategic competitor," and has been struggling to develop a strategy that recognizes the obvious fact that it is both. The only solution is what former defense secretary William Perry, who has spent a lot of time weighing the intentions of China's many competing fractions, calls "prudent hedging."

"During the Cold War we assumed the worst-case scenario, and so did the other side," Perry said to me. "It gets you into a psychology of endless competition, and an arms race. We may end up in confrontation with China someday, but let's not assume we will and make it inevitable."

China is not seeking territory so much as a sphere of influence— and time to cope with other problems. Behind the Olympic spectacle, the country remains preoccupied by the huge challenges it faces at home, challenges that the leadership knows could easily derail the new China Doctrine. As Hu Jintao told George Bush the first time the two sat down for what approached an unscripted dialogue, when the Chinese look at their own rise, they see an era of huge risk.

The biggest single risk is that the Chinese economy, which has somehow avoided every major boulder in its twenty-year-long ride down a raging river, finally hits a big one. There was a reason the Chinese announced a $586 billion economic stimulus in November 2008, as the economic crisis spread. For the Communist Party, an end to the era of growth could quickly turn into a crisis of legitimacy.

When Americans heard during the opening ceremonies that Beijing had spent $43 billion to stage the Olympics, they had images of an unstoppable locomotive headed down the tracks to run them over. When the Chinese heard that figure, translated into yuan, they saw another jobs program intended to keep the country from running off the rails—part of Hu's effort to create 20 to 25 million new jobs a year as young Chinese stream into the coastal cities looking for new opportunities. Without those jobs, Hu told Bush in that first conversation, the social stability that allows China to grow—and, he might have added, keeps the Communist Party in power—would unravel. Americans were fixated on that shiny locomotive; Hu was worried about the decrepit trackbed. Americans think about the Pratt & Whitney factory that moved jobs out of the American Midwest to China's manufacturing coast; Hu thinks about the 300 million people in Western China who are living on fifteen dollars a month and are desperate for a piece of the Chinese miracle.

For Hu, replacing track, and adding new jobs, is not enough. To keep the growth going, China needs to add enough electrical generating capacity every year to power the equivalent of all of Britain.[2] So even while the Chinese were shutting down factories around Beijing in a determined effort to clear the pollution from the air for the Olympics, out in the countryside they were adding a new power plant every seven to ten days—mostly coal-fired and inefficient. As soon as the Games ended, the turbines were flipped back on.

The Chinese were not eager to highlight those grimy facts during the Olympics. Instead they used the moment to persuade reporters and foreign leaders that the country had a newfound devotion to green technologies. They took visitors on tours of environmentally friendly buildings rising in Beijing and Shanghai and showed their experimental wind farms in Guangzhou, where China's electronics factories are concentrated just across the border from Hong Kong and Macao. They talked about a vision of China in 2020 and beyond, when an increasingly educated workforce will push the country into nonpolluting knowledge industries—designing software and developing alternative fuels and energy-saving urban designs.

It's an impressive plan, but Chinese leaders know there aren't enough windmill sites in southern China to generate anything close to the amount of power they need. As I drove up one spring morning in 2008 from Hong Kong into Guangzhou, I saw newly built coal-burning power plants kicking to life just to keep churning out enough power to light the new factories and housing complexes. (Anyone seeking to grasp the change in Guangdong should look at the famous painting of Mao, made just four decades ago, hiking with peasants as water buffalo grazed in the background.) Those factories and housing complexes are the product of one of the most successful antipoverty programs in modern history. Though the pace of growth slowed dramatically in 2008, local Chinese officials estimate that roughly 18 million factory workers are employed on the assembly lines in the factories just north of Hong Kong. Here's a sobering thought: That's a larger workforce of factory employees than in the entire United States.[3]

No wonder Hu is talking green in Beijing while building coal plants in Guangdong. He knows that alternative energy sources may create the illusion of an energy "revolution" that China craves, and ultimately needs for political accommodation with the West. But over the next twenty or thirty years, alternative energy sources are not sufficient to sustain the miracle. Western leaders who meet with him say Hu is quick to point out that when Britain and the United States went through their industrial revolutions, no one was demanding that they limit their efforts in order to meet environmental standards. China is willing to try, he insists, but he emphasizes the need for patience.

Hu's argument carried the day. For all the administration's talk of having the best relationship in history with the Chinese—working together on reining in the North Koreans, and most recently on mitigating the effects of the 2008 financial crisis—it was not until late in Bush's presidency that he began to engage the Chinese on the hardest challenges of the twenty-first century. We had a chance to think big with the Chinese—and show the world that we could work together on the two linked problems, energy and global warming, that will have the biggest effect on the prosperity of Americans and the growth potential of China. Yet Bush never fully engaged with the Chinese on the issues—perhaps because of ideology, perhaps because he feared the Chinese would use the talks to require environmental changes in the United States that could limit growth.

In short, Bush wasted precious years. Obama is now left with a huge opportunity—if only the political atmosphere in the United States, where China is equated with job loss, enables him to exploit it. Imagine that the new American president, in one of his first meetings with his Chinese counterpart, seizes the initiative with an opening like this:

"President Hu, we Americans are direct—probably too direct for your taste—but let me get right to the bottom line. If you keep building coal-fired plants and pouring factory and mining waste into your rivers at this pace, two things are going to happen. Californians are going to be breathing your pollution—they already are—and we're going to be headed into a big problem. The protests and riots in your villages over kids getting sick are going to get worse—there were about 51,000 demonstrators in 2005, right?[4] Sooner or later, this will result in a threat to the stability of the Communist Party. And it's one you can't solve by sending in the People's Liberation Army to shoot a few protesters.

"So here's an idea. We announce, together, a multibillion-dollar environmental cleanup project. Everything's on the table—our clean-coal technology, electric cars, wind farms—you name it, with the right protections on American intellectual property, of course, because this stuff is a lot more valuable than *Pirates of the Caribbean*. Now, I have to warn you, Congress isn't in a mood to pay to solve China's problems—not when you are running a huge trade surplus, and you might have noticed that Bush left me a trillion-dollar deficit, a bunch of which you've been financing. So you'll pick up most of the tab for this one by recycling those billions you've been building up selling stuff at Wal-Mart. It'll help close the trade gap, which is good for both of us. Maybe we'll even let developing countries join—good for your reputation, good for my image. Best of all, we'll have a common project to work on, which is a hell of a lot more than I have going with Putin. And each of us will have an answer to the right-wingers—those crazy generals in the People's Liberation Army and the cable television geniuses who want to prepare for the great Sino-American confrontation. That's a confrontation that, if we're smart about it, doesn't need to happen."

My guess is that the Chinese would say nothing at first—other than "very interesting"—but in time the offer will have a clear appeal. How they respond might begin to answer the big questions that were left hanging as the Olympic athletes headed home from Beijing. The two most urgent were crystallized by John Ikenberry of Princeton: As Beijing plots out its "peaceful rise" with the same precision and insistence on total control that it charted for the Games, "will China overthrow the existing order, or become part of it? And what, if anything, can the United States do to maintain its position as China rises?"

It is a burning question for software engineers in Silicon Valley and financial analysts on Wall Street. But it was barely touched upon in the 2008 campaign. Wars in Iraq and Afghanistan are vivid and urgent. Iran is easy to vilify. Managing China—or, more precisely, learning to profit from China's rise—seems like a ripe topic for some slow-running congressional commission.

"Think about the two preoccupations in Washington today: countering terrorism and managing China's rise," Joseph Nye, the Harvard professor and originator of the term "soft power," told me one day in 2007. "You couldn't have two more different kinds of problems. It takes entirely different kinds of skill sets to handle each one—and we've put just about all our energy and money over the past seven years into the first. We've never gotten the balance right."

◆

THE TORCH that Hu Jintao held in his hand that brisk Monday morning in March 2008 in Tiananmen Square, with its sleek, sculpted red handle, was designed to symbolize New China, the China of innovation and bold new design.

Its cool lines topped with flame all but shouted, "We're hot, we're global, and everyone should step out of the way." As Hu dipped the torch into the Olympic flame, no one was watching with more interest—or pride—than the freewheeling computer designers in Yao Ying Jia's laboratory at the Lenovo Corporation. At thirty-five, with a buzz haircut and graying sideburns, Yao is constantly on the search for the new—the new design, the hot new gadget. As he races from meeting to meeting, a small team of adoring acolytes moves with him, taking down his ideas. For the young, hip engineers working at Lenovo, success means establishing a new business model for the country. It means making Lenovo an innovator that can take on the best in Japan and the United States, and prove that China's contributions to the world of commerce can be grander than simply being the lowest-cost producer of almost everything. If Hu spends his days worrying about the threat from Taiwan and Tibet, Yao spends his days worrying about how to battle Apple and Dell.

In fact, he looks like he could be working at Apple or Dell, and that is quite deliberate. To get to Yao's R&D center from Beijing, you have to drive past the Summer Palace, the ancient retreat for Chinese emperors, with its lakeside pavilions and soaring pagodas. But Yao's laboratory was designed to evoke the Google dynasty, not the Qing dynasty. The atmosphere is Silicon Valley casual. Just outside Yao's meeting rooms, there is a giant pool table where his designers challenge one another in late-afternoon competitions. The walls are done in glass and sleek fabrics, with just a touch of Chinese accents, including a few decorative wooden doors that resemble those from the kind of charming but barely heated houses that used to dot the outskirts of the city here before it became a high-tech office park. Save for the perpetual Beijing smog, the view out the window might make you think you were in Santa Clara.

The workers clearly imagine that is exactly where they are. Moving between Lenovo's offices in Beijing and its other offices in Raleigh, North Carolina, and Yamato, Japan, Yao and his team of engineers and designers like to think of themselves as citizens of the Internet first and of China second. A distant second.

I discovered this when I casually asked Yao what he thought of the crackdown on the Tibetans, which was splashed across the front pages the morning we met. "We don't talk about politics much," Yao said to me, sounding like a California entrepreneur who can't be bothered with a bunch of Washington guys and their petty power plays. "We've got too much to do."

Yet whether Yao and his team acknowledge it or not, they are living out one of China's greatest political experiments—one testing whether their country is truly ready to go global. Just three years before, in 2005, as Hu was settling into his top post in the leadership compound at Zhongnanhai, Lenovo accomplished something almost no Chinese company had ever done before: It bought out one of the most famous industrial names of the West, the IBM personal computer division. With the purchase came the right to sell computers under the IBM name—at least for a couple of years—and the division's global network of design laboratories.

With only a few years to market computers under the familiar IBM label before the company had to survive using the Lenovo name—a combination of the company's old name, Legend, and *novo*, the Latin word for "new"—Yao and his team had to move fast to create an independent identity for their brand.

Quickly they settled on a strategy for recognition: the Beijing Olympics. The Games were all about showing the world the rise of a new, internationalized, innovative China—one that in just four decades had moved from the insular mind-set of Mao's Cultural Revolution to the sleek, tech-savvy world Yao and his engineers had created north of Beijing. It was the kind of unfettered capitalism that might send Mao spinning in his mausoleum.

Looking to showcase the company on the Olympics' world stage, Yao's industrial designers saw a notice for a national competition to design an Olympic torch, with "Chinese characteristics." This was their chance. Designing the next laptop took a backseat, briefly, to designing a torch. Out of 388 competing designs, Lenovo's entry won—a smooth, curved, distinctively Chinese handle (with the rubbery feel of a laptop computer's outer case), flowing upward into an ethereal representation of a traditional Chinese "lucky cloud." It was designed to stay lit in a robust wind and a drenching rain.

"Pretty cool," Yao said, handing me one of the prototypes just before the real torch began its six-continent, 85,000-mile journey. "You won't be able to look at it without thinking 'China' and 'Lenovo.'"

TEN YEARS AGO, little of this would have been foreseeable—not the buyout of IBM's personal computer operations, not the pool table, not the Olympic torch. But the most interesting element of the Lenovo experiment—and the new challenge for Washington—is that no one seems to be directing it from the top of the Chinese power structure.

Everyone I spoke with at Lenovo insisted that buying up IBM's personal computer division was the company's idea, not the idea of some central planner from the Chinese government. It would be hard to convince many lawmakers of that in Washington, where every step the Chinese take is viewed as part of a grand plan to surpass American industry.

The whole buyout likely would have been doomed if it had happened just a year later, around the time that Dubai Ports World tried to buy the management contracts for some port operations in the United States. By then, Washington was in one of its episodic allergic reactions to foreign ownership of American assets. Democrats and Republicans alike screamed that America was outsourcing its security; it did not help that Dubai Ports World was an Arab firm, based in one of America's few allies in the Gulf, the United Arab Emirates. On television, members of Congress complained that the United States could never let foreigners run our ports. (One of the inconvenient facts of this deal was that the seller was a British company which had been responsible for the management of the ports for years.) Within weeks, Dubai Ports gave in and scrapped the deal.

Just a few months later, Lenovo ran into a similar, but smaller, firestorm. Carrying the Dubai experience to the next step, some members of Congress demanded that the State Department renege on a deal for 16,000 desktop computers purchased from Lenovo. The fear in Congress, supported by dubious evidence, was that Chinese authorities might have stuffed the computers with secret surveillance equipment that would send State Department communications straight to intelligence agencies in Beijing. After many trips to Capitol Hill, Lenovo's American managers defused the situation, and the deal survived, although the computers are supposed to be used only for nonsensitive material.

Taken together, however, the Dubai Ports World debacle and the State Department incident pointed to a huge challenge the Obama administration is going to have to face: Well into our second decade of globalization, Congress still can't think straight about global enterprises—especially those with Chinese or Arab roots. To members of Congress, Lenovo is first and foremost a "Chinese" company, even if it has morphed into an enterprise that is reaching beyond China's shores to buy up foreign laboratories, employing workers in the United States, and hiring American managers.

In fact, no one in Congress or in the Great Hall of the People has ever seen a company quite like Lenovo. Soon after the purchase of the IBM division, Lenovo's chairman of the board, Yang Yuanqing, moved to Raleigh, North Carolina, setting up headquarters in the heart of America. Bill Amelio, the American executive whom

Yang hired away from Dell, runs the company's day-to-day operations from Singapore. In Shenzhen, the Chinese trade zone where Lenovo makes most of its laptops, the manufacturing is overseen by another American, a former IBM-er named John Egan. He gets driven to work every morning from Hong Kong, passing through the giant border station that separates the former British colony from the Chinese mainland, while an endless stream of trucks bearing Chinese goods comes the other way, toward the ships in Hong Kong Harbor.

Together they have created an enterprise that is neither entirely Chinese nor entirely American. Lenovo writes its software and designs some of its ThinkPads in Raleigh, and does other laptop development in Yamato, Japan, another former IBM facility. Yao and his designers operate out of Beijing, coming up with smaller, lighter machines, many for the Chinese market, where Lenovo has about a 30 percent share of the market. There are additional factories in Poland and Mexico, and several are planned for other countries.

Lenovo's experiment—creating a global enterprise with Chinese and American roots—is exactly the kind of experiment that Washington ought to be encouraging. As more global Chinese enterprises emerge, the more globally minded China's behavior is going to become. Lenovo is the New China example we want Old China to follow: an enterprise so integrated into the rest of the world that it will begin to force China to take into account international laws and standards.

But Washington doesn't work that way. Democrats react reflexively—and negatively—to the idea of a Chinese firm buying out an American company. They assume—sometimes correctly, sometimes not—that the result would be a loss of jobs inside the United States. Republicans are equally unhappy. They view each purchase of an American entity by the Chinese as a potential security threat. Business leaders fear the theft of American technology. "The problems with the U.S.-China relationship in the next few years are largely going to be here, not in China," Anne-Marie Slaughter, the dean of

Princeton's Woodrow Wilson School of Public and International Affairs, told me after spending a year living in Shanghai. "They are more ready for the next stage in globalization than we are."

We are going to have to get ready—fast. Like the Japanese in the 1980s, the Chinese today are the world's capital exporter. They are shopping for the best technology and the best talent here, just as American managers shop in China for the most efficient, reliable, and inexpensive factories. The only question is whether we can figure out how to adjust to this new reality.

The good news is that after twenty years, we figured out how to deal with the Japanese. When I reported from Japan in the late 1980s and the early 1990s, we spent most of our time writing about the political uproar that accompanied every major Japanese purchase of an American icon—Universal Pictures, the Empire State Building, the Pebble Beach Golf Club. Today, as I travel around America—to places as different as Alabama and Indiana—the concern is that the Japanese are not investing fast enough. Americans are only beginning to think about China as a potential investor.

When they do, there will be fears in Congress that the Chinese will begin deciding which factories stay open and which are shuttered, which American companies will thrive and which will be left as roadkill in the financial crisis. That is why we need more Chinese companies modeled after Lenovo—with managers and owners from many nations. "The Chinese government plays no role in what we do," Bill Amelio told me from his office in Singapore. The company's boardroom and management, he pointed out, don't even look very Chinese anymore. "When you look around at our board and our top managers, there are a lot of different passports."[5]

The look changes, of course, when you walk inside the doors of the Shenzhen factory, near Hong Kong. At its upper reaches, the company may be full of freewheeling designers who are jetting off to Yamato and Raleigh, but down in the manufacturing center of China, when it comes to producing as cheaply as possible, Lenovo looks like every other computer maker in the country.

The factory is tucked in amid plants run by the Chinese firms that churn out Apple's iPhones and iMacs, and a dizzying array of Japanese and European-branded computers. But what is most striking about the Lenovo factory is how un-automated it all is. Young women, no more than twenty or twenty-one years old, spend all day doing welding that could be done by a robot. But it is cheaper to have the young Chinese laborers perform the work. That enables the company to change models instantly without reprogramming all their equipment. The workers told me they made about $300 a month, a pittance by American standards, but ten or twenty times what they might make at home. It is boring, repetitive work, but they all told me they felt lucky to have the job.

The bustling Shenzhen plant explains a lot about why Lenovo thrives in the capitalist authoritarian state of China. The unspoken bargain today is that as long as companies keep generating jobs, no one in the government is going to tell them how to run their businesses. "As long as we keep employing people, and expanding, the Chinese will stay off our backs," one American who works in Lenovo's senior management told me. "They don't want to be deciding where we build factories, or where we sell our stuff."

He paused. "What we don't know," he said, "is whether that freedom goes away if China stumbles." We may be about to find out. By the end of 2008, with a recession looming in the United States, some of those factories were slowing down and laying off workers.

THE SECOND PART of the bargain in a capitalist authoritarian state, of course, is that Chinese knowledge workers—highly educated, highly compensated, free to travel the world—are expected to keep their heads down when it comes to challenging the government on sensitive issues like "splittism" or human rights. So far, it looks like many Chinese are willing to take that deal. I discovered that one morning in Beijing when I was having tea with Lenovo's freewheeling laptop designers.

The day I arrived at the Lenovo R&D center, China's efforts to quell the uprising in Tibet suffered another setback. A group of dissident monks in Lhasa, in a brilliant move, infiltrated a press tour of the capital for foreign reporters. The tour was one of those stage-managed visits that the government organizes, under tight controls, to convince Western correspondents that the tales of violence, burning cars, and mass arrests have been greatly exaggerated. But this effort backfired.

They chose the famous Jokhang Monastery, one of Tibet's holiest shrines, which, according to Tibetan legend, dates back to 647 CE— around the time that China was the political powerhouse of the world. Even then, Tibet was worried about its autonomy, and the temple was built under the reign of a Tibetan king, Songtsän Gampo, who sought good relations in the neighborhood by marrying both a Nepalese princess and a princess from the Tang Dynasty in China. Reflecting the strange mix of Tibet itself, the temple today is a four-story-high combination of Tibetan, Nepalese, and Chinese architecture, spread over six acres.

Long before the protests, a substantial Chinese military presence existed throughout the city. There were troops at the mountaintop monasteries, to make sure that the Buddhist ceremonies did not turn into anti-Chinese rallies. The monks sometimes take American visitors aside to show them hidden pictures of the Dalai Lama—tucked away in a busy mural, or secreted inside a locket.[6] But the Chinese have a deeper problem than surreptitious veneration of the Dalai Lama. A new generation of Tibetans seems to chafe at the Dalai Lama's call for peaceful resistance. Much as they honor His Holiness, they fear his Gandhi-like approach over the past four decades has accomplished nothing—except creeping Chinese domination.

For the press tour, of course, the Chinese authorities were confident they could keep evidence of those tensions under wraps.

They were wrong. As the reporters toured the monastery, a group of red-robed monks suddenly appeared and yelled, "Tibet is not free!"

Weeping, they accused the government of planting fake monks in their midst to give the reporters a glowing account of life in Tibet under Chinese rule. The Chinese guides froze. They knew if they shoved the monks away, or clubbed them, the violence would become the news story—hardly what they had in mind. So for a while the Chinese guides seethed, until finally demanding that the journalists just get out.[7]

The monks' protests dominated the papers the next day—though the version in the *International Herald Tribune* didn't read much like the version in the government-run *China Daily*. At Lenovo, sipping tea with Yao's team, I gingerly raised the subject of the Tibetan protests—and the farce of the government press tour. The designers appeared stricken. Looking at each other, they shrugged—each waiting for the other to go first.

"We don't like it," one of the twentysomething women on Lenovo's industrial design team said to me as we started walking through the laboratory. She looked around to make sure none of her colleagues saw us talking about the subject. "But it is in a different place," she said, "and it is not our business. We design the newest laptops."

She was part of the post–Tiananmen Square generation, probably about five or six years old when students took over the center of the city in a direct challenge to the Communist Party. I was in China a few weeks after Tiananmen, when young people her age were outraged at the repression and the government's effort to minimize the death toll. But that was nineteen years ago.

Members of the Lenovo generation had learned to avert their eyes. They have grown accustomed to a system that allowed plenty of economic liberalization but only the most limited political dissent. They understood the unspoken deal: In the New China of capitalist authoritarianism, you can do whatever you want—start up a new company, change jobs, travel abroad, vent your frustration in a blog post—as long as you don't veer out of the clear lane markers. You do not challenge or question the legitimacy of the Communist Party, especially to visiting reporters. When asked, you offer up the standard talking points about how greater economic freedom will lead, over time, to greater political freedom with "Chinese characteristics." You explain that in a country of 1.3 billion people, unfettered democracy would lead to chaos. After work, you go out drinking, but you stay away from meetings to plan demonstrations. The Lenovo generation does not camp out in front of the Great Hall of the People; there is too much to lose the next morning back at the Great Hall of the Product.

But, try as they might to shield their eyes, it was impossible for members of Yao's team to ignore what was happening in Tibet. Whatever they thought about Hu Jintao's crackdown, they knew that perceptions of China's action abroad would be taken out on the torch relay—*their* torch—as it raced through twenty-one nations. Within days, their fears turned into reality. The "One World, One Dream" slogan that sounded so inclusive on the streets of Beijing seemed to lose something in translation. Suddenly, Lenovo's R&D staff got a quick education in how the rest of the world viewed China.

One of the worst receptions was in London on April 6, when the torch was run for seven hours through the city to the site of the 2012 Olympics in Stratford. Protesters went after the torch with fire extinguishers, unsuccessfully trying to wrestle the torchbearer for control of the flame.[8]

The next day in Paris, 3,000 police were needed to protect the torch, especially from demonstrators who had watched the fire-extinguisher trick in London and decided to try it en masse. Fearful that the torch would be extinguished on global television, the authorities reached for the hidden on-off switch in the Lenovo torch and doused the flame themselves. Then they put the torch on a bus to run it to its next destination in the city. The whole day was a cat-and-mouse game between torchbearers and torch protesters.

368 ♦ David E. Sanger

As Lenovo's staff watched in disbelief, many other young Chinese reacted in anger. Zhu Xiaomeng, a student at Beijing's Foreign Studies University, helped organize a boycott of Carrefour, the French retailer, in reaction to the Paris protests. Online petitions gathered 20 million electronic signatures. "China used to be known as the sick man of Asia," she told my colleague Andrew Jacobs. She was determined to turn the tables on Western countries, using the power of China's consumers to demonstrate that the country would tolerate no disrespect. "After five thousand years, we're not so soft anymore," she said.[9]

When I asked Amelio a few weeks later about the reactions inside his company—with its split loyalties between China and the West—he turned quite cautious, realizing that he was stepping on shaky ground. He clearly did not want to give the Chinese government reason to think they had provided the foreigners running Lenovo a bit too much license.

"We had to talk a lot of people in the Lenovo team through this one," Amelio conceded. "Some of our Chinese team members understood, some didn't." He quickly pointed out to me that he had personally carried the torch, briefly, when a shortened relay was run through the streets of San Francisco, the only stop in the United States. (The city canceled the closing ceremony to avoid further protests.) Amelio was a big supporter of the Beijing Games and, of course, Lenovo's sponsorship. But by lacing up for the run, he demonstrated to the Chinese that he was on Beijing's side of the Great Torch Standoff.

Unfortunately for Lenovo, it wasn't relay-runners like Amelio who were capturing the headlines. All of the front-page pictures showed the team of Chinese agents in blue-and-white Olympic track suits, who had trained for a year at China's Armed Police Academy to protect the flame. In their signature dark black sunglasses, and in their stoic demeanor, they looked like extras in a Jackie Chan movie, shoving people aside and making sure no protester got close enough to the flame to extinguish it or steal it. This group of super-fit guardians had a wonderful name: "Olympic Sacred Flame Protection Unit." Its members were clearly hand-picked for the job: The average height of the thirty members of the squad was reported at six feet three inches. Quiet street diplomacy was not their forte: If Central Casting had ordered up some thugs to represent Old China, these would have been the guys.[10]

In June the Chinese executed the most daring torch run of all—through the streets of Lhasa, the same streets that three months before had erupted in violence. The ceremonies were held at the Potala Palace, the historic seat of the exiled Dalai Lama, with Chinese troops stationed every few feet along the route. The Communist Party secretary of Tibet, Zhang Qingli, left no doubt who was in charge. "Tibet's sky will never change and the red flag with five stars will forever flutter high above it," he declared. "We will certainly be able to totally smash the splittist schemes of the Dalai Lama clique."[11]

But by then the talk among Western leaders about whether to boycott the opening ceremonies to express their displeasure had dissipated. After the earthquake in Sichuan Province in May, there had been an understandable outpouring of sympathy for the Chinese people, and suddenly no one was thinking about boycotts. Bush, who had entertained the Dalai Lama in the residence of the White House several times—a way of avoiding an "official" meeting in the Oval Office—made clear he was going to Beijing, after issuing the ritual calls for the Chinese leadership to open up a dialogue with the exiled Tibetan spiritual leader. When I asked Condoleezza Rice one afternoon why Bush was so quick to reaffirm that he would attend, she gave me an answer I don't think I would have heard from her, or from Bush, in 2001.

"I didn't think that made much sense," she said of boycotting the opening ceremony. "I told the president that it wouldn't only be an insult to the Chinese leaders, it would be an insult to 1.3 billion Chinese people."

She was probably right. But Bush never made a serious effort to square that decision with his "freedom agenda," which he insists will be the lasting legacy of his administration. Nor did he square it with his decisions to tighten restrictions on the odious regimes in Burma or Cuba. He had come to the same conclusion that his predecessors had: We simply need China too much, on too many critical elements of the American agenda, to risk a real confrontation on human rights. In short, we do not have the leverage to reward New China and punish Old China. They are inseperable; they are symbiotic.

"Both are the real China," Jeffrey Garten, a longtime Asia expert who shaped the Clinton administration's strategy for dealing with rising economies before he became the dean of the Yale School of Management, told me during the torch run. "And Americans have to get used to that. We have to shed our habit of separating the world into good guys and bad guys and recognize that some countries are both. Unless we consider China an economic partner on one hand, and a political and military problem on the other, and unless we deal with each dimension on its merits rather than mortgaging one to the other, our policies will veer from one extreme to the other, and we'll fail to achieve any of our objectives. It's a new world for America's relationship with the country that will be most important to it, and I just hope we are up to the challenge."

FOR THE BETTER PART of the past sixteen years, over two administrations, Washington seemed befuddled about how to deal with the two Chinas. Both Bill Clinton and George W. Bush argued, time and again, that New China would invariably strangle Old China—that a country so in love with the fruits of capitalist enterprise would soon hunger for an end to authoritarian rule. So far the theory remains unproven. For now, the argument that New China will soon subsume Old China remains what James Mann, once a China correspondent for the *Los Angeles Times,* terms "The China Fantasy."[12]

Whether it is a fantasy or, as I suspect, just a prayer for the future, every modern American president has embraced it. They have no choice.

When Bill Clinton took office in 1992, he was still threatening to limit China's trading rights unless it got serious about human rights. It's one of those lines that gets huge cheers on the campaign trail, particularly when delivered in a state hard-hit by Chinese competition, like Michigan or Ohio. Then reality set in. Within the first year of his presidency, he abandoned that talk and ended up articulating George H. W. Bush's policy—the complete separation of trade from human rights issues—more forcefully than his predecessor in office had ever explained it. By the time he left office in 2001, Clinton had dragged his party, kicking and screaming, toward a new American strategy: He argued that the magic of the Web spread freedom and undermined the Communist Party in ways that no military action, no trade agreement, and no democracy-promotion program ever could. During trips to China and during debates at home over whether to let China join the international trading system, Clinton talked endlessly about how the Old China problem would solve itself as villagers logged on, and began to discover how their fellow citizens were dealing with such issues as polluted water, corrupt officials, and elections. Inevitably the Communist Party's monopoly on information would erode. When it did, its authority would erode too.

Clinton used the Internet logic to argue why the United States should let China join the World Trade Organization, despite the complaints that he was "rewarding" a repressive regime. He made a compelling case that by integrating China into the global economy, America would be forcing it to adopt the rule of law. (It was the same argument that Clinton made, more delicately, about Russia.) It was only a matter of time, he told an audience of American and Chinese students in March 2000, before a Net-savvy, rising middle class would begin to demand its rights, because "when individuals have the power not just to dream, but to realize their dreams, they will demand a greater say." [13] After all, Clinton said, it had happened in

South Korea, which shook off years of military rule. Why not China?

It sounded so logical that Democrats and Republicans alike voted for China's admission to the World Trade Organization, despite their many misgivings. That turned out to be a good thing: WTO membership forced China to open many of its markets, and paved the way for American insurance companies, automakers, and others to compete.

A decade later, the Chinese are freer to express their opinions than ever before—within limits. They create chat rooms to vent their frustrations about corruption. The government tries to keep the dissenting chatter under control, but it is a little like fighting the tides: As my colleague Nick Kristof has pointed out, in the cat-and-mouse game between censors and bloggers, "the mice are winning this game, not the cats." When censors take down one or two sites, the material gets posted on fifty more. Yet the truth is that none of this venting appears to have undermined the authority of the party, at least yet. Few authoritarian governments have figured out how to turn the Internet to their advantage better than the Chinese. It took a while, but they have learned the importance of letting their own populace use the blogs to blow off steam. They have learned, reluctantly, to let foreign news pour into the country via the Web—also within limits.

Determined Web trollers, of course, can get anything. One day in an Internet café in Shanghai during Bush's trip there in 2001, just after 9/11, I tried to get on the *Times* website, only to discover that many stories were blocked. A young boy, no more than fourteen or fifteen years old, sidled up next to me and asked, "Mister, what you need?" I explained, and with a few strokes of the keyboard he routed the request through a foreign server and called up the Web page I sought.

"Great!" I said. "I can't thank you enough!"

He held out his hand. "Five bucks," he said with a smile.

I paid up happily, figuring I was supporting the subversion of an authoritarian regime. But if Chinese teenagers have learned how to turn the Web to their advantage, so have Chinese industrial spies. At the same time that they are controlling access at home, they are exploiting the openness of the Web abroad. At the Pentagon and inside American intelligence agencies, officials watch, as Chinese computer operators sweep up what one senior American intelligence official described as "terabytes of data" every week from American corporations and government sites. Most of it is lying there in the open, and the Chinese presumably sift through it for anything that might give the country a competitive leg up. It is this astounding mix—the ability to mine the databases of the Pentagon while blocking access to YouTube videos of Chinese police beating monks senseless in Lhasa—that has given China its reputation for harnessing the political and economic muscle of the Web. It is Old China and New China, cohabiting on the same hard drive.

GEORGE BUSH'S backflips on China outdid Clinton's—which was no small feat. In 2000, during the presidential campaign, he famously kept talking about treating China as a "strategic competitor." In two separate interviews I conducted before 9/11, two of Bush's aides actually used the phrase "the Red Chinese" to describe the government in Beijing. In six years of living in and covering Asia, I don't think I had heard that phrase once, except maybe in old newsreels about the Korean War. China was many things when Bush came to office, but "red" was not one of them.

The phrase, though, reflected a mind-set when Bush took power. The neoconservatives who had arrived in their new offices in the White House were determined to describe China in the most threatening terms. And the Chinese helped fuel their arguments by mounting a huge espionage operation in the United States, scooping up corporate data, weapons information, and, of course, whatever they could learn about American policy toward Taiwan. Many around Bush, including Secretary of Defense Donald Rumsfeld, pushed for a far more aggressive approach toward "containment" of Chinese power, using the flawed comparison between China today and the Soviet Union of 1981.

To his enduring credit, Bush rejected the containment crowd. "China was the exception to the rule in the White House because Bush saw it in transformational terms," Chris Hill noted at the end of the administration. China was one of the few countries that Bush had visited as a young man, when his father was the U.S. representative there prior to the opening of formal diplomatic relations. "He was often telling people about riding around on a bicycle in Beijing, and he would marvel at the changes." His travels through China at that formative moment of his life gave him a comfort and an affection for the Chinese people that ended up defusing several potential collisions with the Chinese throughout his presidency. Unfortunately, China was the exception. As a young man Bush never went bicycling in Tehran, Pyongyang, Havana, or Rangoon.

# CHAPTER 13
# THE PUNCTURE STRATEGY

ON JANUARY 11, 2007, the same week that Bush announced the "surge" in Iraq, Old China and New China briefly joined forces in an experiment designed to jolt Washington. With no warning, Chinese military forces sent an anti-satellite missile aloft and blew up one of their own weather satellites, just as it was about to fall out of orbit five hundred miles above Earth. They did it just to prove they could.

It was quite a feat for a country that forty years earlier was on the brink of starvation and anarchy, gripped by the terror of the Red Guards. It was also a long way from Mao's military strategy of a "People's War," in which the country's enemies—he was thinking mostly about the Soviets—would be lured into Chinese territory and destroyed in a war of attrition. The space test marked the reversal of Mao's doctrine; in this new strategy, China's enemies are to be blinded and intimidated long before military forces make it near the mainland.

To the China hawks in Washington, the anti-satellite test seemed to validate every warning they had issued for years about the "China threat." At the very moment the Pentagon was fixated on the low-tech but lethal techniques of the militants in the deserts of Iraq and the mountains of Afghanistan, the Chinese had, in a single missile launch, demonstrated how they could defeat the highest-tech, highest-flying systems in the American arsenal.

The satellite the Chinese shot down—on the somewhat thin pretext that it could pose a danger if it fell on a populated area—was traveling at a far higher altitude than the satellites that aim America's precision weapons, run its GPS systems, keep cell phone calls connected, warn of troop movements, detect nuclear sites, and transmit financial data around the world. Presumably, if Beijing could take out the weather satellite, it could turn off America's lights in space.

Because they gave no warning of the anti-satellite test, the Chinese violated the usual protocol that you should at least notify the world when you are about to create hundreds of pieces of space junk that will be tracked for years. (In this case, it was no small issue; NASA later determined that the test added about 10 percent to the total amount of debris floating around in near-space and said it would take roughly a century for all of it to fall out of orbit.)[1] But inside the White House, the complexity of the situation, which American spy satellites had followed minute by minute, went well beyond tracking space junk. The test revealed how little we know, even today, about the relationship between China's civilian leaders and its military.

When I went to see Steve Hadley, the president's national security adviser, about ten days after the test, he said he still did not know if Hu Jintao had ordered the satellite shot down or whether the Chinese leader learned about it from reading the newspaper.

"The question on something like this is, at what level in the Chinese government are people witting, and have they approved?" he said to me. The wave of diplomatic protests that followed the test, he said, was partly an effort to make sure the Chinese military's actions "get ventilated at the highest levels in China."[2]

For nearly two weeks the Chinese leadership responded to Washington's queries with nothing but stony silence. When Beijing finally acknowledged that it had shot down the satellite, the description of the event left the regime's intentions highly ambiguous. "This test was not directed at any country and does not constitute a threat to any country," Liu Jianchao, the spokesman for China's foreign ministry, insisted to reporters. "What needs to be stressed is that China has always advocated the peaceful use of space, opposes the weaponization of space and an arms race in space." He seemed to be hinting that this was a shot across Bush's bow. A few months earlier the White House had issued a new space policy that declared the United States would "preserve its rights, capabilities and freedom of action in space."[3] China's message seemed clear: We can play this game too.

But there was a deeper meaning to the Chinese statement. While the United States spent the first years of the new millennium probing al Qaeda's vulnerabilities, the People's Liberation Army spent those same years probing ours. Like al Qaeda and the Taliban, the Chinese were looking for America's Achilles' heel, the hidden vulnerabilities in the world's biggest military and economic machine. Al Qaeda and the Taliban were thinking small: Their idea of asymmetric warfare was to plant roadside bombs and other improvised explosives, or send suicide bombers to the gates of American embassies and hotels. Their tactics were tragically effective at generating headlines and producing casualties (mostly innocent Muslims), but as asymmetric warfare goes, roadside bombs represent amateur hour. Absent a true weapon of mass destruction, al Qaeda and the Taliban are restricted to disabling a few personnel carriers at a time and hoping that the grievous injuries and fear they sow in the streets of Baghdad and Kabul will eventually drive out the Americans.

The Chinese are thinking big. They recognize that America's vulnerability lies in its high-tech infrastructure. So while the Taliban labored away in basements building magnetic IEDs to stick under cars, the Chinese labored away in computer labs and missile sites. No one gets hurt in an antimissile attack. But China's military strategists know they can do far more damage to the United States by threatening to take out the military and civilian satellite systems than by threatening a nuclear confrontation.

"Unlike the Soviets, the Chinese decided early on that nuclear weapons have a limited utility in the world," Kurt Campbell, an Asia expert who served as a defense official in the Clinton administration, told me. "But they recognize how sensitive we are to strategic competition. So they look for the subtle edge." Antisatellite missiles provide that edge: We have a far larger number of vulnerable satellites circling the globe than the Chinese do. The anti-satellite missile launch was asymmetric warfare, New China style.

The change in strategy was years in coming, a product of China's two biggest assets: its persistence and its growing wealth. In the early 1990s, the People's Liberation Army spent a lot of time studying the Persian Gulf War. Their shock at how far behind they were triggered the first wave of big annual increases to fund military modernization. As America's brief "unipolar" moment peaked in the late 1990s, China's feeling of inferiority mounted. Nothing sent a bigger chill through Zhongnanhai, the leaders' residential compound, than the image of American B-2 bombers lazily lifting into the air over Missouri at midday, flying an 11,000-mile, thirty-two-hour mission to drop laser-guided weapons over Belgrade, and arriving back in time for the pilots to have dinner at home the next evening.[4] When one of those bombs went astray and destroyed the Chinese embassy in downtown Belgrade, the blunder not only touched off anti-American protests in the streets of Beijing but also produced huge skepticism on the part of the People's Liberation Army that the attack could have been anything but deliberate. A senior Chinese official told Thomas R. Pickering, the American diplomat sent to Beijing to apologize for the bombing, that the United States had gotten involved in Kosovo for one reason only: to test its latest armaments.[5]

This concern about American military superiority grew with the rapid destruction of Saddam Hussein's much-feared Republican Guard in 2003, a sobering reminder of the fate of those who try to confront the American military directly, force-on-force. And for the past few years, visiting delegations of Chinese military officers have said they are fascinated by the use of unmanned Predator drones in Iraq and along the Pakistan-Afghanistan border, particularly by the thought that the planes were being flown by a young pilot with a joystick who was sitting in a trailer in the Nevada desert.

"They looked at what we were doing by remote control from Bagram Air Base," one senior official in the Pacific Command told me, referring to the huge outpost in Afghanistan where many of the Predators are launched, "and you could see them calculating what we could do over China someday from our bases in Japan."

It's no surprise that the People's Liberation Army spent the past two decades focusing on America's heavy dependence on the intelligence, computer, and communications technology that give American military forces global eyes and global reach. Chinese military planners quickly began searching for inventive ways to shut it down, investing in cyberwarfare and sea-skimming ballistic missiles that could threaten, from hundreds of miles away, any American carrier fleet that might one day head to the Taiwan Strait in a crisis over China's claims to that last, wealthy artifact of the Cold War. It is all part of a broader strategy, as two of America's top experts on the subject wrote, to "puncture American dominance wherever possible."[6]

When he became secretary of defense, Gates examined this new strategy and emerged concluding that China's buildup was a reason for concern—but not reason for panic. "They want to have a capability to hold us at risk," Gates told me when I asked him about China's intentions. (Rumsfeld's holdovers, no surprise, had a darker, more expansive view of China's ambitions.)

The "puncture" strategy is a direct challenge to the Bush Doctrine, enunciated by the White House in its first "National Security Strategy," published in September 2002.

The doctrine is best known, of course, for its emphasis on preemption against states amassing weapons of mass destruction that could threaten the United States—an approach that went awry in its first application, with the invasion of Baghdad six months later.* But for the China hawks—and for the Chinese—the most important sentence of the document lay elsewhere, in the section meant to address America's approach to dealing with rising great powers. "Our forces will be strong enough," the document said, "to dissuade potential adversaries from pursuing a military buildup in hopes of surpassing, or equaling, the power of the United States."

At the time, Russia seemed so financially hobbled that the statement seemed clearly aimed at the Chinese and their expanding conventional and nuclear forces. When I was first reporting on the new National Security Strategy—and its declaration that no "peer competitor" would be allowed to take on the United States—Condoleezza Rice was very clear about Bush's objectives. "The president has no intention," she told me, "of allowing any foreign power to catch up with the huge lead the United States has opened since the fall of the Soviet Union more than a decade ago."[7]

The Chinese are a long way from catching up, but the test in January 2007 left little doubt that the Chinese leadership viewed Bush's vow as bluster. With American troops bogged down on the other side of the globe, the U.S. defense budget under pressure, and huge U.S. deficits financed largely by the willingness of the Chinese government to lend Washington the money to keep paying the bills, Hu Jintao banked on the proposition that the United States could do little to prevent China from developing a twenty-first-century military that targeted America's vulnerabilities. He was right. Even if we had not gone into Iraq, even if the country were not deeply in debt, it would have been difficult to dissuade China from building a military that reflects its new influence in the world.

---

* In interviews, Rice and others have argued that the invasion of Iraq was not an example of preemption because Saddam Hussein had so blatantly ignored a series of United Nations resolutions. Thus, they do not consider it a test of the Bush Doctrine. Most Americans and much of the rest of the world, however, considered it to be a preemptive strike, largely because Bush, Cheney, and Rice had warned in vivid terms of the dangers of Saddam's weapons.

The White House reaction to the antisatellite test was almost as fascinating as the test itself. If Iran or North Korea or Iraq in Saddam's day had conducted such a test, Bush would have denounced it from the South Lawn and threatened retaliation. He never did in China's case. But he also never budged from his space policy, which declared that the United States would "deny, if necessary, adversaries the use of space capabilities hostile to U.S. national interests."[8] The White House however, did quietly order the military to prove that it could perform the same feat. A little over a year later, in February 2008, the United States launched an interceptor—a version of what it designed for the antiballistic-missile system—to destroy a U.S. satellite that was falling out of orbit with 1,000 pounds of highly toxic fuel.

Earlier, the United States had said the fuel posed no threat and that the military would simply let the satellite fall, hoping it would sink to the bottom of some ocean. Then, when the Air Force and others realized there was an opportunity to match the Chinese accomplishment and to show off the ABM technology, they declared that the toxic fuel posed too great a risk. They proceeded to do exactly what the Chinese had done: They took the satellite out with a single shot. With that accomplishment, both countries crossed into dangerous new territory.

Apart from the space junk—theirs and ours—no one did serious damage with these tit-for-tat shots. But as America tries to manage the Old China–New China tensions, it is incidents such as these that give one pause. In public, both Chinese and American leaders say roughly the same thing: The world is a big place, and there's plenty of room for both of us. But in reality, the Pentagon and the People's Liberation Army are pursuing their own versions of a "hedging strategy" just in case the world really isn't that big, after all.

America hedges by keeping bases in Japan and South Korea and by patrolling the region with its carriers and submarines. The Chinese hedge by talking incessantly about their "peaceful rise" while testing weapon after weapon to send the message that Beijing will tolerate no interference in its sphere of influence, especially near Taiwan.

China used to wrap those weapons programs and tests in total secrecy, save for the May Day parades of missiles and tanks, a holdover from the Communist era of muscle-flexing when military power was still measured in throw-weights. But these days, many in the Chinese leadership prefer a different expression of power. In gradual increments, they have been dispatching their navy to farther destinations. "They want us to see them everywhere—in the Pacific, in the Indian Ocean," an Indian admiral told me during a visit to New Delhi. "It would be years before they would be able to run a war far from China—they simply can't do it. But they want us to get used to seeing them," he said, so that years from now no one will question their right to patrol Asia's waters.

To show off their new capabilities, the Chinese have started publishing photos of their second-generation nuclear-powered attack submarines and announcing big increases in defense spending, upward of 18 percent per year. (The Chinese insist their defense budget is $45 billion; the Pentagon thinks the real number is more than $100 billion. That's a big number, but even the higher figure would amount to less than a quarter of the American defense budget.)* The Chinese have disclosed, or made obvious to American spy satellites, about ten different varieties of ballistic missiles—including nearly 1,000 short-range missiles based opposite Taiwan. The Chinese Navy is developing its own aircraft carrier, after concluding that the Russian ships they were buying were built to Russian standards. The list goes on: new laser weapons, new missiles with sophisticated guidance systems, and new submarines.

Still, many experts in Washington say that what they worry about in China is what we don't see. "There is scandalously little intelligence

---

* Congress agreed to $462.8 billion for defense programs for fiscal year 2007. This does not include the supplemental budget packages for funding the wars in Iraq and Afghanistan.

on their weapons systems," one senior intelligence official complained to me in the fall of 2008, "because it's simply tied up elsewhere."

What really grabs the attention of the China hawks in Washington, however, is the gradually increasing size and sophistication of the country's nuclear arsenal—and the number of weapons aimed at the United States.

Americans have never known quite what to make of the Chinese nuclear arsenal. In the mid-1960s, the prospect of Mao with nuclear weapons seemed so terrifying that President Johnson briefly considered teaming up with the Soviets for a joint strike on the country's nuclear facilities before the first Chinese test in 1964. (That debate closely paralleled the current arguments about whether the world can live with an Iranian nuclear weapon or should strike before one is built.) The risks seemed wildly high, and the idea, fortunately, was dropped. For the rest of the Cold War, the Chinese nuclear arsenal was something of a strategic footnote. The country was satisfied with a "minimum deterrent" of just a couple of hundred warheads, compared with thousands in the United States and the former Soviet Union. The Chinese were far more enlightened on this issue than either Washington or Moscow; China knew it needed just enough to create a credible deterrent. It had other priorities for its money.

New riches have ushered in a slightly changed approach. In 2005 a National Intelligence Estimate circulated to the top layer of the national security leadership but never publicly discussed by the Bush administration, warned that the Chinese were increasing the size of their nuclear arsenal by about 25 percent—a number that sounded big but didn't amount to many more weapons. More important, the Chinese began deploying a new, mobile-launched, land-based missile—called the DF-31A—that is difficult for American forces to target and, perhaps more worrisome, can reach just about the entire United States. American intelligence officials estimated that by 2015, China will have 75 to 100 warheads aimed at American territory—not exactly how you treat a "strategic partner."[9]

"They have thought out their strategy very carefully, as you might expect," one of the key Pentagon analysts assessing the Chinese buildup told me. "They know that credibility is the coin of the realm, so they've built a very, very credible force. But they still have a hard time integrating their security interests with their economic interests. So we really don't know how they plan to use all this power."

In a parting shot just as the Bush administration was packing up and getting ready to leave Washington, Paul Wolfowitz, the former deputy secretary of defense who gained fame arguing that the invasion of Iraq could be done on the cheap because oil revenues would pay for the reconstruction of the country, made the argument that the United States cannot allow China to gain nuclear parity.

"China's military modernization is inspired in part by growing nationalism and pride, by the goal of checkmating U.S. military power while expanding its own presence and capabilities in Asia and the Pacific, by its increasing international commerce, and by Beijing's desire to be perceived as a serious player on the world scene," he wrote in a report to Condoleezza Rice in his capacity as chairman of a State Department advisory board. After years of humiliation by Korea, Japan, and the United States, he wrote, China's leaders "probably believe that, with rising nationalism under way, any similar humiliation in the future would be a threat to the regime from within."

Wolfowitz's solution was to rebuild and modernize America's nuclear infrastructure, because "the United States cannot risk China perceiving the United States as either unprepared or unwilling to respond to Chinese nuclear threats and use." He called for better missile defenses and making it clear that Washington "will not accept a mutual vulnerability relationship with China."[10]

Wolfowitz was giving voice to a strand of thinking in Washington that the United States must be "second to none." If China is allowed to challenge the United States in the number of deployed nuclear weapons, that theory goes, Iran or Pakistan or India will be right behind. Such thinking dominated the White House in the Bush years, driving its determination to talk about eliminating nuclear weapons as a long-term goal—much like paying off the national debt—that everyone loves in theory and has no interest in pursuing in practice. Nowhere in Wolfowitz's report to the secretary of state was there mention of the option of opening up talks with the Chinese about reducing the size or potency of their arsenal and ours.

THE MAN RESPONSIBLE for figuring out how to deal with these threats is Admiral Keating. A warrior with an imposing presence but a friendly demeanor, he has spent his life engaging his Asian military counterparts at endless receptions where the defenders of the world's most vibrant economies eye one another over mai tais. Keating grew up in landlocked Dayton, Ohio, graduated from the Naval Academy in Annapolis, and has, for the better part of the past thirty-five years, been floating and flying across the Pacific. During 9/11 and the Iraq War, he headed the North American Aerospace Defense Command—NORAD, the famed mountain fortress—before commanding the newly created Northern Command, the military unit created to focus on homeland defense.

But in early 2007, after Donald Rumsfeld was shown the door and the more thoughtful, less confrontational Robert Gates settled into the job of secretary of defense, Keating returned to his roots. He was made commander of all American forces in the Pacific.

From his perch over Pearl Harbor, where he can just make out the sunken remains of the USS *Arizona*, still bubbling oil nearly seven decades after the Japanese attack that brought America into World War II, Keating devotes more time to understanding our Asian rivals' intentions than to counting ther ballistic missiles. It's an approach that might have benefited his predecessors in the late 1930s. Yet it is not much easier to figure out which of many competing factions in Beijing will emerge on top than it was to determine which of the battling factions in Tokyo would win out in 1941.

"When I ask my Chinese colleagues," Keating told me, "they say, 'We only want to protect those things that are ours.' We say, 'Fair enough.' When you rely as much as they do on importing precious metals, and oil, and exporting their goods, having a maritime presence makes sense. But why sixty-five submarines that can shoot a missile a hundred kilometers? That's a different kind of navy—and a different kind of air force—than you might create if you were only interested in protecting those things that are yours."[11]

Keating has concluded that—at least for now—the Chinese are largely interested in creating what he calls "an area of denial," a zone around the mainland and Taiwan that they can keep American forces from entering, especially if a nasty confrontation develops between Beijing and Taipei. If he had been in the same job ten years ago, when the Clinton administration was focused on the "big emerging markets" and diplomacy centered far more on the Pacific, Keating would have been constantly fending off officials from Washington. But to Keating's relief, the Bush administration was so wrapped up in Iraq and Afghanistan that it couldn't be bothered to focus on pesky extraneous issues such as managing military interchanges with China. You can't take the time to think about long-term threats, he told me, if you are waking up every morning in a cold sweat about how to handle short-term threats.

"There is the unmistakable focus by Washington on matters Middle Eastern, largely Iraq, secondarily Afghanistan, maybe the Levant," he said, the last a reference to the area that encompasses Israel, Syria, Lebanon, and Jordan. Those are the three areas that Bush associated with terrorism. "The issues with which we deal aren't in the top three," he said, "and we are six time zones away, so everyone's stayed out of our hair."

The results are startling to anyone who travels the globe these days measuring the mood about America. In the Pacific, there is far more concern about whether the United States is turning protectionist than about whether it is turning loose the captives in Guantánamo. Wherever I travel in Asia—back to my old haunts in Japan, in Thailand, in India—top officials nervously ask whether I think America is gradually withdrawing from the Pacific and surrendering the region to China's influence.

Maybe they like us, or maybe they just like having us there. It is easy to understand why. As Keating and I talked, we peered down from his office window as sailors and Air Force personnel were rushing to put together "earthquake kits" for victims of the huge disaster in China's Sichuan Province that destroyed whole cities and brought down shoddily built schools. It was the latest of a series of humanitarian operations that Keating was overseeing. He had just returned from a trip to the border of Myanmar where he tried to persuade the paranoid Burmese junta to allow the United States to provide aid to victims of a cyclone. Always suspicious, the Burmese were reluctant. Keating found himself attempting to reassure the leaders of the military regime that America was not interested in occupying the country. "We don't want Burma," he says he told them.

The exchange with the Burmese was not unusual. The Indonesians have made it clear they do not want the hospital ship *Mercy* bobbing conspicuously offshore during emergencies; to them, its appearance is a sign of national weakness. The Philippines had the same worry about American counterinsurgency forces that arrived to help clear out Islamic extremists. In both cases Keating learned the importance of delivering help silently, invisibly, even if it meant that the United States military did not get credit on the evening news.

As we talked I kept thinking back to Bush's confident-sounding lectures during the 2000 presidential campaign about why American troops should never be used for nation-building. The refutation of that view was unfolding below Admiral Keating's window: It's the best single way to make use of America's soft power while delivering a subtle message about America's hard power.

"It's a different kind of American presence, and it works," Keating told me. The speed with which the aid arrives and the accuracy with which it is airdropped, leave an impression. These operations remind people, Keating said, that "we're still the predominant military power out here, and we intend to stay that way." He recalled an incident from the winter of 2007, when two American C-17 cargo planes were dispatched to Guangzhou Province in China with blankets because the area had been hit with a brutal cold spell that threatened mass deaths from exposure. It took less than seventy-two hours, he said, between the time the Chinese asked for some help and the arrival of the first American planes, which immediately offloaded pallets full of blankets.

"There was a Chinese general there," Keating recalled. "And the first thing he said was, 'I can't believe you got here so quickly.'"

The real message of the Chinese general's surprise is that humanitarian operations give the United States a chance to make a point about our speed and our reach—wordlessly. "We don't want to fence them in," Keating said. "We want to draw them out, let them see the capabilities we have, coax them to let us see their capabilities, and assure them we mean them no ill will." He paused.

"And we want to convince them," he said, "that if it ever came down to soldier-to-soldier, airplane-to-airplane, ship-to-ship, we are not going to lose. So don't waste your money, don't waste your time. Come with us, let us operate together. Send your kids to West Point, and we'll send our guys to the Guangzhou Military Academy."

EVEN IF YOUNG Chinese officers end up at West Point, the leaders of Old China have no intention of giving up the "puncture strategy" to deal with the United States, any more than Lenovo intends to surrender the laptop market to Dell and Apple. But at the same time, I detect no desire among the Chinese, even the hardliners of Old China, to engage in direct confrontation with the United States. It is the last thing they want—and their behavior during the Bush years suggests they have concluded that it is completely unnecessary.

Hu Jintao and his colleagues have plenty of problems these days—from tainted milk to desperate water shortages, protests over new chemical plants and toxic rivers, and tens of millions of restive unemployed workers. But when they look across the Pacific, they see a superpower consumed by woes of equal magnitude. With the publication of every new State Department assessment of China's human-rights record, Chinese diplomats gently ask when waterboarding became an acceptable American interrogation technique. They rarely miss a moment to point out that the America that preached to China about fiscal "transparency" and the wonders of efficient markets amid the Asian financial crisis in 1998 ignored its own advice before the American financial crisis in 2008.

Now, for the first time in the history of Chinese-American relations, we are the ones with our hands out—for diplomatic help with unruly rogue states like North Korea, and for desperately needed capital.

When the United States reached its last, unsatisfactory deal with North Korea on nuclear inspections in October 2008, Condoleezza Rice was on the phone to her Chinese counterparts trying to get assurances that Beijing would enforce compliance. The same week, private investment houses and banks were turning to Chinese investors, hoping that Beijing would find them an exit ramp from financial calamity. So was the U.S. government, which knew that if the Chinese chose not to show up for the Treasury auction, the White House was going to have trouble raising the cash for its bailout of the banks. Naturally, the American concern that China would stop lending was all fodder for the daily debate in Beijing, where the question of whether America is in decline is a constant subject of self-interested discussion. The Chinese are not sure of the answer, but they are certain the United States is suffering from the triple plagues of debt, distraction, and global overreach.

The Chinese like to overstate our dependency on them. American politicians want to understate it. But the fact is we need them as much as they need Wal-Mart. Under these circumstances, American efforts to stop China from becoming a "peer competitor" are bound to fail. We can delay the day, but we can't stop it. If we view our relationship with China as a zero-sum game, in which one nation is on top, and one is pursuing the brass ring, the relationship will be defined by a constant series of confrontations.

That strategy simply does not make sense. If American exceptionalism meets Chinese exceptionalism, we'll end up in two camps. The best thing we have going for us right now is that the relationship with China is fundamentally unlike the old relationship with the Soviet Union. The coin of the realm is not the number of strategic weapons, but the number of strategic partnerships. That means encouraging more purchases like Lenovo's buyout of the personal computer division of IBM. It means letting more Chinese engineers into the country, even at the risk of displacing some American jobs. The more China is invested in America, the more likely it is to think twice about confrontation. As one of America's top intelligence officials said to me about cyberwarfare, "I'm more worried about Russian teenagers than I am about the Chinese Army. You think twice about shutting down our Federal Reserve if you've got a few hundred billion tied up in Treasury bills."

None of this intermingling of interests guarantees peace and harmony. After all, Germany went to war with France and Britain twice in the first half of the twentieth century, despite deep commercial interconnections. Yet in China's case, there is an additional incentive to avoid conflict. The Communist Party knows that preserving internal stability—and its own hold on power—depends on the country's ability to keep exporting. That's why the Party itself has absorbed into its ranks so many entrepreneurs, university students, and professionals—the people who forty years ago would have been sent to camps to be "reeducated." Without trade, without rising prosperity, that stability is threatened.

"This is a very reflective party," David Shambaugh, a longtime China scholar, said at the opening of the Olympics. "They are adaptive, reflective, and open, within limits. But survival is the bottom line. And they see survival as an outcome of adaptation."[12]

That survival instinct gives President Obama a surprising amount of leverage with the Chinese—if only he can learn to use it.

America has an opportunity to rewrite the first big diplomatic engagement between America and Beijing: the "Open Door Policy" first created by John Hay, Lincoln's personal secretary during the Civil War and the secretary of state just as America was becoming a power in the Pacific with the annexation of the Philippines. At the time it seemed that many European countries would seek to partition a weak China. Hay sought everyone's agreement to preserve China's territorial rights, an effort that failed when the Japanese couldn't help themselves and seized Manchuria.

The new Open Door Policy has to work in reverse: It has to open *our* doors wider to China, in return for a Chinese agreement not to carve up Asia, global energy supplies, outer space, or the atmosphere to satisfy its own growth agenda. We have much that the Chinese desperately want: universities that are brimming with ideas, companies that are developing new technologies. That gives the new president leverage. But he has to learn how to use it and learn how to move fast, because the Chinese are placing their bets all over the globe.

In 2003, the year of the Iraq invasion, China's investments in foreign mergers and acquisitions totaled a couple of billion dollars a year. By 2008 those investments hit $45 billion, more than half of that amount in companies around the world that can provide China with natural resources, from Australia to Syria.[13] They've been busy in Brazil, buying up iron ore and timber and manganese, along with copper in Chile, a country that now sends more of its exports to China than to the United States. And they have been very busy in the Sudan and Chad, one of the most isolated corners of Africa, buying the rights to vast new exploration zones and promising that unlike the preachy Americans they will offer no lectures on human rights. Nigeria, Angola, and the Ivory Coast all have embraced the Chinese investment boom, in part because its cash comes free of the restrictions attached to loans from the World Bank and the International Monetary Fund. (Chinese firms are building a new capital for the Ivory Coast, in the wonderfully named Yamoussoukro, just as they built a new capital for East Timor.) The residents of Khartoum, Sudan's dusty capital, point to their paved roads—something many Sudanese have never seen before—as the product of deals struck with Beijing, not with Western financial institutions. In northern Cambodia, Chinese firms are building bridges across the Mekong to their new Silk Road, a 1,200-mile route down to the Gulf of Thailand.

China isn't pursuing these ventures because the Great Hall of the People has suddenly been taken over by the Sisters of Charity. It is extracting what Beijing hopes will be exclusive deals that will ensure a steady supply of oil and commodities to fuel Shanghai and Guangdong, even if global energy crises hit. "They are buying long-term supplies wherever they find them, including in unsavory places like Sudan, Iran, and Burma, where we won't buy," Bush's former China adviser, Michael Green, said to me. "They say it is benign, because they don't interfere with the internal affairs of other nations. And we say it is anything but benign."

Yet astoundingly, the Bush administration fired only one warning shot about this practice, just before Hu Jintao arrived in Washington in 2006. That visit is remembered mostly for a series of diplomatic disasters on the South Lawn, when ceremonies for the state visit opened with the announcement of the playing of the national anthem for the Republic of China—the formal name for Taiwan. The Chinese delegation nearly walked out. A few minutes later a protester from Falun Gong interrupted Hu's speech with shouts. Hu paused for a long while, as if to say, "I'll wait a few moments while you shoot this miscreant," but Bush nudged Hu to go on.

The administration's warning to China about its efforts to scoop up the world's energy supplies was buried in a revision of the National Security Strategy in 2006. The document, approved by Bush, explicitly cautioned China's leaders against "acting as if they can somehow 'lock up' energy supplies around the world or seek to direct markets rather than opening them up, as if they can follow a mercantilism borrowed from a discredited era."[14]

As the Chinese quickly pointed out, mercantilism was a European and an American invention, and a series of weak Chinese regimes were on the receiving end of it a century ago. But curiously, Bush himself never issued a public complaint beyond that single line in the National Security Strategy, a document read mostly by diplomats, policy wonks, and professors. "With the Chinese," Stephen Hadley said when I raised the question, "some things are better done privately."

Perhaps so, but history suggests that China responds, grudgingly, to public pressure. It has begun to pressure the Sudanese government about Darfur because of international criticism. It releases imprisoned human-rights leaders when the heat gets too high. And it has embraced environmental cleanup largely because of public protests.

For the next president, it is this last category—climate change and environmental cleanup—that affords the greatest opportunity for an alliance with both New and Old China, if only we seize the chance.

Hardly a week goes by without some group in the United States, Europe, or Asia issuing a report enumerating the terrifying statistics about China's growth, starting with a thousand new cars on the roads around Beijing every day. So many new cement factories are being constructed that the country is now using half of all the cement made in the world and spewing out toxic dust and smog along the way. Satellites are beginning to track those deadly clouds as they move around the globe.

In April 2006, researchers who sample air on the tops of mountains in Oregon and Washington began to pick up sulfur compounds and carbon residue that they traced back to coal plants across the Pacific. When air filters in Lake Tahoe start turning black with Chinese particulates, globalization takes on a very different, darker hue.[15]

Remarkably, the Chinese are now openly acknowledging the environmental problem, and that marks a dramatic change from just a few years ago. They don't like to hear specific numbers about the costs of their growth—particularly the World Bank's estimate that pollution leads to 750,000 premature deaths every year in China—but they have started publishing their own stark warnings about the dangers of doing nothing.[16] Of course, while the national government says all the right words, local officials and businesses are still buying up wildly inefficient old steel mills from ThyssenKrupp in Germany and moving them halfway around the world to increase the economic growth of their provinces.[17] That is the reality of modern-day life in China: centralized instructions from the top, decentralized resistance below.

But for Washington and Beijing, rarely has there been such a ripe chance to forge a profitable collaboration. China is desperate for clean-coal technologies, new, low-emission power plants, nuclear power, and expensive experiments in carbon sequestration—pumping carbon emissions back into the earth or sea. American companies, of course, will complain at first that they can't run the risk that the Chinese will steal some of their technology. But it is a risk we will have to take—because it is the only way into the market.

The Chinese, of course, will argue that the United States polluted the world for decades when its industrial base was growing, so it needs some patience—say, a century or so—while China catches up. But that argument is already being chipped away as Chinese entrepreneurs embrace clean-energy technologies that also save them money by running plants more efficiently. The central problem will be who pays the bill for all this technology. It's difficult to imagine Congress, strapped by demands to pay for Wall Street's sins and new health-care programs, agreeing to finance environmental projects that will benefit Chinese companies.

"We're going to say you are the developed country and we are the developing country," a senior Chinese diplomat in Washington said to me one day. "And you're going to say, 'Yes, but we're broke.' I'm not sure how we get past that." That may be where President Obama begins his dialogue with the Chinese.

PRESIDENCIES ARE ABOUT setting priorities. Bush got several of his China priorities right: He coaxed the Chinese into dealing with North Korea (the process was better than the results), and he ignored members of his own party who were eager to make China the enemy. But when it came to energy policy, he favored showing off prototypes of hydrogen-powered cars instead of putting real money into alternative energy research.

His biggest mistake was wasting years denying, then ignoring, the science around climate change. Imagine what he could have done for the image of the United States around the world if he had championed an American-subsidized program to sell China far more efficient, far less polluting coal-fired power plants. During the height of the Chinese boom—which roughly matched the years Bush was most absorbed in Iraq—the United States could have been at the forefront of a global effort to help China grow at 10 percent per year without adding the equivalent of Britain's carbon emissions. No single action would have done more to combat global warming. No single action would have done more to promote American exports. Yet Bush never tested the Chinese or pushed them. He could have launched a truly broad program with Beijing to cap our emissions together—with the world's largest economy and the world's largest new consumer of energy each bearing a share of the cost, and each benefiting from the creation of the hottest new industry on Earth. There would be no better way to encourage the rise of New China. There were many lost opportunities in the Iraq years; this one may have been the most consequential.

Eight weeks before the presidential election in 2008, five former secretaries of state gathered at George Washington University to talk about the agenda for the next president. They disagreed on much, from how to handle Iran to how to pursue Mideast peace. But they agreed on one thing: The Chinese will not move on environmental cleanup until we force the issue.

"You're not going to get it done if the president of the United States doesn't lead the charge," one of the former secretaries said. The other four—Henry Kissinger, Madeleine Albright, Colin Powell, and Warren Christopher—nodded in agreement. The speaker was James A. Baker III, the man who led the legal team that, in 2000, won the recount in Florida for George W. Bush.

Compared to the other problems the next president faces, the China problem is a blessing. It does not require the threat of confrontation, and it may not require a huge investment beyond what we would make anyway in energy technology. It is all about leadership, partnership, and confidence—the confidence that America is strong enough to manage the rise of another superpower and secure enough not to become paranoid about the prospect that America's lead over one of its biggest competitors is shrinking. Over time that was bound to happen. It isn't a sign of weakness. It's a sign of progress.

# PART VI

❖

# THE THREE VULNERABILITIES

# CHAPTER 14

# DETERRENCE 2.0

*The bomb was in the back of a Mini.*

*The car was parked in the lot on the edge of the Reflecting Pool, just across from the Jefferson Memorial, where locals and tourists parked to stroll through the cherry blossoms. Between the trees on the path around the calm waters, you can sometimes see the Truman Balcony of the White House, just off the president's living quarters.*

*The weapon the terrorists had put together was remarkably simple. The basic design was Los Alamos circa 1944, similar to the one sketched out by Manhattan Project scientists. It was relatively straightforward, two small hemispheres of highly enriched uranium sitting inside either end of an old artillery tube. When smashed together, the hemispheres would initiate a nuclear reaction, a smaller and more primitive version of the bomb dropped on Hiroshima.[1]*

*The detonation system was Baghdad circa 2006, the same kind of remote-triggering, via cell phones, that made it so easy for militants to plant and detonate roadside IEDs.*

*It took two years and considerable stealth and sophisticated bribery schemes to put together enough chunks of highly enriched uranium—30 kilograms in all—to make the bomb. In the end, sleeper agents in Pakistan's weapons labs made all the difference.[2] By comparison, getting the components into the United States was a breeze. The uranium was shipped in a few kilos at a time, heavily shielded, mixed in with old industrial parts; the terrorists were betting that the technology the Bush administration had deployed in the days after 9/11 for domestic nuclear detection was fundamentally useless for detecting weapons fuel. Their assumption was correct. Once the various shipments made it inside the United States—one across an obscure back road through the open border between Maine and Canada, another through one of the busiest crossings on the Mexican border— UPS handled the rest of delivery, bringing the boxes one by one to a suburban house in New Jersey. The "gun-type" device was assembled in the basement, put tenderly into a crate, and driven to Washington.*

*Scouts had surveyed the city and determined that parking near the White House was too risky. The Secret Service had a heavy presence, and a fully loaded nuclear detection truck was permanently parked at one end of West Executive Avenue, its sensors arrayed on the roof.*

*Instead the terrorists settled on the parking lot near the Jefferson Memorial, where the images of devastation would be dramatic. This was, in the end, more about creating televised chaos than about causing casualties. It was early April, and the cherry blossoms were in full bloom, drawing tourists, joggers, lovers, and hot-dog vendors to the pathways around the Tidal Basin. The trees were a gift from the Japanese early in the twentieth century, and survived efforts during World War II to have them chopped down. They were a symbol of friendship, sur- vivors of a challenge to American power that had started with the surprise attack at Pearl Harbor and ended, three and a half years later, with the only two deto- nations of nuclear weapons on civilian populations. Until now.*

*When it went off, it was nothing like Hiroshima or Nagasaki. Like the North Korean nuclear test in 2006, it was half explosion, half fizzle. But the North Ko- reans conducted their test deep in a cave. This one happened within view of the blue Oval Room in the White House, where tourists making their way through public rooms saw the flash outside the windows. They survived, at least the initial explosion, because the deadly radiation ring stopped just short of the South Lawn. But in milliseconds the Reflecting Pool was gone, and there was no sign of the tourists, the hot-dog vendors, or the black-barked cherry trees. The memorial was blackened but half standing; the statue of Jefferson was melted on one side.*

*The president was out of town. Just like President Bush on the morning of 9/11, his successor had a difficult time getting reliable, real-time information. The only thing he knew for sure was that a thousand miles away, the capital of the United States was burning for the first time since the British invaded in 1812. The city's residents had not been instructed to find out which way the wind was blow- ing—the most important single piece of information for determining whether people should flee or seek shelter for two or three days in their basements or the subways. So they jumped in their vehicles, triggering deadly traffic jams as the fallout began to descend. Everything ground to a halt; parents were unable to get to their children at school; emergency vehicles were immobilized.*

The newly built Continuity of Government center, off Route 66 in Virginia, became the new capital. Inside that underground facility officials watched helplessly as a single square mile of devastation—a horror, but a contained horror—created a global panic in major cities and in world financial markets.

As images of the National Mall engulfed in flames were being broadcast around the world, Al Jazeera began playing a tape that had mysteriously appeared at the network's headquarters. In it, a young, round-faced, bearded man, describing himself as the leader of an obscure militant group, began ticking off a long list of America's alleged offenses. Then he added, "This was our first weapon, but not our last. Tomorrow afternoon, a similar bomb will go off in Los Angeles. If Americans have not left Afghanistan by the weekend and swear never again to enter the tribal lands of our ancestors, New York will suffer the same fate. If you attack us, know that we have planted more devices, in Atlanta, Chicago, and Dallas. Our fellow martyrs are living among you, and they know what to do."

A bluff? Probably. Getting enough nuclear material for a single bomb is incredibly difficult, and the early indications were that this was a "subkiloton" explosion, a fraction of what went off at Hiroshima or Nagasaki. The national security adviser told the president that the intelligence community doubted that the terrorists had enough fuel for a second bomb.

But such estimates didn't matter. In America's biggest cities, the panicked exodus began. While a parade of officials—most never before seen by Americans—urged calm, and warned that more people would be killed evacuating the cities than died in the initial attack, no one listened. Even the president was unconvincing as he urged everyone to stay home. After all, he wasn't home, so why should they be?

The explosion wasn't intended to wipe out Washington. It was designed to create a chain reaction of terror and economic meltdown. The terrorists' investment in the device, bribes included, was $525,000. As world markets plummeted and credit markets froze, they knew that the cost to the West would be measured in the trillions of dollars.

Within hours a white-suited "nuclear attribution" unit from the Pentagon headed into the new Ground Zero to gather radioactive samples that might indicate where the bomb originated—an urgent issue if the government had any hope of *stopping a second attack. The scientists conducting the investigation knew that testing could take days or weeks, though the White House was demanding answers now, and on Fox News, two commentators were declaring that the president must order the annihilation of whichever country was responsible for providing the bomb material, wittingly or not.*

*The Russian and Pakistani governments had already sent assurances that all their nuclear material was accounted for, along with offers of help. Their truthfulness was hard to assess. But the White House would need their help urgently in coming days to determine if the terrorists' claim that they posessed more weapons was plausible.*

*"You know," the president said to his national security adviser, "during the Cuban Missile Crisis, at least Kennedy knew who to threaten. Would one of you geniuses tell me who I'm supposed to talk to? Or how you bomb a country that probably didn't know its nukes were missing?"*

THE MAN with the job of keeping this horror—and twenty easily imagined variants of it—from ever being realized sits in an office in downtown Washington, D.C., that is, by his own admission, within the blast zone.

"What's even more hilarious," says Vayl Oxford, a trim, fifty-six-year-old former Air Force officer with short-cropped hair and a bit of a twinkle in his eye, "is that our evacuation plan for this building calls for everyone to go that way . . ." He gestured out the window, toward the nearest subway stop. "We head toward the White House," he said with a tight smile. "We may need to revamp our plans."

That is not the only plan Vayl Oxford has tried—with only limited success—to revamp since he settled into his office on the twelfth floor of a bland glass office building whose other occupants include lobbyists and trade associations. If you wandered in off the elevators and looked around the Department of Homeland Security's Domestic Nuclear Detection Office, you might think the employees were selling insurance. It doesn't look like the place created by the Bush administration to prevent a nuclear 9/11.

The truth is that things are not going very well in the

Armageddon-prevention business. Oxford *is* selling a form of insurance; he oversees the construction of the last line of defense against the entry of a bomb—or the fuel for one—into the United States. The employees in the cubicles are in charge of designing, testing, purchasing, and deploying the detectors that are supposed to ring the alarm if a truck coming into Manhattan through the Lincoln Tunnel is carrying a nuclear weapon. They are setting up the "portals" that scan containers at the giant port at Long Beach, California, and in the cargo hold at Kennedy Airport. They don't have much margin for error. If a weapon makes it as far as their detectors, it means the "layered defense" system that the Bush administration designed in 9/11's aftermath has already failed, probably more than once.

The first layer belongs to the intelligence agencies, which are monitoring phone calls and e-mails around the world and paying informants, in hopes of getting some warning of a pending plot. Cargo headed to the United States, and elsewhere, is supposed to be scanned before it leaves ports in Europe and Asia. Manifests are supposed to be checked, with special attention to anything that wasn't packed by a "trusted carrier." The detectors at the ports and in the tunnels are the last layer. If they fail to sound the alarm, the bomb is in a basement—or a parked car.

That's the plan, anyway. The reality is a little different.

In September 2008—as Capitol Hill was consumed with designing the bailout bill to save reeling financial institutions—Oxford had to acknowledge to a Senate subcommittee that the government's detection programs had gone seriously awry. The aging technology that the Bush administration rushed into place after 9/11 to provide some measure of reassurance was based on 1980s designs and was never intended to detect a nuclear weapon.

The current detectors are, as Oxford puts it, "basically big Geiger counters" built for industries that need to make sure that irradiated scrap metal does not make it into factories. He describes those outdated detectors with care because their shortcomings are classified so that potential terrorists don't understand what is detectable and what is not. But Oxford notes, "if you had HEU [highly enriched uranium] in traditional cargo, the current system would have great difficulty in detecting the amount of material we are told we would have to identify." Put more simply, the old detectors simply can't pick up a few kilograms of the most common bomb fuel that terrorists would likely employ. When pressed, Oxford concedes that if you put Little Boy—the atomic bomb that destroyed Hiroshima in 1945—through one of the existing radiation detectors, it probably wouldn't set off alarms. The casing of the bomb itself would probably create enough shielding. I went to another nuclear expert who does not work for the government—but once did—to ask him if this could be true. He stopped for a moment, and said: "Five 'Little Boys' wouldn't register with the junk we've put at the ports."

That is not to say the system is useless. There are cargoes that do set off the current detectors. Giant loads of bananas coming into the United States from Latin America trigger alarms all the time; the high potassium levels give off trace amounts of radiation. Slabs of granite, imported to remodel kitchens from Scarsdale to Beverly Hills, frequently emit a radioactive signature. So do porcelain toilets. Kitty litter makes the needle on the big detectors hop, and so does wood from trees that grew downwind from Chernobyl. It should be no surprise that at the port of Los Angeles/Long Beach, there are 400 to 600 false alarms a day—115,000 a year. In fact, the sensors currently deployed will pick up almost anything that is radioactive, except for an atom bomb.

"You can't change the laws of physics," said Lisa Gordon-Hagerty, who tackled this problem for both the Clinton and Bush administrations. "The reality is that a real weapon doesn't create much of a radioactive signature." It is one of those inconvenient facts that President Bush neglected to mention when he, and other members of the administration, boasted that 98 percent of the 11 million cargo containers that enter the United States are now "screened." It was a carefully worded claim—one deliberately designed to leave Americans (and terrorists) with the impression that in the post-9/11 age, we've solved the problem of detecting a nuclear device or fuel hidden in a cargo container. We haven't—but if someone attempts to attack America with kitchen countertops, the Department of Homeland Security has us covered.

Technology problems aside, there are many other obstacles to detecting nuclear material—starting with the first line of defense, which is overseas. The Bush administration made much of its "Megaports" initiative, which is supposed to scan cargo as it is being loaded onto ships bound for the United States. The plan makes a lot of sense, because by the time the cargo pulls into the port of Long Beach, it may be too late to stop the attack.

But it turns out that many countries don't want U.S. Customs inspectors on their territory, and working at their ports. Shippers don't want to slow the process of loading the ships—time is money, and inspections take time. And of course the scanning equipment we are installing around the world doesn't pierce containers any better than the scanning equipment we are installing at home.

Just as the Bush administration was winding down in October 2008, Michael Chertoff, the secretary of homeland security, told Congress that it was impossible—and maybe even unwise—to fulfill the legislative mandate to make sure all cargo is scanned for radioactivity while it is still abroad. Instead, he said the focus should be on improving the "trusted shipper" program and the review of manifests detailing the contents of every container. And just as most people worry more about street crime in rough neighborhoods than in leafy suburbs, Chertoff seemed more worried about loose nukes in some parts of the world than in others. "I'm not terribly concerned someone's going to build a nuclear bomb in England" and smuggle it into the United States, he said. "But I might be more concerned about South Asia."[3]

Somehow, Chertoff's reassuring words didn't make me sleep

much better. Anyone smart enough to make a bomb is probably smart enough to figure out that you don't want to ship it directly out of Pyongyang or Natanz. The containers transporting the centrifuges A. Q. Khan built for the Libyans (in Malaysia, not a place Mr. Chertoff might worry about very much) were transferred at least once, from one freighter to another, in Dubai.

So in 2012, the year Congress mandated this effort be complete, the "layered defense" envisioned by the Bush administration will still be as porous as a coffee filter. But there has been some progress. New York City—recognizing that it is target number one—has roughly 1,000 officers a day moving around the five boroughs with mobile detection units and radiation wands. Greeting parties are sent out to cargo ships when they enter New York Harbor—and are still far from the city—to inspect incoming ships. "It works better than you might think," said Richard Falkenrath, who was a homeland defense official inside the White House before he took command of the effort for the New York City Police Department. He had praise for Oxford's operation. "You hear a lot of horror stories about the Department of Homeland Security, but the domestic nuclear detection guys do a pretty good job."

Oxford's office now spends $500 million a year struggling to find solutions to the myriad problems with detection. Considering the importance of the mission, it's worth questioning whether that budget is woefully inadequate. In 2008, we were spending $12 billion a month in Iraq, a war that was originally justified as a way to keep a nuclear 9/11 from happening on our soil.[4] If you asked most Americans whether they think that even a twentieth of that amount might be better spent on detectors that had a chance of telling the difference between Little Boy and kitty litter, I suspect I know how they would answer.

The closest thing to a solution is a new generation of detectors, called Advanced Spectroscopic Portal monitors, or ASPs, in acronym-crazed Washington. They are not just big Geiger counters. The ASP was designed to solve the banana and kitty litter problem by discriminating between harmless sources of radiation and potentially dangerous ones.

Similar detectors have been operating at the White House for several years, as I once discovered after making the mistake of taking a medical test involving a radioactive isotope and then going to an appointment in the West Wing. I got no farther than just inside the main doors when alarms started blasting, and a Secret Service agent moved in on me. With one phone call to a command center—and one eye on my briefcase—the agent learned exactly which isotope had triggered the alarm, and knew that it was one used for medical purposes. Everyone relaxed, save for the fact that they couldn't figure out how to turn off the sirens.

The good news is that Oxford wants to protect America's cities with the kind of technology that safeguards the West Wing against radioactive journalists. The bad news is that even the newest detectors have many of the same problems when it comes to finding a well-shielded lump of highly enriched uranium. Like the old detectors, the ASPs can be fooled. As Thomas Cochran, a scientist with the Natural Resources Defense Council and a critic of the administration's efforts, told Congress, a terrorist who knew what he was doing could "defeat these systems almost 100 percent of the time." Fortunately, most terrorists don't know what they are doing. But that was not exactly the kind of reassuring message the Bush administration wanted to advertise.

If, by a stroke of good luck, the ASPs do find a radioactive shipment, they should be able to tell the difference between the granite countertop you just ordered from Home Depot and a 10-kiloton bomb. Yet by the time Bush left office, seven years after 9/11, there was a raging argument over whether the ASP technology was worth the price. Not a single next-generation detector had been deployed in an American port. A couple of them were being tested. A backup system, designed to X-ray cargo to determine if part of a shipment has been shielded to defeat the radiation detectors, was shelved as too expensive, too inaccurate, and too slow. The bottom line is that at America's borders, it is probably as easy to ship a few kilograms of HEU into the country as it is to ship in a few kilograms of heroin.

"Failure is not an acceptable option," Senator Joseph Lieberman warned Oxford during a hearing in 2008. "I want to know what's transpired over the last two years which has left us basically where we were two years ago."[5]

OXFORD BEGAN looking at America's post–Cold War nuclear defenses when he was in the White House in the panicky years after the 9/11 attacks. "It was a mess," he told me one day in his office. "Here we knew there was a low-probability chance of a truly catastrophic event, and there was no real government plan."

Today there is a semblance of a plan. But as Oxford is the first to volunteer, "there is more to be done than just scanning containers," or even meeting ships before they enter New York Harbor. "We are not even close" to managing the threat, he says.

When I went to see Oxford, he had just spent the preceding few days examining one of the many holes in the net of defenses. He asked what if someone flew a nuclear weapon into the United States on a private plane—and detonated it in the air over a major city, rather than landing at an airport? No one had a reassuring answer to his question. "My worry is that you wouldn't even have to land the jet," Oxford noted.

America's domestic detection infrastructure, he pointed out, depends on trying to keep track of shipments before they leave a foreign port and then inspecting them once they arrive. But as any pilot of a private jet—and many passengers—will tell you, most countries make assumptions about the safety of private aviation that they would never make about the commercial sector. (The White House press corps can testify to this fact. Although our baggage and cameras were always searched before we went aboard *Air Force One*, at the airport closest to the president's ranch we walked aboard our chartered jet without ever passing through a metal detector.) Oxford, ever the pragmatist, soon began focusing on a program to screen private jets that take off from abroad before they depart for the States. Of course, the plan requires tremendous confidence in the skills and focus of foreign inspectors.

THE PROBLEM of defending the homeland is complicated by the fact that many departments in the U.S. government seem to have a piece of the Armageddon business. Yet no one really runs the show.

The Department of Homeland Security and the FBI are supposed to deal with threats inside the United States—tracking down terrorists and detecting, finding, and disabling weapons. But the Energy Department has most of the expertise in these matters, including the nuclear-emergency response teams that are the stuff of so many movie dramas, and the "render safe" teams, meant to defuse weapons, described to me by one Energy Department official as "one of those jobs that make it hard for you to buy life insurance."

While the Pentagon is responsible for thinking about how to reduce the threat, the intelligence agencies have created a new "counterproliferation center," part think tank, part "action tank," where officials can cull all of their knowledge about how to stop terrorists from obtaining the most powerful weapons in the world. Ken Brill, the lanky diplomat who runs the center, tries to put together the government's many pockets of expertise—at the CIA and the Defense Intelligence Agency, inside the Energy Department and the National Laboratories, at the largely defunct Arms Control and Disarmament Agency, and at the State Department—as they try to come up with new ways of defeating rogue states and terrorists.

Brill used to be America's representative to the IAEA, meaning he understands the limitations of inspections of countries determined to hide their weapons programs. "I'd rather not rely on that," he said to me. "We have to develop our own ways to find out. That's what intelligence agencies are all about."

Who puts all these different elements together to avoid the

kind of turf battles that contributed to the failure to find and thwart the 9/11 plotters? No one. Bush signed more than thirty presidential directives that dealt with some aspect of combating WMD, but many of them were overlapping, inconsistent, or integrated with the previous directives. One of the main conclusions of the 9/11 Commission was that the United States desperately needed a single senior official, inside the White House, with the president's ear, who has the responsibility of ensuring that everything is being done to prevent a devastating attack on the country—and who has thought at length about how the United States should respond if a bomb does go off. President Bush signed the legislation to create the job in August 2007. As his term approached its last two months, he had yet to appoint someone to the post.

"It's incredible to me," said Rolf Mowatt-Larssen, the Energy Department's intelligence chief, who met with Bush many times during the nuclear terror scares of the first term. "You want somebody right by the president's elbow who knows this stuff. Because it's more likely to happen now than it was in the Cold War."

WHEN GEORGE BUSH was running for president in 2000, he made clear he was thinking about the evolving nature of nuclear weapons. In a speech in May of that year in Washington, he declared that "the emerging security threats to the United States . . . now come from rogue states, terrorist groups, and other adversaries seeking weapons of mass destruction, and the means to deliver them. Threats also come from insecure nuclear stockpiles and the proliferation of dangerous technologies."[6] He sounded as if he was preparing to remake American nuclear strategy as soon as he took office. "The Cold War logic that led to the creation of massive stockpiles on both sides is now outdated." Bush proclaimed, "We should not keep weapons that our military planners do not need. These unneeded weapons are the expensive relics of dead conflicts. And they do nothing to make us more secure."

Eight years later, after a war fought against one of the only rogue states not driving toward a weapon, and after more than a few panic attacks about terrorists with bombs, it's worth assessing how Bush performed on his own set of goals. The answer is that, as in so many things in his presidency, he got off to a fast start and then forgot what he was trying to accomplish.

Bush's first step was to abandon the Anti–Ballistic Missile Treaty, angering the Russians and displaying the administration's contempt for international agreements. Though this decision led to predictions of disaster, it did not result in the antimissile arms race that Bush's many critics anticipated. Bush let Powell quickly negotiate a major arms reduction agreement with Putin, the Strategic Offensive Reductions Treaty, which the two presidents signed inside the Kremlin with considerable fanfare. Both men hailed the agreement as a simpler, faster, more cordial model for dispensing with the problem. Nuclear weapons were no longer the centerpiece of Washington's relations with Moscow. It was the right move, and it had the potential to be a great start to reshaping the relationship.

But almost as soon as the treaty was signed, all the energy went out of the effort. Both countries shrank their arsenals, but they never had the follow-on talks that might have allowed them to get down toward a truly minimum deterrent. They never fully engaged with the Chinese, the one major power that is beginning to increase the size and sophistication of its arsenal and a player that clearly needs to be part of any larger agreement to reduce the nuclear threat. The failure to follow up was a huge mistake. As Russia became richer and more nationalistic, its relations with Washington became frostier. By the end of Bush's presidency, Russia had resumed occasional "bomber patrols"—one of the most memorable symbols of the Cold War—and, in 2008, began giving speeches about building a more potent nuclear arsenal. Whatever momentum Bush had created was lost.

Putin's aggressiveness was matched by Bush's seeming indifference to the issue after the Moscow Treaty was signed. One might think that when four serious cold warriors—Henry A. Kissinger, George P. Shultz, Sam Nunn, and William Perry—come together to argue that the United States can now safely begin to negotiate its way down to an arsenal of zero weapons, eliminating the weapons all four helped to amass, the president of the United States might be interested in hearing out their logic. Instead, Bush barely engaged with them and never publicly addressed their central argument: that if the United States is going to get other nations to give up nuclear ambitions, it is going to have to move in the direction of deep reductions. There are legitimate counterarguments to be made, but Bush never articulated them. He was simply absent from the debate.

That became clear in the winter of 2007, when a group of Russians and Americans, Nunn included, went to see Bush at the White House as part of an annual high-level exchange program between the two countries.

"The Russians started talking about this effort, and then Nunn explained briefly the elements of the plan," one participant in the conversation told me later. Nunn noted that the president himself had often pointed out that the threat America faces had changed and he had embraced the goals of deeper arms reductions. He noted Bush's call for a halt on new countries going into the enrichment business and had expanded American efforts to lock down weapons and fuel around the world. (That program is named for Nunn and Senator Richard Lugar, who created the effort immediately after the end of the Cold War.) A courtly Southerner, Nunn was very diplomatic, but he made it clear that Bush and other world leaders had failed to follow through on their grand pronouncements. With the exception of the program to speed up the securing of nuclear material in Russia, there was no schedule, no diplomatic push, no leadership on the issue. And this was Bush's signature goal—making sure weapons and nuclear fuel were kept out of the hands of terrorists.

"It was really astonishing—here we were, sitting in the Roosevelt Room, yards from the Oval Office, and we were talking about how we could dismantle the threat that hung over our lives for seventy years," an observer to the conversation noted. And Bush, he said, "couldn't have shown less interest. He jotted a few notes, looked up over his glasses—and then he asked a question about something else." (Nunn had a different memory, saying that he thought the president *had* listened.)

Perhaps Bush's failure to lead the charge to drive down the size of the American and Russian arsenals grew out of his belief that America could never let another country become a "peer competitor" that could challenge American power. Inside the Bush White House, Hadley and other aides argued that retaining American supremacy meant keeping upward of 1,200 to 1,500 nuclear weapons in our arsenals. "Do you really want the Chinese to feel they have equivalent power?" one of Bush's aides asked me one afternoon. "Do you really want the Iranians to think, 'Gee, if we get to three hundred, we can be a superpower too?'" Bush, another official said, respected Kissinger and Shultz, two lions of the Republican foreign policy establishment, "but on this one, he thinks they don't understand what we're up against."

THOUGH HE WAS suspicious of arms control treaties, Bush deserves credit for making progress in one area: counterproliferation. In the years after 9/11, the White House feverishly churned out new strategies to combat weapons of mass destruction, and the president signed new, classified "National Security Directives" to move the bureaucracy into action. The Proliferation Security Initiative, which joined countries together to interdict weapons on the high seas or in the air, was so innovative that both Senator Obama and Senator McCain praised the project and promised to continue it. With U.S. pressure there was a UN resolution requiring all countries to lock down their loose nuclear material (few have complied). Congress agreed to pay for radiation portals at key land crossings around the world, many concentrated in Eastern Europe, where the bulk of the more than 1,000 cases of illegal trafficking in nuclear materials have occurred over the past fifteen years. The detectors, of course, suffer from the same limitations as the technology used in the United States. But they are better than nothing. Bush also created another program, the "Global Threat Reduction Initiative," a project designed to reduce and protect vulnerable nuclear material at civilian sites worldwide, and joined up with Russia to create a "Global Initiative to Combat Nuclear Terrorism," building the capacity of partner nations to improve accounting, control, and security of nuclear materials.

Astoundingly, Bush did little to prepare the country for the need for this new kind of nuclear deterrence. After A. Q. Khan's arrest, Bush gave a major speech describing a series of sensible ways to keep new countries from adding to the world's oversupply of nuclear material, including international "fuel banks" that would sell the fuel to any country that wanted to build nuclear power plants—and would take back the waste product to make sure it isn't turned into bombs. But he put little effort into the diplomacy to make the plan work, and it was quietly shelved by the allies.

As the Bush administration prepared to leave office, it assembled a sizable inventory of these and other projects to hand off to its successors. "It's a good list," Hadley told me one day in September 2008.

Yet the programs were wildly underfunded. One member of an independent commission that examined the programs noted that "the Global Threat Reduction Initiative, which provides a detailed list of the world's nuclear sites and weapons, so that the most vulnerable could be locked down first, has less federal manpower than a light infantry rifle company."[7] In 2008—seven years after President Bush told the country, "our highest priority is to keep terrorists from acquiring weapons of mass destruction"—Congress was informed that the list of places those terrorists could steal the weapons or fuel from was still being compiled.

As with so many projects in the Bush administration, ideology became the enemy of practical solutions. Making lists of vulnerable sites seemed a lot less urgent than invading Iraq to prevent Saddam Hussein from reconstituting a nuclear program the IAEA had largely dismantled.

At the end of his presidency, one big nuclear initiative seemed to catch Bush's interest: a plan to put missile defense in Poland and the Czech Republic, even at the cost of outraging the Russians. The system—referred to as "Rumsfeld's Revenge" inside the Pentagon—was supposed to deter the Iranians in case they ever developed a nuclear warhead to fit atop their long-range missiles, which could reach Israel or Europe. Bush sold the effort as an insurance policy—despite the fact that it was designed to counter a threat that does not yet exist, with a technology that may not work.

Not surprisingly the Russians were convinced the missile defenses were secretly aimed at them. So when Putin visited Bush at Kennebunkport, the summer home of the president's parents, the Russian leader offered to have the missile defenses installed on Russian territory, jointly manned and operated by American and Russian personnel. "It was a serious offer," one of Bush's senior aides, who was present for the meeting, told me later. "But the president never really considered it seriously, because there was a caveat." The condition: the United States could not build missile defenses on Russia's borders, particularly in Poland and the Czech Republic. The missile defenses could be inside Russia pointing out, but not outside Russia pointing in.

The Bush administration's excuse for rejecting Putin's offer out of hand was that Rumsfeld had already made a commitment to Poland and the Czech Republic. It was a thin argument—and a major mistake. Though Bush spent roughly $10 billion a year on missile defense—or about twenty times more than the government has dedicated to deploying domestic radiation detectors—the antimissile technology envisioned for Europe will not be deployed for years. It is simply not ready. Yet a deal with Putin would have put Washington and Moscow on the same side of the effort to contain Iran's nuclear ambitions. Suddenly, the two Cold War rivals would have been partners in designing a defense for Europe. Given what happened twelve months later—the Russian attack on Georgia—it's doubtful that Bush's successor will have a similar opportunity.

IN FEBRUARY 2008 Hadley revealed that Bush had quietly rewritten American deterrence policy but hadn't told anybody, including the terrorists he was seeking to deter. After a year and a half of debate inside the White House, Bush had decided that the threat he had made against North Korea—that he would hold North Korea "fully accountable" if it was found to be the source of a terrorist weapon—would now be expanded to the rest of the world.

"The president has approved a new declaratory policy to help deter terrorists from using weapons of mass destruction against the United States, our friends, and allies," Hadley told a small group at Stanford University. Under the president's new directive, he said, "the United States will hold any state, terrorist group, or other non-state actor fully accountable for supporting or enabling terrorist efforts to obtain or use weapons of mass destruction."[8] Back in the days of the Cold War, "fully accountable" suggested the United States reserved the right to use nuclear weapons in response. With this new policy, not only would states be held responsible, but in the aftermath of the revelations about A. Q. Khan, individuals would be held accountable as well. Their actions would justify retaliation on a grand scale if they assisted a terrorist group in obtaining a weapon of mass destruction. The directive invited a question that the White House declined to discuss: How do you threaten devastating retaliation against a group with no territory of its own, one that might be working out of a basement, armed with little more than a laptop? And what does it mean to be held "fully accountable" after North Korea shipped nuclear technology to Syria and has never been held accountable?

Few news organizations noted Hadley's declaration, which he repeated a few months later at a meeting in Washington on halting nuclear proliferation. Curiously, Bush himself never announced his decision, although it constituted one of the largest changes in American nuclear policy since the end of the Cold War. This was "declaratory policy" without a declaration. For a while there was talk of having the president give a speech on the subject, but his days in the White House were waning, and the country—and much of the world—had stopped listening to him. Markets were melting down. With Pakistan in chaos and relations with Russia slipping back toward open hostility, some feared he might seem to be pouring oil on a burning world.

When I asked the White House for a copy of the new policy, I was told that if it existed anywhere, it was probably classified. That's great, I said, but wasn't the whole point to have the president make a declaration that the world would notice—and heed? I was told I could dig up Hadley's speech on the White House website. A few days before the 2008 presidential election, the White House asked Robert Gates to amplify Hadley's declaration, and he did—finally generating some headlines. But Bush himself never issued the warning.

Imagine that. Five years ago, Bush talked incessantly about grave threats in the runup to a war against a dictator who did not possess weapons of mass destruction. He left office facing several countries that had these weapons or were building them, and said little about it. Perhaps there was no more vivid evidence of how Bush's credibility—and America's leverage—had diminished.

ON A BRILLIANT April day in 2007, when those cherry blossoms around the Jefferson Memorial were near their brilliant peak, about fifty of the top military, Homeland Security, and intelligence officials of the United States gathered in Washington to think anew about the unthinkable.

During the Cold War, Pentagon officials and civil defense analysts used to meet all the time to discuss what a full-scale nuclear exchange with the Soviet Union would look like. Fortunately, no one ever had to discover how accurate these forecasts were. But the challenges posed the day after a small nuclear device is detonated in an American city—an event everyone in the room said they thought was now far more likely than a nuclear exchange during the Cold War—were entirely different. The bombing itself would be horrible, everyone agreed, though not as horrible as a single Soviet weapon would have been.[9] But as the participants talked about how they or their organizations would react, it became evident that the government needed to think this one through again.

One Homeland Security official discussed the contingency plans for immediately putting some of their top officials on television or radio to give instructions about where the wind was blowing, who should stay in place, and who should flee the radioactive plume. "You realize," one of the participants said, "as soon as you guys go on television instead of the president, everyone's going to assume the president is dead?" From the response, it appeared that no one had thought much about that.

But the biggest discovery arose from the fact that the government's plans all focused on a single place and event into which emergency help would be poured—a new Ground Zero. "They thought it was going to be like Hurricane Katrina," said Ashton Carter, who helped organize the event. "And it won't. It will feel like it's an attack everywhere, because if San Francisco is hit, the next question will be whether to evacuate Washington."

"The terrorist who says he's got another weapon will have enormous credibility" even if it's a bluff, Carter noted. The financial impact will be instantaneous—and calamitous.

And more than ever, the United States will need its allies—and maybe even some enemies—to figure out whether additional weapons or fuel are missing, and where they might be. Threatening retaliation, Cold War–style, may be the first instinct for angry talking heads on television. But instant retaliation may not help us survive the worst moments of the Second Nuclear Age.

# CHAPTER 15

# THE INVISIBLE ATTACK

*They had gathered from around the country, 100,000 people marching along the San Francisco waterfront to protest what they believed to be an impending Israeli-American air attack on Iran's nuclear facilities. As protesters held aloft signs declaring* NO MORE IRAQS! *a few aging Hollywood stars lectured to the crowd, reminding everyone that they had failed to stop a war in 2003—and could not fail again. The San Francisco rally was the first of three scheduled for that weekend; the next day the scene would be repeated in Chicago and New York.*

*The protesters wanted to make sure they were heard, and vendors were ready with just the thing: air horns, which sent a blast from a canister of compressed air. All afternoon, the air horns blared—so loudly that people turned away. They did not see the mist as each canister was emptied.*

*These air horns, it turned out, were blasting out more than noise. Several of the canisters had been deliberately contaminated with* Yersinia pestis, *bacteria that, once inhaled, causes the pneumonic plague, which is fatal if untreated.*

*The attackers had time on their side. Although the symptoms of the plague can show up quickly, it initially resembles a cold or flu—headaches, coughing, a fever. And while San Francisco was one of the first cities equipped with detectors under the federal government's BioWatch program, the warning that an attack had occurred would not come for hours. Biodetectors don't go off like smoke detectors; a technician has to come around daily to remove a filter, and it takes hours to get the sample analyzed. That left plenty of time for repeat attacks in Chicago and New York, where more air horns were being handed out.[1]*

*It was Tuesday, a day after people began to fall ill and arrive at hospital emergency rooms, before the Centers for Disease Control began to figure out what had happened. Then the system kicked into action: Fortunately, the needed antibiotics—primarily streptomycin, gentamicin, or one of a number of tetracyclines—had been stockpiled in strategic warehouses across the country. Radio and television messages warned those with symptoms to go to the nearest hospital and cautioned everyone else on how to reduce their chances of exposure.*

*Still, the combination of hundreds of truly infected victims and millions who were concerned that they might have contracted a disease that sounded like the terror from the Middle Ages led to panic. Hospitals around the country were soon overwhelmed. Government officials offered reassurances that almost all of the patients who received the antibiotics relatively soon after exposure would be fine. They should have known that the statistics didn't matter. Millions feared they or their children would not get the antibiotics in time. Few went to work for fear of exposure to the disease. Schools were closed. People stayed out of supermarkets and malls. Even with the government doing just about everything right—telling people how to protect themselves, distributing medicine, isolating the sickest—the economy came to a screeching halt.*

SEVEN YEARS AFTER 9/11, the United States is in far better shape today to respond to a biological attack than it ever has been before. After the anthrax attacks in 2001, the government initiated a program called BioWatch that collects air samples to detect biological agents in the air above major cities across the United States. Life-saving drugs are strategically stockpiled around the country, even if there is still debate about the most effective way to distribute them. Yet despite these advances, we remain almost as vulnerable as before, largely because almost everything about a biological attack is different from other types of terrorism.

Though politicians tend to talk about nuclear and biological attacks in the same breath, they have almost nothing in common. We invest in nuclear detection to protect ourselves from a detonation; after it happens, it's way too late. Biological attacks are almost undetectable in real time. There's no boom, no mushroom cloud to tell you that an aerosol can has just dispersed anthrax or pneumonic plague. The dirty little secret of those BioWatch detectors is that they are designed to tell you what happened a few hours ago, not what's happening now.

To catch a bioterrorist, the authorities would have to get pretty lucky. Conventional explosives leave a residue on the clothing of a bomb-maker or a bomb-carrier. That, of course, is what airport security officials are looking for when they swab a briefcase or a piece of hand luggage and put it in a sniffing machine at security checkpoints. But if your briefcase contained a package of dry anthrax material, enough to kill thousands, the machines would detect nothing. The helpful guard from the Transportation Security Administration would hand you back your computer bag, apologize for delaying you, and wish you a safe flight.

The professionals in the business all understand that we probably won't be able to stop an attack from happening; the real question is how good we can be at mitigating the effects. But astoundingly, years after Dick Cheney took an emergency trip to the Centers for Disease Control to try to lock down America's biological vulnerability—probably his most constructive act in a largely destructive term in office—no politicians or Homeland Security officials want to explain the real dangers, or the plan, to the American people. The scenarios simply sound too scary, the government too helpless. Merely having the conversation would prompt speculation that government officials have evidence of an imminent attack, even if they didn't. But it's a conversation we cannot afford to ignore. If there is a nuclear attack, there's not much that ordinary citizens can do to protect themselves from the radiation; the choices are to lock yourself in your duct-taped basement or flee. If there is a biological attack, individuals can do plenty to protect themselves, especially if they are prepared and informed. But the Bush administration did not want to discuss the subject. They didn't even want to fund it: The one major program the administration created, which sought to train Americans on what to do during an attack and created a Medical Reserve Corps of professionals who could administer antibiotics, saw its funding halved during Bush's second term.*

Richard Danzig, who served as secretary of the Navy under President Clinton, captured the problem elegantly in a report he wrote in May 2008. After seven years of work, he concluded, the effort to defend Americans against bacteria, viruses, and toxins "is an agglomeration of tactics presented as a strategy."[2]

During the Clinton administration, Danzig had developed a fascination with the challenges of preparing for bioterrorism, and he negotiated an uneasy accord with the Bush administration that allowed him to keep pushing both government and academic institutions into action. By early 2007 Danzig had signed on as one of Barack Obama's top foreign-policy advisers, telling him he was convinced that the Illinois senator, then the longest of long shots, was the right man for the job. He also told Obama that he would almost certainly lose the Democratic nomination. "So much for my political predictions," the white-haired Danzig told me as the campaign wound down. "Maybe I should stick to biodefense."

Danzig had worked for a president whose interest in bioterrorism was piqued by reading a novel: Clinton reportedly asked the FBI to tell him whether a biological attack of the kind Richard Preston wrote about in *The Cobra Event* could actually happen.[3] But Clinton left his successor with a flurry of reports and few action plans, and until the 2001 anthrax attacks, the problem got little attention. When Bush's National Security Council was first forming, recalls Kenneth W. Bernard, a member of Clinton's national security staff who would later serve as Bush's special assistant for biodefense on the Homeland Security Council, "There was a general sense that health wasn't a real security issue."

It soon became one. In October 2001, an envelope arrived at the office of Tom Daschle, then the Senate majority leader, with a return

---

* The program funding went from about $40 million to about $20 million annually.

address for the nonexistent "4th Grade, Greensdale School." Another letter was mailed to Senator Patrick Leahy of Vermont, with just a gram of anthrax—which amounts to about one trillion spores. That would be enough to kill, in theory, 100,000 people if it had been spread outdoors under perfect conditions. One study later concluded that if a kilogram or two were released in a city like New York, and sucked into the air handlers of skyscrapers, the result could make the buildings uninhabitable for more than four decades. (Later, the number was revised to three hundred years. The fact is, no one knows for sure.)[4]

As it was, about thirty workers on Capitol Hill and several more postal workers tested positive for anthrax exposure. That was enough to shut down the House of Representatives and the Senate office buildings; across the street, the Supreme Court was evacuated. And that was from just a few grams of powder, contained in a few envelopes.

Soon Cheney and his staff were seized with the threat of a possible biological attack. Intelligence reports indicated that North Korea, Iraq, and Russia had undeclared samples of smallpox virus. (So did France, the intelligence indicated. "The one country that Cheney trusted less than Iraq," one White House aide joked darkly.) Cheney pushed for a mass inoculation of the entire country, despite warnings that the inoculations themselves would kill about three hundred people. He concluded that was better than having thousands, or tens of thousands, die in an attack—if one ever happened.[5]

"This was the moment when I first saw the president split away from Cheney," one White House official who was in the room told me. "He just wasn't ready to see three hundred people die for a low-probability event, even if Cheney was."

Bush went for something more modest: a flurry of new presidential directives, of the kind already issued regarding counterproliferation programs and counterterrorism operations. The initiative was called "Biodefense in the 21st Century."[6]

Bush and Cheney deserve significant credit for kicking the federal bureaucracy into action. Lawrence M. Wein, a professor of management science at Stanford's Graduate School of Business who constructed the mathematical models about how long it would take to decontaminate New York, credits the administration with stockpiling enough vaccine for everyone in the country in the event of a smallpox attack.

"While it would cause a lot of panic, we would not see anywhere near 100,000 people dying," Wein said. "We would see hundreds or a couple of thousand at most. I think that's one we've taken off the table as a catastrophic scenario." Unfortunately, there are many others still on the table.

WHEN RICHARD DANZIG explains the biological threats that the government needs to be prepared to face, he breaks them down into four categories, each requiring a different response, each a different strategy. "We've got many of the tools, we've made some progress," he told me one day on his back deck in Washington, "but this is all about preparation, and I don't think you can say that at this point we're anywhere near prepared. We've got huge disconnects in the system—mostly between the federal government and localities that will be doing the treatment. We haven't figured out how to engage people in thinking about this without panicking them." And, he added, "if you are going to have a strategy, you need to think about how this fits into a broader concept of terrorist threats."

The first entry in Danzig's catalog of four threats is viruses, of which smallpox is the best known. Viruses can be enormously contagious, and getting people vaccinated fast enough would be the main challenge.

Danzig's second category is poisonous toxins, such as botulin, a neurotoxin that can be found in badly preserved meats or vegetables and that could be deliberately introduced into the food supply. Unlike smallpox and other viruses, toxins are not contagious, but the trick is finding the poisoned food in time—which could cause huge disruptions and food shortages.

His third category is an indirect agent such as foot-and-mouth disease, a highly contagious virus that can affect cattle, sheep, goats, pigs—but almost never humans. People could eat meat from an infected animal with no worries. But the disease itself can devastate herds and wipe out food supplies. It's highly transmissible; it can be carried on clothes, shoes, even a handkerchief if it got close enough to a cow or pig with the disease. So anyone who has been on a farm in an affected area would have to be disinfected and put under travel restrictions to prevent wider spread of the disease.*

Each of these problems requires a different response: efficient vaccination for smallpox; food screening and destruction for botulin and other toxins; quarantines and herd slaughters for foot-and-mouth disease. Each taxes an overburdened medical system in different ways. But it is the fourth category for which we remain significantly underprepared—largely because by the time we recognize an attack is under way, several others may have already taken place.

That fourth category is anthrax, the bacterium that consumes Homeland Security planners. A gram inside each of several envelopes killed five people in the 2001 attacks—two postal workers in Washington, a New York hospital worker, a Florida photo editor, and an elderly woman in Connecticut. Seven years later, what worries Danzig is the primitive state of our detection capability, which slows the response time and creates a huge opportunity for repeated attacks before anyone realizes we've been struck.

"Reload," Danzig said to me, letting the word hang in the air a moment. "By the time you realize an attack is happening, whoever did it has time to reload."

---

* When foot-and-mouth disease hit Britain in 2001, many animals were slaughtered, an election was delayed, and quarantines were imposed. It was inconvenient and very expensive, but containment worked.

It's not easy to refine the production process to make anthrax in a form that can be turned into an aerosol weapon. It would cost tens of thousands of dollars and require a good deal of expertise. But once the facility is created, you don't need a big, easy-to-find factory to make a few hundred grams of anthrax. Nuclear terrorists may have one bomb; a bioterrorist could have plenty of anthrax to hit multiple cities sequentially. That's the crux of the reload problem. "It's a campaign of terrorism you have to worry about," Danzig explained. "Suppose a determined terrorist sprays an aerosolized form of anthrax in one city and then moves on to Minneapolis or Chicago or Dallas. Just think about what that does: You have a crisis in one part of the country, and then in another and another, and you don't know how to stop it or how to spread your resources to treat it." It took the better part of two months, he notes, to find a couple of snipers who terrorized Washington in the fall of 2003, and they were operating in only one metropolitan area.

Reload is also a problem because of the primitive state of the detection technology. There are now thirty-one cities that have BioWatch detectors installed; for obvious security reasons, the federal government does not name all of them. They sniff the atmosphere, but their filters still have to be physically collected and sent off to labs. It's a labor-intensive, time-consuming process. As a practical matter, it only tells you what happened yesterday or the day before, and the detectors cannot pinpoint the source of the attack. That isn't much solace if you are an air traveler squeezed into the middle seat of a crowded plane with nothing to eat but a measly bag of airline peanuts, sitting next to a carrier of the pneumonic plague, fresh from an antiwar demonstration.

If this worries you, get a job in the Pentagon. Not because it's the place that plans out counterterrorism attacks, but because it is the only large building in the country right now protected by an experimental new technology that can warn, in real time, of an approaching cloud of anthrax.[7] Once the kinks are worked out (there are still too many false alarms, including from diesel exhaust) these devices will be able to map a cloud as it envelops a city and point authorities to the cloud's source. LIDAR—think radar for toxic clouds—gives the authorities a decent chance of capturing the terrorists before they can move on to the next attack. It also would enable a warning to be sent out immediately to other cities—potentially creating the 9/11 effect, where passengers on the flight headed for Washington, realizing what had happened to the other planes, were able to overpower the hijackers.

Danzig compares where we are now to where the British were in the 1930s, facing the Luftwaffe. "They didn't think they could stop long-range German bombers," he wrote. "But they built an air defense system—and they had it mostly in place for the Battle of Britain."[8]

WHEN I WAS a correspondent in Japan in the early 1990s, the cult group Aum Shinrikyo was experimenting with anthrax. But the police in the area had no idea about what was going on, even when faced with unexplained events, including the deaths of a number of farm animals near the Aum compound. It turned out that while the Aum desperately wanted to use anthrax to attack Tokyo, they made some big mistakes, employing a vaccine form that was essentially harmless as a weapon.

They got away with the experiments for so long because the local authorities were clueless. (So were the foreign correspondents.) Japanese police will come by your house to measure that your parking space is bigger than your car (you cannot buy a car in Tokyo unless you can prove you have a place to park it, a law that would spark rioting in many American cities), but when confronted with bioweapons, they did not know what questions to ask. Ultimately, Aum turned to an easier terror weapon to handle: sarin gas, a chemical weapon, which they used to conduct a deadly attack in the Tokyo subways. Though it didn't seem so at the time, the Aum attacks could have been much worse. The gas did not go very far in the subway tunnels. Anthrax would have made those tunnels uninhabitable for years.

But the next time we, or the Japanese, may not be so lucky. The fact that the anthrax attack in Washington in 2001 proved so deadly, even though it was never released on a large scale, demonstrated the power of the weapon. Authorities were able to close off mailrooms on Capitol Hill and in newsrooms around the country. But you can't shut down the atmosphere.

The reality is that we can't prevent a biological attack, but we can prepare to deal with it—and to mitigate its effects. And so far, the preparation of the general public has been miserable. There has been little effort to get communities to talk about how to distribute vaccines or antibiotics quickly. One of the best ideas, promoted by Lawrence Wein and others, involves using the United States Postal Service to deliver antibiotics directly to Americans' doorsteps.[9] Under the plan, postal carriers—the same people who were the target of the 2001 attacks—would travel the same paths they traverse each day to distribute the drugs. Trials in Seattle, Boston, and Philadelphia have shown, according to Wein, that antibiotics could be distributed to a large chunk of the population in fewer than eight hours.

"Here you have a federal asset that specializes in doing something like this every day," Wein said in his office at Stanford. "It would be one less headache for the local health community to think about."

Contagious pathogens such as the plague or smallpox would be a more complex problem: Some people cannot be safely vaccinated, including pregnant women, small children, and people with immune deficiencies. In the days after 9/11, cities and states were encouraged to work with doctors and specific hospitals to develop their own plans for handling the vast lines of people who would suddenly seek vaccination. But that is clearly not enough: As Wein observes, "It's clear that very few of these cities are capable of doing this."

The next president can get them ready. Like stopping a stock-market panic, stopping a biological threat begins with creating confidence in the system—confidence that the disaster can be dealt with effectively. That is why the Bush administration's approach—

leave the preparation to professionals, and say little to the public—has been so damaging. But in the Bush administration's view of the world, fighting the war on terror was supposed to be a job for the Special Forces and the CIA, not ordinary citizens. That attitude also explains how Bush blew the chance to get Americans to conserve oil. And it explains why most Americans know little more about what they should do in the aftermath of a biological attack than they knew at the end of 2001.

# CHAPTER 16
# DARK ANGEL

*It began with what seemed like a simple blackout. But something was odd: Cell phones didn't work because the cell towers were also dead—despite their battery backup systems. Then it suddenly became evident that ATMs were out of order not just in Chicago, where the blackout began, but across the nation. When people around the country tried to log in to their bank and brokerage accounts, their screens were frozen.*

*Then came the deluge—starting with the collapse of the 9-1-1 systems across the country. Emergency call centers were flooded with false alarms—almost all computer-generated, so that dispatchers could not tell real emergencies from the phantoms. Air traffic control systems mysteriously shut down; like the cell towers, they were supposed to have backup systems. There were rumors of oil and gas pipeline shutdowns, but operators were having trouble telling whether the flow had really stopped or their computer links had been severed. If there was any doubt that the country was under attack, it was resolved within the hour, as three-quarters of the American power grid crashed and transformers began to blow up. Though they said nothing publicly, plant operators knew that meant six months of national darkness, save for places with emergency generators.*

*The president scrambled fighter jets to patrol over American cities, just as Bush had done on 9/11—but there was nothing to see, much less shoot down. Markets around the world first plunged, then closed. If trades couldn't be cleared in the United States, they couldn't happen anywhere else.*

*Cyber experts had been warning the government for years that the daily barrage of attacks on computers from the Pentagon to Citigroup were likely "probes" looking for weaknesses and vulnerabilities in the nation's computer networks.*

*Now, this seemed like the inevitable follow-on attack. Corporate America was largely unprepared: While virtually all companies had installed protective software against hackers, little had been invested against an attack of this scale, one so sophisticated that it probably required the help or financing of a state. But inside the government's new cyber-security centers in Virginia, analysts knew that it would be harder to trace where the attack had come from than it would be to trace the origins of a terrorist's nuclear bomb. In this attack the timing was exquisite. The crippling of emergency response systems, backup systems, and communications systems was a prelude to the attack on the primary targets: the banks, the markets, and the power plants.\* By comparison, the Russian attacks on Estonia in April 2007 and on Georgia in August 2008 were sophomoric pranks.*

*When the National Security Council met that afternoon in the Situation Room—one of the few places in Washington that still had lights—the president was told he would soon face a choice. Once the National Security Agency narrowed down where the attack originated from, the president would have a few options, all unsatisfactory. He could decide to try to absorb the damage, appealing for swift action from his counterpart in the country where the attack originated, and focus on getting things switched back on as fast as possible. There was a more aggressive option: He could order an American-led cyberattack on the country that was responsible for the devastation, an eye for an eye, a byte for a byte. Or he could initiate a conventional military attack on the country that crippled America, if it appeared the cyber-aggression had state sponsorship.*

*"Will we ever know for certain who is responsible?" the president asked his national security adviser.*

*"Probably not, sir," was the answer. "If it's like the few attacks we've seen before, we'll probably never know for sure."*

IF A MOMENT like this happens on the next president's watch, no one will be able to say the White House wasn't given ample warning. In February 2002, five months after the 9/11 attack, a group of about fifty scientists, engineers, and former intelligence and de-

---

\* Like the nuclear scenario, this one is based on an exercise in September 2002, by a panel of experts that attempted to outline a cyberattack that would trigger panic, disorder, and economic collapse. The scenario was called Dark Angel and was widely circulated, in unclassified form, around the government.

fense officials sent a letter to President Bush. It was patterned, deliberately and more than a little ostentatiously, after the two-page letter Albert Einstein wrote to "F. D. Roosevelt" on August 2, 1939, warning him for the first time that "it may become possible to set up a nuclear chain reaction in a large mass of uranium" that would lead to the construction of a new generation of bombs. He noted evidence that Hitler might be trying to get there first.

The 2002 letter to President Bush was equally stark. It warned that the next chain reaction he needed to worry about was not at the atomic level. It would start in cyberspace—and America was a wide-open target. "The consequences of successfully exploiting these vulnerabilities," the letter read, "would be significant damage to the U.S. economy, degraded public trust with concomitant long-term retardation of economic growth, degradation in quality of life, and a severe erosion of the public's confidence that the government can adequately protect their security." The authors asked for the same kind of response that the Einstein letter generated: a Manhattan Project–type undertaking that would recruit top scientists and require billions of dollars of federal money. The first task would be to sort through the complexities of how to defend against a cyberattack that was aimed primarily at such "soft" targets as banks, credit markets, power stations, and cell phone networks—networks the federal government did not own and could not control.

FDR had responded to Einstein right away, but Bush had more immediate threats to worry about. There had just been an anthrax attack. There were rumors of loose nukes. "As far as I can tell, I don't think it was read," one of the lead authors, O. Sami Saydjari, the president of the Cyber Defense Agency, told me six years later. "I don't think it made his priority list."

Saydjari received a standard letter of thanks for corresponding with the White House and an invitation for his panel of experts to review a draft version of the forthcoming 2003 National Strategy to Secure Cyberspace. The experts read the strategy, Saydjari recalled, and concluded, "Nice try."

"It could probably stop a fourteen-year-old," he said. "But it's not a national strategy that can be used against the nation's great adversaries."

Saydjari began appealing to members of Congress, but the subject was too complex, the threat too distant. A smattering of hearings generated little news and did not result in any meaningful legislation. "I would characterize the reception as lukewarm," Saydjari told me. "Cyber just did not have traction, at least in the administration."

The few people inside the government who were interested told Saydjari to put up or shut up: to come up with a cyberattack scenario that would be realistic enough to convince the country's leaders that there was a threat out there as big as nuclear and as nasty as anthrax. Saydjari hesitated. "'We don't think you want us to put this together on an unclassified level,'" he recalled telling administration officials.

"They said, 'Yes, we do.'"

The result was Dark Angel, the code name for a sophisticated cyberattack scenario drawn up in thirty days by experts from the transportation, electrical, and financial industries, and vetted by others who vouched for its plausibility. Its details were similar to the events outlined at the opening of this chapter, only much worse. Dark Angel assumed three years of preparation by a state or a transnational terrorist group with $500 million to spend. That's serious money, but if the attack was launched with the help of a government, a good deal of the cash would be spent trying to cover their tracks so that it would be hard for the United States to retaliate.

In Dark Angel, the main goal of the attack was to trigger economic collapse. But most immediate damage would be psychological: When the lights go out, the e-mail goes down, and the power stations blow up, panic and fear and looting are sure to follow. Every community in the country is affected, and everyone feels vulnerable. That was the real lesson of the scenario, Saydjari told a congressional panel in April 2007, and it was the real lesson in Estonia and Georgia after they were hit by Russian cyberattacks.

"It would be hubris to think our adversaries don't already have a plan in place that's substantially better than our brief sketch, or that their capabilities to execute such an attack aren't improving," Saydjari said.[1]

By then, one of the signatories of the 2002 letter had returned to government and was greeting President Bush in the Oval Office every morning to deliver the 8:00 a.m. intelligence briefing: J. Michael McConnell.

BUSH WAS AWARE of computer threats long before he asked Mc-Connell, in late 2006, to leave his profitable consultancy at Booz Allen, and return to government as director of national intelligence. But Bush rarely thought much about computer technology: He told visitors to the White House residence that he decided to give up e-mailing as soon as he became president; there was no sense in having electronic copies of private presidential musings zipping through the blogosphere, or subpoenaed in a trial. The result was that his familiarity with modern computing was distant, at best. He once told an interviewer that "one of the things I've used on the Google is to pull up maps," mostly of the Crawford ranch.[2] (The use of the definite article "the" left many with the impression that he was not a frequent Googler.) His former aides tell me that his primary cyberspace obsession centered on the rise of jihadist websites, particularly those on which al Qaeda spread its propaganda, sought new recruits, and ran grainy, gruesome videos of American convoys in Iraq as they were blown up by roadside bombs.

"This would drive him up the wall," one of Bush's Iraq strategists told me. "He'd ask: 'Why are they using the Internet better than we are? Didn't we invent this thing?'"

Gradually, though, Bush began to discover the world of cyber espionage. The President's Daily Brief, a digest of the most critical intelligence that landed on Bush's desk every morning, often referred to information based on computer intercepts, from the communications of al Qaeda members to the cracking of Iran's nuclear plans to the possibilities of altering information flowing to terror groups. But when McConnell arrived back in Washington, after an absence of a decade, he was shocked by two discoveries. The first was how little had been done to consolidate the eighty or more intelligence databases that sixteen disparate agencies—from the CIA to the Defense Intelligence Agency to the Drug Enforcement Administration—had assembled. (That is beginning to be solved at the new National Counterterrorism Center in the building next to McConnell's own office, all part of a secure new office park built a few miles away from the CIA campus in northern Virginia.) The second was how little had been done to protect the country against cyberattacks, and how little thinking had gone into the strategic implications of engaging the United States in cyberwarfare.

The Pentagon and the CIA were tracking those jihadist websites, of course, building elaborate databases to show who was signing on—and trying to pinpoint where they were located. The NSA had broken new ground intercepting coded e-mails and conversations among young jihadis, even to the point of delving into the "chat" in online video games, where some of them met electronically to exchange messages that they thought would evade detection. But to McConnell, all this was just updating an old art form. "We've been doing this same thing since we were breaking German code" in World War II, McConnell told his colleagues and visitors to his office.

To push the issue to the next level, McConnell quickly hired some of the staff at Booz Allen who had put together studies of the vulnerabilities of major financial institutions, the first step in getting hundreds of millions of dollars in contracts to plug those gaps. Soon they were developing similar studies of the federal government's vulnerabilities, trying to cut down on the number of "portals" through which invaders could enter federal computer systems. Melissa Hathaway, one of McConnell's hires, came up with some scary examples of actual attacks, including the moment in 2006 when "a disgruntled Navy contractor inserted malicious code into five computers at the Navy's European Planning and Operations Command" in Naples, Italy, and knocked two computers out of action. Had the other three been disabled, she reported, the networks that track U.S. and NATO ships in the Mediterranean would have been blinded. She raised the question of whether an adversary could "insert erroneous data that would cause weapons, early warning systems, and other elements of national security to fail" at a critical moment. And, with an eye on Chinese firms—especially companies like Huawei, which makes network control equipment to compete with American firms like Cisco—she asked, "What if malicious code were secretly installed during the manufacture or shipping of computer equipment, to be activated at some future date? How would we even know what threats we face?"[3]

What Hathaway was saying in public was a much watered-down version of what her boss was saying in private. "The Chinese are just having us for lunch right now," McConnell would tell visitors to the sprawling new intelligence campus in Virginia. "We're going to have to rethink this partnership thing," he would argue, because "they're also leaving little telltale capabilities back in our systems. So if we ever do have a little dustup, they can remotely turn them on." The Chinese, of course, are convinced we are doing the same to them.

IN HIS PRESENTATIONS to the administration about cyber threats, McConnell usually started by reaching for a poster-size map of the flow of Internet traffic around the world. (He kept the map leaned up against the wall by the conference table in his office.) It showed a huge bulge in the middle, where the United States was. The message was clear: For good and ill, America is the world's biggest switching center for Internet traffic.

A few years ago, Michael Hayden, the director of the CIA, liked to say that the fact that the United States was the giant stationmaster of the Internet was "our home-field advantage." When a terrorist in Iraq wanted to e-mail his buddy in Waziristan, or an Iranian nuclear engineer had a question for a physicist in Stuttgart, there was a good chance the communication was passing—unbeknownst to the sender and receiver—through a server in the American Midwest. Time and again, that fact gave America's spies access to all kinds of vital data, and McConnell and Hayden often used this map in presentations on Capitol Hill to make their argument in favor of the need for greater latitude as they rewrote the 1978 Foreign Intelligence Surveillance Act, or FISA, which governs the tapping of any "wired" communications—voice or computer—by citizens or foreigners inside the United States. A version of the same map had been part of the administration's effort to convince the *Times* not to reveal that the president had ordered Hayden and other top intelligence officials, in the weeks after 9/11, to ignore the law, circumvent the FISA court, and tap in to communications that flowed through the United States or involved American citizens. The paper, and soon the rest of the world, called that order the administration's "warrantless wiretapping" program. The president, arguing that he was acting within his powers as commander in chief, quickly came up with a different name to sell the effort: the "Terrorist Surveillance Program."

Eventually, the law was rewritten, in a compromise that many Democrats—including Barack Obama—signed on to. Warrants would no longer be required for purely foreign communications passing through the United States. But Americans—no matter where they were in the world, at home or abroad—would be protected. If an American was a participant in the intercepted conversation, there would have to be a warrant. The rewritten law took domestic wiretapping off the table as a political issue before the 2008 elections.

But even before the law was changed, McConnell was using his map for a different purpose: to demonstrate America's growing vulnerability to cyberattacks. The same technology that gave us home-field advantage, he argued, made us far more vulnerable to having our field destroyed—or at least put out of action for months.

In a meeting with many members of the Cabinet in May 2007, McConnell finally raised the issue with Bush. With Henry Paulson, the new Treasury secretary, and Michael Chertoff, the secretary of Homeland Security, at his side, he described how a country or a sophisticated terror group could attack many government agencies and shut down much of the private sector—the markets, the banks, the power stations. Then he got to his punch line. "If the 9/11 perpetrators had attacked one single bank in the United States and damaged it to the point that it couldn't recover data, that they didn't know what they had, it would have had an order of magnitude greater impact on the global economy" than the attacks on the Pentagon and World Trade Center.

That got Bush's attention. McConnell later told visitors that the president looked at him like he "had two heads."

Then Bush looked at Paulson. "Is this right, Hank?" he asked. Paulson did not hesitate. "It was what kept me up at night when I was chairman at Goldman Sachs. It was my greatest single worry, because everything's based on confidence."

A year later, of course, Paulson confronted such a crisis of confidence in the markets and stepped in to save Bear Stearns from collapse, the first of a series of bailouts. Inside the government, McConnell kept citing the Bear Stearns example. Here was a company whose own mistakes brought it down, he said. But look at the ripple effect—and think about what would happen if a cyberattack created twenty Bear Stearns–like crises, or two hundred, at once.

WHEN MCCONNELL explained the threats he was worried about to Bush or other members of the national security team, he often grabbed a piece of paper and drew a little chart—to show what the intelligence community already does and what it needs to learn to do.

On the far left, he created a category called COMMS for "communications." This was the old-fashioned stuff—tapping in to calls, e-mails, ATM transactions, online video games. The intelligence community spends billions of dollars a year on these tactics, and they've gotten better and better: If you sit in a "forward operating post" in Afghanistan, on the screens in front of the commanders there are often transcripts running—translated into English—of nearly real-time cell-phone conversations happening in the outskirts of Kandahar. It would look great in a James Bond movie, but it's essentially old-style wiretapping, improved and sped up to deal with the world of al Qaeda.

McConnell's next category was labeled EXPLOIT. By the time of the first Persian Gulf War, he would explain to Bush and others, the exploitation of intercepted messages had turned into a fine art. "'Wow, look what we can do,'" McConnell would tell them. "'We can attack. We can turn off their air defense system remotely!'"

The Persian Gulf War was before the Internet explosion, before an American president could turn to "the Google," and before America's challengers had the sophistication to launch cyberattacks on the United States. So the last two boxes on McConnell's chart for Bush read ATTACK and DEFEND. This was his pitch about the future of cyberwarfare—and it was jammed with thorny decisions that President Obama will likely have to confront.

Naturally, the U.S. government doesn't talk much about the scenarios in which we attack other countries in cyberspace, especially because we are still more vulnerable than our adversaries. Yet inside the intelligence agencies and the Pentagon, offensive capabilities are a subject of regular, impassioned debate.

Unfortunately, most of that debate during the Bush administration—at least at senior levels—focused on the turf war, not the strategy. Everyone agreed that America has to be able to wage cyberwar. But who gets to command the fight? The military or the computer geeks at the National Security Agency?

McConnell quickly found himself enmeshed in this internecine battle. The Pentagon insisted that since cyberwar was still war by other means, it must be within its territory. The Department of Homeland Security said that it didn't want to play offense. But when it came to protecting domestic banks, financial institutions, 9-1-1 systems, and power grids—where 95 percent of the targets exist—well, that's where Congress put DHS in charge. The National Security Agency, McConnell's old shop, said cyberwar is all about code-breaking and code-making and electronic surveillance and penetrating other nations' computer systems. Since the NSA is the repository of that particular expertise, everyone else should stand aside and leave this to the professionals. Everyone was spending their days arguing about who was in charge. "You could never get a holistic approach," McConnell complained.

In typical Bush administration fashion, no one was openly debating the big questions. The first was obvious: If a cyberwar breaks out, is offense the best defense? And if so, should part of that strategy be preemptive war—the theory Bush promulgated in the 2002 National Security Strategy and that he later discredited in Iraq in 2003?

The argument for preemption in cyberwarfare is simple: By the time a sophisticated cyberattack happens, it's probably too late to defend against it effectively. We can build better network filters and early warning devices and add new firewalls around the computers that keep America humming. But in cyberwar, attackers have almost all of the advantages. They get to pick from thousands of possible attacks. Defenders have to protect against everything, including attacks they can't imagine.

In March 2007, just before McConnell's meeting with Bush, researchers at the Idaho National Laboratory launched an experimental cyberattack on a power station—just to see what damage they could do. It turned out they could do a lot, and in September 2007, a previously classified video made its way to CNN. It showed what happened when the power station's big diesel generator was deliberately driven out of kilter. It started shaking and smoking, and then it stopped. Permanently.

"It was done by a bunch of kids in the critical infrastructure section of DHS," an intelligence official said to me. "Whatever next set of players come in here have to understand that." People started crunching the numbers. By one estimate, if one third of the country lost power for three months, the economic price tag would be about $700 billion—the size of your ordinary, once-in-a-century Wall Street bailout.[4]

McConnell persuaded Bush to start up a five-year program, rumored to cost more than $15 billion, called the Comprehensive National Cyber-Security Initiative. Like its price tag, the details are classified, so no one can assess whether it matches the challenge or is largely a boon for a new generation of defense contractors. It's not the only classified part of the great new cyberwar games. On January 8, 2008, Bush approved a presidential directive designed to be the guiding document in cyber defense and offense for the United States. Unfortunately, because it was never published in open literature, the private sector—where 95 percent of the targets are located and defended—has little idea what it says; only at the end of the administration did McConnell and Hathaway and others begin to hold private briefings for American businesses. But it's all reminiscent of Bush's "declaratory policy" for nuclear terrorism: At home, no one is quite certain what the defensive plan is; abroad, adversaries are not warned about the devastating response if they get caught launching an attack.

Congress passed Bush's request for the $15 billion cyber-security initiative in September 2008, just as Wall Street was melting down. It would have gone through even without the freezing of credit markets, but the crisis didn't hurt, especially after McConnell told members of Congress that "the ability to threaten the U.S. money supply is the equivalent of today's nuclear weapon." A few months before, he might have been viewed as hyping the threat. No more. Congress had seen its first financial mushroom cloud.

But the question that Bush never discussed with Congress, at least in the open, centered on preemption—a word he could not utter in public after Iraq. Secretly, he had already authorized at least two preemptive cyberattacks. In the months leading up to the March 2003 invasion of Iraq, cyberwarfare experts waged an e-mail assault against Iraq's leadership, urging them to break away from Saddam Hussein's government.[5] The move was a relatively benign form of information warfare. But to reach the right audience, the United States infiltrated Iraqi networks, not only siphoning off information but also manipulating the flow of information to key Iraqi officials.

Then, a few years later, came a more devastating cyberattack—against al Qaeda in Mesopotamia, the al Qaeda affiliate that had moved into Iraq to take on the Americans.

The officials I interviewed were reluctant to discuss the attack in detail, for fear of revealing their capabilities. But this one seemed to involve the alteration of data and databases on a computer used by al Qaeda operatives and its associates. That manipulation, in turn, helped lure them into a trap. It worked, and those militants won't be building any new databases.

Of course, making the decision to launch a cyberstrike against al Qaeda is easy—it would have a hard time striking back from the unwired corners of Pakistan. Making the decision to do the same against China or Russia is a whole different matter. There, a preemptive strike—even against a rogue programmer or terror group or business—would carry many risks, including the likelihood that the confrontation could escalate, quickly, into a traditional war.

Bush administration officials say that his January 8, 2008, cyberwar strategy did not deal with "first use" or attack capabilities. But at the end of their time in office, some inside the Bush administration began to consider some preemptive-strike scenarios, just to think through the possibilities. The most common concerned China. Suppose the National Security Agency, poking around in China's computer systems, detected a cyberattack in the making. If they got inside the Chinese computer systems, they could watch, silently, as Chinese computer hackers—maybe members of the People's Liberation Army, maybe just talented twenty-year-olds—put together an ingenious attack to bring down American financial networks. Then commanders would have to make the same decision that George Washington had to make when scouts reported that they had seen

Redcoats massing, or that Eisenhower had to make after U-2s saw the Soviet Union's missiles being deployed. Do you attack first? Do you prepare yourself but let the other side fire the first shot?

The less aggressive answer, already kicked around inside the NSA and the Pentagon, would be to exploit the intelligence to design "inoculations" that would protect both private and public computers in the United States—a sort of anticipatory form of virus protection. Sounds like a great idea, if it works. That strategy, of course, depends on perfect intelligence gathering. And, as with flu shots, there's no guarantee it will work against the next strain of the virus.

McConnell and his aides began to debate whether the United States should be ready to do far more. If authorized by the president, should the U.S. government be ready to disable another nation's computer networks before they disable ours? How would you prepare for "escalation," cyber-style? If we take out Gazprom's networks, do they take out Citigroup's? And is it possible to deter some countries with the knowledge that to take out our financial system is to gravely harm their own? As one senior intelligence official said to me, if the cash registers at Wal-Mart flip off, it's only a matter of time before China's exports take a hit. If the markets freeze up, it's going to be hard for the Chinese finance ministry to sell off their American treasury bills. "They're deterred," one top official insisted when I asked about Chinese cyberattacks. "It's the rest of the world I worry about."

# EPILOGUE

# OBAMA'S
# CHALLENGE

Never, at any moment, even the most grotesque, in the exercise
of 1960, had he believed that men were powerless to ask new
questions or define new rules, or that individuals were helpless
as the "engines of history" rolled toward them. He had always
acted as if men were masters of forces, as if all things were
possible for men determined in purpose and clear in thought—
even the Presidency.

This perhaps is what he had best learned in 1960—even
though he called his own victory a "miracle." This was what he
would have to cherish alone in the White House, on which an
impatient world waited for miracles.

— Theodore H. White, *The Making of the President, 1960,*
describing John F. Kennedy as he assumed office

IF EVER Barack Obama faced an impatient world, it was over Thanksgiving weekend in 2009.

His presidency was only ten months old. He had successfully
navigated the worst of the global financial crisis. The Great Recession no longer seemed likely to trigger something far worse, a second Great Depression that had appeared to be a real possibility
when he took office. While Obama's conservative critics still complained that the president was enthusiastically embracing a new era
of Big Government, the facts were more complicated. The rescue of
Wall Street banks and the nationalization of General Motors appeared to have worked, at least for the time being, and a handful of

the saved, eager to free themselves of government control, were paying back their loans early. Clearly, Obama was trying to wind down expensive government intervention and the trillion dollars in additional deficits they triggered.

But unemployment was higher than 10 percent, and suddenly within his own constituency Obama faced the disappointed and the doubters. Black and Hispanic congressional leaders, along with many members of Congress from the Midwest states where unemployment was much worse than the national figures suggested, were demanding another round of economic stimulus. His liberal base complained that Obama had backed down, again and again, on health care in a desperate effort to win Republican support. And throughout the country, supporters who thought they had elected an antiwar candidate, only to discover that they had elected an anti–Iraq War candidate, were disheartened by the reality: The president was about to send 30,000 troops to Afghanistan, boosting the American commitment to roughly 100,000. It was nearly the size of the commitment in Iraq. Obama himself was clearly having a hard time answering the question that Gen. David Petraeus once asked about Iraq: "Tell me how this ends."

The administration's infighting over strategy was playing out each day on the front pages. A team once known for its discipline and tight loyalty was now leaking the content of discussions taking place inside the Situation Room. Anyone following the debate even casually knew that Vice President Joe Biden and Obama's political advisers feared that committing significantly more combat troops would alienate Obama's base and slow the effort to get a corrupt, incompetent Afghan government to defend itself. But perhaps the cautionary words that carried the most weight with Obama came from Karl Eikenberry, the former military commander whom Obama had sent back to Afghanistan as his ambassador. Now viewing the same war from the other side—the civilian side—Eikenberry was struck by the reaction to America's military presence as he traveled the country. In the Afghan cities and towns where that presence was most heavy-handed, the earnest new ambassador, an unusual blend of Harvard, Stanford, and the Army, could hear the resentments growing among the Afghan people, even those who had welcomed American troops in 2002. In areas where there was a big civilian American presence building roads and schools—not many places, since there were only nine hundred American civilians assigned to Afghanistan, or about one-seventieth of the military personnel deployed there—the reaction was almost the opposite. Sure, we need more troops, Eikenberry told the president, but let's not forget what we're here to do: help a desperately poor country pull itself out of centuries of backwardness.

The Biden-Eikenberry camp was arrayed against the current American military commander, Gen. Stanley McChrystal, who warned in a memorandum to the president—leaked in late September—that without a major commitment of additional forces the eight-year-long mission in Afghanistan "will likely result in failure."

McChrystal was Obama's personally selected commander of Afghanistan forces. Obama and Defense Secretary Gates had unceremoniously removed his predecessor, Gen. David McKiernan. McChrystal's first assignment was to come up with a new strategy, amid plentiful evidence that the course the Bush administration had pursued was failing. His sixty-six-page memorandum to Obama, delivered just as the president was headed to Martha's Vineyard for a late-August vacation, made a persuasive case for a full-scale counterinsurgency operation—not the kind of lightning strikes that the Special Forces are known for, but slow, patient protection of local populations, so that they could resist the Taliban.

The objective was to make Afghanistan's population centers feel secure despite a surprisingly effective summer onslaught by the Taliban. A civilian presence was essential, McChrystal wrote, but impossible without enough troops to keep the Taliban at bay. But the price would be high: After too many years of neglect—the Bush legacy—Obama would need another 40,000 troops or more. It was a far higher figure than Obama had in mind even months before. No one called Afghanistan "the good war" anymore. Now it was referred to as "Obama's war." Casualties in Afghanistan were already running far higher than in Iraq. Soon the number of troops committed would do so as well. And for the first time, polls showed that a bare majority of Americans were coming to the conclusion that the war was no longer worth the sacrifices.

Obama was determined not to make the Bush mistake: He would not give the generals whatever they asked for, not without examining, and reexamining, a strategy that clearly had not worked for the past eight years. "What general ever asked for fewer troops?" one of Obama's top national security aides fumed to me one afternoon at the White House. Obama knew the political risks of giving McChrystal less than he asked for, and his aides saw the president chafe at his poor choices. "He wouldn't show it outwardly, until the decision got close," one of the participants in the debate said. "And then he just kept sending us back for another scenario." When yet another strategy came off the drawing board, he told me, Obama's reaction was to ask for "another one."

By Thanksgiving, the reexamination of options had dragged on for three months. And whether one viewed it as deliberative or as dithering, or merely a demonstration that Obama would not make gut decisions the way his predecessor did, the delay was not cost-free. Obama's repeated assurance that he would not involve the United States in an "open-ended commitment" led many to question whether he really was committed at all. The Pakistani military and intelligence services certainly doubted he would stay. Afghans voted with their feet and their cash: They searched for exit ramps of their own out of the country, fearing that even if Obama committed new troops, their deployment would simply be a prelude to retreat.

In Washington, Obama's debate over sending new troops was conducted in a haze of comparisons to Vietnam—not only on television, but in the White House. Rahm Emanuel, the chief of staff who made no secret of how much he loathed the idea of sending tens of thousands of additional troops, distributed to the senior staff at the White House a recently published book: Gordon M. Goldstein's *Lessons in Disaster: McGeorge Bundy and the Path to War in Vietnam*. Most didn't need to read past the title page, but those who did found cautionary tales of what happens to very smart leaders who pour troops into places they do not fully understand and convince themselves that there is a pathway out.

In late June 2009, Obama invited a half-dozen historians to dinner at the White House; not until they arrived did they realize several had written about Johnson, and the escalation of the Vietnam War. Although Obama never said so explicitly, he was acutely aware that he faced the same risks that LBJ confronted in 1965. Obama came into the room the night of the dinner looking relaxed and smiling, but as usual he kept small talk to a minimum. He started with a general question: What have you discovered that would apply to this moment in history, to this presidency?

Several offered variations on a single theme: Wars can kill ambitious domestic agendas. After the shock of the Kennedy assassination had abated, Johnson had envisioned an ambitious expansion of his Great Society program. Much of that plan proved another casualty of the escalating war in Vietnam. Obama, of course, had already launched a Johnson-sized agenda. In public, at least, Obama was still talking about winning passage of landmark health-care reform, energy and environmental legislation that would revive talks on global warming, and the remaking of the financial regulatory system—all before Christmas. These would have been virtually impossible timetables even without the prospect of sustaining 100,000 soldiers in Afghanistan, over the strong objections of leaders in his own party.

The historians looked at one another, and then at Obama, searching for anything in his facial expression that would reveal how he was leaning. They didn't get much. But the scene was a little spooky. Johnson had debated Vietnam strategy in the same dining room, forty-four years earlier. "All I could think of when I was sitting there and this subject came up was the setting," said Robert Caro, who has devoted much of his life to recording LBJ's rise and fall. "You had such an awareness of how things can go wrong."[1]

VIETNAM ANALOGIES are seductive and dangerous. At the peak of the Vietnam War, there were more than 500,000 American troops in Indochina. (The number killed in action was roughly ten times greater than the number of American forces who died in Iraq and Afghanistan combined between 2001 and the end of 2009.) Johnson feared that if Vietnam collapsed, other dominoes would fall to Communism. There is no such fear about the Taliban—a collection of local extremists with no superpower patrons—but losing Afghanistan could well embolden attacks on a far more important target: Pakistan and its expanding nuclear arsenal.

Obama's bigger challenge, however, may be the calendar. Eight years after 9/11, the grand mission that Bush had laid out—democracy for Afghanistan, Marshall plans for Afghanistan, victory in Afghanistan—now looks completely unachievable. From the first weeks of his presidency, Obama tried to narrow the objectives. No one in the White House talks about building a democratic Afghan state as an American goal; it is certainly nothing the United States can engineer. Some of Obama's aides even bridled at the use of the phrase "nation-building." As Secretary of State Hillary Clinton bluntly put it, "Our primary focus is on the security of the United States of America."[2]

No one was a bigger skeptic of Afghanistan's president, Hamid Karzai, than Clinton herself. In her first few weeks in office, she made it clear that Karzai was hopeless and his government incurably corrupt. But there was no alternative on the horizon.

Clinton knew that a Defense Department report written just as Obama was coming into office concluded that "building a fully competent and independent Afghan government will be a lengthy process that will last, at a minimum, decades." For his part, Obama felt hemmed in, partly by his own campaign argument that the real war on terror was in Afghanistan, not Iraq.

In the first few weeks of Obama's presidency, eager to make good on his commitment not to under-resource the war, he committed another 21,000 troops to secure the country before a presidential election that was supposed to put Afghanistan on the road to self-sufficiency. Even then, Obama had his reservations, but he figured it was worth the risk: If he gave the military everything they asked for, they would not be able to come back for more in 2009. It was a bet he lost twice. They did come back for more. And Karzai turned out to be more craven than Obama and Clinton feared, turning the election into a debacle of fraud and corruption. Obama had put the United States in the position of coming to the defense of an Afghan leader who could barely claim he was legitimately elected. It didn't help that an embittered Karzai, on the eve of his inauguration, told my PBS colleague Margaret Warner, "The West is not here primarily for the sake of Afghanistan. It is here to fight the war on terror." He pointed out that the United States had abandoned Afghanistan twenty years before, after the Soviets beat a retreat, and did not return until after the 2001 terror attacks. "Afghanistan was troubled like hell before that, too. Nobody bothered about us."

Now, inside the White House, there was talk that history could replay itself. As Gen. James L. Jones, the national security adviser, told me just before the summer, "I figure we've got about eighteen months to turn this around." And then what? He would not say, but his implication seemed to be that, without success by 2011, American and NATO forces would pull back and simply keep enough firepower in place to keep Afghanistan from becoming a launching ground for 9/11-style attacks. The problem, of course, is that Bill Clinton tried and failed with such an approach in the late 1990s—pinprick attacks on al Qaeda bases in Afghanistan.

The changed thinking in Washington could be seen in Obama's restatement of America's goals. In March 2009 he announced that the mission was to "to disrupt, dismantle, and defeat al Qaeda and other extremist networks around the world." By October, his spokesman, Robert Gibbs, was saying that the primary target was groups "that can strike our homeland, strike our allies," or provide a safe haven for them.[3] The Taliban, of course, were a local force with little ability to reach American shores. Gradually, they became a secondary target.

The depth of the change was driven home to me when, battling the leak of the McChrystal report, a senior White House official tracked me down to describe how radically the war strategy was being reframed in those Situation Room debates.

"We don't have to kill every Taliban," the official said. The Situation Room review, he argued, cemented the reality that the Taliban could never be wholly removed from Afghanistan; they were part of the landscape, embedded in every village, and always would be. The trick was to contain their influence and limit their territory. Already, he said, the United States was pulling out from the small posts it had set up in villages around the country; they had become easy target practice for Taliban militants. The idea was to reverse that momentum, and make the Taliban the target for surprise attacks. Obama was persuaded that the right focus was to hold on to the population centers, starting with Kabul, of course, and Kandahar, long the spiritual center of the Taliban. Afghanistan's other big cities, like Mazār-e Sharīf, Herat, and Jalalabad all made the list.[4]

"The argument now," one military official told me as the list was being composed, "is over where you draw the line. What can we afford to lose, without losing Afghanistan?" Inside those population centers, the strategy would be to kill the "unreconcilables"— the hard-core Taliban—and persuade or pay off the majority of the Taliban forces who saw the movement not as a jihad but as a way of scratching out a living. In the rest of the country, the U.S. military would conduct pinpoint attacks on Taliban forces—many launched from drones, as well as some ground attacks led by American and NATO "trainers"—as they tried, once again, to create a real army from the ranks of the Afghan military.

But the reality was that a quarter of the Afghan army's recruits went AWOL every year. Even before Obama announced his new strategy, the Pentagon had already created a new "Community Defense Initiative," an effort to support local tribal militias that could take on the Taliban. Of course, these militias are law unto themselves and, as such, were the opposite of building up the army. But there was no time left for democratic niceties. Obama had to bet that these militias could succeed where the Afghan army had repeatedly failed.

WHEN OBAMA BEGAN his intensive review of Pakistan and Afghanistan in September, he was highly skeptical of McChrystal's case for more than 40,000 additional troops. He was careful not to tip his hand, but in off-the-record discussions with columnists, scholars, and retired officials, he dwelled on the human and financial costs. He described his job as one of balancing competing interests, and this war was not affordable over the long term.

But at each Situation Room meeting, the long-term cost of *not* adding troops on the ground became more vivid. The new American ambassador, Karl Eikenberry was shocked at how much territory the Taliban had regained since he lived in Kabul as military commander. He reported that the situation was "dire." The National Intelligence Council delivered roughly three dozen intelligence assessments that painted an equally grim picture. Some of the reports explored what might happen if Kabul fell and destabilization spread over the border in Pakistan.

But what really moved Obama was Gates himself. Until the summer of 2009, Gates had been a skeptic of adding more forces, fearing their presence would only enflame the Afghan allergy to foreign occupation. McChrystal, however, convinced him, as Gates said later, that "it wasn't the number of troops, but how they were used." And Gates reminded a White House that had little experience with the military that the top officers would have to buy into Obama's decision with enthusiasm. Otherwise, Obama would get the worst of all worlds: democratic rebellion about committing more troops, military rebellion about committing too few. In late October, Gates gave the president what he thought was the magic number: 30,000 additional troops, bringing the American total to just under 100,000. NATO, now at 40,000 troops, agreed to muster another 7,000. Biden was unhappy, but after weeks of haggling they came up with what Obama later called the "max leverage plan": Rush in 30,000 troops at breakneck pace—about six months—but declare they would begin to depart in July 2011, exactly two years after the first Marines landed in Helmand Province.

Gates, fearing this timeline would signal to the Taliban that it could disappear for two years and return, insisted on one last tweak: The pace of withdrawal would depend on "conditions on the ground." In other words, heading into the 2012 election, Obama would be able to claim that he had withdrawn from Iraq and was beginning to withdraw—maybe very slowly—from Afghanistan.

Meanwhile, Obama had come to the conclusion that the analogies to Vietnam were flawed. Just hours before he announced his decision, he told a group of columnists and reporters that the circumstances of the Afghan war were radically different. The Vietnamese were fighting a civil war; they had never attacked American soil; Johnson had never put a time limit on the American commitment.

"To pretend that somehow this is a distant country that has nothing to do with us is just factually incorrect," he insisted.

Wouldn't the hard deadline for withdrawal simply invite the Taliban to wait him out? Obama was asked. "This is an argument I don't give a lot of credence to," Obama replied, because by that logic, "you would never leave. Right?"⁵ The deadline, he argued, would force the Afghans to finally take on the fight themselves. Many in the room left unconvinced.

Within hours, Obama was at the United States Military Academy at West Point. Facing four thousand cadets, many of whom would be in Afghanistan in just months, he gave a speech that began describing his inheritance from Bush. The war in Iraq "drew the dominant share" of our resources, while the Taliban made alarming gains in Afghanistan, and engaged "in increasingly brazen and devastating acts of terrorism" against Pakistan.

"Afghanistan is not lost, but for several years it has moved backwards." He restated his goal in Bush-like terms: to "disrupt, dismantle, and defeat al Qaeda in Afghanistan and Pakistan, and to prevent its capacity to threaten America and our allies in the future."

But leaving Afghanistan, he insisted, was the ultimate goal. We simply could not afford to stay—words that Bush never would have uttered. Iraq and Afghanistan had already cost $1 trillion, and "that is why our troop commitment in Afghanistan cannot be open-ended—because the nation that I am most interested in building is our own."

It was the first time in years an American president had said that some conflicts, no matter how morally worthy, are simply not worth the cost—even some "wars of necessity."

But that recognition also opened a chink in Obama's armor: It made him sound less than committed, as if one day, after examining the budget impact, he might throw in the towel.

"This approach is not open-ended 'nation-building,'" Gates explained the next morning. "It is neither necessary nor feasible to create a modern, centralized, Western-style Afghan nation-state the likes of which has never been seen in that country. Nor does it entail pacifying every village and conducting textbook counterinsurgency from one end of Afghanistan to the other."

BUT THERE REMAINED a hole in Obama's strategy: Pakistan. The main mission for the United States, he argued in January and again in his West Point Speech, was defeating al Qaeda. Only al Qaeda had the motive and the means to strike the United States. And defeating al Qaeda was a goal every American could understand and support.

"The problem we've never gotten around is that al Qaeda isn't in Afghanistan," one of the president's key strategists told me as Obama moved toward his decision. "They're in Pakistan. And so far, our new strategy for Pakistan is a lot like our old strategy for Pakistan: Have the Pakistanis take the lead."

Without question, the Pakistanis were now far more motivated to fight than they had been a year before, when Cheney and Mc-Connell and Hayden were making regular trips there. In the spring, the Pakistanis fought a bloody campaign to oust the Taliban from the Swat Valley. It was a crucial struggle, because Swat is less than one hundred miles from the capital, Islamabad, and within striking distance of some of the military bases where parts of Pakistan's nuclear arsenal are believed to be stored. The government wrested back control of the area but created a crushing flow of two million refugees who fled to escape the fighting. And when the Obama administration offered up humanitarian aid, the Pakistani government took it on the condition that no American officials, and no American airplanes, could be directly involved in distributing the food or emergency goods.[6] Few incidents underscored more clearly the depth of the anti-American mood or the Pakistani government's fears that it was vulnerable to charges of acting as an American colony.

Then, jolted into action by attacks on the military headquarters in downtown Rawalpindi—the garrison city that was no garrison—and a bombing of the ISI's offices in Peshawar, the Pakistani military sent 12,000 troops into the no-man's-land of Waziristan, along the Afghan border. But they had done little to take on the targets high on the Americans' list, including Mullah Omar's operation in Quetta, where plots were hatched daily to attack American troops over the border in Afghanistan, or the Haqqani network that was directing attacks in eastern Afghanistan and in Kabul.

In early November 2009, as Obama traveled in Asia, General Jones headed off on his own for a quiet trip to Islamabad. He carried a two-page letter from Obama. The letter made the case that no matter how many troops Obama sent to Afghanistan, the strategy would fail unless Pakistan broadened the fight to take on the Taliban leaders who were using Pakistani cities to launch attacks on American forces over the border. Jones brought with him a briefcase full of inducements: promises of more military equipment, more jointly coordinated drone strikes, more intelligence cooperation. But he also issued a warning: If the Pakistani military could not wipe out Mullah Omar and the other Taliban leaders who were operating from Pakistani cities, the United States would.

The Pakistanis gladly accepted the offer of more help. But they also told Jones exactly what they used to tell President Bush and his parade of emissaries: We're doing what we can, and we're gradually doing more. No sooner had Jones left than the Pakistanis, in private conversation, resumed questioning the depth of Obama's commitment. When Obama says he is not willing to make an "open-ended commitment," one Pakistani asked me, is it unreasonable to conclude that he's planning to leave sometime soon?[7]

THE LETTER TO Mohamed ElBaradei arrived at the headquarters of the International Atomic Energy Agency on a Monday evening in mid-September, just as the IAEA chief was headed to the airport to fly to New York. It came from Iran. ElBaradei didn't read it until he had settled into his seat on the plane.

In a single paragraph, with no details, the Iranians admitted that they had been at work for years on a secret nuclear site—a "pilot plant," they wrote, to make it sound as benign as possible—that no inspector had ever visited. It was a uranium enrichment plant, they said, built as a backup in case the Israelis or the Americans attacked the main facility at Natanz that ElBaradei's inspectors visited regularly.

ElBaradei was flabbergasted and angry. The Iranians made no apologies for lying to the inspectors for so many years. After three United Nations Security Council resolutions insisting that the Iranians cease enriching uranium—all of which were ignored by Tehran—the mullahs were only now admitting that they had long been hiding another plant. Though Iran would argue later that they had renounced the part of their agreement with the IAEA that required them to reveal new facilities before construction began, everyone understood the country's obligations. This was a plant originally intended, ElBaradei thought, to be cloaked from the world—a place to manufacture nuclear fuel away from the prying eyes of his inspectors. The Iranians wouldn't have revealed its existence unless they had suspected they were about to be caught.

As ElBaradei later learned, the plant was tunneled into a mountainside, on an Iranian Revolutionary Guard base, and surrounded by antiaircraft guns. "They called it a passive defense to protect their technology," ElBaradei told me and my colleague Bill Broad one evening in New York. "I guess if you read every day that you are going to be bombed, what else are you going to do?"

When ElBaradei landed and was whisked off to the United Nations, he showed the letter to American officials, including Obama's coordinator for weapons of mass destruction, Gary Samore. The letter said nothing about where the facility was, or why the Iranians were revealing it then. Samore thought he knew the answer to both questions.

The facility may have been news to ElBaradei, but it was hardly news to American intelligence agencies. When intelligence officials told me in the summer of 2008 that they were looking at suspect facilities in Iran, the one the Iranians turned out to be referring to in the letter—just outside the holy city of Qom—was first on their list. A few months later, at Obama's first national security briefing in Chicago in early September 2008, the candidate had been told about the mysterious site.

Later, as president, he was shown the detailed satellite images. There was a huge amount of construction underway on the mountainside. From the satellite imagery, it appeared as though Iran was building a small replica of Natanz. There were human sources as well, who had provided information to the British, the Israelis, and the Americans. Qom was not yet operational, Obama was told. But the plant—mostly the secrecy around it—was the strongest evidence yet that the Iranians were lying about the true purpose of their nuclear ambitions. From the look of it, the Qom plant was too small to make fuel for nuclear power plants. But it was big enough to turn out sufficient bomb material for one or two weapons a year while the IAEA inspectors were occupied at Natanz, the only enrichment plant the Iranians had previously acknowledged.

Samore and the deputy national security adviser, Tom Donilon, went to tell Obama about the Iranian letter the next morning. The president was in New York, preparing for his first speech to the United Nations. He was not surprised by the news. He and his advisers began to ponder how to outflank the Iranians and use the disclosure to persuade other countries to support the case for stronger sanctions against Iran. "This was our moment," one of Obama's aides said, "to end any doubts that the Iranians had a secret program, and that their intent was to have a weapons capability." He added: "Everybody's been asking, 'Where's our leverage? Well, now we just got that leverage."

Obama, Donilon, and Samore were not surprised that the Iranians had decided, belatedly, to make the existence of this new site public. In late spring 2009, American intelligence agencies determined that the Iranians knew that the secrecy of Qom had been breached. They had prepared for the possibility that the Iranians would try to preempt an embarrassing announcement by revealing the news themselves, spinning the disclosure as a voluntary gesture despite the fact that they had been working on the plant for six years.

"We knew that sooner or later we were going to have to present the evidence about Qom to the world," one of Obama's top aides told me later. By early summer, Obama had ordered that the CIA work with the British, French, and Israelis to come up with a common evaluation of the evidence. He didn't want another Iraq—with different intelligence agencies fighting over the significance of the evidence.[8]

Obama was scheduled to meet Dmitry Medvedev, the Russian president, that afternoon, and he told him about the discovery. The following day, Obama chaired a meeting of the U.N. Security Council, a previously scheduled session that was dedicated to debating how to tighten the rules on nuclear proliferation. The White House had scripted the session carefully and did not want to turn it into a moment for bashing Iran or any other individual nation. Obama said nothing in public that day about the Iranian revelation, even though the president of France, Nicolas Sarkozy, wanted to spill the beans. By late that evening the news was leaking, and the next morning, Obama, Sarkozy, and Britain's prime minister, Gordon Brown, appeared at the G20 economic summit in Pittsburgh to declare that the Iranians had been caught deceiving inspectors and must open the Qom site in two weeks. The Iranians did so—but they waited a bit more than two weeks because, as they told ElBaradei, they didn't like meeting American deadlines.

Qom turned out to be the turning point in Obama's experiment with engaging the Iranians. He had run for office declaring that he would restart direct negotiations with Tehran, exactly the kind of no-preconditions talks that Bush had rejected. Soon after taking office, Obama appealed directly to the Iranian people in a New Year's greeting and sent two private letters to Iran's supreme leader, Ayatollah Khamenei, expressing his respect for the country and urging him to sweep away thirty years of distrust. He got back only one response, "mostly a laundry list of past grievances," said one official who had read it. The Iranians were not biting.

The White House saw a chance for a breakthrough after Iran's presidential elections in June 2009, when Ahmadinejad was up for reelection. But no one could have predicted what followed: accusations in Iran that the election was fixed, followed by massive street protests. Suddenly, people were taking to the streets, yelling not "Death to America" but "Death to the Dictator." As the protests grew, the Revolutionary Guard and their thuggish allies decided that the uprising was a threat to the regime, and they set out to crush it. To the disappointment of many who thought they might finally be witnessing the crumbling of the Iranian regime, the forces of repression won out—at least for the moment. By year's end, there were accounts of protesters who were tortured, or executed, for challenging the regime.

Obama found himself boxed in. Desperately as he may have wanted to support the street protesters, he knew the risks. In Cairo earlier in the year, he had alluded to the CIA's meddling in Iranian politics in the 1953 coup that overthrew a democratically elected leader, Mohammed Mosaddeq, and ultimately replaced him with the Shah. He did not exactly apologize, but he made clear that those days were over. Now he had to keep his hands off. "Anything we said would feed into the Iranian narrative that this was all an American plot," one of Obama's Iran strategists argued, as calls were rising for the president to rally support for the dissidents.

Over the long term, the 2009 election undoubtedly did lasting damage to Khamenei, and to his fellow mullahs. For the first time, their legitimacy was questioned by their own people. Divisions in the leadership became evident to all, played out in text messages and Internet sites read all over Iran and around the world. Try as they might, the Iranians could not stop every image of the crackdown from seeping out of the country on cell phone networks and Facebook. Every few months, new protests surfaced, even at the celebration of the thirtieth anniversary of the takeover of the American embassy in Tehran. It seemed unlikely that the mullahs would ever fully recover their authority.

But as America had been reminded after Tiananmen Square, not every uprising results in social revolution. The clerics may have been backwards hardliners, but the Revolutionary Guard and the rest of the military seemed completely on the side of the supreme leader and Ahmadinejad.

In the short term, the divisions made it even more difficult for

Obama to negotiate with the Iranians. A first meeting of Iranian and American officials was finally held on October 1, in Geneva, the site of so many Cold War negotiations. It was four months after the elections, and Iran clearly wanted to show that the ugly street incidents were in the past. But the Iranian leadership was brittle and scared. The only accomplishment of the session was an agreement in principle by the Iranians to ship some of their nuclear fuel out of the country for new enrichment in Russia, where the fuel would be converted for use in a medical research reactor in Tehran that was running out of fuel. It was a deal that Ahmadinejad himself had once proposed—perhaps speaking off the top of his head—and that the Americans had immediately embraced.

The advantages for Obama were obvious. If Iran shipped a big chunk of its stockpile out of the country, it was highly unlikely that it could race to build a bomb over the next year—the dreaded "breakout scenario" that North Korea pulled off successfully six years earlier. With the fuel out of Iran, Obama would have some time and political space to work out a broader deal with the Iranians while holding off the inevitable Israeli pressure for an attack on Iran's nuclear facilities. But within two months, the deal fell apart. The Iranians rejected an agreement hashed out between the West and Iran's representatives at IAEA headquarters in Geneva. After weeks of public bickering that revealed divisions in the Iranian leadership, Khamenei himself denounced the agreement as a Western plot. That killed it. "We think their leadership is in such chaos that they can't make a decision to give anything up," one of Obama's aides told me. "The good news is that maybe they are in such chaos that they can't decide to move ahead with making a weapon, either."

Maybe so, and maybe not. At his last meeting with the IAEA board before retiring from his post, ElBaradei declared that the effort to get Iran to respond to the evidence it once worked on—or is still working on—designing nuclear weapons was at a "dead end." The board passed a resolution demanding that the country suspend its work on the Qom enrichment center—a demand even the Russians and Chinese echoed. The Iranians responded by declaring they would build ten more enrichment plants—more bluster than real threat, given the trouble they've had building two. But the direction seemed clear: Iranian leaders had concluded that at a time of political infighting, no Iranian leader could afford to be seen bending to American-led pressure.

Obama faces, in 2010, the prospect of a major confrontation with Iran. In the spring of 2009, with Prime Minister Benjamin Netanyahu of Israel at his side, Obama declared that if no progress was made with Iran by the end of the year, he would reevaluate his options and consider moving ahead with what Secretary of State Clinton once called "crippling sanctions." It is questionable whether he could bring the Russians or the Chinese along—or whether they would enforce the sanctions even if they vote for them. And there is little doubt that without help from Russia, China, and the Latin American nations that have developed close ties to Iran, the sanctions would be ineffective. Obama was running up against the limits of engagement policy: It is one thing to declare that America is no longer the sole superpower and that the rest of the world must step up to its responsibilities. It is another to figure out what to do if America's partners shy away.

The Iranians are preparing for the worst. At the end of November 2009, they organized several days of military drills specifically intended to demonstrate their ability to protect their nuclear facilities. Those drills, of course, were largely for show, all for the cameras. But as 2009 closed, there was reason to question whether Obama's engagement strategy, through no fault of his own, had jumped the tracks. And plan B, though wrapped in diplomatic niceties, would be more about confrontation than negotiation.

IF IRAN WAS Obama's biggest nuclear headache, North Korea turned out to be his first strategic surprise.

When the new president came to office, the North seemed to be an intractable problem—but not an urgent one. He thought it could safely be put on the back burner. With Kim Jong-Il reportedly desperately sick, the country would be consumed by a power struggle that could go on for years. Before they took office and were required to toe the official line that the United States would never tolerate or recognize North Korea as a nuclear-weapons state, several of Obama's top advisers acknowledged that the North would not give up its one source of leverage—no matter how big the bribe.

"Just because Kim Jong-Il is very ill," one of Obama's Asia experts said to me before formally entering the government, "it doesn't follow that he's lost his mind." Neither Kim nor his successor, he added, is likely to give up an arsenal whose cost had all but bankrupted his country. "Would you?" he asked.

Obama's team decided on a policy that might be best described as calculated neglect. To fill Chris Hill's role as the chief American envoy to the North Korean nuclear talks, they picked a graduate school dean who was told he could do the job part-time. There were no new offers on the table; Obama simply expected the North Koreans to carry out the deal Hill had negotiated at the end of the Bush administration. The North Koreans had a different idea. No sooner had Obama been sworn in than they began dismantling the deals Hill had painstakingly put together.

They announced that the "disabling" of Yongbyon would be reversed. In part, that was a bluff: The reactor was like a rusted-out '65 Chevy. But it didn't take long to revive the facilities needed to reprocess the remaining fuel in North Korea's possession, turning it into weapons-grade plutonium. Obama, not wanting to take the bait, all but ignored the provocation.

Kim was determined to up the ante—and perhaps prove that he was still alive and in charge. On Memorial Day, the North set off its second nuclear test, one designed to prove that it had fixed what went wrong in the 2006 test that fizzled.

Obama knew that he couldn't ignore the test—not after his declarations that he was going to end the post–Cold War cycle of proliferation. By the time he came back to Washington from Camp David, where he'd been for the holiday weekend, his advisers, who had been meeting on and off all day, had concluded that it was a moment to stand up to a rogue state—but to do it Obama-style, not Bush-style. Obama appeared briefly in public to declare that he would "take action" in response to what he called "a blatant violation of international law." But all the initial action was largely at the United Nations. Obama put his hard-driving ambassador, Susan Rice, to the task of seizing the moment. The idea was to get the Security Council to authorize countries essentially to shut down North Korea's ability to ship weapons—something that Bush had never managed to achieve after the first nuclear test.

Rice was partially successful. A few weeks later, the Security Council unanimously authorized sanctions that required all nations to cooperate in searching North Korean vessels suspected of carrying weapons whenever those vessels entered their territorial waters or sought to refuel at a port. But the resolution stopped short of allowing countries to stop and board those ships. That was enough to get the Russians and Chinese to join—a significant diplomatic victory. "I think we were all impressed with the fact that the Russians and the Chinese denounced [North Korea] so strongly," Rahm Emanuel told me, predicting that this was the beginning of a new era of cooperation among former Cold War rivals.

The resolution passed just as Iran's streets were erupting in protest, and the dramatic images from Tehran overshadowed the action against North Korea. With so many rogue states erupting at once, several of Obama's national security aides invited me to the conference room just outside the entrance to the Situation Room, where they tried to make the case that Obama was being prudent in both incidents: hanging back so that the Iranians could not accuse him of meddling in their disputed election and putting the screws to the North Korean economy. In fact, the resolution on North Korea was less muscular than the administration would have wanted; it did not allow North Korean ships to be flagged down for inspection in international waters. But as a practical matter, no one in the White House was eager to board ships and risk a firefight that could quickly escalate. "The chance that the North Koreans could do something stupid when a bunch of Special Forces landed on their deck is pretty high," one said.

Shortly thereafter, the White House scored a rare victory against the North: It tailed a cargo ship, believed to be carrying some kind of contraband weapons, as it left North Korea and headed toward the South China Sea. The intelligence agencies guessed it was headed toward Burma, where the North has long been helping prop up an odious regime. Perhaps the only country in the world as isolated as North Korea itself, Burma has long been suspected of trying to build a rudimentary nuclear capability of its own, with North Korean help.

After days of a slow chase—really more like a shadowing—the North Korean vessel turned around and went home. "There was a lot of coordination on this," Adm. Timothy Keating, the head of Pacific Command, told me later. "But we never did quite figure out what they were up to."

Belatedly, the administration established a modest set of goals with North Korea. Publicly, they still talked about negotiating "complete, verifiable, irreversible" surrender of all of the North's weapons and nuclear facilities. Clearly, that wasn't going to happen. But when former President Bill Clinton was sent to North Korea in August 2009 to win the release of two young American women who, in a journalistic reporting trip gone wrong, had been seized by the North along the border with China, it seemed to reconfirm that the North's ambitions had shrunk as Kim was fading.

Ill and insecure, Kim was using the drama of drawing a former American president onto his own turf to demonstrate that the Americans were still willing to send a high-level envoy to pay homage. (Clinton came back and quietly met with Obama, reporting that Kim was recovering from a stroke but still appeared fully in charge and in command of his faculties.)

But the truth is that by the time Obama came to office, North Korea no longer instilled much fear—in Washington or in Asia. Its threats rang increasingly hollow. Fifty years after the outbreak of the Korean War, neither the South Koreans nor the rest of Asia believe there is even a remote possibility of another invasion of the South. It would be regime suicide.

This reality lends weight to the Obama administration's instinct to "break the cycle" of the Clinton and Bush eras, in which the North's serial nuclear provocations lead to a payoff and an agreement that then falls apart, leading to another crisis and another payoff. "I am tired of buying the same horse twice," Defense Secretary Gates said after the North Korean nuclear test. "I think this notion that we buy our way back to the status quo ante is an approach that I personally think we ought to think very hard about."

While the administration said it was open to resuming negotiations, its strategy amounted to classic containment. "We just want to make sure the government of North Korea is operating within the basic rules of the international community," Obama said on his trip to Asia at the end of the year. The language sounded benign, but what it means is stopping North Korea from exporting reactors to Syria, or helping the Burmese learn the secrets of bomb-making. Sure, Obama will engage in diplomacy—but his expectations are limited. Like every American president before him, he is hoping for his adversary's collapse.

Containment may be the best choice available. But it doesn't eliminate the nuclear stockpile in North Korea's hands. Two Bushes, two Clintons, and Obama himself have vowed that the world will never tolerate a nuclear North Korea. Yet as 2009 came to a close, it was evident that we were learning to live with it. And the Iranians have definitely noticed.

◆

BY THE END of Obama's first year in office, he could boast several successes. He had repudiated the ideological certainties of the Bush era and replaced them with a flexible pragmatism—the pragmatism that led him to conclude that Americans could put terrorists on trial rather than lock them away in violation of American judicial principles, and that even a "war of necessity" was subject to cost limitations. This same pragmatism also led him to nationalize the country's largest car maker to save jobs but to ignore advice, much of it from his own party, to nationalize the banks. He changed—sometimes radically, sometimes incrementally—America's image around the world. He reached out to enemies, recognizing that until Washington made a bona fide effort to find diplomatic solutions to long-simmering crises such as Iran's nuclear program, there was no hope of organizing the rest of the world to enact harsh sanctions—or something more severe. He completely turned around the debate on climate change and nonproliferation, putting America into the front of the pack rather than declaring that the rules were different for the world's biggest power. These were huge changes, but mostly tonal ones.

What he had not yet demonstrated is that his engagement, dialogue, patience, lengthy analysis, and reliance on alliances can produce significantly better results. Nor had he convinced his allies or his skeptics that he was developing a broader strategic plan that would keep the United States at the center of world power, with the leverage it needs to persuade allies and keep challengers at bay. By the end of 2009, looking back at a decade that started with 9/11 and ended with a financial crash whose roots were distinctly domestic, many Americans feared our most powerful and prosperous days were behind us. Obama's challenge is to reverse that perception, even as he helps Americans adjust to a world in which cooperation with other powers is paramount.

It turned out that the easiest step was undoing the damage to

America's reputation. He went to Cairo, where al Qaeda found many of its intellectual roots, to make his appeal to the Muslim world. He quoted from the Koran, sprinkled his speech with bits of Arabic. No one could remember the last time an American president began a speech with "*Salaam aleikum*," or "Peace be upon you," the traditional Arab greeting.

By declaring that he would close the prison at Guantánamo Bay—even though he missed his own deadline to shutter it within a year of his inauguration—he started to narrow that yawning gap between America's ideals and its behavior. By acknowledging that the United States could not demand that the rest of the world forsake nuclear arms while clinging to its own outsized arsenal, he has defused one of the easiest critiques of America's atomic double standard. As Mohamed ElBaradei said as he was preparing to leave office, Obama recognized that the days were over when America could "lecture people on stopping smoking while a cigarette hung from its lips."

He envisioned a new international order, in which the United States was first among nations, but willingly ceded space—and authority—to rising powers. He showed no interest in clinging to the outdated pecking order created at the end of World War II. The financial crisis had proven the old order simply would not work: The most critical decisions were not the ones made between the United States and Europe, or even the United States and the world's second biggest economy, Japan. For good or bad—and it rankled many Americans—these were decisions that had to be made with newly empowered G20 nations, nearly half of which border the Pacific. The United States is first among this group, but China, rather than Japan or a European power, is clearly second.

The first time Obama ever set foot on Chinese soil—his trip in November 2009—he declared that the two countries carry a "burden of leadership" on issues ranging from climate change to nuclear nonproliferation to the management of the world economy. "I will tell you, other countries around the world will be waiting for us," he said. These were exactly the words the Chinese had been waiting centuries to hear. They reveled in their central role in pulling the world out of recession, and their new powers of influence. In a few months, Obama had buried, at least for the time being, sixty years of talk in the United States about "containing" China's power. He rightly concluded that containment was a loser's game—and he said so on Chinese soil.

That trip to China underscored both the enormous power of and the lingering concerns about the Obama brand around the world. He drew huge crowds: Everywhere he went, the Chinese lined the streets for a glimpse of his motorcade, and, until the Chinese government banned them, they snatched up T-shirts that bore an iconic likeness of Obama in Mao's clothes.

More important, a new generation of Chinese with no memory of Mao and a fascination with Obama's life story listened to and tweeted and blogged about what he said. They easily outwitted crude attempts by the Chinese leadership to limit the reach of his voice and the power of his message. China insisted, for example, on carefully controlling the environment of a question-and-answer session with students in Shanghai—they were largely handpicked members of the Communist Party who endured days of training about what to ask and which subjects to avoid. But one student brushed up against the limits of China's continuing rigid controls on the Internet and free speech, asking, "Should we be able to use Twitter freely?" Obama paused, then gave an answer that carefully skirted any direct criticism of the Chinese or their heavy-handed control of dissent—while still sending a message that resounded up and down the Chinese coast.

"I have a lot of critics in the United States who can say all kinds of things about me," he told the students. The cacophony of criticism, he said, "makes me a better leader because it forces me to hear opinions that I don't want to hear." Bland as it was, this comment touched off a huge amount of chatter on Chinese websites and hit the top-10 list of searches on China Google. Of course, the Chinese government tried to stuff the genie back into the bottle. Within a day, much of this traffic mysteriously disappeared, and one had to explore the back corners of the Chinese Web to find a transcript of his remarks. But while many in the United States criticized Obama for not forcing the Chinese to broadcast his comments around the country, in fact he ended up demonstrating to the Chinese elite that their leadership, for all its talents, remains ridiculously paranoid. It still fears letting a popular foreign leader communicate directly with the Chinese people.

At the same time, like Clinton and Bush before him, Obama seemed in his public comments to buy into the theory that the Internet would spur political freedom in China. It's a theme that sounds great to visiting American politicians—a demonstration of how American-invented soft power, or at least Google power, will change the world. But it ignores the evidence that, over the past twenty years, China has skillfully used the Net as an instrument of political control.

Many of Obama's exchanges with the Chinese were refreshing: They made clear that he believes the era of the sole American superpower is over. That is a truth that past presidents, and many Americans, did not want to hear—on Twitter or anyplace else. It revealed perhaps the biggest shift from the Bush era. Bush clung to the old order because he had a difficult time imagining a world in which the United States did not decide every major issue and punish violations of the global rules; his idea of "building consensus" was dragging other nations either to go along, or get out of our way. When the United States was engaged in a project that it could manage by itself, this approach worked. When it turned out the project was too big and the price too high, the rest of the world left us hanging. Obama's message was that almost every future project is too big for America alone—from taming Afghanistan to regulating financial markets and nuclear black markets—so we'd better start acting like we have a grip on reality.

Obama's vulnerability now is his risk of veering to an anti-Bush extreme. He is so determined to tread lightly, to recognize America's limitations, that some of America's rivals (and a few of our allies) read his consensus-building as an absence of conviction, or of retreat. Where he fell short in his first year was in projecting American resolve, exhibiting a steeliness that matches his analytic, bluster-free tone.

Obama's critics seized on the China trip to make the case that he was too deferential to his hosts. They cited his willingness to stand alongside President Hu at a "press conference" at which no questions were permitted and his caution against talking about China's continuing human-rights violations. Not surprisingly, Obama's aides were testy about the flood of criticism. They insisted that in private sessions, where it can do the most good, he was blunt and direct with China's leaders, particularly on human rights. They further maintained that he pressed on the issues that mattered most—and got some results. Days after Obama left China, Beijing voted to demand that Iran cease work on its newly revealed enrichment plant at Qom, and then issued a detailed proposal for reducing its carbon emissions. The proposal fell far short of what is needed to reach a global accord. But it was more than Bush got out of the Chinese on the same subject.

In the end, Obama managed his Asian hosts well. A trip that was derided in the United States was well received in the most populous region of the world. But the reaction was also a cautionary tale for a new president. His every move abroad will be examined in Washington for signs of weakness or inexperience. And even minor gestures—bowing to the Emperor of Japan, for example, a ritual of respect performed by many previous presidents—will be held up as an example of a new president ceding American preeminence.

But in more significant ways, the testing of Barack Obama is just beginning.

How else can one read Israel's open defiance of Obama's demands that they stop all growth of settlements in the disputed West Bank territories until the boundaries of an Israeli and Palestinian state are negotiated? Or Iran's bet that even Obama, with his famous skills of persuasion, will never entice the Russians and the Chinese to invoke sanctions that would truly hurt—or make good on his campaign warning that, if pushed too far, the United States might impose an embargo on Iranian oil exports? There is no other convincing way to explain North Korea's retreat from agreements it had made just the year before, testing Obama's insistence that it stick to past agreements to dismantle its nuclear facilities, no other explanation for Iran's refusal to abide by the United Nation's Security Council's resolutions demanding an end to uranium enrichment. The Chinese were too polite to say it during Obama's trek through the Forbidden City and across the Great Wall, but a country that has borrowed $2.2 trillion dollars from Beijing, and may need more, does not have a lot of leverage.

For Obama, the test will be whether he can find the elusive balance between strategic patience and conviction, whether he can find a way to marry the smart power that America has failed to use for so many years with the hard power that it has overused. When a visitor to the White House asked the president, then in office about ten months, whether allowing the Taliban to operate freely in parts of Afghanistan was a sign of a lack of determination, Obama shot back that the Taliban was not exactly equivalent to the Nazis. He was right, of course. Nonetheless, the Taliban's success would send an unmistakable message to the Muslim world that with the passage of time and enough suicide bombs, American willpower crumbles.

"The problem for Obama is how to handle the 'irreconcilables'—whether they are Taliban or rival states," one of the president's aides told me at the end of 2009. He might have added the other irreconcilables on Obama's agenda: Wall Street banks that want to go back to the way things were a few years ago, and an unemployment rate and multitrillion-dollar debt that threatens Obama's domestic agenda. Henry Kissinger remarked at the end of Obama's first year that the new president reminded him of "a chess grandmaster who has played his opening in six simultaneous games" but so far hadn't finished any of them. Between the end of his first year and the end of his first term, how he finishes a few of those games—especially against the world's irreconcilables—will be the test of how well he turns a fraught inheritance into a new start for the nation.

# ACKNOWLEDGMENTS

A book like *The Inheritance* emerges from a lifetime of reporting, and reporting is a team sport. I have been privileged to work with the best—the most talented reporting and editing staff in the world, the women and men who turn out the daily miracle that is *The New York Times*.

Bill Keller and Jill Abramson, the executive editor and managing editor for news at the paper, granted me a leave to pursue this project and they poured on good ideas over breakfasts, lunches, and dinners. Bill's ability to frame just the right question and Jill's investigative zeal—and her resiliency as Washington bureau chief during some of our toughest journalistic endeavors from 9/11 through the Iraq war—make them the kind of editors that reporters cherish.

Dean Baquet, the Washington bureau chief, repeatedly gave me the time and encouragement to get this book written. His predecessor, Phil Taubman, a veteran intelligence reporter, kept pressing for more and deeper reporting. So did Susan Chira, the paper's foreign editor, and Nick Kristof, our unparalleled op-ed columnist, who have lost none of the inquisitiveness and drive for news that drew us together in college three decades ago and led to many adventures together in Asia.

Bill Broad, my colleague since the days when we covered the investigation into the space shuttle *Challenger* in 1986, has been an indispensable partner on all things nuclear—from the investigation into the A. Q. Khan network to assessing Iran's capabilities to the story of the Israeli attack on Syria. Matt Purdy and Paul Fishleder, extraordinary editors at the *Times* investigations desk, turned our discoveries into stories.

Felicity Barringer, Warren Hoge, Mark Mazzetti, Helene Cooper, Steve Erlanger, Douglas Jehl, David Johnston, Steve Myers, Jim Risen, Sheryl Stolberg, Elaine Sciolino, and Steve Weisman have all been partners in peeling the onion of the Bush administration's national security policy. Thom Shanker and Eric Schmitt, two of the most persistent, inquisitive, and congenial reporters in Washington, were partners in covering the hardest stories of all—the overt and covert wars of the Bush administration.

There are few jobs in Washington more exhausting, frustrating, and ultimately rewarding than covering the White House, particularly in historic times. During my seven-year tenure as White House correspondent, I worked alongside two of the best: Dick Stevenson and Elisabeth Bumiller, astounding reporters with Kevlar skins and remarkable skills for getting to the ground truth. I learned as much from them every day as from any sources.

During my travels for this book, I had the benefit of help from many friends. In China, Joe Kahn, Jim Yardley, and James Fallows provided excellent advice and generously shared sources. Somini Sengupta unlocked India. In Pakistan, the brave duo of Jane Perlez and Carlotta Gall guided me through one of the world's most fascinating powder kegs. David Rohde was my coauthor in a lengthy examination of what went wrong in Afghanistan that formed the basis for a key section of this book.

Sources inside and outside the government generously provided guidance, critiques, and fresh thinking. They are too numerous to mention, and many would be embarrassed—or fired—if their names appeared here. A few tutors, however, require special thanks. Gen. Brent Scowcroft has brought both a sense of history and a delicious sense of irony to understanding the world of the Bush White House. Joseph Nye and Graham Allison of Harvard conducted their national security seminars on some of the best trout streams in America. Ash Carter, also of Harvard, was generous as always with his expertise. So were David Donald and Ernest May, two of the country's finest historians. Scott Sagan of Stanford and Gary Samore of the Council on Foreign Relations tutored me as an undergraduate, and are still at it a quarter-century later. Michael Beschloss, the most extraordinary presidential historian of our generation, was a constant source of good ideas and critiques. Glenn Kramon, one of the best newspaper editors in the business, read chapters and honed ideas.

The Center for a New American Security, a young think-tank filled with some of the brightest national security minds in Washington, gave me office space and support as a writer in residence. I thank Kurt Campbell and Michèle Flournoy, the center's founders and good friends, for their ideas, their advice, and their willingness to provide funding for this effort. Their staff of scholars and researchers were a great help, and great fun.

The Hon. Lee Hamilton, president of the Woodrow Wilson International Center for Scholars, along with Michael Van Dusen, the center's deputy director, and Robert Litwak, the director of international security studies, took me on as a visiting scholar as this project entered its last six months and provided wise counsel.

Three extraordinary young scholars made this book possible. Michael Zubrow, a 2007 graduate of the University of Pennsylvania, was in on the ground floor of this effort and worked tirelessly, raising the right questions and constantly digging deeper. Laura Marie Stroh, a graduate student at Georgetown University's School of Foreign Service, combined her understanding of intelligence issues, her Arabic abilities, and her editing skills to make every page sharper. Theo Milonopoulos, a senior at Stanford University, joined us for the summer of 2008 and contributed deep insights. I was privileged to have the chance to work with all three of them; I fear they taught me a lot more than I taught them. Without them, you wouldn't be holding this book in your hands. As they head off into bigger things in the world, America is lucky to have their talents.

My agent and friend, Michael Carlisle of Inkwell Management, turned inchoate ideas into a real project and went far beyond the call of duty by sticking with each chapter along the way. At Harmony, I learned why John Glusman has a reputation as one of the best editors in the business, one who knows what's news, knows what's missing, and knows when to spare the reader. Amy Boorstein, Linnea Knoll-mueller, Nancy Field, David Wade Smith, Rachelle Mandik, Anne Berry, and Kate Kennedy cheerfully created order out of the chaos of the bookmaking process. Shaye Areheart, the publisher of Harmony, and Jenny Frost, the president of Crown, championed this book from the beginning.

As always, I am thankful to my parents, Ken and Joan Sanger; my sister, Ellin Sanger Agress; and brother-in-law, Mort Agress, for their support and love.

The biggest thanks go to the love of my life and my best editor, Sherill, who not only shaped chapters but took on the uncelebrated burdens of parenting while I was buried behind a computer screen. Her talent and grace remind me every day how lucky I was to find her. Our sons, Andrew and Ned, kept us laughing throughout the process and joined some of the reporting—from the snowy depths of the New Hampshire primary to hikes along the Great Wall. In a troubled world, they are sheer joy.

# NOTE ON SOURCES

*The Inheritance* is based on reporting that stretches back to the beginnings of the Bush administration, which I covered from its first day. Readers of the Endnotes will see that for some historical material I drew heavily from my own writings and those of my colleagues and competitors. After I took a leave from the *Times* in September 2007 to work on this book, I conducted scores of interviews with current and former senior officials, with the understanding that they were speaking for a book that would not be published until days before the administration's end. For some, this agreement allowed a new level of candor. For others, it did not.

Many senior administration officials were generous enough to allow multiple interviews, especially on issues that were evolving quickly during the work on this book: Iran, Afghanistan, Pakistan, and North Korea. Most insisted that they speak on "background," meaning that they could not be quoted by name unless they specifically approved. A number of intelligence and military officials also agreed to talk, but with the understanding from the beginning that they would never be quoted by name.

Readers of America's major newspapers are rightly suspicious of anonymous sources. Whenever they see a phrase like "according to an administration official," they are concerned that the reporter is being spun. Many are concerned that they cannot independently evaluate the source's motives or believability. Reporters, too, dislike the practice of granting anonymity; it undercuts the credibility of what we do.

But the reality of reporting at this moment in history is that background conversations are the currency of everyday conversation, especially in Washington and especially on matters that touch on national security and intelligence collection. This is a bad habit, and every day I worked on this project I pressed sources to put their comments on the record. In a number of cases, I succeeded. In others, I failed. There are no hard and fast rules here. In many cases I discarded information that I received on background and could not independently verify from sources with a different perspective or interest. I gave significantly greater weight to individual sources who have a long track record of accuracy, and significantly less weight, or none, to sources who, in my experience, are more generous with spin than with facts or insight. When faced with a choice between using only on-the-record information and describing essential intelligence information, events, or conversations that I received on a background basis from trusted sources, I chose the latter path. There is no other way I know of to paint a picture of what has transpired in the past eight years, or the difficult choices facing the new administration.

In a handful of instances involving current intelligence information, I discussed at length with senior government officials the potential risks of publication. I withheld some details that they feared might jeopardize individuals or ongoing operations.

# Suggested Reading

Allison, Graham. *Nuclear Terrorism: The Ultimate Preventable Catastrophe.* New York: Henry Holt and Company, 2004.

Armstrong, David, and Joseph Trento. *America and the Islamic Bomb: The Deadly Compromise.* Hanover, N.H.: Steerforth Press, 2007.

Baker III, James A., and Lee Hamilton, co-chairmen. *The Iraq Study Group Report.* New York: Random House, Inc., 2006.

Barnett, Thomas, P.M. *Blueprint for Action: A Future Worth Creating.* New York: G.P. Putnam's Sons, 2005.

Benjamin, Daniel, and Steven Simon. *The Next Attack: The Failure of the War on Terror and a Strategy for Getting It Right.* New York: Henry Holt and Company, 2005.

Berman, Ilan. *Tehran Rising: Iran's Challenge to the United States.* New York: Rowman and Littlefield Publishers, Inc., 2005.

Bumiller, Elisabeth. *Condoleezza Rice: An American Life: A Biography.* New York: Random House, Inc., 2007.

Campbell, Kurt M., and Michael E. O'Hanlon. *Hard Power: The New Politics of National Security.* New York: Basic Books, 2006.

Carter, Ashton B., and William J. Perry, *Preventative Defense: New Security Strategy for America.* Washington, D.C.: Brookings Institution Press, 1999.

Chollet, Derek, and James Goldgeier. *America Between the Wars: From 11/9 to 9/11.* New York: PublicAffairs, 2008.

Chollet, Derek, Tod Lindberg, and David Shorr, eds. *Bridging the Foreign Policy Divide.* New York: Routledge, 2008.

Chua, Amy. *Day of Empire.* New York: Doubleday, 2007.

Cohen, Stephen P., *The Idea of Pakistan.* Washington, D.C.: Brookings Institution Press, 2004.

Coll, Steve. *The Bin Ladens: An Arabian Family in the American Century.* New York: The Penguin Press, 2008.

Corera, Gordon. *Shopping for Bombs*. Oxford: Oxford University Press, 2006.

Daalder, Ivo H., and James M. Lindsay. *America Unbound: The Bush Revolution in Foreign Policy*. Washington D.C.: Brookings Institution Press, 2005.

DeYoung, Karen. *Soldier: The Life of Colin Powell*. New York: Alfred A. Knopf, 2006.

Doyle, Michael W.; Stephen Macedo, ed. *Striking First: Preemption and Prevention in International Conflict*. Princeton, N.J.: Princeton University Press, 2008.

Drogin, Bob. *Curveball: Spies, Lies, and the Con Man Who Caused a War*. New York: Random House, Inc., 2007.

Fortier, John C., and Norman J. Ornstein, eds. *Second-Term Blues: How George W. Bush Has Governed*. Washington, D.C.: Brookings Institution Press, 2007.

Frantz, Douglas, and Catherine Collins. *The Nuclear Jihadist*. New York: Twelve, 2007.

Friedman, Thomas L. *Longitudes and Attitudes: Exploring the World after September 11*. New York: Farrar, Straus and Giroux, 2002.

_____. *The World Is Flat: A Brief History of the Twenty-First Century*. New York: Farrar, Straus, and Giroux, 2006.

Galbraith, Peter W. *The End of Iraq: How American Incompetence Created a War Without End*. New York: Simon & Schuster Paperbacks, 2006.

Goldstein, Morris, and Nicholas R. Lardy. *Debating China's Exchange Rate Policy*. Washington, D.C.: Peter G. Peterson Institute for International Economics, 2008.

Gordon, Michael R., and General Bernard E. Trainor. *Cobra II: The Inside Story of the Invasion and Occupation of Iraq*. New York: Pantheon Books, 2006.

Haass, Richard. *The Opportunity: America's Moment to Alter History's Course*. New York: PublicAffairs, 2005.

Hachigian, Nina, and Mona Sutphen. *The Next American Century: How the U.S. Can Thrive as Other Powers Rise*. New York: Simon & Schuster, 2008.

Hormats, Robert D. *The Price of Liberty*. New York: Henry Holt and Company, 2007.

Jafarzadeh, Alireza. *The Iran Threat: President Ahmadinejad and the Coming Nuclear Crisis*. New York: Palgrave Macmillian, 2007.

Kagan, Robert. *Dangerous Nation: America's Foreign Policy from Its Earliest Days to the Dawn of the Twentieth Century*. New York: Alfred A. Knopf, 2006.

_____. *The Return of History and the End of Dreams*. New York: Alfred A. Knopf, 2008.

Kaplan, Fred. *Daydream Believers: How a Few Grand Ideas Wrecked American Power*. Hoboken, N.J.: John Wiley & Sons, 2008.

Kean, Thomas H., and Lee Hamilton. *The 9/11 Commission Report: Final Report of the National Commission on Terrorist Attacks Upon the United States*. New York: W. W. Norton and Company, 2004.

Kessler, Glenn. *The Confidante: Condoleezza Rice and the Creation of the Bush Legacy*. New York: St. Martin's Press, 2007.

Langewiesche, William. *The Atomic Bazaar: The Rise of the Nuclear Poor*. New York: Farrar, Straus and Giroux, 2007.

Levy, Adrian, and Catherine Scott-Clark. *Nuclear Deception: Pakistan, the U.S. and the Secret Trade in Nuclear Weapons*. New York: Walker and Company, 2007.

Lewis, Bernard. *The Middle East: A Brief History of the Last 2,000 Years*. New York: Simon & Schuster, 1995.

Lilley, James. *China Hands*. New York: PublicAffairs, 2004.

Litwak, Robert S. *Regime Change: U.S. Strategy Through the Prism of 9/11*. Washington, D.C.: Woodrow Wilson Center Press, 2007.

Mann, James. *The China Fantasy: How Our Leaders Explain Away Chinese Repression*. New York: Viking, 2007.

Margulies, Joseph. *Guantánamo and the Abuse of Presidential Power*. New York: Simon & Schuster Paperbacks, 2006.

Matthews, Mark. *The Lost Years: Bush, Sharon and Failure in the Middle East*. New York: Nation Books, 2007.

Mayer, Jane, and Doyle McManus. *Landslide: The Unmaking of the President, 1984–1988*. Boston: Houghton, Mifflin and Company, 1988.

Musharraf, Pervez. *In the Line of Fire: A Memoir*. New York: Free Press, 2006.

Nasr, Vali. *The Shia Revival: How Conflicts Within Islam Will Shape the Future*. New York: W. W. Norton and Company, 2007.

Nixon, Richard. *1999: Victory Without War*. New York: Simon & Schuster, 1988.

Nixon, Richard M. *The Real War*. New York: Warner Books, 1980.

Oberdorfer, Don. *The Two Koreas*. Reading, Mass: Addison-Wesley, 1997.

Oren, Michael B. *Power, Faith, and Fantasy: America in the Middle East 1776 to the Present*. New York: W.W. Norton and Company, 2007.

Packer, George. *The Assassins' Gate: America in Iraq*. New York: Farrar, Straus and Giroux, 2005.

Podhoretz, Norman. *World War IV: The Long War Against Islamofascism*. New York: Doubleday, 2007.

Powell, Colin L., and Joseph E. Persico. *My American Journey*. New York: Random House, Inc., 1996.

Pritchard, Charles L. *Failed Diplomacy: The Tragic Story of How North Korea Got the Bomb*. Washington, D.C.: Brookings Institution Press, 2007.

Reiss, Mitchell. *Without the Bomb*. New York: Columbia University Press, 1988.

Rhodes, Richard. *Dark Sun: The Making of the Hydrogen Bomb*. New York: Simon & Schuster, 1995.

Ricks, Thomas E. *Fiasco: The American Military Adventure in Iraq, 2003–2005*. New York: The Penguin Press, 2006.

Risen, James. *State of War: The Secret History of the CIA and the Bush Administration*. New York: Free Press, 2006.

Ross, Dennis. *Statecraft and How to Restore America's Standing in the World*. New York: Farrar, Straus and Giroux, 2007.

Sandalow, David. *Freedom from Oil: How the Next President Can End the United States' Oil Addiction*. New York: McGraw Hill Companies, 2008.

Silberman, Laurence H., and Charles S. Robb (co-chairmen). *The Commission on the Intelligence Capabilities of the United States Regarding WMD, Report to the President of the United States*. Washington, D.C.: Commission on the Intelligence Capabilities of the United States Regarding Weapons of Mass Destruction, March 31, 2005.

Slavin, Barbara. *Bitter Friends, Bosom Enemies: Iran, the U.S., and the Twisted Path to Confrontation*. New York: St. Martin's Press, 2007.

Stewart, Rory. *The Places in Between*. New York: Harcourt Books, 2004.

Suskind, Ron. *The One Percent Doctrine*. New York: Simon & Schuster, 2006.

Takeyh, Ray. *Hidden Iran: Paradox and Power in the Islamic Republic*. New York: Henry Holt and Company, 2006.

Tenet, George. *At the Center of the Storm: My Years at the C.I.A.* New York: HarperCollins, 2007.

Whitney, Craig R., ed. *The WMD Mirage: Iraq's Decade of Deception and America's False Premise for War*. New York: PublicAffairs, 2005.

Wit, Joel S., Daniel B. Poneman, and Robert L. Gallucci. *Going Critical: The First North Korean Nuclear Crisis*. Washington, D.C.: Brookings Institution Press, 2004.

Woodward, Bob. *Bush at War*. New York: Simon & Schuster, 2003.

Wright, Lawrence. *The Looming Tower: Al-Qaeda and the Road to 9/11*. New York: Alfred A. Knopf, 2007.

# ENDNOTES

*Where there are attributed quotes in the text that are not cited in the notes, they derive from personal interviews.*

## INTRODUCTION: THE BRIEFING

1. In both public and private comments, McConnell and the director of the CIA, Michael Hayden, noted that the first bombing of the World Trade Center in 1993 came in the first year of the Clinton administration, and 9/11 in the first year of the Bush administration. Whether that was coincidence or part of a strategy of striking when administrations are new is a subject of considerable debate.

2. Remarks by the Director of National Intelligence at the United States Geospatial Intelligence Foundation, October 30, 2008.

3. According to intelligence officials, a number of the reports for the candidates were distilled in part from new National Intelligence Estimates that were being prepared around the same time.

4. Mark Mazzetti, "C.I.A. Chief Says Qaeda Is Extending Its Reach," *The New York Times,* November 13, 2008, p. A12.

5. "Hackers and Spending Sprees," *Newsweek*, November 5, 2008.

6. A fascinating history of intelligence briefings for presidential candidates can be found on the CIA's website, at https://www.cia.gov/library/center-for-the-study-of-intelligence/csi-publications/books-and-monographs/cia-briefings-of-presidential-candidates/index.htm.

7. The difference was that Kennedy acknowledged the mistake in the case of Cuba, whereas Bush spent years denying he miscalculated about Iraq. Kennedy ruefully noted later: "If someone comes in to tell me this or that about the minimum wage bill, I have no hesitation in overruling them. But you always assume that the military and intelligence people have some secret skill not available to ordinary mortals." Quoted in Kurt M. Campbell and James B. Steinberg, *Difficult Transitions: Foreign Policy Troubles at the Outset of Presidential Power*, Brookings Institution Press, Washington, D.C., 2008, pp. 26–27.

8. Gates resigned from the group when he was appointed Defense Secretary, so he never signed its final report. Fellow members of the commission, however, say they heard no dissent from him about its major conclusions.

## PART I: IRAN
### THE MULLAHS' MANHATTAN PROJECT

CHAPTER 1 · DECODING PROJECT 111

1. Some details of the network penetration have been omitted at the request of senior intelligence officials.

2. This account of the description Bush was given is based on interviews with a number of officials who were involved in vetting the intelligence and passing it on to the White House, along with interviews of White House officials. But none directly witnessed the conversation—they heard about it later—and none would agree to be named because of the highly sensitive nature of the intelligence.

3. McCain interview on *Face the Nation*, January 15, 2006. He repeated versions of the statement several times throughout the presidential campaign.

4. See Seymour Hersh, "Shifting Targets," *The New Yorker*, October 8, 2007; Seymour Hersh, "The Redirection," *The New Yorker*, March 5, 2007; Seymour Hersh, "The Next Act," *The New Yorker*, November 27, 2006; Seymour Hersh, "Last Stand," *The New Yorker*, July 10, 2006; and Seymour Hersh, "The Iran Plans," *The New Yorker*, April 17, 2006. Hersh also wrote that consideration was being given to use nuclear weapons to wipe out Iran's facilities, an idea dismissed by several top military officials as highly unlikely, in part because conventional weapons could do the trick and in part because it would put the United States in the position of employing nuclear weapons to prevent a nuclear war.

5. Several of the authors of the National Intelligence Estimate on Iran agreed to be interviewed for this chapter. Except as noted later in the chapter, most refused to be named because they remain in their jobs in the intelligence agencies.

6. Lawrence Wright, "The Spymaster," *The New Yorker*, January 21, 2008.

7. Author interview with senior intelligence official, December 2007.

8. In January 2008, after the NIE was published, Israeli intelligence officials handed a secret dossier to the authors of the report to make the case that the report's authors had underestimated the threat. "A little late and nothing new," one of the Americans who reviewed it said to me later, dismissively.

9. Author interview with a senior Israeli official, January 2008.

10. Author interview with a senior intelligence official, December 2007.

11. Bush press conference, October 17, 2007.

12. The Iranians were referring, accurately, to Article IV of the Nuclear Non-Proliferation Treaty, "Nothing in this Treaty shall be interpreted as affecting the inalienable right of all the Parties to the Treaty to develop research, production and use of nuclear energy for peaceful purposes without discrimination and in conformity with Articles I and II of this Treaty." Many of the debates about whether the treaty needs to be amended center on this sentence, which creates a loophole for any nation that pursues a civilian program, to renounce the treaty and uses their nuclear material for weapons. In the parlance of nuclear experts, this is called "breakout."

13. Lawrence Wright, "The Spymaster," *The New Yorker,* January 21, 2008.

14. Author interview with former intelligence official, spring 2008.

15. Jim Rutenberg and David E. Sanger, "Overhaul Moves White House Data Center into the Modern Era," *The New York Times,* December 19, 2006.

16. Unclassified key judgments of the National Intelligence Estimate entitled, "Iran: Nuclear Intentions and Capabilities," p. 1.

17. Author interview with Thomas Fingar, January 25, 2008.

18. After McConnell told a conference on intelligence analysis in Washington on October 13, 2007, that he planned to reverse the practice of releasing "key judgments" of NIEs, one of his deputies, David R. Shedd, told reporters that McConnell had issued a directive to discourage declassification. "It affects the quality of what's written," he said. "Spy Chief Makes It Harder to Declassify NIE's," *Washington Post,* October 27, 2007.

19. David E. Sanger, "Bush Says U.S. Will Not Tolerate Building of Nuclear Arms by Iran," *The New York Times,* June 19, 2003.

20. Author interview with a senior Egyptian official, fall 2007.

## CHAPTER 2 · REGIME-CHANGE FANTASIES

1. Robert Gates, *From the Shadows* (New York: Simon & Schuster, 1996).

2. Author interview with Robert Gates, April 22, 2008.

3. Robert Gates, *From the Shadows* (New York: Simon & Schuster, 1996).

4. Author interview with Robert Gates, April 22, 2008.

5. "Iran's Strategic Weapons Programmes: A Net Assessment," International Institute for Strategic Studies, 2006, p. 12.

6. "Nuclear Black Markets: Pakistan, A. Q. Khan and the Rise of Proliferation Networks, A Net Assessment," International Institute for Strategic Studies, 2007.

7. John Lancaster and Kamran Khan, "Pakistanis Say Nuclear Scientists Aided Iran," *Washington Post,* January 24, 2004.

8. The best description of these meetings appears in Doug Frantz and Catherine Collins's excellent book about Khan and his network, *The Nuclear Jihadist* (New York: Twelve Books, 2007), p. 154–61.

9. Doug Frantz and Catherine Collins, *The Nuclear Jihadist* (New York: Twelve Books, 2007), pp. 211–13.

10. The exact nature of the threat has been reported in several different versions, but there are accounts in two excellent books, Steve Coll's *Ghost Wars: The Secret History of the CIA, Afghanistan and Bin Laden, from the Soviet Invasion to September 10, 2001* (New York: Penguin, 2004), 220, and in Doug Frantz and Catherine Collins, *The Nuclear Jihadist* (New York: Twelve Books, 2007).

11. Interview with Benazir Bhutto for "Nuclear Jihad: Can Terrorists Get the Bomb?" a *New York Times*/Canadian Broadcasting/Discovery Channel documentary, first broadcast April 20, 2006. My thanks to our producer, Julian Scher, who conducted the interview.

12. Author interview with John McLaughlin, February 2008.

13. Bush made his comments during a meeting with reporters at the White House in February 2007.

14. "Leading Conservative Ayatollah Condemns Slaughter of Innocent People," *Financial Times*, September 15, 2001.

15. A good discussion of these tensions appears in Barbara Slavin's account of America's ill-fated relationship with Iran, *Bitter Friends, Bosom Enemies* (New York: St. Martin's Press, 2007), pp. 90–91.

16. I would cite David Kilcullen's work on disaggregating terrorist threats. He wrote a CNAS Solarium paper on the subject and a great article called "Countering Global Insurgency," available from http://smallwarsjournal.com/documents/kilcullen.pdf.

17. The President's State of the Union Address, available from http://www.whitehouse.gov/news/releases/2002/01/20020129-11.html.

18. Ibid.

19. David E. Sanger, "Bush, Focusing on Terrorism, Says Secure U.S. Is Top Priority," *The New York Times*, January 30, 2002, p. 1.

20. Karen DeYoung, *Soldier: The Life of Colin Powell* (New York: Knopf, 2006).

21. David E. Sanger, "Bush Aides Say Tough Tone Put Foes on Notice," *The New York Times*, January 31, 2002, p. 1.

22. Ibid.

23. Michael Slackman, "All Sides in Iran Seize on Bush's Condemnations," *Los Angeles Times*, July 20, 2002.

24. Todd S. Purdum and David E. Sanger, "It Was Clinton at Waldorf Instead of Dessert," *The New York Times*, February 5, 2002, p. 1.

25. Glenn Kessler, "Front Firms Aided Iran Nuclear Bomb Effort, Sources Say; India and China Said to Provide Materials," *Washington Post*, December 19, 2002.

26. National Intelligence Council, "Regional Consequences of Regime Change in Iraq," ICA 2003-03, p. 18, available on the website of the Senate Intelligence Committee.

27. Nicholas Kristof, "Iran's Proposal for a 'Grand Bargain,'" NYTimes on the Ground Blog, April 28, 2007.

28. The text of the letter is available from the Inter Press Service News Agency website, at http://ipsnews.net/iranletterfacsimile.pdf.

29. Author interview with a senior administration official, July 2008.

30. Author interview with Richard Haass, January 2008.

31. Glenn Kessler, "In 2003, U.S. Spurned Iran's Offer of Dialogue," *Washington Post,* June 18, 2006.

32. John Bolton, interview for a PBS *Frontline* episode, "Showdown with Iran," http://www.pbs.org/wgbh/pages/frontline/showdown/themes/grandbargain.html.

33. Joby Warrick, "Iran Given Deadline to Lay Bare Nuclear Program," *Washington Post,* September 13, 2003.

34. Nazila Fathi, "Iran Cleric Suggests Nation Quit Nuclear Nonproliferation Treaty," *The New York Times,* September 20, 2003.

35. See Glenn Frankel and Keith B. Richburg, "Europeans Seek Arms Accord in Tehran; Iran Would Get Aid on Civilian Nuclear Program," *Washington Post,* October 21, 2003; and Elaine Sciolino, "Iran Will Allow UN Inspections of Nuclear Sites," *The New York Times,* October 22, 2003.

36. David E. Sanger and Steven Weisman, "U.S. and Allies Agree on Steps in Iran Dispute," *The New York Times,* March 11, 2005.

37. Author interview with Condoleezza Rice and Stephen J. Hadley, June 2, 2006.

## CHAPTER 3 · AHMADINEJAD'S MONOLOGUE

1. This strained credulity. Both before and after Ahmadinejad's talk, American forces were capturing members of the elite Quds Force, part of the Iranian Revolutionary Guard, inside Iraq. See David E. Sanger and Michael R. Gordon, "Rice Says Bush Authorized Iranians' Arrest in Iraq," *The New York Times,* January 13, 2007.

2. The most detailed public account of the contents of the laptop—though the computer itself is not mentioned—is in the IAEA's report to its board of governors, dated February 22, 2008, and available on www.iaea.org.

3. The first detailed account of the acquisition of the laptop was reported by the author and Bill Broad, and appeared as "The Laptop: Relying on Computer, U.S. Seeks to Prove Iran's Nuclear Aims," *The New York Times,* November 13, 2005, p. 1. Carla Anne Robbins wrote an earlier account: "U.S. Gives Briefing on Iranian Missile to Nuclear Agency," *Wall Street Journal,* July 27, 2005, p. A3. Both current and retired intelligence officials have since filled in additional details, and the data on the laptop was revisited during the compilation of the National Intelligence Estimate in late 2007. It concluded that although the description of the program contained in the computer

was largely accurate, the program was suspended after the laptop left Iran.

4. "The Commission on the Intelligence Capabilities of the United States Regarding Weapons of Mass Destruction: Report to the President of the United States," March 31, 2005, p. 305. The commission said almost nothing about Iran and North Korea in its unclassified report, but had eleven findings that it included in the classified version.

5. Author interview with John McLaughlin, January 2008.

6. The statement was reported to the author by two senior administration officials during the course of separate interviews.

7. William J. Broad and David E. Sanger, "The Laptop: Relying on Computer, U.S. Seeks to Prove Iran's Nuclear Aims," *The New York Times*, November 13, 2005.

8. Presidential news conference, December 18, 2005.

9. Author interviews with senior American officials, June 2006.

10. Much of the account of the American effort to sabotage the Iranian program first appeared in a story with my colleague Bill Broad, whose reporting contributed greatly to our understanding of the American effort. William Broad and David E. Sanger, "In Nuclear Net's Undoing, A Web of Shadowy Deals," *The New York Times*, August 25, 2008, p. 1. Souad Mekhennet aided us from Frankfurt, and Uta Harnischfeger from Zurich.

11. *Ayande-ye Now*, January 6, 2007.

12. Iranian officials talked briefly about the power-supply incident but said they were moving to build their own. All the evidence suggests they have solved the problem, and at the beginning of 2008 they showed IAEA inspectors a second generation of centrifuges—called the P-2—that they were preparing to install in coming years. The P-2, also a Pakistani design, should énable the country to enrich uranium faster, more efficiently, and more reliably. The first detailed explanation of this transition appeared in a German news service, "*Iran is bereit für nächsten wichtigen Schritt im Atomprogramm*," APA Online, January 25, 2008.

13. Remarks by Condoleezza Rice at State Department ceremony, April 10, 2008.

## CHAPTER 4 · THE ISRAEL OPTION

1. Elaine Sciolino and William J. Broad, "To Iran and Its Foes, an Indispensable Irritant," *The New York Times*, September 17, 2007, p. A1.

2. My thanks to Elaine Sciolino and Bill Broad, who conducted much of the reporting on the Heinonen briefing. Several diplomats who attended the session shared their notes. In addition, David Albright has posted useful details at http://www.isis-online.org/publications/iran/IAEA_Briefing_Weaponization.pdf.

3. Ahmadinejad's statement was reported on the Iranian presidency's website on December 5, 2007. It is also quoted in Dennis Ross's excellent paper "Diplomatic Strategies for Dealing with Iran," included in *Iran: Assessing U.S. Strategic Options* (Washington, D.C.: Center for a New American Security, June 2008).

4. David E. Sanger, "Why Not a Strike on Iran?" *The New York Times*, January 22, 2006, p. 1.

5. Robert Gates's Senate hearing for confirmation as secretary of Defense, December 5, 2006.

6. My colleague James Risen documented several of these efforts in *State of War: The Secret History of the CIA and the Bush Administration,* (New York: Free Press, 2006).

## PART II: AFGHANISTAN
## HOW THE GOOD WAR WENT BAD

### CHAPTER 5 · THE MARSHALL PLAN THAT WASN'T

Much of the initial reporting for this chapter was conducted with my *Times* colleague David Rohde, an extraordinary journalist with a deep understanding of Afghanistan. Our joint project resulted in a lengthy *Times* investigation, "Losing the Advantage: How the 'Good War' in Afghanistan Went Bad," published in *The New York Times* on August 12, 2007. Many of the original sources for that story have been re-interviewed, and many others have been added since, to update the account. My thanks to David for his reporting and his advice; the editorial conclusions about the administration's successes and failures are, of course, my own.

1. Author interview with Gen. Dan McNeill, June 16, 2008.

2. M. K. Bhadrakumar, "Afghanistan: Why NATO Cannot Win," *Asia Times*, September 30, 2006; Tim Shipman, "US Officials 'Despair' at Nato Allies' Failings in Afghanistan," *The Telegraph*, June 22, 2008.

3. I cited Bush's political use of the Afghan war in "At All Bush Rallies, Message Is 'Freedom Is on the March,'" *The New York Times*, October 21, 2004, p. A1.

4. Author interview with Lt. Gen. Douglas Lute, June 2008.

5. Adm. Mike Mullen, testimony before the House Armed Services Committee on Security and Stability in Afghanistan: "Status of U.S. Strategy and Operations and the Way Ahead," December 11, 2007.

6. David Rohde and David E. Sanger, "How a 'Good War' in Afghanistan Went Bad," *The New York Times*, August 12, 2007.

7. Ibid.

8. President Bush's speech at the Virginia Military Institute, April 17, 2002.

9. Author interview with James Dobbins, June 7, 2008. Dobbins wrote about the experience in his book *After the Taliban* (Dulles, VA: Potomac Books, 2008).

10. Author interview with President Bush, January 14, 2001.

11. David Rohde and David E. Sanger, "How a 'Good War' in Afghanistan Went Bad," *The New York Times*, August 12, 2007.

12. Author interview with Condoleezza Rice, April 28, 2003.

13. E-mail exchange with Colin Powell, July 2007.

14. David Rohde and David E. Sanger, "How a 'Good War' in Afghanistan Went Bad," *The New York Times*, August 12, 2007.

15. Ibid.

16. James F. Dobbins, *After the Taliban* (Dulles, VA: Potomac Books, 2008).

17. Author interview with John McLaughlin, June 2007.

18. David Rohde and David E. Sanger, "How a 'Good War' in Afghanistan Went Bad," *The New York Times*, August 12, 2007.

19. Ibid.

20. Mark Mazzeti and David Rohde, "Amid U.S. Policy Disputes, Qaeda Grows in Pakistan," *The New York Times,* June 30, 2008.

21. David Rohde and David E. Sanger, "How a 'Good War' in Afghanistan Went Bad," *The New York Times*, August 12, 2007.

22. Author interview and e-mail exchange with Lt. Gen. Karl Eikenberry, June 2008.

23. Lt. Gen. Karl Eikenberry's written testimony to the House Armed Services Committee, February 13, 2007.

24. David Rohde and David E. Sanger, "How a 'Good War' in Afghanistan Went Bad," *The New York Times*, August 12, 2007.

25. Ibid.

26. Bush and Musharraf meeting at the White House, February 13, 2002.

27. Douglas Jehl, "A Nation Challenged: Journalists; Pakistan Officials Arrest a Key Suspect in Pearl Kidnapping," *The New York Times*, February 13, 2002.

28. Remarks by President Bush and President Musharraf at Camp David, June 24, 2003.

29. David E. Sanger, "Bush Offers Pakistan Aid, but No F-16's," *The New York Times,* June 25, 2003.

30. David Rohde and David E. Sanger, "How a 'Good War' in Afghanistan Went Bad," *The New York Times*, August 12, 2007.

## CHAPTER 6 · THE OTHER "MISSION ACCOMPLISHED"

1. Author interview with Gen. Dan McNeill, June 16, 2008.

2. Remarks by Secretary Rumsfeld in Kabul, Afghanistan, May 1, 2003.

3. Carlotta Gall, "Warlords Yield to Afghan Leader, Pledging to Hand Over Funds," *The New York Times*, May 21, 2003.
4. Linda D. Kozaryn, "U.S. Focus Turns to Afghanistan's Reconstruction," American Forces Press Service, U.S. Dept. of Defense, January 16, 2003.
5. David Rohde and David E. Sanger, "How a 'Good War' in Afghanistan Went Bad," *The New York Times*, August 12, 2007.
6. Ibid.
7. Ibid.
8. Ibid.
9. Mark Mazzeti and David Rohde, "Amid U.S. Policy Disputes, Qaeda Grows in Pakistan," *The New York Times,* June 30, 2008.
10. David Rohde and David E. Sanger, "How a 'Good War' in Afghanistan Went Bad," *The New York Times*, August 12, 2007.
11. Mark Mazzeti and David Rohde, "Amid U.S. Policy Disputes, Qaeda Grows in Pakistan," *The New York Times,* June 30, 2008.
12. Eric Schmitt and David S. Cloud, "U.S. May Start Pulling Out of Afghanistan Next Spring," *The New York Times*, September 14, 2005.
13. David S. Cloud, "Europeans Oppose U.S. Plan for NATO in Afghanistan," *The New York Times*, September 13, 2005.
14. Ibid.
15. David Rohde and David E. Sanger, "How a 'Good War' in Afghanistan Went Bad," *The New York Times*, August 12, 2007.
16. Kenneth Katzman, "Afghanistan: Post-War Governance, Security, and U.S. Policy," CRS Report RL30588, July 11, 2008, pp. 59–60.
17. David Rohde and David E. Sanger, "How a 'Good War' in Afghanistan Went Bad," *The New York Times*, August 12, 2007.
18. Ibid.
19. Mark Mazzetti and David Rhode, "Amid U.S. Policy Disputes, Qaeda Grows in Pakistan," *The New York Times,* June 30, 2008.
20. Carlotta Gall, "Musharraf Pledges to Pursue Qaeda and Taliban Insurgents," *The New York Times*, September 8, 2006.
21. Carlotta Gall and Ismail Khan, "Taliban and Allies Tighten Grip in North of Pakistan," *The New York Times*, December 11, 2006.
22. Musharraf's interview with Wolf Blitzer of CNN, September 26, 2006.
23. Private dinner meeting at the White House with Bush, Karzai, and Musharraf, September 27, 2006.
24. Mark Mazzetti and David Rohde, "Amid U.S. Policy Disputes, Qaeda Grows in Pakistan," *The New York Times,* June 30, 2008.
25. The account of Townsend's meeting is based on interviews with several participants.
26. Carlotta Gall and David E. Sanger, "Civilian Deaths Undermine Allies' War on Taliban," *The New York Times*, May 13, 2007, p. 1.

27. Testimony of Robert Gates before the House Armed Services Committee, December 11, 2007.

28. Author interview with Gen. Dan McNeill, June 16, 2008.

29. Thomas Schweich, "Is Afghanistan a Narco-State?" *New York Times Magazine,* July 27, 2008.

30. Pervez Musharraf, *In the Line of Fire,* New York: Free Press, 2006, 273–74.

31. Mark Mazzetti and David E. Sanger, "Bush Advisers See a Failed Strategy Against al Qaeda," *The New York Times,* July 17, 2007, p. 1.

32. David Rohde and David E. Sanger, "How a 'Good War' in Afghanistan Went Bad," *The New York Times,* August 12, 2007.

33. Ibid.

34. Author interview with David Kilcullen, December 2007.

## PART III: PAKISTAN
## "HOW DO YOU INVADE AN ALLY?"

### CHAPTER 7 · SECRETS OF CHAKLALA CANTONMENT

1. Author interview with Khalid Kidwai, April 2008.

2. Khan made his comments to the Associated Press, which ran them in a series of dispatches on July 4, 2008.

3. "Fareed Zakaria's Interview with President Pervez Musharraf," *Newsweek,* January 12, 2008.

4. Author interview with Rolf Mowatt-Larrsen, April 2008.

5. Ron Suskind, "The Untold Story of al-Qaeda's Plot to Attack the Subway," *Time,* June 19, 2006.

6. Author interview with Adm. Timothy Keating, May 15, 2008.

7. Bush expressed this concern to the author and other reporters in February 2007.

8. Tim Weiner, "After an Anguished Phone Call, Clinton Penalizes Pakistanis," *The New York Times,* May 29, 1998.

9. Author interview with Pervez Musharraf by the author, September 12, 2005, at the Roosevelt Hotel in New York.

10. Bhutto described her father's insistence on starting the bomb project during an interview in London conducted for a *New York Times*/Canadian Broadcasting/Discovery Channel documentary, "Nuclear Jihad: Can Terrorists Get the Bomb?"

11. Author interview with Gen. Talat Masood, April 6, 2008, in Islamabad.

12. Ibid.

13. The first detailed story on Mahmood's meeting and the American effort to understand it appeared as part of the first investigations we conducted at the *Times* about Pakistan's involvement with al Qaeda and the Taliban.

See Douglas Frantz, James Risen, and David E. Sanger, "Nuclear Experts in Pakistan May Have Links to al Qaeda," *The New York Times*, December 9, 2001, p. A1.

14. Peter Baker, "Pakistani Scientist Who Met Bin Laden Failed Polygraphs, Renewing Suspicions," *Washington Post*, March 3, 2002, p. 1.

15. Some of the most detailed accounts of Mahmood's life and adventures, to the extent they are understood, were recounted in David Albright and Holly Higgins, "A Bomb for the Ummah," *Bulletin of the Atomic Scientists*, March 2, 2003. Also, Graham Allison has an account in *Nuclear Terrorism: the Ultimate Preventable Catastrophe* (New York: Times Books, 2004), pp. 20–24, and Doug Frantz and Catherine Collins explore the issue in *The Nuclear Jihadist* (New York: Twelve Books, 2007), pp. 263–71.

16. David Albright and Holly Higgins, "A Bomb for the Ummah," *Bulletin of the Atomic Scientists*, March 2, 2003.

17. George Tenet, *At the Center of the Storm: My Years at the CIA* (New York: HarperCollins, 2007), p. 268.

18. Patrick Tyler, "Powell Suggests Role for Taliban," *The New York Times*, October 17, 2001.

19. George Tenet, *At the Center of the Storm: My Years at the CIA* (New York: HarperCollins, 2007), 265.

20. Ibid.

21. Author interview with Colin Powell, March 18, 2008.

22. Pervez Musharraf, *In the Line of Fire* (London: Simon and Schuster, 2006).

23. Author interview with Pervez Musharraf in September 2005 for a New York Times/Canadian Broadcasting/Discovery Channel documentary, "Nuclear Jihad: Can Terrorists Get the Bomb?"

24. David E. Sanger, "So, What About Those Nukes?" *The New York Times*, November 11, 2007, p. 1.

25. Ibid.

26. Ibid.

27. Author interview with an official who was a member of the delegation.

28. I am indebted to my colleague Bill Broad for explaining the intricacies of PALs systems, and to the guidance of a number of current and former American officials who requested that they not be named.

29. David E. Sanger and William J. Broad, "U.S. Secretly Aids Pakistan in Guarding Nuclear Arms," *The New York Times*, November 18, 2007.

30. Richard Ullman, "The Covert French Connection," *Foreign Policy*, no. 75 (Summer 1989).

31. David E. Sanger and William J. Broad, "In Nuclear Net's Undoing, A Web of Shadowy Deals," *The New York Times*, August 24, 2008.

32. "Nuclear scientist says he confessed to 'save' Pakistan," *Agence France-Presse*, April 7, 2008.

33. "A. Q. Khan says he confessed to 'save' Pakistan," *Daily Times* (Islamabad), April 8, 2008, p. 1.
34. The quotes are from a private communication from A. Q. Khan shared with the author.

### CHAPTER 8 · CROSSING THE LINE

1. The broad outlines, and some specifics, of Bush's secret decisions about Pakistan are described in this account. A few specific details have been withheld at the request of officials who made a persuasive case that they could compromise ongoing intelligence or military operations.
2. Remarks by Ted Gistaro, National Intelligence Officer for Transnational Threats, The Washington Institute for Near East Policy, August 12, 2008, at www.dni.gov/speeches.
3. The reconstruction of what happened that night was put together brilliantly by my colleague Carlotta Gall in "Taliban Gain New Foothold in Afghan City," *The New York Times*, August 27, 2008, p. 1.
4. Several intelligence officials confirmed that they had seen intelligence reports in which General Kayani was reported to have described Haqqani in those terms. A senior Pakistani intelligence official used the same term to describe Haqqani to a *Times* reporter several years ago.
5. Mark Mazzetti and Eric Schmitt, "Pakistanis Aided Attack in Kabul, U.S. Officials Say," *The New York Times*, August 1, 2008, p. 1.
6. Dexter Filkins, "The Long Road to Chaos in Pakistan," *The New York Times*, Week in Review, September 28, 2008.
7. Mark Mazzetti and Eric Schmitt, "U.S. Study Is Said to Warn of Crisis in Afghanistan," *The New York Times*, October 8, 2008, p. 1.
8. Ibid.

### PART IV: NORTH KOREA
### THE NUCLEAR RENEGADE THAT GOT AWAY

### CHAPTER 9 · KIM JONG-IL 8, BUSH 0

1. Author interview with Robert Gates, April 22, 2008.
2. Author interview with Condoleezza Rice, May 8, 2008.
3. Stephen J. Hadley at the editorial board of *The New York Times*, September 2007.
4. Helene Cooper, "Bush Rebuffs Hard-Liners to Ease North Korean Curbs," *The New York Times*, June 27, 2008, p. 1.
5. Author interview with a senior administration official, May 30, 2008.

## Chapter 10 · Cheney's Lost War

1. Author interview with Adm. Timothy J. Keating, May 15, 2008.
2. For more of these encounters, see "North Korea Asks Investors to Look Beyond Bleakness of Communist Decay," *The New York Times*, May 21, 1992.
3. Ashton B. Carter and William J. Perry, *Preventive Defense: A New Security Strategy for America* (Washington, D.C.: Brookings Institution Press, 1999).
4. Author interview with Jim Steinberg, December 11, 2007.
5. A good summary of the Vulcans' debate is contained in James Mann, *The Rise of the Vulcans: The History of Bush's War Cabinet* (New York: Viking, 2004), 277–81.
6. Helene Cooper, "A New Bush Tack on North Korea," *The New York Times*, December 7, 2007, p. A1.
7. Notes from conversation with Condoleezza Rice, March 5, 2001.
8. David E. Sanger, "Bush Tells Seoul Talks with North Won't Resume Now," *The New York Times*, March 8, 2001, p. 1.
9. Ibid.
10. Khan appeared to have been trying to implicate President Pervez Musharraf in the case, perhaps out of revenge for Khan's house arrest. "Pakistani Says Army Knew Atomic Parts Were Shipped," *The New York Times,* July 5, 2008, p. 8.
11. David E. Sanger and William J. Broad, "U.S. Concedes Uncertainty on Korean Uranium Effort," *The New York Times*, March 1, 2007, p. 1.
12. David E. Sanger, "Administration Divided Over North Korea," *The New York Times*, April 21, 2003, p. A15.
13. Author interview with Gen. Richard Myers, April 2006.
14. Chairman Donald H. Rumsfeld, *Report of the Commission to Assess the Ballistic Missile Threat to the United States,* July 15, 1998.
15. Conversation with Stephen Hadley, December 2002.

## Chapter 11 · "Everything Is Appomattox"

1. Siegfried S. Hecker, testifying during a Senate Foreign Relations Committee hearing on "Visit to the Yongbyon Nuclear Scientific Research Center in North Korea," January 21, 2004.
2. Hecker recounted his experiences in "The Nuclear Crisis in North Korea," *Bridge* (Summer 2004). This account is supplemented by his public speeches and two conversations.
3. Sigfried S. Hecker, "The Nuclear Crisis in North Korea," *Bridge* (Summer 2004).
4. Author interview with a senior administration official, September 2006.
5. Helene Cooper and Norimitsu Onishi, "Rice Says North Korean Missile Test Would Be a 'Provocative Act,'" *The New York Times*, June 20, 2006.

6. Author interview with Adm. Timothy J. Keating, May 15, 2008.

7. Norimitsu Onishi and David E. Sanger, "Missiles Fired by North Korea; Tests Protested," *The New York Times,* July 5, 2006.

8. In 2008, Stephen J. Hadley, Bush's national security adviser, gave two speeches that appeared to broaden the policy beyond North Korea.

9. Thom Shanker and Warren Hoge, "Rice Asserts U.S. Plans No Attack on North Korea," *The New York Times,* October 11, 2006.

10. Warren Hoge, "Security Council Supports Sanctions on North Korea," *The New York Times,* October 15, 2006.

11. Joseph Kahn and Helene Cooper, "North Korea Will Resume Nuclear Talks," *The New York Times,* November 1, 2006.

12. Thom Shanker and David E. Sanger, "Making Good on North Korea Vow Will Take Detective Work," *The New York Times,* October 13, 2006.

13. David E. Sanger, "For U.S., a Strategic Jolt After North Korea's Test," *The New York Times,* October 10, 2006.

14. Author interview with Condoleezza Rice, July 3, 2008.

15. Discussion with Bush, February 2007.

16. Jane Perlez, "Albright Greeted with Fanfare by North Korea," *The New York Times,* October 24, 2000.

## PART V: CHINA

### CHAPTER 12 · GENERATION LENOVO

1. Juliet Macur and David Lague, "China Won't Alter Olympic Torch Path," *The New York Times,* March 20, 2008.

2. My thanks to Keith Bradsher, the *Times*'s Hong Kong bureau chief, for assistance on this information.

3. Exact numbers are hard to come by. Data from 2004, from the *Guangdong Statistical Yearbook,* show that there were 14.9 million factory workers in the province. Overall job growth since then has exceeded 20 percent. That would make the 18 million number, so widely repeated in Guangdong, entirely plausible.

4. Elizabeth C. Economy, "The Great Leap Backward?" *Foreign Affairs,* September/October 2007.

5. Author interview with Bill Amelio, June 23, 2008.

6. For the description of the temples and monasteries of Tibet, I am indebted to one of my research assistants, Laura Stroh, who traveled the region.

7. David Barboza, "Protesting Monks Interrupt a Scripted Press Tour in Tibet," *The New York Times,* March 28, 2008, p. A6. The *Times* account was based on wire and pool reports because the paper was banned from the tour.

8. John F. Burns, "Protests of China Make Olympic Torch Relay an Obstacle Course," *The New York Times*, April 7, 2008, p. A12.

9. Andrew Jacobs and Jimmy Wang, "Indignant Chinese Urge Anti-West Boycott over Pro-Tibet Stance," *The New York Times*, April 20, 2008, p. A8.

10. The best account of the training of the Sacred Flame Protection Unit appeared in the *Times* of London. Jane Macartney and Richard Ford, "Unmasked: Chinese Guardians of Olympic Torch," *The Times* (London), April 9, 2008.

11. Jim Yardley, "Olympic Torch's Tibet Visit Is Short and Political," *The New York Times*, June 22, 2008.

12. James Mann, *The China Fantasy: How Our Leaders Explain Away Chinese Repression* (New York: Viking, 2007).

13. David E. Sanger, "Democracy, Limited," *The New York Times Book Review*, May 18, 2008, p. 20.

## CHAPTER 13 · THE PUNCTURE STRATEGY

1. For a good discussion of the test, see Bruce W. MacDonald, "China, Space Weapons and U.S. Security," *Council on Foreign Relations Report No. 38,* September 2008.

2. David E. Sanger and Joseph Kahn, "U.S. Officials Try to Interpret China's Silence Over Satellite," *The New York Times*, January 22, 2007, p. A3. (Months later, Hadley and other administration officials concluded that the Chinese leadership had been taken by surprise—and surmised that embarrassment may have explained their unwillingness to answer Washington's questions.)

3. United States National Space Policy, August 31, 2006.

4. For more discussion of the reactions of the Chinese, the Russians, and the others to America's technological dominance in the late 1990s, see David E. Sanger, "Agony of Victory: America Finds It's Lonely at the Top," *The New York Times*, July 18, 1999, p. 1.

5. Ibid.

6. Ashton B. Carter and William J. Perry, "China on the March," *The National Interest*, March/April 2007, p. 18.

7. David E. Sanger, "Bush to Outline Doctrine of Striking Foes First," *The New York Times*, September 20, 2002.

8. United States National Space Policy, August 31, 2006.

9. For the best unclassified estimates of the Chinese arsenal, see Robert S. Norris and Hans M. Kristensen, "Chinese Nuclear Forces, 2008," *Bulletin of the Atomic Scientists*, July/August 2008.

10. "China's Strategic Modernization," *Report from the ISAB Task Force*. As of October 2008, the report had not yet been published, but was widely distributed.

11. Author interview with Adm. Timothy J. Keating, May 15, 2008.

12. Jim Yardley, "China's Leaders Are Resilient in Face of Change," *The New York Times*, August 7, 2008, p. A1.

13. Exact numbers are suspect. See Rick Carew, "China Deals Extend Global Push," *Wall Street Journal*, September 26, 2008, p. B4.

14. For further discussion, see David E. Sanger, "China's Rising Need for Oil Is High on the U.S. Agenda," *The New York Times*, April 19, 2006, p. A1.

15. Keith Bradsher and David Barboza, "Pollution from Chinese Coal Casts a Global Shadow," *The New York Times*, June 11, 2006.

16. David Barboza, "China Reportedly Urged Omitting Pollution-Death Estimates," *The New York Times*, July 5, 2007.

17. Joseph Kahn and Mark Landler, "China Grabs West's Smoke-Spewing Factories," *The New York Times*, December 21, 2007.

## PART VI
## THE THREE VULNERABILITIES

### CHAPTER 14 · DETERRENCE 2.0

1. This description of a nuclear device detonated on the edge of downtown Washington is fictional, but hardly fanciful. It draws heavily on Scenario #1 in "National Planning Scenarios," a guide created by the Department of Homeland Security in April 2005, and updated since then. That scenario describes the effects of a 10-kiloton, gun-type weapon, with a core of highly enriched uranium smuggled into the United States. The government document posits that it was "stolen from a nuclear facility in another country" and "assembled near a major metropolitan center" inside the United States. In the scenario, the weapon is detonated in a delivery van and casualties run into the hundreds of thousands. The description appearing in this chapter imagines a far smaller, less capable weapon, yielding only 1 kiloton. By way of comparison, the crude device tested by North Korea in October 2006 produced less than a 1-kiloton yield.

2. In the official "National Planning Scenario," the fuel is also pieced together, and the scenario contained this chilling line: "The latest theft of 5 kilograms will likely be discovered at the next quarterly inventory at the primary facility, but by then the bribed security official, the UA [Universal Adversary] terrorists, and the HEU will be long gone."

3. Mimi Hall, "2012 Deadline to Scan All Port Cargo Won't Be Met," *USA Today,* October 21, 2008.

4. Charles J. Hanley, "Studies: Iraq Costs US $12B Per Month," Associated Press, March 9, 2008.

5. Hearing of the Senate Committee on Homeland Security and Governmental Affairs, "Preventing Nuclear Terrorism: Hard Lessons Learned from Troubled Investments," September 25, 2008.

6. George W. Bush, "Remarks on New Leadership on National Security," Washington, D.C., May 23, 2000.

7. Charles B. Curtis, "Preventing Nuclear Terrorism—Our Highest Priority—Isn't," National Defense University Foundation, May 21, 2008.

8. Remarks by the National Security adviser, Stephen Hadley, to the Center for International Security and Cooperation, Stanford University, Palo Alto, California, February 8, 2008.

9. The conference was sponsored by the Preventive Defense Project, a research collaboration of Stanford and Harvard Universities that is run by former defense secretary William J. Perry and Professor Ashton B. Carter. The readings were unclassified but sensitive; the entire discussion was unclassified, but the comments of individual participants could not be directly quoted. The author was one of the participants.

## CHAPTER 15 · THE INVISIBLE ATTACK

1. This is a fictional scenario, but the infection times and the frailties of the detection systems are real. Some details were described by Jeffrey Stiefel, director, Early Detection Division, BioWatch Program Executive at the Department of Homeland Security, at a Joint CBRN Conference, June 25, 2008.

2. Danzig has written several reports on the threat of bioterrorism. His latest is "Preparing for Catastrophic Bioterrorism: Toward a Long-Term Strategy for Limiting the Risk," Washington, D.C.: Center for Technology and National Security Policy, May 2008.

3. Margo Nash, "Where Terrorism Meets Optimism," *The New York Times*, November 24, 2002.

4. Lawrence M. Wein, Yifan Liu, and Terrance J. Leighton, "HEPA/Vaccine Plan for Indoor Anthrax Remediation," *Emerging Infectious Diseases,* vol. 11, No. 1 (January 2005): p. 71.

5. For a good discussion of this debate, see Barton Gellman, *Angler: The Cheney Vice Presidency,* (New York: Penguin Press, 2008), pp. 343–44.

6. National Security Presidential Directive 33, "Biodefense for the 21st Century," April 28, 2004.

7. The technology is called LIDAR, for Laser Imaging Detection and Ranging. For a more detailed discussion, see Shane D. Mayor, Paul Benda, Christina E. Murata, and Richard J. Danzig, "LIDARs: A Key Component of Urban Biodefense," *Biosecurity and Bioterrorism: Biodefense Strategy, Practice, and Science,* Vol. 6, No. 1 (2008).

8. Richard Danzig, "Preparing for Catastrophic Bioterrorism," Washington, D.C.: Center for Technology and National Security Policy, May 2008, p. 18.
9. Lawrence M. Wein, "Neither Snow, Nor Rain, Nor Anthrax . . ." *The New York Times*, October 13, 2008.

## CHAPTER 16 · DARK ANGEL

1. O. Sami Saydjari, "Addressing the Nation's Cyber Security Challenges: Reducing Vulnerabilities Requires Strategic Investment and Immediate Action," testimony before the House Committee on Homeland Security Subcommittee on Emerging Threats, Cybersecurity and Science and Technology, April 25, 2007.
2. Interview with Maria Bartiroma, CNBC, October 23, 2006.
3. With McConnell's agreement, Hathaway began to speak publicly in the fall of 2008.
4. Jeanne Meserve, "Sources: Staged Cyber Attack Reveals Vulnerability in Power Grid," CNN, September 26, 2007. The video is available through CNN's website.
5. Thom Shanker and Eric Schmitt, Firing Leaflets and Electrons, U.S. Wages Information War," *The New York Times*, February 23, 2003.

## EPILOGUE: OBAMA'S CHALLENGE

1. Peter Baker, "Could Afghanistan Become Obama's Vietnam?" *The New York Times*, August 22, 2009.
2. Interview on ABC's *This Week*, November 15, 2009.
3. Press briefing by Press Secretary Robert Gibbs, October 7, 2009.
4. Thom Shanker, Peter Baker, and Helene Cooper, "U.S. Weights Afghan Strategy of Protecting Population Hubs," *The New York Times*, October 28, 2009, p. 1.
5. The best on-the-record account of the lunch appears in David Ignatius, "Surge, Then Leave," *Washington Post*, December 2, 2009, p. A23.
6. Jane Perlez and Pir Zubair Shah, "In Refugee Aid, Pakistan's War Has New Front," *The New York Times*, July 1, 2009, p. 1.
7. Eric Schmitt and David E. Sanger, "U.S. Asks More from Pakistan in Terror War," *The New York Times*, November 16, 2009, p. 1.
8. For the best account of how the administration handled the runup to the announcement, see Helene Cooper and Mark Mazzetti, "Cryptic Note Ignited an Iran Nuclear Strategy Debate," *The New York Times*, September 26, 2009, p. 1.

# INDEX